Software Portability
with imake
Second Edition

Software Portability
with imake
Second Edition

Paul DuBois

O'REILLY™

Beijing · Cambridge · Köln · Paris · Sebastopol · Taipei · Tokyo

Software Portability with imake, Second Edition
by Paul DuBois

Copyright © 1996, 1993 O'Reilly & Associates, Inc. All rights reserved.
Printed in the United States of America.

Editor: Adrian Nye

Update Editor, Second Edition: Gigi Estabrook

Production Editor: Clairemarie Fisher O'Leary

Printing History:

July 1993:	First Edition.
December 1993:	Minor corrections.
August 1994:	Minor corrections. Appendix added.
September 1996:	Second Edition.

This book is printed on acid-free paper with 85% recycled content, 15% post-consumer waste.
O'Reilly & Associates is committed to using paper with the highest recycled content available consistent with high quality.

ISBN: 1-56592-226-3

Table of Contents

Preface

The hungry sheep look up, and are not fed…
—John Milton, *Lycidas*

This handbook is about *imake*, a UNIX tool that helps you write portable programs.

Most program development under UNIX is done with *make*, using a *Makefile* to direct the build and install processes. But Makefiles aren't portable, and it's often difficult to rewrite them by hand to accommodate machine dependencies for different systems. *imake* provides an alternative based on a simple idea: describe the dependencies for various systems in a set of configuration files and let a program generate the *Makefile* for you after selecting the dependencies appropriate for your machine. This frees you from writing and rewriting Makefiles by hand and helps you produce portable software that can be built and installed easily on any of the systems described in the configuration files.

imake has been used successfully to configure software such as the X Window System (Version 11), Motif, and the Khoros software development environment. X11 in particular is a large project that, despite its size and complexity, is remarkable in its portability. Much of this portability is due to the use of *imake*, which is thus arguably one of the reasons X11 has been so successful.

Nevertheless, despite the fact that it's freely available and runs on a variety of systems, *imake* isn't as widely exploited as it could be. There are at least two reasons for this:

- *imake* itself is a simple program, but the configuration files it uses sometimes are not. In particular, most people first encounter *imake* through the configuration files distributed with X. The X11 files are powerful and flexible, but they're also complicated and forbidding, and don't provide a very accessible entry point into the world of *imake*.

- *imake* documentation has been sparse. Normally when you don't understand how to use a program, you turn to the documentation. But for *imake* there hasn't been much available, which compounds the difficulty of learning it. Consequently, *imake* remains a mystery, leaving potential *imake* users in the predicament of Milton's sheep—seeking help in vain.

I freely acknowledge that *imake* can be difficult to make sense of. But it doesn't *need* to be so, nor should you have to become an initiate into the Eleusinian mysteries to be granted an understanding of how *imake* works.

Why Read This Handbook?

The goal of this handbook is to show how *imake* can help you write portable software and to make it easier for you to use *imake* on a daily basis. Then you'll be able to see it as a tool to be used, not a stumbling block to trip over.

If you don't know how to use *imake* at all, this handbook will teach you. If you already use *imake*, you'll learn how to use it more effectively. The handbook provides assistance on a number of levels, and you'll find it useful if you're in any of the situations below:

- You wonder what *imake* is and how it works.

- You couldn't care less what *imake* is or how it works. (As in, "I just got this program off the Net. What do I do with this *Imakefile* thing? I'm not interested in *imake*, I just want to get the program built!")

- You're curious about the relationship between an *Imakefile* and a *Makefile*.

- You're faced with the task of using *imake* for the first time and are finding it less than obvious.

- You're trying to use *imake* but you need help diagnosing problems that occur. For example: "I just generated my *Makefile*, but *make* says it contains a syntax error; what do I do now?"

- You're tired of editing your Makefiles every time you move your programs from one machine to another.

- You've inherited projects that were developed using *imake* and you need to understand how they're configured so you can maintain them.

- You've been able to use *imake* to configure, build, and install the X Window System on your workstation using the instructions provided with the X11 source distribution, but it all seemed like magic. You want to better understand what goes on during that process.

- You're planning to write X-based software. It's best to do this using an *Imakefile* (since X11 itself is *imake*-configured), and you'll be required to provide one anyway if you plan to submit your software to the X Consortium for inclusion in the X11 *contrib* distribution.

- You admire the portability of X11 and want to achieve the same for your own software, but you've found it difficult to use *imake* without a copy of X11 nearby. You suspect it's possible for *imake* to stand on its own, but you're not sure how.

- You're looking for a general-purpose tool for long-term software development and are considering using *imake* to that end.

Scope of This Handbook

This handbook is divided into three parts. Part I provides an overview of *imake* and how to use it, a basic description of the operation of configuration files, and how to write and troubleshoot Imakefiles. Part II describes how to write your own configuration files. Part III consists of appendices containing reference material or covering special topics. Each chapter and appendix is described briefly below: use this information to navigate to those of most interest to you.

Part I

Chapter 1, *Introduction*, describes what *imake* is and what it does. It also discusses why *make* is inadequate for achieving software portability. Read this to find out what problems *imake* attempts to solve.

Chapter 2, *A Tour of imake*, is an *imake* tutorial. In this chapter, I assume that you're not particularly interested in details about how *imake* works, you just want to know how to use it to do specific things: how to write a simple *Imakefile* to specify programs you want to build, how to generate the *Makefile* from the *Imakefile*, etc. Instead of starting from "first principles," you use *imake* to run through some basic exercises to get a feel for what it does and how to make it do what you want.

Chapter 3, *Understanding Configuration Files*, describes the principles governing the design of configuration files that you need to know to understand their structure and content—what's in them and how they work together. You don't need to read this chapter if you're a casual *imake* user, but you should if you want to employ *imake* more effectively or if you plan on writing your own configuration files. In this chapter I assume you want to understand *imake*'s workings in more detail—not just what it does, but how and why.

Chapter 4, *Writing Comments*, describes how to write comments in configuration files and Imakefiles, and how to deal with problems that arise in connection with commenting. The issue here, as in Chapter 3, is how to write down information about project configuration, so that it is useful to people rather than to programs.

Chapter 5, *The X11 Configuration Files*, discusses the configuration files from the X Window System, relating them to the general principles described in Chapter 3 and pointing out some of their unique features. This isn't an X book, but the X11 configuration files are the best-known instance of the use of *imake* to date. As such, they provide a fertile source of examples and discussion. It would be unwise not to take advantage of the lessons they provide.

Chapter 6, *Writing Imakefiles*, describes how to write Imakefiles for programs configured with the X11 configuration files. This chapter provides simple examples that require little or no knowledge of the X11 files, as well as detailed discussion to increase your practical understanding of how the X11 files work.

Chapter 7, *Imakefile Troubleshooting*, discusses things that can go wrong when you write Imakefiles and how to fix them.

Part II

Chapter 8, *A Closer Look at Makefile Generation*, examines the process by which *imake* builds Makefiles, including a discussion of how the `Makefile` and `Makefiles` target entries work.

Chapter 9, *A Configuration Starter Project*, shows how to convert the X11 configuration files into a starter project you can use as a jumping-off point for developing new projects or new sets of configuration files.

Chapter 10, *Coordinating Sets of Configuration Files*, discusses the problems that arise in a world populated by multiple sets of configuration files and how to solve the problems so you can manage those files easily. This chapter traces the design of *imboot*, a general-purpose *Makefile* bootstrapper, and shows how to use it with various sets of configuration files, such as those from X11, Motif, and Open-Windows. The chapter also develops an alternative approach to generating the `Makefile` target entry.

Chapter 11, *Introduction to Configuration File Writing*, shows by example how to write a set of configuration files. It provides a general description of the various ways you can specify the contents of configuration files.

Chapter 12, *Writing Rule Macros*, continues the discussion begun in Chapter 11, focusing on the design and implementation of *imake* rules.

Chapter 13, *Configuration Problems and Solutions*, discusses several configuration problems and shows how to solve them using the principles and techniques described in Chapters 11 and 12.

Chapter 14, *Troubleshooting Configuration Files*, discusses things that can go wrong when you write configuration files and how to fix them. It complements Chapter 7, *Imakefile Troubleshooting*.

Chapter 15, *Designing Extensible Configuration Files*, discusses how to design configuration files to be shared easily among projects, while allowing individual projects to specify their own particular requirements by extending or overriding the information in the shared files. This extensible architecture reduces the need to write new configuration files for a project when existing files don't quite match a project's configuration requirements.

Chapter 16, *Creating Extensible Configuration Files*, describes a procedure you can use to convert existing project-specific configuration files to the extensible architecture.

Chapter 17, *Using Extensible Configuration Files*, shows how to develop new projects that take advantage of the flexibility afforded by the extensible architecture.

Chapter 18, *Using imake on Non-UNIX Systems*, covers some of the issues you must address if you're trying to port *imake* to a non-UNIX system. It also discusses writing Imakefiles and configuration files to be less UNIXcentric and so is useful even if your own interest is primarily in UNIX but you wish to make it easier for your projects to be ported to non-UNIX systems by others.

Part III

Appendix A, *Obtaining Configuration Software*, describes how to get the software described in this handbook. *imake* isn't always included as part of the software distributed with the UNIX operating system, but anyone with World Wide Web or FTP access on the Internet can get it. *imake* is also available by electronic mail.

Appendix B, *Installing Configuration Software*, discusses how to build and install the software described in this handbook.

Appendix C, *Configuration Programs: A Quick Reference*, documents the software described in this handbook, using an abbreviated manpage format.

Appendix D, *Generating Makefiles: A Quick Reference*, briefly describes how to build a *Makefile* from an *Imakefile*.

Appendix E, *Writing Imakefiles: A Quick Reference*, briefly describes how to write an *Imakefile*.

Appendix F, *Writing Configuration Files: A Quick Reference*, briefly describes how to write configuration files.

Appendix G, *Basics of make and cpp*, provides brief overviews of *make* and *cpp*. Since *imake* produces Makefiles, you need to understand a little about *make*. You should also understand something about *cpp*, because *imake* uses *cpp* to do most of its work.

Appendix H, *A Little History*, describes how *imake* came into being.

Appendix I, *Other Sources of Information*, lists some other references on *imake*, *make*, and *cpp*. It also provides instructions for getting on the *imake* mailing list.

Appendix J, *Using imake with OpenWindows*, describes some special problems with using *imake* under OpenWindows, and how to handle them.

imake and the X Window System

imake is part of the distribution of the X Window System, Version 11, a product of X Consortium, Inc. X11 (and hence *imake*) is owned and copyrighted by X Consortium, Inc., but is freely available. For more information, the X Consortium is reachable on the World Wide Web at:

```
http://www.x.org
ftp://ftp.x.org
```

Or by surface mail at:

```
X Consortium, Inc.
201 Broadway
Cambridge, MA 02139-1955
USA
```

You don't need to have or use X11 to use *imake*. Nevertheless, X11 has a strong presence in the *imake* world. In particular, the X11 configuration files are very popular, and I refer to them often. When the first edition of this handbook was published, the current release of the X Window System was Version 11, Release 5 (denoted as X11R5, or just R5). For the second edition, Release 6 (X11R6) was current during most of the revision period and Release 6.1 (X11R6.1) was issued shortly before publication.

R6.1 is used as the reference release for most of the discussion in this handbook, but R5 and R6 are mentioned on occasion as well. The default pathnames for program and configuration file installation directories are shown for each release in Table 1. You can use these pathnames to recognize on sight which release particular examples refer to.

Table 1: *Default X11 Program and Configuration File Installation Directories*

X11 Release	Program Directory	Configuration File Directory
X11R5	*/usr/bin/X11*	*/usr/lib/X11/config*
X11R6	*/usr/X11R6/bin*	*/usr/X11R6/lib/X11/config*
X11R6.1	*/usr/X11R6.1/bin*	*/usr/X11R6.1/lib/X11/config*

Conventions Used in This Handbook

The following typographical conventions are used in this handbook:

Italic

is used for file and directory names when they appear in the body of a paragraph, for program and command names, and for options to commands.

`Constant Width`

is used in examples to show the contents of files or the output from commands; and to indicate environment variables, rules, entries, and targets.

Constant Bold

is used in examples to show commands or other text that should be typed literally by the user. For example, **rm myfile** means to type "rm myfile" exactly as it appears in the text or example.

Constant Italic

is used in code fragments and examples to show variables for which a context-specific substitution should be made. The variable *filename*, for example, would be replaced by some actual filename.

Acknowledgments

Many people contributed in various ways to both editions of this handbook; those listed here were especially helpful.

Thanks are due to Todd Brunhoff, Jim Fulton, Bob Scheifler, Stephen Gildea, and Kaleb Keithley for their willingness to answer my myriad questions about *imake* and the X11 configuration files.

David Brooks, Steve Dennis, Gary Keim, Jim Kohli, Steve Kroeker, David Lewis, Miles O'Neal, Andy Oram, and Tom Sauer provided helpful review comments.

Mary Kay Sherer waded through early drafts and refused to be nice to them. But faithful are the wounds of a friend; her criticisms helped weed out many incomprehensiblenesses.

The staff of O'Reilly & Associates was a pleasure to work with. Adrian Nye provided editorial guidance and oversight and is really the one to whom *Software Portability with imake* owes its existence (the book was his idea; I just wrote it).

For the first edition, Laura Parker Roerden copyedited what must have seemed an intractable thicket of words and managed final production with the indispensable help of Clairemarie Fisher O'Leary. Lenny Muellner fielded a constant stream of *troff* questions. Ellie Cutler wrote the index. Jennifer Niederst provided design support. Jeff Robbins produced the figures. And Edie Freedman designed the book and the cover with that marvelous snake. For the reprint of this handbook, Nicole Gipson entered new edits, Chris Reilley designed the figure for the new appendix, and Chris Tong prepared the index.

For the second edition, Gigi Estabrook pulled the various pieces together, and Clairemarie Fisher O'Leary coordinated the production. David Sewell copyedited the manuscript, and Nancy Kotary and Evan Garcia made the edits. Seth Maislin helped to update the index. Lenny Muellner fielded yet more *troff* questions, and Chris Reilley did the figures.

Most of all I'd like to thank my wife Karen, who endured author's-widow tribulations with considerable grace and understanding. And patience; she listened while I rehearsed often and at length my thoughts about the topics in this book, even though she "cared for none of those things." This was invaluable in helping me sort out what I was trying to write. Her contribution was significant, and greatly appreciated.

We'd Like To Hear from You

We have tested and verified all of the information in this handbook to the best of our ability, but you may find that features have changed (or even that we have made mistakes!). Please let us know about any errors you find, as well as your suggestions for future editions, by writing:

O'Reilly & Associates, Inc.
101 Morris Street
Sebastopol, CA 95472
1-800-998-9938 (in the US or Canada)
1-707-829-0515 (international/local)
1-707-829-0104 (FAX)

You can also send us messages electronically. To be put on the mailing list or request a catalog, send email to:

info@oreilly.com

To ask technical questions or comment on the handbook, send email to:

    bookquestions@oreilly.com

To correspond directly with the author, send email to:

    dubois@primate.wisc.edu

1

Introduction

There is no such thing as portable software, only software that has been ported.
—Unknown

The problem of how to write portable software confronts a broad spectrum of developers—from the lone programmer seeking to move a single program from one machine to another, to commercial enterprises seeking to port large, complex projects to run on several systems to maximize the market for their product. In each case, the common aim is to move software from one system to another without investing substantial time and effort in code revision.

In the UNIX world, software development typically involves *make*, using a *Makefile* describing how to build and install the programs in which we're interested.[*] The *Makefile* lists targets (for example, programs to be built) and associates each target with the commands that build it. When you invoke *make*, it determines which targets you want to build, and for each one that's out of date, recreates it by executing the commands associated with it. This process is recursive: if a target depends on other prerequisite targets being up to date, *make* first executes the commands associated with the prerequisites as necessary.

In essence, *make* functions as a command-generating engine, and the *Makefile* controls which commands to generate for specific targets. This is a tremendous convenience for the programmer, since it eliminates the need to type a bunch of commands each time you want to build something. The *Makefile* serves as a repository for your knowledge, encoded in such a way that arbitrarily complex command sequences can be called forth and reenacted at will simply by naming targets.

---

* If you're unfamiliar with *make* and Makefiles, see Appendix G, *Basics of make and cpp.*

Unfortunately, Makefiles aren't portable. The commands that *make* so conveniently generates at the drop of a hat are subject to variation from system to system, so a *Makefile* that works on my system may not work on yours. Under ideal circumstances we could take a software distribution, plop it on another machine, compile and install it, and it would run. But it doesn't always work that way.

Suppose we're writing a small C program, *myname*, consisting of a single source file *myname.c*:

```
#include <stdio.h>
int main ()
{
char    *getenv ();
char    *p;
    p = getenv ("USER");
    if (p == (char *) NULL)
        printf ("cannot tell your user name\n");
    else
        printf ("your user name is %s\n", p);
    exit (0);
}
```

The *Makefile* for the program might look like this:

```
myname: myname.o
    cc -o myname myname.o
install: myname
    install myname /usr/local
```

To build and install *myname*, we'd use these commands:

```
% make myname
cc -c myname.c
cc -o myname myname.o
% make install
install myname /usr/local
```

The first *make* command does two things: it compiles *myname.o* from *myname.c* (*make* has built-in intelligence about producing *.o* files from *.c* files), and it links *myname.o* to produce an executable *myname*. The second *make* command installs *myname* in the */usr/local* directory.

All our friends are astonished at the usefulness of this program and immediately begin hectoring us mercilessly for the source code. We give it to one of them, together with the *Makefile*, and he lopes off to install it on his machine. The next day he sends back the following report:

- We don't have any *install* program, so I used *cp*.

- Our local installation directory is */usr/local/bin* rather than */usr/local*.

He sends back a revised *Makefile*, having made the necessary changes, and also having conveniently parameterized the things he found to be different on his system, using the *make* variables[*] INSTALL and BINDIR at the beginning of the *Makefile*:

```
# set following variables appropriately for your machine
INSTALL = cp
 BINDIR = /usr/local/bin

myname: myname.o
    cc -o myname myname.o
install: myname
    $(INSTALL) myname $(BINDIR)
```

This is a step forward. The installation program and directory as specified in this *Makefile* are no longer correct for our machine, but now they're parameterized and thus easily located and modified. We change the values back to *install* and */usr/local* so they'll work on our machine, and both we and our friend are happy.

Alas, our idyllic state of mind doesn't last long. We give the program to another friend. She builds it and reports back her changes:

- I prefer to use *gcc*, not *cc*.

- Our C library is broken and doesn't contain *getenv()*; I have to link in *−lc_aux* as well.

- Our system uses the environment variable LOGNAME rather than USER.

She, too, sends back a revised *Makefile*, further parameterized:

```
# set following variables appropriately for your machine
        CC = gcc
EXTRA_LIBS = -lc_aux
    BINDIR = /usr/local
   INSTALL = install

myname: myname.o
    $(CC) -o myname myname.o $(EXTRA_LIBS)
install: myname
    $(INSTALL) myname $(BINDIR)
```

The *Makefile* solves her first two problems, as they involve variations in building and installing the program. The third problem involves a nonportability in the program source itself. Our friend took the easy way out and simply edited *myname.c*, changing the parameter passed to the *getenv()* call from USER to LOGNAME.

---

[*] What I'm calling *make* variables are sometimes referred to as *make* macros. In this handbook, the word "macro" always means a *cpp* macro, not a *make* macro.

Unfortunately, that means she'll have to remember to edit the source every time we release a new, latest-and-greatest version of *myname*. It would be better to use the *Makefile* to make the nonportability explicit.

It's easy to solve the problem using some of *make*'s built-in intelligence. The default command that *make* executes to produce an object file *x.o* from a C source file *x.c* looks something like this:

```
$(CC) $(CFLAGS) -c x.c
```

The default command may vary somewhat from system to system, but will include $(CFLAGS) in it somewhere. We can use CFLAGS to control whether *myname* attempts to reference USER or LOGNAME at run time. First, we change the line in *myname.c* where the *getenv()* call occurs, from this:

```
p = getenv ("USER");
```

to this:

```
#if USE_LOGNAME
    p = getenv ("LOGNAME");
#else
    p = getenv ("USER");
#endif
```

Then we define CFLAGS appropriately in the *Makefile*. To select LOGNAME, write this:

```
CFLAGS = -DUSE_LOGNAME=1
```

To select USER, write this instead:

```
CFLAGS = -DUSE_LOGNAME=0
```

Now, with a simple change to the *Makefile*, *myname* can be compiled on machines that use either environment variable. This is encouraging. Using our vast-and-ever-increasing porting experience, we can easily build *myname* on more machines now—three! And the revised *Makefile* is better than the original:

- It parameterizes all the nonportabilities we've encountered so far.

- Nonportabilities are identified explicitly at the beginning of the *Makefile*.

- They're easily modified by editing the *Makefile*.

However, we begin to notice uneasily that the number of things that might need changing from machine to machine is increasing. There were only two differences between machines when we built *myname* on two systems. Now we can build it on three systems, but the number of differences has increased to five. How many differences will we find when we try to port *myname* to additional systems? As the *Makefile* editing job gets bigger, it becomes more difficult. Each nonportability adds another increment to the burden incurred each time *myname* is built on a different machine.

Also, it's becoming clear that we'd better keep a list of parameters appropriate for each type of machine on which the program is known to run, or we'll forget them. When we distribute the program to other people who want to build it, we need to give them the list as well so they can see how they might need to modify the *Makefile* on their systems.

The Nature of Nonportability

The preceding example illustrates that even simple programs must be adapted to variation, both in the way their source code is written and in the way they're built and installed. *myname* is by no means an exotic program, but we encountered several sources of nonportability during its development:

- User environment (USER vs. LOGNAME)

- Program-building tools (*cc* vs. *gcc*)

- System library contents (presence/absence of *getenv()* in the C library)

- Installation tools (*install* vs. *cp*)

- Installation locations (*/usr/local* vs. */usr/local/bin*)

If we encounter this many variations with such an utterly trivial program, you can imagine (and perhaps know from experience!) how much worse the problem is for larger projects. For a project with a *Makefile* and one source file in a single directory, it might be no more than an annoyance to make the necessary changes. But if a project has dozens or hundreds of source files distributed throughout 5, 10, or 50 directories, we have a much more difficult problem on our hands.

Software portability is sometimes approached as an exercise in eliminating machine dependencies from source code. That's a worthwhile goal, but insufficient, because many nonportabilities involve factors other than the program source itself. Our experience of porting *myname* to various systems demonstrated this; only one of the nonportabilities had anything to do with *myname*'s source code. The others involved variations in the build and install process, and the tools used during that process had to be selected and adapted for each system. This means the notion of "portable programs" must include a portable development process that allows us to select those tools easily.

Why Not Just Use make?

It would be advantageous to ensure portability with *make*, since we're already using it. But *make* alone isn't up to the task for the following reasons:

- **There are no conditionals**. If we could assign values to *make* variables conditionally, we could parameterize machine dependencies by assigning variable values appropriate to a given machine type. This would be a useful way of setting CFLAGS when building *myname*, for instance.

  If we could define target entries conditionally, we could build targets in the most appropriate way. For example, on machines with *ranlib*, we'd run it after building a library. On machines without it, we wouldn't. To some extent we can use the shell's *if*-statement syntax to get around lack of conditionals in target entries, but it's clunky to do so.

- **There is no flow control**. Loops and iterators must be done using shell commands to simulate them.

- **It's difficult to make global changes**. For example, suppose you use BINDIR to name your installation directory. You can assign it the proper value in each *Makefile* in your project. But if you decide to change it, you must find and change every *Makefile*. Alternatively, you can assign BINDIR once in the top-level *Makefile* and pass the value to *make* commands in subdirectories using suitable recursive rules. But then you can't run *make* directly in a subdirectory because BINDIR won't have the proper value. Recursive rules are difficult to write correctly, anyway.

  If *make* had a mechanism for file inclusion, global information could be split out into a separate file and included from within each *Makefile*. Then the information would need to be specified in only one file and would be easier to change. Some versions of *make* have in fact been extended to allow file inclusion, but the extension isn't universal and thus is nonportable itself. So we can't rely on it.

- **Header file dependencies for C source files are inherently nonportable**. Different systems organize header files differently. You might even have multiple sets on systems that support development under more than one environment (BSD, System V, POSIX, etc.). This makes it impossible to list header file dependencies statically in the *Makefile*. They must be computed on the target machine at build time.

The *Makefile* is a terrific vehicle for expressing knowledge about building a target on a given system, but it's not especially good for adapting to variation between systems. *make* variables allow the variation to be parameterized, but that makes the Makefiles easier to configure only if you have a mechanism for changing them—and *make* doesn't provide one. In order to adapt to variation, the Makefiles must be changed by some external configuration process.

The Nature of Configurability

The simplest configuration process is the brute force approach: "The person installing the software will edit the *Makefile* as necessary." Using this "method," we distribute a *README* file with the program describing how to manually edit the *Makefile*. The *README* clearly and explicitly expresses what needs to be changed. However, the mechanism for translating that knowledge into a properly configured *Makefile* (hand editing) leaves something to be desired, especially as a project becomes more complex and subject to variation over a larger number of parameters. "Aren't these computers supposed to do the dirty work for us?" becomes the plaintive cry of despair of anyone who tries to configure software this way.

It would be better if we could express what we know about building a project on various systems in such a manner that a program could use our knowledge to reparameterize Makefiles automatically. Then we'd just say *poof!* and the Makefiles would be reconfigured for the machine we're using.

Our difficulties in writing and porting *myname* provide valuable instruction from which we can formulate two principles for portable software development:

- **Our knowledge of configuration requirements must be explicit**. We need to leave a trail by writing down what we know. If we carry our knowledge in our heads it will be lost.

- **Our knowledge must be machine readable**. If we don't write down configuration information in a form a program can use, we'll still end up editing it ourselves each time a project is moved to a different machine. Also, we want to specify the information once, not replicate it manually in every *Makefile*. If any replication is necessary, a program should do it for us.

imake helps us follow these principles. It provides the means to avoid extensive manual *Makefile* rewriting by giving us a method for expressing our knowledge about configuration requirements for various systems in explicit, machine-usable form. When the software is moved to different machines, *imake* automatically uses our knowledge to rebuild Makefiles without manual intervention.

How Does imake Work?

When you're developing software using *make* alone, you write machine dependencies directly into your *Makefile*, using an editor such as *vi* or *emacs*. Then you run *make* to build your programs (Figure 1–1).

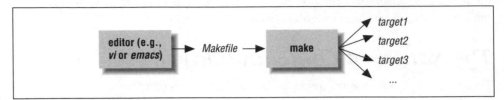

Figure 1–1: Producing software with make alone

With *imake*, you don't write a *Makefile*. Instead you write an *Imakefile*, which is a machine-independent description of the targets you want built. Machine dependencies are centralized into a set of configuration files isolated in their own directory, so they don't appear in the *Imakefile*. This makes the differing requirements for various systems explicit in a well-known place and keeps them out of your target descriptions. *imake* reads the *Imakefile* and generates a properly configured *Makefile* by selecting from the configuration files those dependencies appropriate for your system. Then you run *make* to build your programs (Figure 1–2).

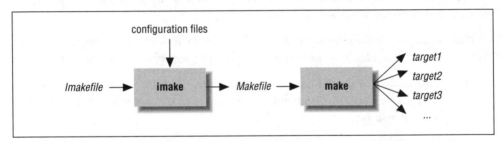

Figure 1–2: Producing software with make and imake

When you move the software to another system, the development process includes porting activity. In particular, a different set of machine dependencies applies, so the *Makefile* is no longer correct. If you're using *make* alone, you edit the *Makefile* by hand again (Figure 1–3). By contrast, if you're using *imake*, you just run it again to generate a new *Makefile* (Figure 1–4).

Figures 1–3 and 1–4 are similar, but there's a big difference between editing a *Makefile* manually and having *imake* generate it for you, especially for multiple-directory projects involving several Makefiles. When you specify configuration information by hand directly in your Makefiles, you have to find and edit information splattered all over your project every time you build it on a different machine. With *imake*, machine dependencies are localized in the configuration files and you run *imake* to replicate that information into the Makefiles automatically.

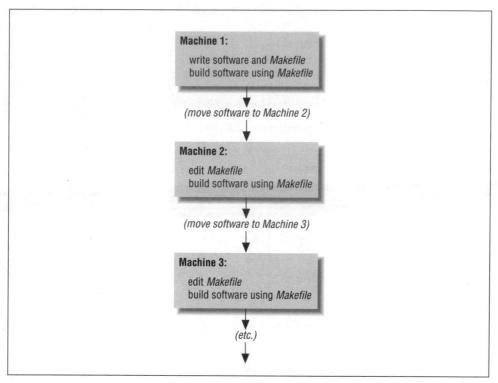

Figure 1–3: Software development and porting with make alone

What Can imake Do for You?

imake isn't a magic bullet that instantly and effortlessly solves all your porting woes. But it can reduce project development and maintenance tasks considerably. Here are some examples of what *imake* does for you:

- *imake* provides a notational convenience. It's easier to write an *Imakefile* than a *Makefile* because it's shorter and simpler.

- If you develop projects in collaboration with people who work on various types of machines, *imake* helps you work cooperatively by making it easier to build the software on the machines involved.

- If you work on a heterogeneous network composed of systems from several different vendors, *imake* helps you cope with your mix of machines by making it easier to build your software on various platforms. This allows you to move your software around to make it more uniformly available.

- If you want to make projects you've written available to others, *imake* helps you configure it to run on many systems, increasing the potential audience for your work.

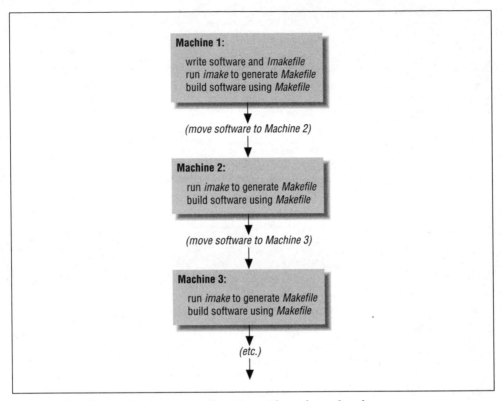

Figure 1–4: Software development and porting with imake and make

- When you want to port an *imake*-configured project to a new platform, *imake* facilitates the process by providing an open-ended mechanism that allows you to incorporate new information into the configuration files. The information is explicitly represented in the configuration files, and, once it's specified, *imake* uses it automatically.

This handbook helps you get started with *imake* without digesting a lot of details first by providing exercises you can do to gain hands-on experience. When you want the details, they're available, but presented in the context of principles that will help you understand them. For instance, *imake*'s configuration files can seem fairly impenetrable, but there are really only two basic principles you need to know in order to decipher them. One is to understand the purpose of each file and how different files relate to each other; the other is to understand the idioms by which their contents are specified. All configuration files consist mainly of the repetition of these idioms in their proper context. When you know how to speak this idiomatic language, you'll be able to use *imake* to its full potential.

You'll also be able to use *imake* for a variety of projects, and, in so doing, move beyond the common (mis)perception of *imake* as just an X tool. *imake* first received extensive exposure as part of the X Window System, so it's often seen as a special-purpose program intended only for that environment. Nevertheless, *imake* isn't limited to X; it's a tool that can be used for general software development. My own experience illustrates this.

Slaying the Beast

Like many people, I first met *imake* through X11. I had obtained a copy of the X11 distribution sometime during the tenure of Release 1 (X11R1), but I just wanted to read the documentation and poke through the source code a bit to see what X11 was all about. I wasn't actually interested in building or using it. Of course, it's difficult to get very far into the X11 distribution before encountering *imake*. For one thing, I was confronted with this thing called an *Imakefile* at every turn. So I decided to investigate *imake* in more detail.

My curiosity was short-lived. As I began to examine the configuration files used by *imake*, I realized I was unable to make the slightest sense of any of them. There were familiar words like CFLAGS, BINDIR, and INCLUDES scattered here and there, but there were also arcana like this:

```
#define InstallMultiple(list,dest)                          @@\
install:: list                                              @@\
    @case '${MFLAGS}' in *[i]*) set +e;; esac; \            @@\
    for i in list; do \                                     @@\
        (set -x; $(INSTALL) -c $(INSTALLFLAGS) $$i dest); \ @@\
    done
```

I don't know what that does for you, but my brain recoiled from it. The general sense is somewhat discernible (it installs programs), but how to use it was a mystery. *imake* seemed a gorgon, turning my thoughts to stone, and I put it aside, horrified. Nevertheless, there remained the suspicion in the back of my mind that a tool capable of configuring a project as large and complex as X11 must have some merit, and that perhaps *imake* would be useful for configuring my own software—if only I could figure out how to use it.

As subsequent releases of X11 became available (R2, R3), I looked them over in turn, reexamining the configuration files each time. These repeated exposures had their effect, and I began to have some slight comprehension. My suspicions about the potential usefulness of *imake* for configuring my own software increased, but I was as yet unable to act on them since my understanding of how it worked was still quite rudimentary.

Sometime between X11R3 and X11R4 I was faced with the need to transport software frequently between two very dissimilar versions of UNIX (a VAX running

Ultrix and a Mips M/120 running RISC/os). The difficulty of accommodating the differences between the machines proved to be extremely frustrating, so I finally decided to force myself to understand *imake*. To that end, I sat down with the X11R3 configuration files (several times!), determined to wrest from them their closely guarded secrets.

Eventually, I was able to configure some of my own projects using heavily modified copies of the R3 files. The result was that I could move those projects back and forth between my machines without concern for rewriting the Makefiles. *imake* took care of that for me. The effort expended had paid off.

Shortly thereafter, X11R4 became available. As before, I obtained a copy of the distribution. As before, I began to examine the configuration files (now with heightened interest) to see if they had changed, and, if so, how. And I found that although they had changed in some significant and important ways, it was a relatively straightforward task to make sense of them—a welcome and pleasant discovery.

I now consider *imake* indispensible and use it for virtually everything I write: program libraries, network client-server applications, bibliographic utilities, data analysis programs, mail servers, and graphics generators. I also use it to develop documentation—including *Software Portability with imake*.

This road was long and difficult, but you need not travel it. In a sense this book is a distillation of my own experience, rearranged and presented in a form suited to easier understanding so you can short-circuit the learning process and begin to use *imake* quickly. I hope the book succeeds in making *imake* accessible and helps you in your own development efforts. I've found *imake* an extraordinarily useful tool. I think you will, too.

However, before you can really do anything with *imake*, you need the proper tools. The next section describes what those tools are and how to make sure they're on your system.

The Essential imake Toolkit

To use *imake*, there are certain crucial minimum requirements:

- *imake* itself and a set of configuration files
- *cpp* and *make*; *imake* uses the former to produce Makefiles for the latter
- *xmkmf* or another program to bootstrap a *Makefile* from an *Imakefile*

A few other programs are closely associated with *imake*:

- *makedepend*, to generate header file dependencies from C source files
- *mkdirhier*, to create directories during file installation operations if your system doesn't support *mkdir −p*
- *bsdinst* or *install.sh*, to install files if your system doesn't have a BSD-compatible *install* program

It's probable that *cpp* and *make* are installed on your system already. The other pieces of the toolkit might also be installed, although it's somewhat less likely. Some suggestions are given below for determining what is and isn't available on your machine. If it turns out that you don't have a complete toolkit, see Appendix A, *Obtaining Configuration Software*, and Appendix B, *Installing Configuration Software*.

imake, *xmkmf*, and related programs tend to be found in X11-related directories, as do the X11 configuration files. If X11 or an X11-derived window system such as OpenWindows is installed on your machine, you probably have *imake* and a set of configuration files already. You can ask your system administrator where they are or try to find them yourself.

To determine whether or not any configuration files are installed on your system, see if you have a *lib/X11/config* directory under */usr* or */usr/X11Rn* (where *n* is a release number). You can also try looking under alternative locations such as */var/X11Rn*, */opt/X11Rn*, or */local/X11Rn*. If you have OpenWindows, look for */usr/openwin/lib/config*.

To locate the configuration programs, try to find *imake*. Assuming you can, *xmkmf* and other related programs are usually installed in the same directory. The *which* command can often tell you where a program is located. In the example below, *which* tells you that *imake* is installed in */usr/X11R6.1/bin*:

```
% which imake
/usr/X11R6.1/bin/imake
```

If *which* doesn't find *imake*, try looking in */usr/bin/X11*, or in any */usr/X11Rn/bin* directory you may have. You can also look in */var/X11Rn/bin*, */opt/X11Rn/bin*, or */local/X11Rn/bin*. If you have OpenWindows, look for */usr/openwin/bin*.

Failing all of the above, you can use *find*:

```
% find / -name Imake.tmpl -print      Look for configuration files
% find / -name imake -print           Look for imake
```

find / searches your entire file system, so it takes a while and is a last resort.

To make sure your shell can find the programs, your search path must include the directory in which they're located. This path is usually set in a shell startup file in your home directory. For *csh* or *tcsh*, look for a *set path* or *setenv PATH* statement in *.login*, *.cshrc*, or *.tcshrc*. For *sh*, look for a *PATH=* statement in *.profile*. (For *sh*-derived shells like *ksh* or *bash*, you might need to look in files like *.kshrc* or *.bash_profile*.)

Add the appropriate directory to the command that sets your search path if it's not already listed there. Suppose the programs are located in */usr/X11R6.1/bin*. If you're using *csh* or *tcsh*, you can use either of the following commands to add that directory to your search path:

```
set path = (dir1 dir2 dir3 /usr/X11R6.1/bin)
setenv PATH dir1:dir2:dir3:/usr/X11R6.1/bin
```

For *sh*, *ksh*, or *bash*, use this command instead:

```
PATH=dir1:dir2:dir3:/usr/X11R6.1/bin
```

See your system administrator if you need more information about setting your path.

In this chapter:
- *The Exercises*
- *What Have You Learned?*
- *Common Problems*

2

A Tour of imake

> *Does the road wind uphill all the way?*
> —Christina Georgina Rosetti, *Uphill*

This chapter discusses how to write a simple *Imakefile* and how to create a *Makefile* from it by running *imake*. It also describes *xmkmf, makedepend,* and *mkdirhier*, three programs that are useful in conjunction with *imake*. The discussion doesn't explain how *imake* works internally. Instead, it provides a set of exercises forming a brief "if you do this, this is what should happen" walk-through. If you've used *imake* before, you may want to skip this chapter. If you haven't used it, or if you're one of those for whom *imake* seems an impenetrable riddle, go through the exercises to get a feel for what *imake* does without wading through a nuts-and-bolts explanation of how it works.

Using *imake* is very much a learn-by-doing experience, so you really should work through the exercises. They give you a chance to observe yourself actually surviving the experience of using *imake* to do something. This is similar to the way new UNIX users can run a simple command like:

```
% who
```

to see that the computer doesn't blow up when they touch it.

The Exercises

The exercises in this chapter are based on the configuration files from the X Window System, Version 11, Release 6.1. If you don't have the X11R6.1 files, there are other options. You can use the files from an earlier version of X11 or from Open-Windows. Or, you can use the TOUR configuration files described in Appendix A, *Obtaining Configuration Software*. They're equivalent to the X11 files for trying out the examples, but simpler. Should you get an irresistible urge to study configuration files directly as you're going through the chapter, you'll find them easier to understand than the X11 files.

The TOUR distribution also contains the Imakefiles and source files described in the following exercises. You can use these files if you don't want to type them in yourself.

It's best to do the exercises in a location devoted to that purpose, so create a work area directory and move into it:

```
% mkdir TOUR
% cd TOUR
```

If you encounter difficulties while doing the exercises, see the section "Common Problems" at the end of this chapter.

Exercise 1: Write an Imakefile and Generate the Makefile

To use *imake*, you need an *Imakefile*. An empty file will do for now. Create one using the following command:

```
% cp /dev/null Imakefile
```

Once you have an *Imakefile*, you generate a *Makefile* from it. In the *imake* world, you normally do this with the command *make Makefile*, which tells *make* to generate the *imake* command needed to rebuild the *Makefile*. That is, you use the *Makefile* to recreate itself. But you can't do that yet because you still have no *Makefile*.

There is a paradox here: you want to use the *Makefile* to run *imake* for you, but you need to run *imake* to get the *Makefile* in the first place. To get around this circularity, you need to know either how to run *imake* manually or how to use a *Makefile*-bootstrapping program that runs *imake* for you. The bootstrapper associated with the X11 files is *xmkmf*, which you use as follows:

```
% xmkmf
imake -DUseInstalled -I/usr/X11R6.1/lib/X11/config
```

After running *xmkmf*, you should have a *Makefile* generated from your empty *Imakefile* and from the configuration files. Notice that *xmkmf* shows you the *imake* command it generates before it executes it. The −I argument tells *imake* where the configuration files are located on your system. It might be the directory */usr/X11R6.1/lib/X11/config*, as shown in the example, or somewhere different, such as */usr/lib/X11/config* or */usr/openwin/lib/config*.

Use the *Makefile* you've just built to try out a few *make* commands:

```
% make clean
rm -f *.CKP *.ln *.BAK *.bak *.o core errs ,* *~ *.a .emacs_* \
    tags TAGS make.log MakeOut "#"*
% make
(no output)
% make Makefile
+ rm -f Makefile.bak
+ mv Makefile Makefile.bak
imake -DUseInstalled -I/usr/X11R6.1/lib/X11/config -DTOPDIR=. -DCURDIR=.
```

The first *make* command runs *rm* to remove various kinds of "garbage" files, such as *.o* files from compiler operations. This command isn't very useful at the moment; we haven't built anything, so there's nothing to remove. The second command produces no output (there's nothing to build yet). The third regenerates the *Makefile*, after saving the current one as *Makefile.bak. xmkmf* isn't necessary at this point because you've got a *Makefile* generated by *imake*, and *imake* will have put the proper *Makefile*-regenerating entry into it.*

Perhaps it seems a little strange that anything at all happens when you run these commands. The *Imakefile* was empty—how could it have contained any information to tell *make* what to do? Why doesn't *make* just spit out error messages?

The reason is that the *Imakefile* isn't the only source of information *imake* uses to generate the *Makefile*. It also uses the configuration files, which supply a number of target entries automatically. Among these are a clean entry, a Makefile entry, and a default target entry named emptyrule that does nothing (the latter target is why *make* with no arguments silently does nothing instead of producing an error message). The amount of information supplied automatically by the configuration files can be surprising, even imposing. For example, on one of the machines I use, the *Makefile* built from an empty *Imakefile* and the X11 configuration files is over 400 lines long and includes entries for nine default targets.

You should consider it a given that *imake* generates Makefiles that are larger than those you'd write by hand. If you find yourself horrified at the difference between the size of an *Imakefile* and that of the resulting *Makefile*, you needn't think, "Oh, no! I've created a monster!" Don't assume that the *Makefile*'s size indicates you've done something wrong. The size reflects only that the configuration files supply a lot of structure in the *Makefile* for you. Besides, when you're using *imake*, you usually don't look at the *Makefile* anyway. You write the *Imakefile* and leave the *Makefile* to *make*, which can digest large Makefiles more easily than you can.

---

* If you make a typo when you edit an *Imakefile*, you'll often find that the resulting *Makefile* is unusable and *make Makefile* won't work. In that case, run *xmkmf* again to bootstrap the *Makefile* after you fix the typo in the *Imakefile*.

Exercise 2: Build a Program

Now let's use *imake* to do some serious software development—the "hello, world" program known and loved by C programmers the world over. Create a file *hello.c* that contains the following program:

```
#include <stdio.h>
main ()
{
    printf ("hello, world\n");
}
```

If you were writing a *Makefile* by hand to build the *hello* program, it might look like this:

```
hello: hello.o
    cc -o hello hello.o
```

Then you'd run *make* to generate the commands that build the program:

```
% make
cc -c hello.c
cc -o hello hello.o
```

To use *imake* instead, edit *Imakefile* so that it contains the following single line:

```
NormalProgramTarget(hello,hello.o,NullParameter,NullParameter,NullParameter)
```

This is a target description, i.e., a specification indicating something to be built. You may find it unedifying at this point. That's okay; with *imake*, nothing is obvious at first. `NormalProgramTarget()` is what's called a rule.[*] When you need a target entry to build a program, you invoke a rule in your *Imakefile*. Then, when you generate the *Makefile* from the *Imakefile*, the rule invocation is turned into an entry that specifies how to build the target.

Rules often take arguments; `NormalProgramTarget()` takes five. The first specifies the name of the program to build. The second specifies the object file or files from which to build it. The third, fourth, and fifth arguments are used when you have more complicated targets that require special information. Since *hello* is a pretty simple program, no more information is necessary. However, we don't just leave the last three arguments empty, because that causes problems on some systems. Instead, to indicate "no value" explicitly, we use the word `NullParameter`. This is a placeholder with a null value.

After you've specified the target you're interested in by invoking `NormalProgram-Target()` in the *Imakefile*, you must regenerate the *Makefile* to reflect these

---

[*] *imake* rules are defined in the configuration files. We'll look at rule definition guidelines in Chapter 3, *Understanding Configuration Files*.

changes. This is a fact of *imake* life: you must rebuild the *Makefile* after each change to the *Imakefile*. Do that now:

```
% make Makefile
```

Now build the program. When you run *make*, it should produce the commands necessary to compile and link *hello*:[*]

```
% make
cc -O -I/usr/X11R6.1/include -c hello.c
rm -f hello
cc -o hello -L/usr/X11R6.1/lib hello.o
```

Run the program and you should see a familar refrain:

```
% hello
hello, world
```

Your mission is now accomplished, so you can clean up:

```
% make clean
rm -f hello
rm -f *.CKP *.ln *.BAK *.bak *.o core errs ,* *~ *.a .emacs_* \
    tags TAGS make.log MakeOut "#"*
```

make clean generates one *rm* command to remove the executable *hello* program, and another to remove general leftover rubble (such as *hello.o*). `NormalProgram-Target()` produces the `clean` target entry that generates the first *rm* command, and the configuration files automatically provide a default `clean` entry that generates the second.

At this point, by working through the preceding exercises, you've engaged in several of the activities common with *imake*:

* Writing an *Imakefile*

* Bootstrapping the initial *Makefile* with *xmkmf*

* Using the *Makefile* to regenerate itself

* Using the *Makefile* to build a program

* Using the *Makefile* to remove debris

---

[*] If you get an error at this point, look in your *Makefile*. If you find `NullParameter` there, you're using a set of configuration files that doesn't define it. See "Common Problems" at the end of the chapter for a fix.

Exercise 3: Examine the Makefile

Gird your loins and prepare for combat: I want you to take a look through the *Makefile*. You'll find that it can be divided into three sections:

- Several zillion lines of *make* variable assignments

- Target entries generated by your *Imakefile*

- Target entries supplied for you automatically by the configuration files

To find the section of the *Makefile* that corresponds to your *Imakefile*, search for a `hello` target entry. You should discover five lines that look something like this:

```
hello: hello.o
    $(RM) $@
    $(CCLINK) -o $@ $(LDOPTIONS) hello.o $(LDLIBS) $(EXTRA_LOAD_FLAGS)
clean::
    $(RM) hello
```

To better understand this, ignore all the stuff about `LDOPTIONS`, `LDLIBS`, etc. In essence, you have two target entries here: a `hello` entry for building your program, and a `clean` entry for getting rid of it. That's all. These two entries resulted from your invocation of `NormalProgramTarget()` in the *Imakefile*.

Everything else in the *Makefile* was put there by *imake* automatically—and it certainly does put a lot there! If you examine an *imake*-generated *Makefile* for anything but the briefest period of time, its contents may prompt you to cry in anguish, "Why is the *Makefile* so complicated?" Attempts to explain this generally derive from one of two schools of thought. One is that *imake* wants to scare you off so you'll leave it alone. The other is that *imake* is trying to knock you insensate by subjecting you to information overload. The effectiveness of both strategies in discouraging developers from using *imake* must be admitted, and it's difficult to choose between the hypotheses because each seems to account for about half of *imake*'s victims.

But *imake* should produce neither fear nor stupor in you. The complexity actually has a different purpose altogether: to provide flexibility. It's unfortunate that flexibility is attained by sacrificing simplicity of the *Makefile*, but that's the way it is. If the complexity tempts you to toss *imake* out the window, consider these two things first:

- The complexity allows the configuration file writer a lot of latitude to parameterize how particular kinds of targets are built on different types of machines. But the complexity in the *Makefile* comes from the configuration files, not from the Imakefiles. If you don't write configuration files (and most *imake* users don't), you don't need to deal directly with the complexity that's in them.

- You don't often deal with the complexity in the *Makefile*, either. Typically you don't even look at it. I'm only having you do so in this exercise so you can see the connection between what you've written in the *Imakefile* and what ends up in the *Makefile*. Normally, when you use *imake*, you work with the *Imakefile* to express what you want to do and let *make* worry about processing the *Makefile*. *imake*-generated Makefiles are like PostScript files: people can read them, but they're really intended for machine processors.

The difference in the complexity of the *Imakefile* and the *Makefile* reflects a difference in the nature of their contents. The *Imakefile* contains the "what" details: what you want to build, and what to build it from. That kind of information doesn't vary from machine to machine, so the *Imakefile* is machine independent. (For instance, you usually don't change the name of a program or the set of source files you build it from as you build it on different machines.)

The *Makefile* contains "what" information, but it also contains the "how" details that come from the configuration files. Those files supply the commands necessary to build the targets in which you're interested, parameterized specifically for your particular machine. The *Makefile* is thus very machine dependent.

In a sense, *imake* takes your simple generic target description file and adds to it all the ugly machine-specific complexity necessary to generate the correct *Makefile* for your system (Figure 2–1). That complexity ends up in the *Makefile*, which therefore becomes machine specific and ugly, too. But since you work with the *Imakefile*, you don't care.

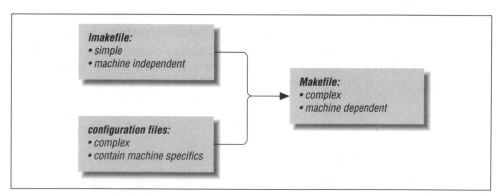

Figure 2–1: Location of complexities

imake generates Makefiles that heavily use *make* variables. Look again at the `hello` and `clean` entries generated by `NormalProgramTarget()`. You'll notice that practically the only things referenced literally in these two entries are the arguments you passed to `NormalProgramTarget()`, namely *hello* and *hello.o*. Everything else is specified using *make* variables: `CC`, `RM`, `LDLIBS`, etc. If you look at the

first section of the *Makefile* (the part containing all the *make* variable assignments),
you should be able to find the lines where each of these *make* variables get its
values. On one of my machines the lines look like this:

```
        CCLINK = $(CC)
            RM = rm -f
     LDOPTIONS = $(CDEBUGFLAGS) $(CCOPTIONS) $(EXTRA_LDOPTIONS) \
                 $(THREADS_LDFLAGS) $(LOCAL_LDFLAGS) $(LDPRELIB)
        LDLIBS = $(LDPOSTLIB) $(THREADS_LIBS) $(SYS_LIBRARIES) $(EXTRA_LIBRARIES)
EXTRA_LOAD_FLAGS =
```

The lines may be different on your system. That's because these variables express
the parameters of your machine's configuration; *imake* figures out from the configuration files which values are appropriate for your machine and writes those values into your Makefiles. Of course, someone has to put the correct parameter
values in the configuration files initially. We'll discuss how this is done in Chapter
3, *Understanding Configuration Files*.

Exercise 4: Compare Makefiles from Different Systems

If you have an account on a second machine running a different version of UNIX,
I suggest you move *hello.c* and *Imakefile* to that machine and build the *hello* program again by repeating Exercises 2 and 3. (You'll need *imake*, *xmkmf*, and the
configuration files on the second machine, of course.) Then compare the Makefiles
from the two systems.

By comparing the Makefiles, you'll see how *imake* individualizes a *Makefile* to the
machine on which it's running, even though the *Imakefile* remains the same. You'll
also see differences in the commands *make* generates when you run it. For example, when I build *hello* on several systems to which I have access, these are the
commands that result:

NetBSD 1.1:

```
% make
gcc -m68040 -Wa,-m68040 -O6 -I/usr/local/X11R6.1/include -c hello.c
rm -f hello
gcc -o hello -m68040 -Wa,-m68040 -O6 -L/usr/local/X11R6.1/lib hello.o
```

SunOS 4.1.1:

```
% make
cc -O -I/usr/X11R6.1/include -target sun4 -c hello.c
rm -f hello
cc -o hello -O -L/usr/X11R6.1/lib hello.o
```

Mips RISC/os 4.01:

```
% make
cc -O -signed -systype bsd43 -Olimit 2000 -Wf,-XNd8400,-XNp12000 \
    -I/usr/X11R6.1/include -DMips -DBSD43 -c hello.c
rm -f hello
cc -o hello -O -signed -systype bsd43 -Olimit 2000 -Wf,-XNd8400,-XNp12000 \
    -L/usr/X11R6.1/lib hello.o -lmld
```

HP-UX 9.05:

```
% make
cc +O1 -Aa +ESlit -I/usr/X11R6.1/include -Dhpux -DSYSV -D_HPUX_SOURCE -c hello.c
rm -f hello
cc -o hello +O1 -Aa +ESlit -L/usr/X11R6.1/lib hello.o
```

Each set of commands differs from the others. This demonstrates two things:

- You as the *Imakefile* writer don't have to think about machine dependencies, so the same *Imakefile* can be used on different systems.

- *imake* does a lot of thinking about machine dependencies, so from a given *Imakefile* produces Makefiles that differ quite a bit from system to system.

The *Makefile* can even vary within a given system if the machine supports multiple development environments. For example, RISC/os supports both the BSD and System V environments. The commands shown for RISC/os above are those for the BSD environment. If the configuration files were set up to select the System V environment instead, the commands would be different. Again, the *Imakefile* wouldn't need to change since the configuration files would take care of the necessary adjustments.

Exercise 5: Generate Header File Dependencies

In the next several exercises, we'll modify the *Imakefile* to handle some other common targets: depend, all, lint, and install. Let's add the depend target first.

If you're building C programs, you need to indicate which targets are dependent on header files: when a header file changes, object files compiled from source files that include that header file must be rebuilt. The problem with this kind of dependency is that it can't be specified statically in the *Makefile* due to differences in the way different systems organize header files. For instance, *hello.c* contains the following #include directive:

```
#include <stdio.h>
```

This means *hello.o* must be recompiled whenever *stdio.h* changes. If *stdio.h* is located in */usr/include*, the dependency line in the *Makefile* looks like this:

```
hello.o: /usr/include/stdio.h
```

If *stdio.h* is located in */usr/sysv/include* instead, the dependency is different:

```
hello.o: /usr/sysv/include/stdio.h
```

The implication is that header file dependencies must be generated dynamically. That's the job of the tool *makedepend*:[*]

- It searches your source files to find #include directives.

- It looks through header file directories to determine where the included files are located.

- It adds the appropriate dependency lines to the end of the *Makefile*.

Of course, you don't want to run *makedepend* by hand, you want *make* to do it for you. That involves two additions to the *Imakefile*:

- Invoke the DependTarget() rule to generate a depend entry.

- Add an assignment for the *make* variable SRCS. DependTarget() has no idea what files you're interested in, so it assumes that SRCS names all the source files to be processed. It's up to you to supply the proper value.

After you make these changes to your *Imakefile*, it should look like this:

```
SRCS = hello.c
NormalProgramTarget(hello,hello.o,NullParameter,NullParameter,NullParameter)
DependTarget()
```

Rebuild the *Makefile* to reflect the changes you just made, then run *makedepend* to generate the dependencies:

```
% make Makefile
+ rm -f Makefile.bak
+ mv Makefile Makefile.bak
imake -DUseInstalled -I/usr/X11R6.1/lib/X11/config -DTOPDIR=. -DCURDIR=.
% make depend
makedepend -- -I/usr/X11R6.1/include -- hello.c
```

Notice that *hello.c* appears in the *makedepend* command generated by the depend target. That's a good sign; it tells you that the value of SRCS was correctly substituted into the command.

---

* There are several programs named *makedepend* floating around. You need the one written for use with *imake*. It's available as part of the *itools* distribution (see Appendix A, *Obtaining Configuration Software*).

The object file *hello.o* is dependent on the header file *stdio.h*, since the latter is #include'd by *hello.c*. So the end of the *Makefile* should look like this when *makedepend* gets done with it:

```
# --------------------------------------------------------------
# dependencies generated by makedepend
# DO NOT DELETE

hello.o: /usr/include/stdio.h
```

If you build a more sophisticated program that consists of multiple source files, or if you build multiple programs using the same *Imakefile*, set SRCS to the names of all the source files for all the programs. However, you still invoke Depend-Target() just once in the *Imakefile*. For example, suppose you have another program *goodbye* compiled from *good.c* and *bye.c*:

good.c:

```
main ()
{
    bye ();
}
```

bye.c:

```
#include <stdio.h>
bye ()
{
    printf ("goodbye, cruel world\n");
}
```

To modify the *Imakefile* to know about the second program, invoke Normal-ProgramTarget() again and add the source files *good.c* and *bye.c* to the value of SRCS:

```
SRCS = hello.c good.c bye.c
NormalProgramTarget(hello,hello.o,NullParameter,NullParameter,NullParameter)
NormalProgramTarget(goodbye,good.o bye.o,NullParameter,NullParameter,NullParameter)
DependTarget()
```

You've changed the *Imakefile* again, so rebuild the *Makefile*:

```
% make Makefile
```

After you do this, take another look through your *Makefile*. You'll discover that it has additional entries to build and remove *goodbye* now, but that the header file dependency information at the end has disappeared into thin air! *imake* doesn't carry that information from one *Makefile* to another, so rebuilding the *Makefile* destroys any dependencies you've generated before. This is another fact of *imake*

life: when you change the *Imakefile*, you must not only recreate the *Makefile*, you
must regenerate header file dependencies. Therefore, your standard procedure
should always be:

```
% make Makefile
% make depend
```

Notice that two separate commands are used here. If instead you tried to combine
the steps into one command:

```
% make Makefile depend
```

you'd find it wouldn't work; no dependencies would be generated. However, if
you then ran that same command a second time, it would work. Why?

When you first assign a value to SRCS in the *Imakefile*, the *Makefile* doesn't yet
know about it. Thus, the first time you run:

```
% make Makefile depend
```

the command is processed using a *Makefile* that contains no value for SRCS. The
depend target is processed using an empty source file list, and no dependencies
are generated.

This is nonintuitive, because it's easy to assume that since the Makefile target is
processed first, the *Makefile* built by it is used to process the depend target. But it
isn't. *make* reads the *Makefile* into memory and processes all targets named on the
command line using the in-memory copy, regardless of what happens to the
Makefile in the meantime.

The command does rebuild the *Makefile*, though, and it puts the SRCS assignment
into it. So the second time you run the command, the depend target is processed
with the new (nonempty) source file list and dependencies are generated correctly.

Lesson: If you need to rebuild the *Makefile* and process other targets as well, it's
better to recreate the *Makefile* first, and then process any other targets in a separate *make* command:

```
% make Makefile
% make other-targets
```

Exercise 6: Add a Default Target

Typically, when you have multiple programs listed in a *Makefile*, you want to be
able to build all of them with a single command, usually one of the following:

```
% make all
% make
```

If you try these commands using the *Makefile* resulting from the Exercise 5, you'll find that they don't work properly. The first gives you an error message ("Don't know how to make target `all`"), and the second builds *hello* but not *goodbye*.

To understand why, consider what's in the *Makefile*. The first instance of Normal-ProgramTarget() in the *Imakefile* generates hello and clean targets. The second instance generates goodbye and clean targets. That's why the commands above don't work:

- *make all* fails because there's no all target.

- *make* (with no argument) builds only *hello* because when you don't specify any target, *make* builds the target associated with the first entry in the *Make-file*. In this case, that's the hello entry.

It's easy to fix the problem. The AllTarget() rule is used when you want to be able to build a target without having to name it explicitly. Invoke AllTarget() in the *Imakefile* before each invocation of NormalProgramTarget():

```
SRCS = hello.c good.c bye.c
AllTarget(hello)
NormalProgramTarget(hello,hello.o,NullParameter,NullParameter,NullParameter)
AllTarget(goodbye)
NormalProgramTarget(goodbye,good.o bye.o,NullParameter,NullParameter,NullParameter)
DependTarget()
```

When you rebuild the *Makefile*, the preceding change results in all entries for each program. This has two effects:

- *make all* causes both programs to be built because each is associated with an all entry.

- all becomes the default target because the first entry in the *Makefile* is now an all entry. Thus, *make* is equivalent to *make all*.

Exercise 7: Check Source Files

If you want to improve your programs by using *lint* to find problems in your source code, invoke LintTarget() in your *Imakefile* to generate a lint entry. LintTarget() is like DependTarget() in that it assumes SRCS is set to the list of all source files of interest; thus, it should be invoked only once per *Imakefile*.

You've already specified the value of SRCS for use with DependTarget(), so you needn't do so again. Just add LintTarget() to the *Imakefile*:

```
SRCS = hello.c good.c bye.c
AllTarget(hello)
NormalProgramTarget(hello,hello.o,NullParameter,NullParameter,NullParameter)
AllTarget(goodbye)
NormalProgramTarget(goodbye,good.o bye.o,NullParameter,NullParameter,NullParameter)
DependTarget()
LintTarget()
```

After you rebuild the *Makefile* (don't forget to regenerate the dependencies, too!), you can use the lint entry to run your sources through the *lint* program:

```
% make lint
lint -axz -DLINT -I/usr/X11R6.1/include hello.c good.c bye.c
```

One problem here is that some of *lint*'s output is superfluous. For example, it will tell you that main is multiply defined. That's because the source for multiple programs passes through a single invocation of *lint*, which therefore sees more than one *main()* function.[*] With a little practice, you'll learn to distinguish useful from nonuseful *lint* output.

Exercise 8: Install the Program

When you write a program, you usually intend to install it somewhere. Your *Imakefile* doesn't help you do that yet because it generates no install entries. To add them, use InstallProgram(). It takes two arguments:

```
InstallProgram(program,directory)
```

program is the program to install and *directory* is the directory in which to install it.

Modify your *Imakefile* by invoking InstallProgram() once for each program:

```
SRCS = hello.c good.c bye.c
AllTarget(hello)
NormalProgramTarget(hello,hello.o,NullParameter,NullParameter,NullParameter)
InstallProgram(hello,$(BINDIR))
AllTarget(goodbye)
NormalProgramTarget(goodbye,good.o bye.o,NullParameter,NullParameter,NullParameter)
InstallProgram(goodbye,$(BINDIR))
DependTarget()
LintTarget()
```

BINDIR is defined in the configuration files as some public installation directory on your system. It usually has a value like */usr/X11R6.1/bin* or */usr/bin/X11*.

_____

[*] It would be better if *lint* were invoked multiple times, once for each program's sources. This is a shortcoming of the X11 rules.

After you rebuild the *Makefile* (and the dependencies), it will have an install target entry for each program. Of course, *hello* and *goodbye* are just toy programs, so we don't really want to install them. But we can see what *make* would do if we were to try. The −*n* ("no execution") flag tells *make* to show us the commands it would generate without actually executing them:

```
% make -n install
if [ -d /usr/X11R6.1/bin ]; then set +x; \
else (set -x; mkdirhier /usr/X11R6.1/bin); fi
install -c hello /usr/X11R6.1/bin/hello
if [ -d /usr/X11R6.1/bin ]; then set +x; \
else (set -x; mkdirhier /usr/X11R6.1/bin); fi
install -c goodbye /usr/X11R6.1/bin/goodbye
```

The *Makefile* generates a sequence of installation commands for each program. As part of the sequence, the installation directory is created if it's missing. *imake* uses *mkdirhier* for directory creation instead of *mkdir* because *mkdirhier* creates intermediate directories if they're missing. (Some systems have a version of *mkdir* that can create intermediate directories if invoked with a −*p* option; if yours is one of them, you might see *mkdir −p* rather than *mkdirhier* in the commands above.)

Your *Imakefile* is now complete. It can build, depend, *lint*, install, and clean up your programs—in just nine lines of instructions. Not bad.

What Have You Learned?

This chapter provides an overview of how to use *imake* and an *Imakefile* to develop programs. Here are some points to remember:

- *Imakefile* writing is primarily an exercise in rule invocation.
- Rebuild the *Makefile* after you modify the *Imakefile*.
- Regenerate header file dependencies after you rebuild the *Makefile*.
- *imake*-generated Makefiles are larger than those you'd write by hand, but normally you don't need to look at them.

Now that you have some experience with *imake*, where do you go from here? To understand how configuration files do their job, read Chapter 3, *Understanding Configuration Files*. To learn about the X11 files in particular, read Chapter 5, *The X11 Configuration Files*. For further discussion about using the X11 files to write Imakefiles, read Chapter 6, *Writing Imakefiles*. If you're anxious to learn more about writing Imakefiles right away, you can read much of Chapter 6 without having read Chapters 3 or 5.

Common Problems

This section describes some problems you might encounter while doing the exercises in this chapter, and how to solve them.

Makefile Generation Failure

If you create the empty *Imakefile* in Exercise 1 and then get the error message "Cannot read Imakefile" from *imake* when you run *xmkmf*, you probably have an X11R6 distribution with too few patches applied. *imake* from R6 rejects zero-length Imakefiles unless it's built from a distribution at patchlevel 4 or higher. As a workaround, just put a blank line in your *Imakefile* and run *xmkmf* again. A better solution is to apply the available patches to your R6 distribution, then rebuild and reinstall *imake*. You can get the patches from *ftp.x.org* in the */pub/R6/fixes* directory. Or you can upgrade to R6.1.

NullParameter Problems

You have a `NullParameter` problem if you see an error message like this in Exercise 2 after generating a *Makefile* and running *make*:

    Make: Don't know how to make NullParameter. Stop.

This means that `NullParameter` in your *Imakefile* isn't being processed properly. If you look in your *Makefile*, you'll find it appearing in your target entries. The cause is most likely that you're using configuration files from X11R4 or files that are based on X11R4, such as older OpenWindows files. (`NullParameter` wasn't invented until X11R5.)

The quickest fix is to define `NullParameter` at the top of your *Imakefile* with a line like this:

    #define NullParameter

A more general long-term solution is to define `NullParameter` in your configuration files, if you have write access to them. Put the `NullParameter` definition at the top of the *Imake.rules* file. That way, `NullParameter` will be available in any *Imakefile* you write. Other solutions are to upgrade to a more recent set of configuration files, or to use the TOUR files (see Appendix A).

XCOMM Problems

Sometimes *make* won't work at all after you generate the *Makefile*. For instance, *make* may quit with an error message like this:

```
make: Fatal error in reader: Makefile, line nnn: Unexpected end of line seen
```

Take a look at your *Makefile*; if you find it littered with XCOMM symbols, you're using the version of *imake* from X11R5 and the configuration files from X11R6 or later. This is a problem because XCOMM is used for writing comments into the *Makefile*, and comment handling changed between R5 and R6 (see Chapter 4, *Writing Comments*, for more information about this). The solution is to replace your version of *imake* with the current version.

3

Understanding Configuration Files

The thing which I greatly feared is come upon me.
—Job 3:25

Now it's time to send you fleeing in terror. In this chapter we tackle the Dread Configuration Files to see what's in them and how they work together. It's possible to write Imakefiles by looking at existing ones and copying the forms you find there, and you can get by this way for a while. However, to write Imakefiles effectively, at some point you'll need to bite the bullet and look at the configuration files you're using and understand how they work.

The more you know about your configuration files, the better you'll know what you can do with them. Sooner or later you'll find yourself trying to use them to develop software having configuration requirements very different from those of the project for which the files were written. When that happens, you'll need to be able to determine whether you can continue to use the files and work around their limitations, or whether you'd be better off writing your own. But you can't make a realistic evaluation of your files if they seem like gibberish when you look them over. You'll need to be able to make sense of them.

This chapter explains how to understand configuration files by showing what goes on behind the scenes as *imake* turns your *Imakefile* into a *Makefile*. I'm not going to start with a set of files used to configure some existing project and explain how they work. Instead I'll use a progressive approach, starting from scratch and showing the process you might go through if you tried to design configuration files yourself. That way you'll see how certain design issues come up and how to resolve them. This will give you a better feel not just for what configuration files do, but for why they do things a particular way.

I'll start with some primitive ways of organizing configuration information. Then I'll point out problems—why simple structures fail to increase portability as much as we might like. That will lead us into more sophisticated organizations that address the problems one by one, until finally we end up with a reasonably capable configuration file architecture.

This is a relatively difficult chapter, and it may not be painless. But by the end, you'll understand the general ideas and concepts used in *imake* configuration files. You should then be able to apply your knowledge to any set of files and determine how they work: despite differences in the way sets of configuration files are designed, there are usually broad areas of agreement.

Basic Principles

The key aspects of the configuration files used by *imake* are the kinds of information in them and the way the files are organized. You should keep in mind two fundamental principles whenever you approach any set of configuration files:

* The way configuration files are organized defines their architecture. Files have specific purposes that you need to determine.

* Configuration files consist of a small number of constructs that are used over and over—the peculiaries of *imake*-speak that are its idioms. To understand the contents of configuration files, you must understand these idioms.

I will proceed to develop several configuration file architectures, introducing the idioms along the way.

Use Machine-Independent Description Files

When you use *make*, you write a target description file called a *Makefile*. However, Makefiles are not portable because the commands needed to build targets vary from system to system. As we saw in Chapter 1, *Introduction*, this is true even for very simple programs. Thus, our first step is to develop an alternative form of description file that doesn't change when you move your software around among different machines.

If we examine *Makefile* target entries, we find that some things remain the same when we port programs to different machines, whereas other things vary. For example, the set of source files from which a program is built usually stays the same no matter what system you build it on. On the other hand, the commands to generate the object files and link them together are extremely likely to vary from system to system—special compiler flags, link options, system libraries, and so forth may be needed.

This tells us that a machine-independent description file will specify what to build and what to build it from. It will not specify the details about how to build it; those are machine dependent. To put this observation into practice, we need a way to abstract target-building instructions out of our target descriptions.

Recognize Target-Building Patterns

Suppose we want to build two programs. The *Makefile* entries might look like this:*

```
proga: proga.o
    cc -o proga proga.o -lm
install:: proga
    install proga /usr/local/bin

progb: progb.o parse.o
    cc -o progb progb.o parse.o -ly
install:: progb
    install progb /usr/local/bin
```

Observe that the programs are built according to one pattern and installed according to another. It's typical of Makefiles that target entries tend to be written using highly redundant patterns. We can exploit these redundancies by using prototypes so that we only need to specify information that varies between entries. For example, the general form of the program-building entry is this:

```
PROGRAM: OBJECT-FILES
    cc -o PROGRAM OBJECT-FILES LIBRARIES
```

This prototype specifies several things: the entry target is the program name, the program's dependencies are its object files, it's built by running the C compiler, etc. The prototype doesn't specify the program name, object files, or libraries for particular targets, although it shows where they should be placed in the entry. Those pieces of information must be supplied on a per-target basis. If we want to generate a target entry, we can copy the prototype into the *Makefile* and substitute

---

* Double colons are used in the `install` target entries. This allows multiple entries to be associated with the target name. The double colon mechanism is not a widely appreciated feature of *make*, but it's essential for writing configuration files. We'll use it frequently in this handbook.

the appropriate information into the correct places. For instance, to produce entries for *proga* and *progb*, we'd make the following substitutions:

For *proga*:

```
      PROGRAM → proga
 OBJECT-FILES → proga.o
    LIBRARIES → -lm
```

For *progb*:

```
      PROGRAM → progb
 OBJECT-FILES → progb.o parse.o
    LIBRARIES → -ly
```

In a similar way, the program installation entries follow a pattern like this:

```
install:: PROGRAM
     install PROGRAM DIRECTORY
```

The prototype indicates the general form of the install entry; to produce entries for particular targets, we'd need to give specific program names and installation directories:

For *proga*:

```
   PROGRAM → proga
 DIRECTORY → /usr/local/bin
```

For *progb*:

```
   PROGRAM → progb
 DIRECTORY → /usr/local/bin
```

Naturally, we don't want to do any of this prototype copying and substitution by hand. The mere thought is enough to make us gag. We want to write specifications that *imake* can process automatically, so we can tell it something like this: "Take these prototypes and generate *Makefile* entries for such-and-such targets, using the following pieces of information." Then we'd expect *imake* to turn our target specifications into full-blown *Makefile* entries for us.

You may have noticed that what we're asking *imake* to do here bears a suspicious resemblance to macro processing:

- Prototypes are like macro definitions
- "Build such-and-such an entry" is like invoking a macro
- Substituting target-specific information into a prototype is like performing macro parameter substitution

Indeed, that's just how *imake* works, although in typical UNIX fashion, *imake* avoids as much work as possible by calling on an existing program to do the work. In *imake*'s case, the choice is *cpp.**

cpp macros with arguments are invoked like this:

```
MacroName(arg_1,arg_2,...,arg_n)
```

Macros describing how to generate *Makefile* entries are called rules. In a macro definition, the macro's name describes what kind of entry to generate, the body provides the entry prototype, and the arguments indicate the per-target information to substitute into the prototype.

If we take the entries in the *Makefile* for *proga* and *progb* and express them using macro notation, they look something like this:

```
BuildProgramTarget(proga,proga.o,-lm)
InstallProgramTarget(proga,/usr/local/bin)

BuildProgramTarget(progb,progb.o parse.o,-ly)
InstallProgramTarget(progb,/usr/local/bin)
```

These invocations comprise the target description file for *imake*—the *Imakefile*. Notice that it's smaller than the corresponding *Makefile*. By taking advantage of patterns in the way we tend to do things, our target descriptions become more concise.

The rule invocations also contain information only about what we want done. They don't say anything about how to do it, i.e., they don't indicate what commands need to be run to build targets. Since machine dependencies tend to be concentrated in those commands, moving the commands out of the target specifications and into the macro definitions has the effect of making our specifications more machine independent. (They aren't completely so; the installation directory is hardwired into them, for instance. We'll deal with that problem in the section "Parameterizing Variation," later in this chapter.)

To produce a *Makefile*, we feed the rule definitions and the *Imakefile* into *imake*, which runs *cpp* to do all the macro processing for it. *cpp* reads the definitions and replaces each invocation with its proper expansion, substituting arguments as necessary. When it's all done, out pops our *Makefile*. That was easy.

Except we haven't said anything yet about what the macro definitions look like. Oops! We'd better do that now.

---

* Another macro processor such as *m4* could have been used. *cpp* was a more expedient choice simply because *imake* is often used to write C programs and C programmers are already familiar with *cpp*. *m4* isn't as well known or widely used. If you happen to be unfamiliar with *cpp*, see Appendix G, *Basics of make and cpp*.

Inventing a Rule Macro Syntax

Let's consider how to write rules, using the target specifications for *proga* as an example. We want the following rule invocations:

```
BuildProgramTarget(proga,proga.o,-lm)
InstallProgramTarget(proga,/usr/local/bin)
```

to turn into these *Makefile* entries:

```
proga: proga.o
    cc -o proga proga.o -lm
install:: proga
    install proga /usr/local/bin
```

cpp macros are specified using #define directives, so our rules should look something like this:

```
#define BuildProgramTarget(program,objects,libraries)
program: objects
    cc -o program objects libraries
#define InstallProgramTarget(program,destdir)
install:: program
    install program destdir
```

The first line of a rule gives the invocation sequence, i.e., the name of the rule and the arguments we must pass to it. The other lines specify the body of the definition, which is what invocations of the rule should expand to. However, these definitions won't work without modification, because *cpp* macro definitions only extend to the end of the #define line unless you put a backslash at the end of lines that should continue to the next. To fix the definitions so they can be spread over multiple lines, we add continuation indicators to all lines of each but the last:

```
#define BuildProgramTarget(program,objects,libraries)         \
program: objects                                               \
    cc -o program objects libraries
#define InstallProgramTarget(program,destdir)                  \
install:: program                                              \
    install program destdir
```

This allows us to write multiple-line input. However, the rules won't produce multiple-line output, because *cpp* collapses all definitions to a single line internally! The resulting macro expansions would look like this:

```
proga: proga.o    cc -o proga proga.o -lm
install:: proga    install proga /usr/local/bin
```

That kind of thing would give *make* indigestion since the entries have target and command lines glued together.

This problem is serious enough that *imake* agrees, grudgingly, to do a little work itself. But it exacts revenge on us by introducing a hideous construction. Rather than using \ to indicate line continuation, we must use @@\ instead:

```
#define BuildProgramTarget(program,objects,libraries)    @@\
program: objects                                         @@\
    cc -o program objects libraries

#define InstallProgramTarget(program,destdir)            @@\
install:: program                                        @@\
    install program destdir
```

I know what you're thinking, and I agree: this syntax is U-G-L-Y. But it's effective. Here's how the @@\ trick works. When *cpp* reads a rule definition, it removes the backslashes and collapses the definition to a single line. Occurrences of @@ are left alone, since they have no special meaning as far as *cpp* is concerned. Any invocations of the rule occurring later in the input are expanded normally (including the @@s). *imake* examines the *cpp* output for @@ sequences and replaces them with line breaks to restore the multiple lines we want.

Let's follow our sample *Imakefile* as it winds its way through this process. *imake* takes the rules and the *Imakefile* and feeds them into *cpp*. *cpp* processes them and disgorges something like this:

```
@@proga: proga.o @@    cc -o proga proga.o -lm
@@install:: proga @@    install proga /usr/local/bin
@@progb: progb.o parse.o @@    cc -o progb progb.o parse.o -ly
@@install:: progb @@    install progb /usr/local/bin
```

imake takes this result and breaks the lines where it sees instances of @@ to produce the intended final output:

```
proga: proga.o
    cc -o proga proga.o -lm
install:: proga
    install proga /usr/local/bin

progb: progb.o parse.o
    cc -o progb progb.o parse.o -ly
install:: progb
    install progb /usr/local/bin
```

Voilà!

In short, the purpose of the strange syntax of *imake* rules is to keep *cpp* from totally destroying the usefulness of its own output for *make* purposes. Thus, although *imake* relies heavily on *cpp*, one of *imake*'s jobs is to undo some of the damage done by *cpp*—an uneasy alliance indeed.

There is nothing inherently special about @@ except that it's not treated specially by *cpp*, and it's unlikely to be used in a *Makefile*. This makes it a pretty safe choice for a symbol whose only role in life is to serve as a transient placemarker.

Of all the dramas played out in *imake*, the role of @@ is surely among the saddest—a tragedy in miniature. Dutifully taking its place in the process of *Makefile*-creation, the @@-symbol serves faithfully and steadfastly without complaint when thrown into the maelstrom of *cpp* processing. Yet its reward at the last is to be thrown out and discarded unceremoniously—refuse cast on the slag heap, unacknowledged and forgotten. Ignominious fate!

imake rules are simultaneously awful and wonderful: awful because the syntax is so bizarre when you're trying to write them, wonderful because once they're written, you can invoke them in your *Imakefile* to concisely express what you want to do without concern for how to do it. If it's any consolation, I assure you that my own eyes glazed over the first few times I tried to understand a set of rules. Take heart: immunity to *imake* rules develops eventually through repeated exposure. The syntax that at first seems deadly becomes second nature.

imake rules can draw on all the power of *cpp*'s macro-processing capabilities, so they're extremely powerful for generating *Makefile* entries. Despite the difficulties of their syntax, rules are the first idiom of the language of *imake*:

Idiom 3-1
_____

> Specify targets in an *Imakefile* using rules defined as *cpp* macros. This lets you specify what you want to do without getting bogged down in the details of how to do it.

What do we gain by using rule macros?

- Rules provide a target description shorthand; it's easier to specify a target to build by invoking a rule in an *Imakefile* than by writing out a full entry in a *Makefile*. Since writing *Makefile* entries can be tedious and error prone, especially for complex targets, specifying targets by invoking rules simplifies the software developer's task.

- Rules help hide machine dependencies by placing the mechanics of target building in the rule definitions rather than in the description file. The definitions can be placed in a configuration file that's located elsewhere (see the next section). As a result, an *Imakefile*, unlike a *Makefile*, contains machine-independent target descriptions, allowing us to concentrate on goal rather than process.

Organizing imake Input

I've been making vague statements about how "*imake* takes the rules and the *Imakefile* and does such-and-such with them." Such statements gloss over certain details. Just how is *imake* invoked? What are its arguments? What is its input? These questions bring us to the topic of configuration file architecture—how the information *imake* uses is organized.

imake gives you a lot of latitude to decide how to organize your information. It assumes you have an *Imakefile* describing the targets you want built, but, other than that, imposes little constraint on the structure of the input you give it. *imake* requires only that you use a template file that describes the input, and lets you specify the template's contents as you like. *imake* accomplishes this by constructing a temporary file, *Imakefile.c* containing the following three lines, then passing *Imakefile.c* to *cpp* for processing:[*]

```
#define IMAKE_TEMPLATE "template-name"
#define INCLUDE_IMAKEFILE <Imakefile-name>
#include IMAKE_TEMPLATE
```

The first two lines of *Imakefile.c* define symbolic names IMAKE_TEMPLATE and INCLUDE_IMAKEFILE for the template file and the target description file. (The default values of these symbols are *Imake.tmpl* and *Imakefile*.) The third line instructs *cpp* to read and process the template.[†]

The structure of *Imakefile.c* gives you freedom as well as responsibility. It gives you freedom by minimizing *imake*'s need to know anything about your configuration files. The template is the only configuration file that *imake* tells *cpp* to read directly. *imake* doesn't know anything about any other files the template might reference—not their names or even whether there are any. This means you can organize the template using any architecture that suits the requirements of your project.

The only file that the template must reference is the *Imakefile*. This is where your responsibility comes in. *imake* provides a symbolic name INCLUDE_IMAKEFILE by which to refer to the *Imakefile*, but doesn't actually cause its contents to be

---

[*] Older versions of *imake* (prior to the version distributed with X11R6) did not use a temporary file *Imakefile.c*. Instead, they wrote the three-line input directly into *cpp*'s standard input. However, some systems have a cranky *cpp* that will process only named files and won't accept input on *stdin*. This occurs under some versions of OSF/1, for example. Using a temporary file that can be named on the *cpp* command line solves this problem.

[†] Line 3 of *Imakefile.c* is an #include directive that uses a macro to specify the name of the file. If you have an older *cpp* that cannot handle this, see Appendix A, *Obtaining Configuration Software*, for information on alternate *cpp*s.

inserted into the input stream anywhere. Therefore, you must put the following line somewhere in the template if you want your description file to be processed:

```
#include INCLUDE_IMAKEFILE
```

Schematically, templates break down as shown in Figure 3–1. The `#include` line must be present somewhere in the template, so you implement your configuration file architecture by deciding what the template does before and after the *Imakefile* is processed.

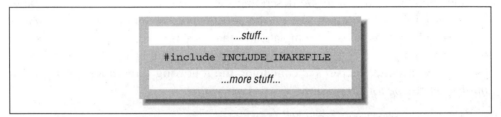

Figure 3–1: Schematic configuration file template architecture

We need to translate the general layout shown in Figure 3–1 into specifics. We have two kinds of information so far: rule definitions that specify how to build targets, and rule invocations that specify which targets to build. The invocations are the basic content of the *Imakefile*. What about the definitions? Where do they go?

If we adopt a modular approach we can separate rule definitions into their own file, *Imake.rules*. Our first version of the template, *Imake.tmpl*, is then quite simple, needing only to refer to the rules file *Imake.rules* and to the *Imakefile*:

```
#include <Imake.rules>            Rule macro definitions
#include INCLUDE_IMAKEFILE        Target descriptions
```

Now that we actually have one, the question arises as to where the template (and the files `#include`'d by it) should be located in the file system. We can decide this on the basis of how widely the files are used.

Each directory in a project is used for a particular purpose, so each *Imakefile* is different. When we're building a *Makefile* in a particular directory, we want to build it from the *Imakefile* in that same directory. By contrast, the template and rules files are the same no matter which directory of a project we're in. They should be placed in a well-known location and shared among all the Imakefiles with which they're used. Let's assume this configuration file directory is */usr/local/lib/myconfdir*.

In order that *cpp* be able to find all the files, *imake* would start it up like this:

```
cpp -I. -I/usr/local/lib/myconfdir Imakefile.c
```

cpp's *–Ipath* option means "look in the directory *path* when searching for files referenced by #include directives." *imake* passes two *–I* arguments to *cpp*. The first, *–I.*, allows *cpp* to find the *Imakefile* in the current directory. The second, *–I/usr/local/lib/myconfdir*, allows *cpp* to find the template and rules files in the configuration file directory.

Since it's a given that the *Imakefile* comes from the current directory, *imake* knows that it should pass *–I.* to *cpp* automatically. But *imake* doesn't know where the configuration file directory is and must find that out from its own command line. That implies *imake* itself must understand *–Ipath* and pass it along to *cpp*. Thus, you invoke *imake* like this:

```
imake -I/usr/local/lib/myconfdir
```

An alternative architecture is to put rule definitions directly in the *Imakefile* rather than in their own file. There are good reasons not to do so, all of which hinge on the distinction between the *Imakefile* as directory specific and rule definitions as shared. Suppose we put the definitions in an *Imakefile*. If we ever wanted to use them in another *Imakefile*, we'd have to copy them from one file to the other. Worse yet, suppose we copy them into several Imakefiles and then find a bug in one of our rules—we'd have to fix it everywhere we've used it.

Keeping the rules in their own file and putting them in a separate directory is a much better policy. The file can be shared, so a rule only needs to be defined in one place, even if it's used by a number of Imakefiles. Should we later find a bug in it, or think of a way to make it better, we edit the definition (once), then use *imake* to rebuild Makefiles automatically. We don't have to edit zillions of Makefiles by hand.

This principle applies more widely, not just to rules, but to any sort of configuration information that needs to be available more generally than in a single directory. The mechanism for sharing information is:

- Make sure that the template knows how to get at the information. The easiest way to do this is to put the information in its own file and #include that file from the template.

- Put the file in a well-known directory.

- Tell *imake* where the directory is, using *–Ipath* when *imake* is invoked.

Parameterizing Variation

Thus far we've developed three files containing three types of information:

- The *Imakefile*, containing machine-independent descriptions of targets to build

- *Imake.rules*, containing target entry prototypes expressed as *cpp* macros

- *Imake.tmpl*, containing a simple template for a configuration file architecture

These files give us a way to move machine dependencies out of our target description file (the *Imakefile*), but they haven't yet really done much to enhance portability.

Rules are a case in point. Rules allow us to generate target entries easily—we just invoke a rule in an *Imakefile* and it turns into a target entry in a *Makefile*. But as we've written them so far, our rules are still machine dependent and don't in themselves give us much help in porting our software. To see this, we need only ask what happens if we want to use our rules to build software on another machine. Consider the present definition of `InstallProgramTarget()`:

```
#define InstallProgramTarget(program,destdir)          @@\
install:: program                                      @@\
    install program destdir
```

If we want to build software on a machine with a missing or broken *install* program, we have to modify this rule, perhaps to use *cp* instead. Now we have an ugly job. How can we know what needs to be changed? We can't just use an editor to globally replace "install" with "cp", because "install" is used both as a target name on the dependency line and as a program name on the command line. It should be changed only where it's used as a program name. This means we must understand each rule that contains "install" and determine from context whether or not to change it. In general, if we write our rules using literal references to machine-dependent aspects of the development process, then whenever we move our rules file to a different machine we'll need to examine all of our rules and figure out how each one might need changing.

The basic problem here is that while nonportabilities are localized in the rules file, they're not explicitly identified in any obvious way (so they're hard to find), and they're written using literal values (so we have to change each occurrence). We should try to find a better way to write our rules.

We can identify nonportabilities explicitly and make them easier to change if we express them as parameters. This is easy to do because *make* has a parameterization facility—it allows us to use variables. We can assign a value to a variable, then use the variable any number of times in a *Makefile*. To affect each use of the variable, we simply change the value assigned to it.

make variables are extremely important. Variable references are visually distinctive, so they're easy to spot. More significant, by changing variable assignments, we can easily effect change throughout the entire *Makefile*. This is one of *make*'s strengths and Idiom 3-2 takes advantage of it:

Idiom 3-2

Any aspect of the software development process that can vary between machines should be a parameter in the configuration files, expressed using a *make* variable.

To use this idiom, we can rewrite our rules in terms of *make* variables. First we choose variables for things likely to be machine dependent and assign appropriate values to them:

```
      CC = cc
 INSTALL = install
```

For modularity, we can keep variable assignments in their own file, *Imake.params*. (It should be placed in the configuration file directory */usr/local/lib/myconfdir* so any *Imakefile* can use it.) Then, instead of writing cc and install literally into our rule definitions in *Imake.rules*, we write the rules to refer to CC and INSTALL:

```
#define BuildProgramTarget(program,objects,libraries)          @@\
program: objects                                                @@\
     $(CC) -o program objects libraries
#define InstallProgramTarget(program,destdir)                   @@\
install:: program                                               @@\
     $(INSTALL) program destdir
```

The template needs to refer to the parameter file now, so we change its architecture slightly:

```
#include <Imake.params>        Default parameter values
#include <Imake.rules>         Rule macro definitions
#include INCLUDE_IMAKEFILE     Target descriptions
```

When we tell *imake* to build the *Makefile* from the *Imakefile* and our current set of configuration files, this is what we get:

```
      CC = cc
 INSTALL = install
proga: proga.o
     $(CC) -o proga proga.o -lm
install:: proga
     $(INSTALL) proga /usr/local/bin
progb: progb.o parse.o
     $(CC) -o progb progb.o parse.o -ly
install:: progb
     $(INSTALL) progb /usr/local/bin
```

What do we gain by parameterization?

- We can completely reconfigure a project by changing the parameter variable assignments and rebuilding the Makefiles.

- When we know something varies among machines, we can use parameter variables to make our knowledge explicit. That can be helpful when we want to configure software on a machine to which it hasn't yet been ported; by looking at the variable assignments, we get an idea of what kinds of things are already known to vary.

- The editing job for configuring software on another machine becomes a lot easier. For instance, instead of changing literal instances of "install" in the rules file several times, we change the "INSTALL=install" variable assignment in *Imake.params* once.

- The rules file becomes more stable. If we write rules in terms of *make* variables, we don't need to change them when configuration information changes; we edit the parameter assignments instead. Stability of the rules file is a good thing. Rules have to obey *cpp* syntax as well as the additional @@\ syntax layered on top of that. They have such a highly constrained format that it's quite easy to make mistakes while writing or revising them.

Parameterization does more than make the rules file machine independent. It also helps us complete the job of making our Imakefiles machine independent. So far we've been generating `install` target entries for our programs, *proga* and *progb*, by invoking these rules in our *Imakefile*:

```
InstallProgramTarget(proga,/usr/local/bin)
InstallProgramTarget(progb,/usr/local/bin)
```

However, we can't really assume that everybody can or wants to install the programs in */usr/local/bin*—that's a machine-dependent thing. To fix this, we can parameterize the installation directory in *Imake.params*:

```
BINDIR = /usr/local/bin
```

Then we write *Imakefile* entries in terms of that parameter:

```
InstallProgramTarget(proga,$(BINDIR))
InstallProgramTarget(progb,$(BINDIR))
```

This makes it easy to change the installation directory: just modify the value of `BINDIR` and rebuild the *Makefile*. Now there's no messing with the *Imakefile* at all. It's completely machine independent.

Selecting Parameters by System Type

Parameterization of variation is a big step forward, but the use of a single parameter file is deficient. It makes configuration requirements explicit only for one machine. This has two shortcomings:

- Configuration still involves a lot of hand editing. The parameter file needs to be changed appropriately each time we move the configuration files to a different machine.

- We know that to configure a project on another machine, we change the parameter file, but we can't tell from looking at that file what the appropriate values should be. We could distribute a *README* file containing that kind of information (e.g., "CC is normally *cc*, but you'll get better results with the GNU C compiler if you have it; in that case, set CC to *gcc*"). However, we want the information in a form that *imake* can use for itself.

Both of these problems can be solved with a simple conceptual change. Right now we have a single parameter file that we edit to the requirements of different machines when we move the software around. Instead, we can keep a separate parameter file for each type of machine on which we want to build software (one for SunOS, one for HP-UX, etc.). Then we select the proper file when we build our Makefiles. On a Sun, we use SunOS parameters; on an HP, we use HP-UX parameters, etc.

To illustrate how this works, let's consider once again the program *myname* from Chapter 1. There we used a *Makefile* to configure *myname* for three different machines. Now we'll configure it using *imake*.

We need to express target rules as macro definitions, but that's done already, because we can use `BuildProgramTarget()` and `InstallProgramTarget()`. We also need to identify machine dependencies—things that differ between systems. We already did that in Chapter 1, where we found five sources of variation. These should be expressed as parameters using *make* variables:

CC	C compiler
CFLAGS	Flags for compilation commands
EXTRA_LIBRARIES	Extra libraries needed for linking
INSTALL	Installation program
BINDIR	Installation directory

Instead of using a single parameter file *Imake.params* and editing it each time we move the configuration files to another machine, we'll use separate parameter files, each tailored for a single machine. So we tell *Imake.params* it's no longer welcome in our architecture, invite it to leave, and create three machine-specific parameter files to take its place.

Suppose we're using a machine from Vendor A, and our two friends who also built *myname* are using machines from Vendors B and C. The parameter files for these systems look like this:

VendorA.cf:

```
          CC = cc
       CFLAGS = -DUSE_LOGNAME=0
EXTRA_LIBRARIES =
      INSTALL = install
       BINDIR = /usr/local
```

VendorB.cf:

```
          CC = cc
       CFLAGS = -DUSE_LOGNAME=0
EXTRA_LIBRARIES =
      INSTALL = cp
       BINDIR = /usr/local/bin
```

VendorC.cf:

```
          CC = gcc
       CFLAGS = -DUSE_LOGNAME=1
EXTRA_LIBRARIES = -lc_aux
      INSTALL = install
       BINDIR = /usr/local
```

The template architecture changes a little, since we're replacing the reference to *Imake.params* with a reference to a vendor-specific parameter file:

```
#include <vendor.cf>            Vendor-specific parameter values
#include <Imake.rules>          Rule macro definitions
#include INCLUDE_IMAKEFILE      Target descriptions
```

vendor.cf will be *VendorA.cf*, *VendorB.cf*, or *VendorC.cf*, according to the type of machine the configuration files are being used on.

This architecture solves one problem: how to specify parameters on a vendor-specific basis. It also creates another: how to select the right version of *vendor.cf*. *imake* handles this by passing to *cpp* a definition for a symbol that uniquely identifies the type of system on which it's being used. That is, in addition to any other arguments *imake* passes to *cpp*, it also passes *−Dvendor*:

```
cpp -I. -I/usr/local/lib/myconfdir -Dvendor Imakefile.c
```

imake knows which symbol to pass because you teach it the right one when you build *imake* on your machine. (See Appendix B, *Installing Configuration Software*, for further details.)

Normally, system-identifying symbols are vendor-OS oriented (ultrix, sun, hpux, ibm, etc.). I'm going to use fake symbols for purposes of illustration: VendorA,

VendorB, VendorC. On a system from vendor C, for instance, *imake* invokes *cpp* like this:

```
cpp -I. -I/usr/local/lib/myconfdir -DVendorC Imakefile.c
```

In this way, *cpp* knows the vendor symbol, and we can take advantage of that knowledge in the configuration files by using *cpp*'s conditional construct to select the vendor file:

```
#ifdef VendorA
#define VendorFile <VendorA.cf>
#endif

#ifdef VendorB
#define VendorFile <VendorB.cf>
#endif

#ifdef VendorC
#define VendorFile <VendorC.cf>
#endif
```

These are called vendor blocks. Each block defines the VendorFile macro as the name of the parameter file for a particular vendor. The file then can be processed by including the following line in the template:

```
#include VendorFile
```

When *imake* is invoked on any of our three machines, it passes −*DVendorA*, −*DVendorB*, or −*DVendorC*, according to which machine it's running on. On a Vendor A system, *imake* passes −*DVendorA*, *cpp* selects the vendor block for Vendor A, VendorFile is defined as <VendorA.cf>, and the directive to include VendorFile effectively becomes the following:

```
#include <VendorA.cf>
```

On a Vendor B system, *imake* passes −*DVendorB* and the directive becomes:

```
#include <VendorB.cf>
```

On a Vendor C system, *imake* passes −*DVendorC* and the directive becomes:

```
#include <VendorC.cf>
```

In each case, *cpp* receives from *imake* the information it needs for selecting the proper machine-specific parameter file, and the *Makefile* is built using the parameters appropriate to that machine.

If we put the vendor blocks in a file *Imake.cf*, the template architecture becomes:

```
#include <Imake.cf>              Vendor blocks
#include VendorFile              Vendor-specific parameter values
#include <Imake.rules>           Rule macro definitions
#include INCLUDE_IMAKEFILE       Target descriptions
```

Only one of the vendor files *VendorA.cf*, *VendorB.cf*, or *VendorC.cf* is selected for any given system. However, in order to make sure that the correct one is available when the configuration files are shipped around to different systems, all vendor files should be distributed together.

What do we gain by vendor-specific parameterization?

- Machine dependencies become more obvious because they are explicitly isolated into files organized according to vendor differences. With a single parameter file, machine dependencies are explicit only for one vendor's systems.

- Parameter information is encoded so that *imake* can use it without human intervention. Using a single parameter file, it's possible to distribute a *README* file indicating what the parameter values should be for other systems, but you still have to do the editing yourself. Vendor files represent that same information in a form that's usable by the configuration process automatically. This makes parameter files more stable because the parameters on one Vendor A machine won't need to change much (if at all) when we move the configuration files to another Vendor A machine.

- It becomes easier to port the configuration files (and thus the configuration process) to a new machine; we write a *vendor.cf* file for it and add another vendor block to *Imake.cf*. That's a simple change that need be done only once, when we first port the configuration files to the new machine. None of the other configuration files change.

Now we have a great deal of flexibility in selecting configuration parameters for various machines and an open-ended mechanism allowing new machines to be included in the porting process. Naturally, we're buoyed by this *fait accompli*— but not so much that we cease to cast a critical eye on our configuration files, searching out other occasions for improvement. And indeed, under scrutiny, they soon reveal another flaw: the parameter files are still written in a way that requires a lot of work—we're specifying every parameter in every machine-specific file. This has two implications, neither appealing:

- If we port the configuration files to a new machine, we must list every parameter in the new vendor file

- If we want to define a new configuration parameter, we must add an assignment for it to every vendor file

This harsh reality quickly dissipates our initial flush of success and causes us to seek a better way to represent parameters in the configuration files.

Assigning Values Conditionally

Instead of listing every parameter in every vendor file, it would be more economical to assign a default value to each parameter. Then the machine-specific files would need to list only the parameters that differ from the defaults. So we apologize profusely to *Imake.params* for our imprudence in dismissing it so hastily and invite it back in to take its rightful place in the architecture—that of holding the default parameter values:

```
#include <Imake.cf>            Vendor blocks
#include VendorFile            Vendor-specific parameter values
#include <Imake.params>        Default parameter values
#include <Imake.rules>         Rule macro definitions
#include INCLUDE_IMAKEFILE     Target descriptions
```

The intent here is to allow parameter values to be picked up from the machine-specific vendor file first, and then from the defaults file for any parameters that remain unassigned. Conceptually, the contents of the defaults file are as follows:

```
if CC has not been specified yet
    CC = cc
if CFLAGS has not been specified yet
    CFLAGS = -DUSE_LOGNAME=0
if EXTRA_LIBRARIES has not been specified yet
    EXTRA_LIBRARIES =
if INSTALL has not been specified yet
    INSTALL = install
if BINDIR has not been specified yet
    BINDIR = /usr/local
```

Unfortunately, *make* doesn't have a conditional construct, so we can't write anything into the *Makefile* that means, "if this variable has not been assigned a value yet, give it such-and-such a value." *cpp* has conditionals (`#ifdef`, `#ifndef`), but we can't use those to test whether a *make* variable has been assigned a value. *cpp* understands very little even about C, the language for which it was designed; it certainly knows nothing at all about *make*.

However, the difficulty is not insuperable, and we can solve the problem by adding an intermediate step. For each *make* parameter variable, we invent a corresponding *cpp* macro. Then, instead of assigning a value to the variable directly, we assign to it the macro value. The macro is given a default value, but only if it has not been set earlier. Thus any definition encountered earlier takes precedence over the default.

Example: If we expect that *cc* will be the most usual C compiler, we use the following construct to set the default value in *Imake.params*:

```
#ifndef CcCmd
#define CcCmd cc
#endif

CC = CcCmd
```

In the absence of any prior definition of CcCmd, CC is assigned the value *cc*. This value can be overridden by providing a different definition in the vendor file, since that file is processed before *Imake.params*. For example, if *gcc* should be used instead of *cc*, the vendor file should contain a line like this:

```
#define CcCmd gcc
```

This causes CC to be assigned the value *gcc* rather than *cc*, because when *Imake.params* is processed, CcCmd already has a value (*gcc*), and the #define line that sets the default value to *cc* is skipped.

The conditional-assignment mechanism has two important effects:

• It becomes possible to override default parameter values on a vendor-specific basis

• It becomes necessary to provide values in vendor files for only those parameters that differ from the defaults

Combining conditionally defined *cpp* macros with *make* variables provides a simple but powerful construct. The idea it embodies is central to effective use of *imake*, which is expressed in our third idiom:

Idiom 3-3

Provide a default value for each configuration parameter, but allow the default to be overridden. Assign the parameter to a *make* variable using a *cpp* macro that is given a default value, and put the macro definition between #ifndef and #endif lines to allow its value to be overridden.

Let's see how we use the macro/variable idiom in practice. Suppose the defaults file *Imake.params* looks like this:

```
#ifndef CcCmd
#define CcCmd cc
#endif
#ifndef CFlags
#define CFlags -DUSE_LOGNAME=0
#endif
#ifndef ExtraLibraries
#define ExtraLibraries /* as nothing */
#endif
#ifndef InstallCmd
```

```
#define InstallCmd install
#endif
#ifndef BinDir
#define BinDir /usr/local
#endif

              CC = CcCmd
          CFLAGS = CFlags
 EXTRA_LIBRARIES = ExtraLibraries
         INSTALL = InstallCmd
          BINDIR = BinDir
```

Then the vendor files *VendorA.cf*, *VendorB.cf*, and *VendorC.cf* need to specify values only for parameters that differ from the defaults. They look like this:

VendorA.cf:

```
/* empty -- the defaults are all correct */
```

VendorB.cf:

```
#define InstallCmd cp
#define BinDir /usr/local/bin
```

VendorC.cf:

```
#define CcCmd gcc
#define CFlags -DUSE_LOGNAME=1
#define ExtraLibraries -lc_aux
```

Note that although the default values are all correct for Vendor A, *VendorA.cf* must still exist (even if only as an empty file). Otherwise *cpp* will issue file-not-found file inclusion errors on Vendor A systems.

What do we gain by the override mechanism?

- The override idiom allows *imake* to use *cpp*'s strengths to compensate for *make*'s weaknesses. You cannot test whether or not a variable already has a value in a *Makefile*. But you can test *cpp* macros and define them conditionally. By assigning *make* variables to conditionally defined macro values you achieve the effect of conditional variable assignment.

- Much of the work of configuring a *Makefile* for a given system consists of determining the proper values for *make* variables. The override idiom provides a lot of flexibility in setting those variables.

- Since any parameter that gets its value using the override idiom is assigned a default value, it's not necessary to provide a value for the parameter in every single vendor file. The default need be overridden only for those systems for which the default is incorrect. This minimizes the information that needs to be contained in the vendor file. That, in turn, makes it easier to create new vendor files when *imake* is ported to a different system.

Writing Rules To Be Replaceable

Parameter macros are defined so they can be overridden, using this conditional construct:

```
#ifndef MacroName
#define MacroName DefaultValue
#endif
```

But rules are defined as macros, too. For maximum flexibility, it's best to enclose rule definitions within #ifndef/#endif so that rules can be overridden as necessary. The two rules we've used in this chapter should therefore be written like this:

```
#ifndef BuildProgramTarget
#define BuildProgramTarget(program,objects,libraries)          @@\
program: objects                                               @@\
     $(CC) -o program objects libraries
#endif

#ifndef InstallProgramTarget
#define InstallProgramTarget(program,destdir)                   @@\
install:: program                                              @@\
     $(INSTALL) program destdir
#endif
```

Note that you don't put @@\ on the ends of the #ifndef or #endif lines because they aren't part of the rule definitions.

In practice, occasions when you need to replace a rule are rare, but by using the override construct, you can do so easily, should it become necessary. For instance, if a rule doesn't work on a particular platform for some reason, you can redefine it in the vendor file for that platform so it does work.

Allowing for Local Convention

The *vendor.cf* files allow us to accommodate the particular requirements of systems from different vendors. However, they're still a bit ill-conceived: a single file holds all machine dependencies for a system. That's parsimonious, but not ideal. There are really *two* kinds of machine-specific values. Some are vendor oriented (such as which environment variable a system supplies, or extra libraries required to compensate for C library deficiencies), but others are user oriented. For instance, the particular kind of system you're using doesn't really have much to do with whether locally installed programs should go in */usr/local* or */usr/local/bin*. Those issues pertain to the local conventions you like to use (or those your system administration ogre imposes on you). The parameters for *myname* break down as shown below:

Vendor-specific parameters:

```
CFLAGS
EXTRA_LIBRARIES
INSTALL
```

Site-specific parameters:

```
CC
BINDIR
```

A distinction between vendor- and site-specific parameters can be implemented by providing a site-specific file *site.def* and placing in it those machine-specific values that aren't vendor oriented. For *myname*, the definitions for CcCmd and BinDir belong in the site file, not the vendor file. When we shuffle the definitions around properly, the vendor files for our three machines look like this:

VendorA.cf:

```
/* empty -- the defaults are all correct */
```

VendorB.cf:

```
#define InstallCmd cp
```

VendorC.cf:

```
#define CFlags -DUSE_LOGNAME=1
#define ExtraLibraries -lc_aux
```

The site file *site.def* changes from machine to machine. You edit it to reflect local convention when you install the configuration files. On the three machines in question, *site.def* looks like this:

Our machine:

```
/* empty -- the defaults are all correct */
```

First friend's machine:

```
#define BinDir /usr/local/bin
```

Second friend's machine:

```
#define CcCmd gcc
```

The architecture of *Imake.tmpl* must incorporate the site file now:

```
#include <Imake.cf>          Vendor blocks
#include VendorFile          Vendor-specific parameter values
#include <site.def>          Site-specific parameter values
```

```
#include <Imake.params>        Default parameter values
#include <Imake.rules>         Rule macro definitions
#include INCLUDE_IMAKEFILE     Target descriptions
```

What do we gain by splitting site-specific values out of the vendor file?

- Configuration parameters vary from vendor to vendor, but many of those parameters tend to be stable among the group of machines running a given vendor's system. Within that group, most of the things that change relate to local convention, so by removing site-related values and putting them in a separate file, the vendor file becomes more stable.

- We also further isolate (to *site.def*, a single, small file) the values likely to need editing when we move the configuration files from machine to machine. The vast majority of the configuration information is now instantiated in a form that the configuration process can use automatically—and in files that don't need editing. Aside from the site-specific values in *site.def*, the configuration files should be pretty usable right out of the box on any machine for which a vendor file exists.

Final Architecture

This chapter describes a step-by-step plan for constructing configuration files. In practice, the process of writing files is not so linear; you'd be using the concepts from each step simultaneously because they interrelate.

We've looked piecemeal at each of the configuration files used in this chapter. Now let's look at them together in their final form. For the architecture we've developed, the final form of the template, *Imake.tmpl*, is shown in Figure 3–2.

The configuration files to which *Imake.tmpl* refers are shown below.

Imake.cf (vendor blocks):

```
#ifdef VendorA
#define VendorFile <VendorA.cf>
#endif
#ifdef VendorB
#define VendorFile <VendorB.cf>
#endif
#ifdef VendorC
#define VendorFile <VendorC.cf>
#endif
```

Imake.params (default parameter values):

```
#ifndef CcCmd
#define CcCmd cc
#endif
#ifndef CFlags
```

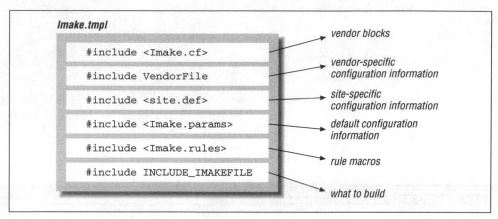

Figure 3–2: Final template architecture

```
#define CFlags -DUSE_LOGNAME=0
#endif
#ifndef ExtraLibraries
#define ExtraLibraries /* as nothing */
#endif
#ifndef InstallCmd
#define InstallCmd install
#endif
#ifndef BinDir
#define BinDir /usr/local
#endif

            CC = CcCmd
        CFLAGS = CFlags
EXTRA_LIBRARIES = ExtraLibraries
       INSTALL = InstallCmd
        BINDIR = BinDir
```

Imake.rules (rule macro definitions):

```
#ifndef BuildProgramTarget
#define BuildProgramTarget(program,objects,libraries)          @@\
program: objects                                               @@\
    $(CC) -o program objects libraries
#endif

#ifndef InstallProgramTarget
#define InstallProgramTarget(program,destdir)                  @@\
install:: program                                              @@\
    $(INSTALL) program destdir
#endif
```

VendorFile (vendor-specific files):

> *VendorA.cf*:
>
> ```
>  /* empty -- the defaults are all correct */
> ```
>
> *VendorB.cf*:
>
> ```
> #define InstallCmd cp
> ```
>
> *VendorC.cf*:
>
> ```
> #define CFlags -DUSE_LOGNAME=1
> #define ExtraLibraries -lc_aux
> ```

site.def (site-specific file; contents vary by site):

> Our machine:
>
> ```
>  /* empty -- the defaults are all correct */
> ```
>
> First friend's machine:
>
> ```
> #define BinDir /usr/local/bin
> ```
>
> Second friend's machine:
>
> ```
> #define CcCmd gcc
> ```

Note that there really isn't much to these files, which is in itself instructive. It's not necessary for configuration files to form a huge, monstrously complex entity. This may surprise you, especially if your exposure to *imake* is primarily through the X11 configuration files.

I said in Chapter 1 that a portable configuration process should be characterized by explicitly represented configuration information in program-readable form. That is exactly what *imake* provides. Our configuration knowledge is represented in the configuration files (not in our heads), and all the configuration files are processed by *imake* or *cpp* without manual intervention.

4

Writing Comments

Sorry, sir.
I seem to be commenting on everything.
—Lt. Commander Data, *Encounter at Farpoint*

Chapter 3, *Understanding Configuration Files*, discusses methods for writing configuration information in a form that programs can use. In this chapter, we'll concentrate instead on ways to put information into configuration files and Imakefiles so people can use it—in other words, how to write comments. Although configuration files are processed by programs, people do sometimes look at them. So a comment here and there is often a good idea, to document the purpose of a parameter, explain a complicated rule construct, etc.

This chapter also discusses problems that can arise when you write comments, and how to solve them.

Types of Comments

When you write down information intended for people rather than programs, you have to write it a different way. The trick isn't how to get the programs (*imake* and *cpp*) to act on the information, it's how to get them *not* to act on it—to ignore the information or pass it through into your Makefiles.

Since *imake* accepts input files in C preprocessor format and produces output files in *Makefile* format, there are two kinds of comments you can use in configuration files and Imakefiles: C comments and *make* comments. Each has a different syntax and a different use.

C Comments

C comments consist of text bracketed by "/*" and "*/". They're deleted from the input by *cpp* and don't appear in the final output (the *Makefile*). C comments are useful for documenting the contents of the configuration files and the *Imakefile*, as in the following fragment:

```
#ifndef StripInstalledPrograms
#define StripInstalledPrograms NO /* leave symbol table just in case */
#endif
```

The comment explains the purpose of the line on which it appears. Since the line is eaten by *cpp* and doesn't appear in the *Makefile*, there's no reason for the comment to appear in the *Makefile* either. A C comment is appropriate in such cases.

C comments are also suitable for commenting out blocks of text when the need arises, since they can span multiple lines. This allows you to disable a portion of an *Imakefile* temporarily without deleting it:

```
/*
 * The following target is disabled
BuildProgramTarget(myprog,myprog.o,-lm)
 */
```

One caveat: C comments do not nest, so any text to be commented out must not itself contain any C comments.

make Comments

make comments begin with a # character and continue to the end of the line. They're useful for documenting the contents of Makefiles. However, since you don't write the *Makefile* yourself when you use *imake*, any *make* comments must be present in the configuration files or in the *Imakefile*, and they must survive the *Makefile*-generation process.

To write *make* comments, don't use the # character. In the *imake* environment, that character is used to introduce *cpp* preprocessing directives. Use the XCOMM symbol instead:

```
XCOMM this is a comment
```

XCOMM has no special meaning to *cpp*, which passes it through unscathed. Then *imake* translates XCOMM to # as part of the postprocessing it does on *cpp* output. The resulting line appears in the *Makefile* as a valid *make* comment:

```
# this is a comment
```

Comment Problems

Comment writing is reasonably straightforward and generally presents few problems. Nevertheless, there are some difficulties you may run into. Their causes and solutions are outlined in the following sections.

Problems Caused by cpp

An easy way to destroy a perfectly good *make* comment is to refer to a rule in it. *cpp* doesn't know anything about *make*, so it doesn't understand that you intend an XCOMM line to be a *make* comment and it merrily expands the rule anyway. If the rule expands to more than one line, goodbye *Makefile*.

Suppose you have a rule named `TouchTarget()` that expands to entries of this form:

```
target::
    touch target
    echo target touched.
```

Then suppose you put a comment like this in your *Imakefile*:

```
XCOMM Update modification time by invoking TouchTarget(xyz)
```

The reference to `TouchTarget()` is processed by *cpp* and your comment ends up looking like this in the *Makefile*:

```
# Update modification time by invoking xyz::
    touch xyz
    echo xyz touched.
```

The *Makefile* is malformed because it appears to contain an entry with no dependency line preceding the command lines. As a result, it's useless:

```
% make
make: line nnn: Unexpected end of line seen
```

You can fix the problem by quoting the invocation:

```
XCOMM Update modification time by invoking "TouchTarget(xyz)"
```

Note that simply leaving the parentheses out doesn't work:

```
XCOMM It does not work to refer to TouchTarget this way
```

cpp issues an "argument mismatch" error, expands the macro as well as it can without the arguments, and still usually succeeds in decimating your *Makefile*.

Another form of *make* comment error occurs when you assume you can use ordinary punctuation. You can't. Some versions of *cpp* complain about invalid C tokens, so if you write this:

```
XCOMM Don't use contractions in your comments
```

cpp may tell you:

```
unterminated string or character constant
```

Write this instead:

```
XCOMM Do not use contractions in your comments
```

Such errors aren't necessarily fatal, since *cpp* may complain but continue to process the input and generate the *Makefile* correctly. Nevertheless, it can be disconcerting to see the error messages during *Makefile* generation, so avoid contractions in comments. This will relieve others who use your Imakefiles or configuration files of the burden of figuring out whether they must attend to such errors or whether they can ignore them.

I suppose as an alternative to avoiding contractions you could go in the other direction and use them to the extreme:

```
XCOMM I'd've thought that this'd've been illegal; it is not.
```

This type of comment doesn't contain any illegal tokens, but it's hardly an aid to understanding, either.

Sometimes *cpp* bites you in ways that are very difficult to catch. For instance, the intent of the following rule is to generate a `clean` target entry that removes all object files in a given directory. It uses the pattern `*.o` to match the appropriate filenames. Do you see what's wrong with it?

```
#define CleanDir(dir)                      @@\
clean::                                     @@\
    $(RM) dir/*.o
```

Give up?

The problem is that `dir/*.o` contains "`/*`", the C begin-comment sequence. From *cpp*'s perspective, this looks like a comment that's missing a terminator.

Problems Caused by *make*

make comments that follow other information on the same line are problematic. Suppose you define three parameters in your configuration files this way:

```
LIBROOT = /usr/lib # some comment about LIBROOT
 LIBDIR = mystuff
LIBPATH = $(LIBROOT)/$(LIBDIR)
```

When putting a comment at the end of a line, it's quite natural (and more readable) to separate it from the preceding information by whitespace. Unfortunately, some versions of *make* treat the whitespace as part of the definition. All versions of *make* ignore the comment, but not all versions ignore whitespace at the end of variable definitions. Thus, if you expect the value of $(LIBPATH) to be /usr/lib/mystuff, you'll be unpleasantly surprised to find that some versions of *make* set it to /usr/lib /mystuff instead (that is, with a space in the middle). The difference is significant. To take an extreme example, consider what happens if you use LIBPATH in a command such as this:

```
rm -rf $(LIBPATH)
```

Depending on how *make* behaves, this command expands in one of the following two ways:

```
rm  rf /usr/lib/mystuff
rm -rf /usr/lib /mystuff
```

The second command has serious consequences for the health of your filesystem, particularly if executed as *root*. To avoid this kind of problem, write the comment on a separate line:

```
XCOMM some comment about LIBROOT
LIBROOT = /usr/lib
 LIBDIR = mystuff
LIBPATH = $(LIBROOT)/$(LIBDIR)
```

Obsolete Commenting Conventions

XCOMM has not always been used for writing *make* comments, nor has *imake* always had the responsibility for turning XCOMM into a # character. The mechanism whereby *imake* translates XCOMM to # actually is relatively recent, having appeared only as of the version of *imake* distributed with X11R6. *make* comment processing prior to R6 has a somewhat spotty record of success, due to problems caused by # being special to both *cpp* and *make*, and to the varying behaviors of different versions of *cpp*.

Several previous commenting methods were found to fail under various circumstances. You may see these methods used in older configuration files and Imakefiles. I'll describe them below so you'll recognize them, and so you'll know why you should avoid them:

- Indent the # character. For older versions of *cpp*, # indicates a preprocessor directive only when it occurs in the first column, so indenting the # by a space fools *cpp* into ignoring it. That doesn't work if you have an ANSI preprocessor, though. Under ANSI rules, # can be preceded by whitespace.

- Hide the # with an empty C comment:

```
/**/# this is a comment for the Makefile
```

The intent is that *cpp* should strip off the C comment and pass the line through without interpreting it as a directive. This construct appears quite often in older configuration files written before ANSI preprocessors became prevalent. It doesn't work under ANSI rules because comments are replaced by a single space before preprocessor directive recognition occurs. Since the # is then recognized as the first non-whitespace character, the line is treated as a directive and doesn't pass through to the *Makefile*. In addition, if the comment doesn't look like a legal directive (and most likely it will not), *cpp* produces an error message.

- Hide the # in a macro and use the macro for writing comments:

```
#define XCOMM #
XCOMM this is a comment for the Makefile
```

This method was used in X11R5; XCOMM was defined as a macro in *Imake.tmpl* with the intent that subsequent instances of XCOMM would be translated by *cpp* to #. This mechanism worked pretty well. However, some ANSI preprocessors interpret the second # in the #define statement as the "convert to string" operator and therefore fail to generate comments in the intended manner.

The conclusion of the matter is twofold: you should always use XCOMM for writing *make* comments, and it's best to replace any pre-X11R6 *imake* with the current version, since that will give you the most reliable behavior.[*]

Version Mismatch Problems

If you find that XCOMM isn't processed at all and ends up in your Makefiles without being turned into #, you're probably using the X11R5 version of *imake* with configuration files from X11R6 or later. In R5, XCOMM is defined as a macro in

---

[*] You can get the current *imake* as part of the X11R6.1 distribution, or as part of the *itools* distribution listed in Appendix A, *Obtaining Configuration Software.*

Imake.tmpl and is processed by *cpp*. Starting with R6, XCOMM isn't a macro and is processed by *imake*. The shifting of XCOMM processing responsibility causes a problem. R5 *imake* expects the configuration files to define XCOMM as a macro that will be handled by *cpp*. R6 configuration files don't define XCOMM as a macro because they expect *imake* to handle it. The result is that no one handles it, and you end up with XCOMM lines in your Makefiles. The solution to this problem is to use a version of *imake* from R6 or later. If you can't do that, then try defining XCOMM as a macro in *Imake.tmpl* using the definition shown in the preceding section. That should allow you to use XCOMM for comments in Imakefiles.

Note that if you're successfully using R5 versions of *imake* and the configuration files now, upgrading to *imake* from R6 or later will not cause you any problems.

5

The X11 Configuration Files

Abandon hope, all ye who enter here.
—Dante, *Inferno*

Chapter 3, *Understanding Configuration Files*, lays out general principles of configuration file design. In this chapter we'll apply those principles to understanding the configuration files from the X Window System. The chapter will also help you if you plan on writing your own configuration files:

- The X11 files are more widely distributed than any other configuration files and exert a considerable influence in the *imake* world. Consequently, many other sets of configuration files trace their ancestry back to the files from some release of X11 or another, and certain aspects of the X11 files are particularly widespread. Among these are the vendor block, token concatenation, and recursive rule conventions. Knowledge of these conventions is useful for designing your own configuration files.

- In being able to configure the X Window System, the X11 configuration files successfully solve a difficult and complex configuration task. Thus they provide many valuable lessons for those who aspire to design configuration files. They also provide many constructs you can copy for your own use rather than reinventing them.

- The X11 files include many vendor files. These provide a measure of the idiosyncrasies of various systems, which can be helpful in assessing and anticipating portability problems you may need to deal with if you write your own configuration files.

The X11 files take some effort to understand, but it's an effort that pays off. You'll find it helpful to have a copy of the X11 files at hand to examine as you work through this chapter. The files described here are from X Version 11, Release 6.1.

The X11 Template

To analyze a set of configuration files you should go straight to the template, since it determines the architecture—how the other configuration files and the *Imakefile* are referenced during the configuration process. The X11 template *Imake.tmpl* is illustrated in Figure 5–1.

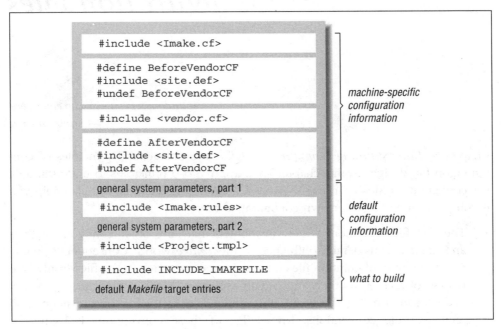

Figure 5–1: X11 configuration file template architecture

The template contains some configuration information itself (e.g., system description, default *make* targets), and it tells *cpp* to draw the rest from several other sources using #include directives. The information contained directly in *Imake.tmpl* or referenced by it falls into three categories:

- **Default configuration information.** This is made up of the system and project parameters sections and the rules file. The system and project sections specify the most likely defaults for most configuration parameters (taken together, they correspond to the use of *Imake.params* in the previous chapter). The rules indicate how to build particular types of targets.

- **Configuration information for your machine**. This consists of the particulars for your machine's operating system (OS) in *vendor.cf* and for your site in *site.def*. Values in these files take precedence over the values specified in the default configuration section.

- **What to build**. Information in the first two categories is of no value by itself; it indicates how to do things (what C compiler to use, where to find header files, etc.), but provides no instruction as to what to do (what programs should be built, where they should be installed, etc.). That information is provided by the *Imakefile* and the default *Makefile* target entries, which specify what to build in the current directory.

I'll discuss the pieces of the template that make up these three categories in more detail in the sections that follow. At the beginning of each section, a diagram of the relevant part of the template is repeated for reference.

Two symbols defined near the beginning of *Imake.tmpl* don't fit into any of the three categories. I'll note them briefly here since references to them are legion throughout the configuration files:

```
#define YES 1
#define NO  0
```

YES and NO are used for true and false, respectively.

Default Configuration Information

The system and project parameters and rules sections of the template define the default configuration values (Figure 5–2). *Imake.tmpl* contains two sections for general system-related parameters. *Project.tmpl* is used for parameters related specifically to X11. The rules file *Imake.rules* defines the default target-building instructions.

General System Parameters—Imake.tmpl

The general system parameter definitions in *Imake.tmpl* are divided into two sections. The first section precedes the inclusion of *Imake.rules* and defines values needed for proper processing of the rules file. The second section is processed after *Imake.rules* and defines the remaining general parameters.

Some parameters describe system characteristics. For example:

- Is the operating system based on BSD or System V?
- Does the system have the *putenv()* library function?

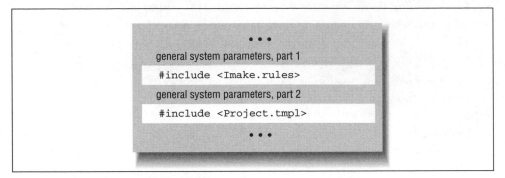

Figure 5–2: Section of Imake.tmpl specifying configuration defaults

- Does it have shared memory?
- Can it execute scripts that begin with "#!"?

These characteristics are usually represented by macros that are given one of the values YES or NO.

Other definitions are related to software building and installation management. For example:

- What is the name of the C compiler?
- What special flags does the loader need?
- How do you make a link to a file?
- What flags are used to install executable or non-executable files?

This kind of information is usually represented by parameters specified using the *cpp* macro/*make* variable idiom (discussed in Chapter 3).

How To Build Things—Imake.rules

The system parameters in *Imake.tmpl* name the tools needed to build and install programs, but don't say how to use them. For that we need the file *Imake.rules*, which describes how to perform particular actions. It contains general-purpose *cpp* rule macros that indicate how to use the tools to build and install particular types of targets, e.g., how to compile a C program, how to install a manual page, how to build a library, etc.

The rules in *Imake.rules* are far too numerous to discuss here in any detail (there are more than 170 of them). General rule syntax is described in Chapter 3, and we'll look at function, use, and implementation of several of the more commonly used X11 rules in Chapter 6, *Writing Imakefiles*. For a paper that catalogs many of the rules and what they're used for, see Appendix I, *Other Sources of Information*.

Project-Specific Information — Project.tmpl

The system parameters in *Imake.tmpl* and the rules in *Imake.rules* are intended to provide general-purpose configuration information that isn't necessarily specific to X11. The file *Project.tmpl*, on the other hand, is very X11 specific. The parameters in *Project.tmpl* provide answers for questions like:

- What is the screen resolution?

- What sorts of connections should the X11 server accept (e.g., UNIX, TCP, DECnet, or STREAMS connections)?

- Should debugging, profiling, or shared versions of X11 libraries be built?

- Where should programs and libraries be installed?

Project.tmpl also contains rule definitions for X11-specific target types, such as how to build a compressed font or install an application-defaults file for an X11 program.

Directory locations

One important purpose of *Project.tmpl* is to describe the layout of the X11 distribution. Another is to define the locations where files are installed after the X11 software has been built. Most location parameter variables are specified using variable names ending in DIR or SRC.

Variables with names ending in DIR specify installation directories. Since you might wish to change these on a system- or site-dependent basis, they're defined via the usual idiom of equating them to the values of *cpp* macros that can be overridden:

```
   LIBDIR = LibDir
  FONTDIR = FontDir
   XDMDIR = XdmDir
   TWMDIR = TwmDir
     etc.
```

Variables with names ending in SRC describe the layout of source directories within the X11 distribution. These variables are assigned values directly without using *cpp* macros:

```
 PROGRAMSRC = $(TOP)/programs
     LIBSRC = $(TOP)/lib
 INCLUDESRC = $(TOP)/X11
  SERVERSRC = $(TOP)/programs/Xserver
     DOCSRC = $(TOP)/doc
       etc.
```

There is no provision for overriding the values of the *SRC variables because the internal structure of the X11 distribution remains constant. The only project location parameter that might legitimately change when the project is put onto different machines is TOP, which indicates the top, or root, of the X11 source tree.

The variable TOP

The *make* variable TOP is important as a reference point because other locations within the X11 project are specified in relation to it. For instance, if the library *libX11.a* is located in the *lib* directory under the project root, we can refer to it as $(TOP)/lib/libX11.a. By anchoring the reference to TOP, we need not be concerned where the project is located within the file system. Nor need we be concerned where our current directory is within the project.

In Chapter 8, *A Closer Look at Makefile Generation*, we'll discuss in more detail how TOP is used and how it gets its value. For now, suffice it to say that TOP is set to the correct value for you by *imake* when the *Makefile* is generated.

A Separation of Powers

The parameters in *Imake.tmpl* and the rules in *Imake.rules* provide general-purpose configuration information. The parameters and rules in *Project.tmpl* provide X11-specific information. For the most part, these two kinds of information don't overlap. So in theory, you could use the X11 files to configure a completely different project by plugging in a different *Project.tmpl* file.

In practice, it's not always easy to achieve a clean separation of configuration information into system and project components. The R6.1 files are much better at making this division than were the R5 files,[*] but there are still some crossovers. For instance, *Imake.rules* contains a ServerTarget() rule for building an X server, which is X11 specific. Conversely, *Project.tmpl* defines a MakeLatexDoc() rule that contains no X11-specific references and thus could be considered a general-purpose rule.

Machine-Specific Configuration Information

Now let's go back to the beginning of the template *Imake.tmpl* (Figure 5-3).

If X11 were configured using only the information provided in the system and project sections of the architecture, its Makefiles would look pretty much the same no matter what machine they were built on. Those sections specify default

---

[*] See the *Minotaur* reference in Appendix I, *Other Sources of Information*. This document, a short excerpt from the first edition of *Software Portability with imake*, describes two instances of intertwining between the system and project sections of the X11R5 configuration files. Both instances were untangled as of R6.

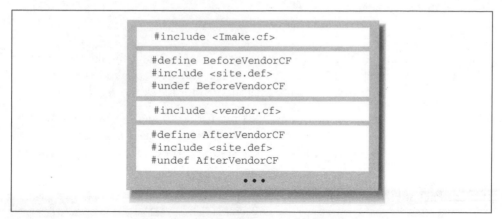

Figure 5–3: Section of Imake.tmpl specifying machine-specific information

configuration values only and provide little in the way of tailoring the build and install processes to a given machine. That kind of tailoring is the function of the machine-specific information, which is given in three places:

- The vendor block file *Imake.cf*, which determines your system type
- A vendor-specific file, *vendor.cf*, that adapts to peculiarities of your system type
- The site-specific file, *site.def*, which adapts to local conventions you use

The ability to specify machine-specific parameters and select them automatically is what makes it possible for X11 to be configured to the requirements of many different systems using the same set of configuration files.

Note that *site.def* is processed twice, once before and once after the vendor file is processed. I'll explain this shortly.

Vendor Block Selection — Imake.cf

Vendor-specific files have names like *sun.cf, linux.cf, hp.cf, sgi.cf*, etc. There is one vendor file for each type of system on which the configuration files may be used.

The vendor file is referenced in two stages. First, the name of the file is determined and used to define the macro `MacroIncludeFile`. Then the template inserts the contents of the file into the input stream using the following directive:

```
#include MacroIncludeFile
```

In effect, this becomes:

```
#include <vendor.cf>
```

Once the name of the file is known, reading it is easy. The difficulty lies in figuring out the correct value of *vendor.cf*. To do that, *imake* needs to determine what type of system you're running. That's what the vendor block file *Imake.cf* is for.

The system type is determined by looking for a trigger—a *cpp* macro that uniquely and unambiguously indicates a given platform. For instance, hpux and linux indicate Hewlett-Packard and Linux systems. The blocks for these systems are shown below:

Hewlett-Packard:

```
#ifdef hpux
# define MacroIncludeFile <hp.cf>
# define MacroFile hp.cf
# undef hpux
# define HPArchitecture
#endif /* hpux */
```

Linux:

```
#ifdef linux
# define MacroIncludeFile <linux.cf>
# define MacroFile linux.cf
# undef linux
# define LinuxArchitecture
# define i386Architecture
# undef i386
#endif /* linux */
```

Some vendor blocks are more complicated, such as this block for Sun systems:

```
#ifdef sun
# define MacroIncludeFile <sun.cf>
# define MacroFile sun.cf
# ifdef SVR4
#  undef SVR4
#  define SVR4Architecture
# endif
# ifdef sparc
#  undef sparc
# define SparcArchitecture
# endif
# ifdef mc68000
#  undef mc68000
# define Sun3Architecture
# endif
# ifdef i386
#  undef i386
#  define i386Architecture
```

```
# endif
# undef sun
# define SunArchitecture
#endif /* sun */
```

Each vendor block is written using a similar pattern. If a block's trigger symbol isn't defined, the whole thing is skipped. If the symbol is defined, *cpp* processes the block and three things happen:

- The name of the associated vendor-specific *vendor.cf* file is defined, for later inclusion by the template.

- One or more architecture-indicator symbols are defined. These symbols are unambiguous and can be used elsewhere in the configuration files to test for particular software or hardware platforms.

- The trigger symbol is undefined to avoid problems with file and directory names. For example, if you have a Sun machine, the symbol sun will be defined (with a value of 1), but it isn't good for sun to remain defined as a macro during the configuration process since references in the configuration files to directories like *mit/server/ddx/sun* and files like *sun.h* and *sun.c* become *mit/server/ddx/1*, *1.h*, and *1.c*, respectively. The Sun vendor block undefines sun to circumvent these problems.

When *cpp* processes *Imake.cf*, it looks at each vendor block in turn, examines it, and ignores it if the trigger symbol isn't defined. If *cpp* finds no trigger symbol defined, it might be that you're trying to use the configuration files on a system for which no vendor block exists (i.e., to which X11 has not been ported). If that's true, you need to write a vendor file and add a vendor block to *Imake.cf* so your vendor file is selected properly.

If there is a vendor block for your system and *imake* still fails, then *imake* probably wasn't built correctly, that is, it doesn't pass a usable trigger symbol definition to *cpp*.

Architecture-indicator symbols that are defined in vendor blocks take the form *System*Architecture. An architecture symbol may refer both to the software and hardware, or separate indicators may be defined. Often both kinds of symbols are necessary to properly describe a given system, since the relationship between hardware and software isn't one-to-one. A given OS may run on multiple hardware types (e.g., NetBSD runs on Intel or SPARC hardware). Conversely, a given hardware type may be used by several different OSes (e.g., MipsArchitecture can be defined for Ultrix, SGI, Sony, or OSF/1 systems; i386Architecture can be defined for more than half a dozen versions of UNIX).

Generally, a vendor block becomes more complex when an operating system runs on more types of machines. For example, the Linux vendor block is simple now, but Linux has been ported to the DEC Alpha and Motorola PowerPC platforms recently. These ports may result in new hardware architecture symbol definitions being introduced into the Linux vendor block.

Once *Imake.cf* has been processed, anything that depends on the system type (including the *Imakefile*) should test the architecture-indicator symbols defined in the vendor block, rather than trigger symbols. The former are more reliable because they're unambiguous, and the latter are undefined by the vendor block, anyway. For example, to test for Hewlett-Packard systems, you should test whether or not HPArchitecture is defined, rather than testing hpux.

Where does the trigger symbol come from?

Since the trigger symbol selects the vendor block and the vendor block specifies the vendor file name, it's pretty important that the proper trigger be defined. Where does this symbol come from?

It depends. On some systems, *cpp* predefines a system-specific symbol that can be used as a trigger. That was the situation for X11R1, when X11 was in its infancy and life was simple; every system on which X11 ran had a *cpp* that predefined a unique symbol. Sun *cpp* predefined sun, Apollo *cpp* predefined apollo, etc. *imake* could assume that *cpp* would select the proper vendor block without any help.

That's no longer true. Triggers must be chosen with care, because it's now more difficult to find symbols that are unique to a single system type. For instance, mips might be defined on any version of UNIX based on Mips hardware. There are several of these, so the mips symbol doesn't unambiguously indicate system type.

Worse yet, the trend in preprocessors seems to be to predefine fewer and fewer symbols. The ANSI standard deprecates predefinition of all but a very few symbols, none of which are for distingushing system types. So ANSI *cpp*s may not predefine anything useful at all. This was already starting to happen during the days of X11R4.

To work around the problems posed by the lack of a unique predefined symbol, *imake* can be built so it passes an explicit trigger definition to *cpp* (using -Dtrigger). The problem of choosing an appropriate symbol is discussed further in Appendix B, *Installing Configuration Software.*

Vendor-Specific Configuration Information — vendor.cf

Each vendor file contains definitions needed to make X11 build and install correctly on systems from a particular manufacturer.[*] Vendor files are often a hodge-podge, because it might be necessary to override defaults of all sorts (system or project parameters, or perhaps even some of the rules). Some types of information you might find in the vendor files are listed below.

Version numbers

If you're using version *xx.yy.zz* of your operating system, this is indicated in the vendor file as:

```
#define OSMajorVersion xx
#define OSMinorVersion yy
#define OSTeenyVersion zz
```

If the operating system version is characterized only by major and minor numbers, there may be no definition for `OSTeenyVersion`.

Some symbol values may be contingent upon the OS version, to accommodate system changes, deficiencies, or bugs. For example, *sgi.cf* contains the following to handle versions of the OS from release 3.3 up:

```
#if OSMajorVersion > 3 || (OSMajorVersion == 3 && OSMinorVersion > 2)
#define NeedVarargsPrototypes    YES
#define NeedConstPrototypes      YES
#define NeedWidePrototypes       NO
#endif
```

For this kind of test to select information correctly, it's important that version numbers in the vendor file accurately reflect your system. You may need to change the values of `OSMajorVersion`, `OSMinorVersion`, and `OSTeeny-Version` in your vendor file if their values are not correct for your system.

Version numbers are also defined for C compilers in some vendor files and used in ways similar to OS version numbers. If necessary, you should change the C compiler version numbers to those used on your system.

---

[*] In some cases, the term "vendor file" is something of a misnomer because there is no "manufacturer" in the usual sense. For instance, Linux and FreeBSD are freely available and not tied to a particular commercial enterprise.

Overall system type

If your system is based on SVR3 (System V Release 3) or SVR4 (Release 4), the vendor file should contain one or the other (but not both!) of the following definitions:

```
#define SystemV  YES /* SVR3-based */
#define SystemV4 YES /* SVR4-based */
```

This is important because many of the default parameter values in later parts of the template depend on the value of `SystemV` or `SystemV4`. *lint* is a good example of this. It often behaves differently on BSD-based systems than on System V-based systems, and the flags passed to it are selected accordingly. For instance, to create a *lint* library, BSD *lint* uses *−C*, whereas System V *lint* uses *−o*, so the following (from *Imake.tmpl*) depends on `SystemV` and `SystemV4` being set correctly:

```
#ifndef LintLibFlag
#if SystemV || SystemV4
#define LintLibFlag -o
#else
#define LintLibFlag -C
#endif
#endif
```

Command workarounds

Vendor files often contain workarounds for commands that are missing, broken, or located in nonstandard places. For instance, *cray.cf* defines `Install-Cmd` with the value of an installation command that emulates BSD *install* properly on Cray machines. *DGUX.cf* defines `UNCOMPRESSPATH` because *uncompress* is found in a nonstandard location. *Mips.cf* defines `InstallCmd` for the same reason.

Rules

Sometimes a rule doesn't work correctly on a given platform. This can be fixed by placing a working definition in the vendor file. For example, *sgi.cf* overrides the default definitions of `NormalLibObjCompile()` and `LibObjCompile()`.

Vendor files and shared libraries

If shared libraries can be built on a vendor's systems, the vendor file includes another file that defines rules about how that is done. For instance, *FreeBSD.cf* and *NetBSD.cf* include *bsdLib.rules*, and *osf1.cf* includes *osfLib.rules*. Each shared library rules file in turn defines the macro `ShLibIncludeFile` as the name of a vendor-related file that *Project.tmpl* includes later to pick up any additional parameters needed for building shared libraries.

Site-Specific Configuration Information — site.def

This file contains site-specific definitions pertaining to local conventions you use that may require different parameter values than those provided by the system, project, or vendor defaults. If you want to override the defaults for parameters such as installation directories, special versions of programs to use during the build, whether to build the server, etc., this is the place to do so.

There is a peculiar relationship between *site.def* and the vendor file. The relevant part of the template is shown in Figure 5–4.

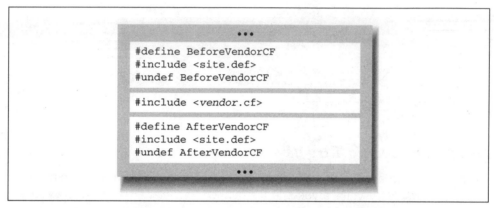

```
#define BeforeVendorCF
#include <site.def>
#undef BeforeVendorCF

#include <vendor.cf>

#define AfterVendorCF
#include <site.def>
#undef AfterVendorCF
```

Figure 5–4: Section of Imake.tmpl specifying site-specific information

site.def is included twice, once before and once after the vendor-specific file, because it's possible that vendor-specific information will depend on a site-specific parameter. The contents of *site.def* are constructed so that only the correct part is processed each time it's included:

```
#ifdef BeforeVendorCF
    /* site-dependent parameters the vendor file needs to know about */
#endif /* BeforeVendorCF */

#ifdef AfterVendorCF
    /* all other site-dependent stuff */
#endif /* AfterVendorCF */
```

Site-specific settings typically go in the AfterVendorCF part of *site.def*, but there are a few exceptions. In particular, if HasGcc or HasGcc2 are YES, some systems need special flags for *gcc* or it won't compile things properly. But the vendor files for those systems can't determine whether to use those flags unless they know your (site-specific) preference for using *gcc* or not. This means HasGcc and Has-Gcc2 must be defined in the BeforeVendorCF part of *site.def* if *gcc* is used.

Note that you cannot rely on the values of SystemV or SystemV4 in the Before-VendorCF part of *site.def*, because they don't have any meaningful values until after the vendor file has been processed.

What To Build

The final section of the template specifies the target entries to generate (Figure 5–5).

Figure 5–5: Section of Imake.tmpl specifying target entries

Directory-Specific Targets — Imakefile

The last file referenced by the X11 template is the *Imakefile* from the current directory. An *Imakefile* usually invokes rules defined in *Imake.rules* to specify target entries to generate in the *Makefile*. If the *Imakefile* uses rules that rely implicitly on the values of *make* variables, it must also assign values to those variables. For instance, DependTarget() generates a target entry that determines header file dependencies, but requires that you set the variable SRCS variable to the list of all source files used in the current directory. Chapter 6 explores these issues further.

Default Makefile Target Entries

The last section of *Imake.tmpl* adds some common entries to the *Makefile*, such as a Makefile target entry to regenerate the *Makefile* itself, and default tags and clean entries.

Recursive install, install.man, clean, tags, Makefiles, and includes target entries are generated if the directory has subdirectories and the *Imakefile* contains these lines:

```
#define IHaveSubdirs
#define PassCDebugFlags
SUBDIRS = subdirectory-list
```

The *make* variable SUBDIRS lists subdirectories in the current directory to which recursive rules apply, e.g.:

```
SUBDIRS = include lib apps man doc
```

This mechanism is extremely important because it makes it possible to issue commands such as:

```
% make clean
% make depend
% make install
```

from any directory within the X11 source tree and have them apply to the entire subtree from that point down. This makes it relatively effortless to apply far-reaching operations to extensive portions of the X11 distribution. Multiple-directory project management using the X11 configuration files is discussed further in Chapter 6.

Miscellaneous Topics

This section describes token-concatenation conventions as implemented in the X11 files. These conventions aren't part of the architecture as such, but their use is pervasive throughout the files, so it's useful to know how they work. The section also discusses how the X11 configuration files allow for Motif support and for host-specific configuration.

Token Concatenation

It's often necessary to construct a token by concatenating other tokens (this is also known as token pasting). As an example, you might have a macro LibBaseName defined as the basename of a library you're working with:

```
#define LibBaseName mylib
```

If you want to construct the full name of a library *libmylib.a* by concatenating the basename, the prefix "lib", and the suffix "a", how would you do it?

It's easy enough to concatenate the basename and the suffix, since you can put a "." between them:

```
LibBaseName.a
```

The value of the concatenation is mylib.a. However, to concatenate the prefix "lib" onto this to complete the name, you can't simply write the following:

```
libLibBaseName.a
```

The preprocessor does not recognize `libLibBaseName` as two separate tokens because there's nothing between them. One way to separate tokens in this situation is by putting an empty comment between them as a "fake" token:

```
lib/**/LibBaseName.a
```

This works for preprocessors that process comments by deleting them entirely (e.g., most older versions of *cpp*). *cpp* recognizes `lib` and `LibBaseName` as separate tokens, deletes the empty comment, and performs the desired substitutions to produce the value `libmylib.a`.

However, empty comments don't work for token pasting under the preprocessing rules defined by the ANSI standard: each comment is replaced by a space instead of being completely deleted. If we try to define the library name using an empty comment, the resulting value is "`lib mylib.a`" (with a space in the middle). The ANSI standard does provide a concatenation operator `##`, though, so we can construct the library name as follows:

```
lib##LibBaseName.a
```

This gives us two different methods for token pasting, but since only one works on any given system, we need a way to choose between them appropriately. The X11 files select the method by defining a `Concat()` rule in *Imake.rules* as follows:

```
#if (__STDC__ && !defined(UnixCpp)) || defined(AnsiCpp)
#define Concat(a,b)a##b
#else
#define Concat(a,b)a/**/b
#endif
```

Using `Concat()`, we can construct the name `libmylib.a` easily:

```
Concat(lib,LibBaseName.a)
```

It's important not to put any spaces in the arguments to `Concat()`. If you do, they'll be propagated into the macro result, which of course defeats the purpose of the macro.

The definition of `Concat()` that's chosen depends on `__STDC__` (ignore `UnixCpp` and `AnsiCpp` for a moment). The ANSI standard says `__STDC__` should be defined as 1 if an implementation conforms to the ANSI standard, so ANSI token pasting is selected for ANSI preprocessors, and the empty-comment method is selected otherwise. However, the construct sometimes selects the wrong method.

That can happen due to the ambiguity of `__STDC__`. The ANSI standard says that an implementation claiming to follow ANSI rules should define `__STDC__` as 1. But non-conforming implementations aren't bound by the standard, of course, and can do anything they want with `__STDC__`. For example, if an implementation defines it as 0 to indicate partial conformance, the empty-comment method is selected. This is incorrect if ## token pasting is included in the preprocessor's level of conformance.

When the wrong token-pasting method is selected, you'll see one of two symptoms:

- **Pasted tokens end up with ## between them**. If this happens, the ANSI method was selected when it shouldn't have been. This is where UnixCpp comes in. You can force the empty-comment method to be used by defining UnixCpp in your vendor file:

  ```
  #define UnixCpp /* as nothing */
  ```

- **Pasted tokens end up with a space between them**. If this happens, the empty-comment method was selected when it shouldn't have been. In this case you define AnsiCpp (the counterpart to UnixCpp) to force ANSI token pasting to be used. Place the following in your vendor file:

  ```
  #define AnsiCpp /* as nothing */
  ```

In addition to Concat(), *Imake.rules* also contains Concat3() and Concat4() rules for pasting three or four tokens together. These rules provide an alternative to nested Concat() invocations, which are excessively ugly and don't work under ANSI rules, anyway, due to vagaries in the way ANSI token-pasting behavior interacts with macro expansion. As Kernighan and Ritchie say of the ANSI standard, "Some of the new rules, especially those involving concatenation, are bizarre."

You can't use the Concat() family of rules in vendor files or in *site.def* because the rules aren't defined until after those files have been processed.

Motif Support

Imake.tmpl contains #include directives for two files that I haven't mentioned yet. These are referenced near the point at which *Project.tmpl* is included:

```
#include LocalRulesFile
#include <Project.tmpl>
#include LocalTmplFile
```

By default, both LocalRulesFile and LocalTmplFile are defined as the empty file *noop.rules*, but you can redefine them in *site.def*. This allows you to extend the template to include information beyond that provided by the X11 files. This is important because without changing any X11 configuration files other than *site.def*, you can use them to configure a wider variety of projects than in the past.

For example, to use Motif with X11R6.1, you install the Motif-specific files *Motif.rules* and *Motif.tmpl* in the directory where you installed the R6.1 configuration files, and add the following to *site.def*:

```
#define LocalRulesFile <Motif.rules>
#define LocalTmplFile <Motif.tmpl>
```

At the moment, however, the current version of Motif (2.0) is designed for use only with X11R5. Presumably Motif will be updated to use the current X11 files at some point. For now, if you want to use Motif with X11R6.1, you must make other changes to the configuration files. See the Motif configuration document listed in Appendix I for further details.

Host-Specific Configuration Information — host.def

host.def is a configuration file that is new as of X11R6. It can be used as a means of setting parameters that vary from host to host within a given site. *host.def* is referenced in both the `BeforeVendorCF` and `AfterVendorCF` parts of *site.def*. By default, *host.def* is unused because the lines that reference it are commented out:

```
/* #include <host.def> */
```

If you want to use *host.def*, you have to create it yourself. Its contents should be written in two pieces, much like *site.def*:

```
#ifdef BeforeVendorCF
    /* host-dependent parameters the vendor file needs to know about */
#endif /* BeforeVendorCF */

#ifdef AfterVendorCF
    /* all other host-dependent stuff */
#endif /* AfterVendorCF */
```

Modify *host.def* as you wish, then uncomment the two lines in *site.def* that reference it so they look like this:

```
#include <host.def>
```

host.def can be used to good effect when configuration files on a master host are shared by other hosts using shadow link trees.[*] Suppose a host needs to modify definitions to supply values that apply only to itself. The link to the default *host.def* should be replaced on that host with a real file containing the definitions. This allows per-host modifications without affecting other machines at the site.

---

[*] You can create shadow link trees using the *mkshadow* or *lndir* utilities included in the X11R6.1 distribution, or in the *itools* distribution mentioned in Appendix A, *Obtaining Configuration Software*.

For example, you might have several machines running a common OS. If they don't all run the same version of that OS, you can set the OSMajorVersion, OS-MinorVersion, and OSTeenyVersion macros in *host.def* appropriately on each machine to affect how the *vendor.cf* file is interpreted on that host.

Be careful if you use *host.def* in a situation not involving shadow link trees. For example, if you copy a set of configuration files that uses *host.def* from one machine to another, you may need to modify *host.def* on the second machine, or disable it by re-commenting the lines in *site.def* that include it.

6

Writing Imakefiles

The easiest way to write an Imakefile is to find another one that does something similar and copy/modify it.

—xc/config/cf/README (X11R6.1)
— mit/config/README (X11R5)

This chapter describes how to write Imakefiles using the X11 configuration files. If you're not interested in X11, don't be deterred from reading the chapter. You can use the X11 configuration files to write Imakefiles for non-X programs, and many of the concepts and ideas presented here apply to any set of configuration files.

Most of the chapter centers around how to use the rule macros defined in the X11 *Imake.rules* file. There are more than 170 such rules; the discussion here covers just a few. But once you understand those few, you should be able to look at *Imake.rules* and understand many of the other rules, too.

When I describe a given rule, I discuss it at two levels. First, I present some basic information—the purpose of the rule, how to use it. Read just this part of the discussion if you don't care how rules work and you just want to get your programs built. This might be the situation if you've skipped directly to this chapter from Chapter 2, *A Tour of imake*, for example.

Second, I present more detailed information—how the rule is defined, how it works. You should read this part of the discussion if you want to gain a greater understanding of the X11 configuration files, learn how to choose between rules in situations where more than one seems applicable, or write your own configuration files. To get the most out of this part of the discussion, it's best to be familiar with rule syntax and the X11 configuration architecture. (See Chapter 3, *Understanding Configuration Files*, and Chapter 5, *The X11 Configuration Files*.)

General Strategy

To write an *Imakefile*, you invoke rules: concise specifications of the types of targets you want to build, such as executable programs, shell scripts, or libraries. *imake* reads your *Imakefile* and expands the rules into *Makefile* target entries. Then you run *make* to build your targets.

Invoking Rules

To invoke a rule, you name it and pass it any arguments necessary:

```
RuleName(arguments)
```

RuleName is the name of the rule and *arguments* lists any arguments you pass to the rule.

There are a few guidelines you should follow when you invoke rules in an *Imakefile*:

- The argument list may be empty or consist of one or more arguments. When there are multiple arguments, separate them by commas, as shown in the following examples:

```
DependTarget()
SimpleProgramTarget(myprog)
InstallLibrary(mylib,$(BINDIR))
NormalProgramTarget(myprog,$(OBJS),$(DEPXLIB),$(XLIB),-lm)
```

- When a rule has a non-empty argument list, you must specify something for each argument. Missing arguments are not allowed. The X11 configuration files provide the symbol `NullParameter` to specify arguments with no value:

```
ComplexProgramTarget_1(myprog,,-lm)                /* incorrect */
ComplexProgramTarget_1(myprog,NullParameter,-lm)   /* correct */
```

- A cosmetic reason to use `NullParameter` is that it makes invocations more readable. Compare the following instances of `CppScriptTarget()`. Without some close inspection, it may not be apparent that the last argument in the first instance is empty:

```
CppScriptTarget(x,x.cpp,'-DDIRS="/a/b,/g/h"',)
CppScriptTarget(x,x.cpp,'-DDIRS="/a/b,/g/h"',NullParameter)
```

- Don't add extra whitespace around arguments:

```
NormalLibraryTarget(mylib,$(OBJS))       /* correct */
NormalLibraryTarget(mylib ,$(OBJS))      /* incorrect */
NormalLibraryTarget(mylib, $(OBJS))      /* incorrect */
NormalLibraryTarget( mylib , $(OBJS) )   /* VERY incorrect */
```

The whitespace may end up as a part of your target entries in an unpleasant way. This is discussed further in Chapter 7, *Imakefile Troubleshooting*.

- Whitespace within an argument is allowable when the argument consists of a list of items such as file names, libraries, or flags:

```
NormalLibraryTarget(mylib,a.o b.o c.o)
ComplexProgramTarget_1(myprog,$(XMULIB) $(XLIB),-ly -lm)
SpecialCObjectRule(file,NullParameter,-DFLAG1 -DFLAG2)
```

- You cannot split a rule invocation across lines:

```
/* incorrect */
NormalProgramTarget(prog1,$(OBJS1),$(DEPXLIB),$(XLIB),\
    NullParameter)
/* correct */
NormalProgramTarget(prog1,$(OBJS1),$(DEPXLIB),$(XLIB),NullParameter)
```

Building Your Project

Once your *Imakefile* is written, a typical sequence of commands to build and install a project looks like this:

```
% xmkmf          Generate the Makefile (xmkmf calls imake)
% make clean     Remove any leftover debris
% make depend    Generate header file dependencies
% make           Build the software
% make install   Install the software
```

If the project consists of multiple directories, the sequence is similar except that the initial *Makefile*-generating step is followed by:

```
% make Makefiles
```

A shortcut is to use *xmkmf -a*, which does most of the above steps for you including:

```
xmkmf
make Makefiles
make includes
make depend
```

Remember that if you change an *Imakefile*, you must rebuild the *Makefile* and regenerate header file dependencies:

```
% make Makefile
% make depend
```

You can test whether your intentions in the *Imakefile* are realized in the *Makefile* by using the *−n* option. This tells *make* to show what commands it would generate to build a particular target, without actually executing them. For example, to verify that targets will be installed where you expect, run this command:

```
% make -n install
```

For the preceding commands to work, the X11 configuration files must be available on your machine, as well as the programs *imake, xmkmf, makedepend,* and *mkdirhier.* If you need any of these, see Appendix A, *Obtaining Configuration Software,* and Appendix B, *Installing Configuration Software.*

The rest of this chapter shows how to select and use the rules you invoke in your *Imakefile* for the targets you want to build. The discussion covers several common situations:

* Building a single program from a single source file
* Building a single program from multiple source files
* Building two or three programs
* Building an arbitrary number of programs
* Building a library
* Installing files

I'll also discuss some related issues such as how to refer to libraries, use of some common *make* variables, and management of multiple-directory projects.

As you read, remember the advice given in this chapter's epigraph, which summarizes an important principle of *Imakefile* writing: it's almost always true with *imake* that it's easier to copy something that works and modify it to suit your own purposes than to write it from scratch. Consider the Imakefiles in this chapter as working examples. Select one that's close to what you want, copy it, modify it, and use it as a basis for your own work. Or you can examine Imakefiles from existing projects to find one that you can use.

Building One Program

To build a single program in your *Imakefile*, you have a choice of two rules. If the program is built from a single source file, use `SimpleProgramTarget()`. If it's built from multiple source files, use `ComplexProgramTarget()`.

Building a Single Program (One Source File)

The simplest case of all is when you're building one program from one source file. If your program fits the bill, use `SimpleProgramTarget()` and your *Imakefile* will be easy to write:

```
SimpleProgramTarget(prog)
```

prog is the name of the program. The source file must be named *prog.c*.

`SimpleProgramTarget()` generates targets for all the following commands:

```
% make all
% make prog
% make install
% make install.man
% make depend
% make lint
% make clean
```

You can also specify libraries to link into the final executable. See the section "Specifying Libraries," later in this chapter.

The definition of `SimpleProgramTarget()` looks like this:

```
/*
 * SimpleProgramTarget - generate rules for compiling and linking programs
 * that only have one C source file.  It should only be used in Imakefiles
 * that describe a single program.
 */
#ifndef SimpleProgramTarget
#define SimpleProgramTarget(prog)                          @@\
        OBJS = prog.o                                      @@\
        SRCS = prog.c                                      @@\
                                                           @@\

ComplexProgramTarget(prog)
#endif /* SimpleProgramTarget */
```

`SimpleProgramTarget()` is actually quite lazy: it foists off onto `ComplexProgram-Target()` most of the work of generating entries to build and install the program. `SimpleProgramTarget()` deigns only to assign the names of the program's source file and object file to `SRCS` and `OBJS`, because `ComplexProgramTarget()` expects those values to be set. `SimpleProgramTarget()` automatically determines `SRCS` and `OBJS` on the basis of the fixed relationship assumed between the name of the program and the names of its source and object files.

Building a Single Program (Multiple Source Files)

If you're building a single program from more than one source file, you can't use
`SimpleProgramTarget()`. Use `ComplexProgramTarget()` instead, which makes
no assumptions about how many files your program is built from or what they're
named. This gives you the freedom to use an arbitrary set of files. However, SRCS
and OBJS still need to be set, and their values cannot be determined from the program name. You must assign them yourself. For example, to build a program
myprog from *main.c*, *connect.c*, and *display.c*, the *Imakefile* looks like this:

```
SRCS = main.c connect.c display.c
OBJS = main.o connect.o display.o

ComplexProgramTarget(myprog)
```

`ComplexProgramTarget()` generates the same targets as `SimpleProgram-`
`Target()`.

If your program needs to have libraries linked into it, see the section "Specifying
Libraries."

The definition of `ComplexProgramTarget()` is more elaborate than that of
`SimpleProgramTarget()`:

```
/*
 * ComplexProgramTarget - generate rules for compiling and linking the
 * program specified by $(OBJS) and $(SRCS), installing the program and its
 * man page, and generating dependencies.  It should only be used in
 * Imakefiles that describe a single program.
 */
#ifndef ComplexProgramTarget
#define ComplexProgramTarget(prog)                                      @@\
        PROGRAM = prog                                                  @@\
                                                                        @@\
AllTarget(prog)                                                         @@\
                                                                        @@\
ProgramTargetHelper(prog,SRCS,OBJS,DEPLIBS,$(LOCAL_LIBRARIES),NullParameter) @@\
                                                                        @@\
DependTarget()                                                          @@\
LintTarget()                                                            @@\
                                                                        @@\
clean::                                                                 @@\
        RemoveFile(ProgramTargetName(prog))
#endif /* ComplexProgramTarget */
```

Like `SimpleProgramTarget()`, `ComplexProgramTarget()` relies on several other
rules to do most of its work. The main helper is `ProgramTargetHelper()`, which

is the rule that actually generates target entries to build and install the program. It looks like this:[*]

```
#ifndef ProgramTargetHelper
#define ProgramTargetHelper(prog,srcs,objs,deplib,locallib,syslib)      @@\
ProgramTargetName(prog): $(objs) $(deplib)                               @@\
    RemoveTargetProgram($@)                                             @@\
    LinkRule($@,$(LDOPTIONS),$(objs),locallib $(LDLIBS) syslib)         @@\
                                                                        @@\
InstallProgram(prog,$(BINDIR))                                          @@\
InstallManPage(prog,$(MANDIR))
#endif /* ProgramTargetHelper */
```

ComplexProgramTarget() and the rules it invokes expand to several entries in the *Makefile*:

- AllTarget() generates an all entry for *prog* so that *make all* compiles the program. The all entry appears first in the resulting *Makefile*, so all becomes the default target and *make* with no arguments is equivalent to *make all*.

- The ProgramTargetHelper() rule generates several targets:

  — A *prog* entry that specifies that the target program depends on its object files and libraries and indicates how to link it to produce the final executable. (The name of the entry is the name of the program, not "prog".) SRCS and OBJS are the source and object file lists. LOCAL_LIBRARIES and DEPLIBS specify link and dependency libraries; they're discussed in the next section, "Specifying Libraries."

  — InstallProgram() and InstallManPage() generate install and install.man entries for installing the target program and its manual page in their respective directories.

- DependTarget() produces a depend entry for running *makedepend* to generate header file dependencies. This rule expects that SRCS names all of the program's source files.

- LintTarget() generates a lint entry for checking the program's source files. It, too, uses SRCS implicitly.

- The clean entry clobbers the compiled program. The configuration files automatically produce a default clean entry that removes .o files, but that entry doesn't know the name of the program built by ComplexProgramTarget(). So ComplexProgramTarget() provides a clean entry to remove the executable explicitly.

---

[*] I've deleted some lines from the definition of ProgramTargetHelper(). Those lines generate special-purpose target entries for use with some specialized development tools, none of which concern us here.

Besides SRCS and OBJS, which we've already discussed, ComplexProgram-Target() and the rules it invokes use a number of other *make* variables, such as LDOPTIONS, LDLIBS, BINDIR, and MANDIR. You can ignore all of them. PROGRAM is set by ComplexProgramTarget() itself; the others are assigned values as necessary by the configuration files.

Specifying Libraries

Programs often use functions contained in libraries, so the *Makefile* must specify how to link in those libraries when the final executables are produced. This section describes what to put in your *Imakefile* so that happens correctly.

SimpleProgramTarget() and ComplexProgramTarget() don't provide any way to specify libraries in the argument list when you invoke them. Instead, you use a trio of *make* variables: LOCAL_LIBRARIES, SYS_LIBRARIES, and DEPLIBS. The first two variables name the libraries in a form the linker can use. The third names them in a form *make* can use for dependency checking.

Link Libraries

LOCAL_LIBRARIES and SYS_LIBRARIES name libraries that need to be linked in when the final executable is created. The X11 configuration files don't give either variable any default value; if libraries are needed, you must assign values yourself or the link step will fail.

Libraries can be specified for the linker either by pathname or by using −*l* notation. Typically, you use a pathname when you know the location of a library, for example, when it's built within your project. You assign this kind of library to LOCAL_LIBRARIES. Use −*l* notation when you want the linker to find the library for you, for example, for a system library. Libraries specified like this are assigned to SYS_LIBRARIES.

Dependency Libraries

DEPLIBS names the libraries your program needs, but in dependency form. This addresses a common *Makefile* deficiency: program-building entries that list the program's object files as dependencies, but fail to list the libraries necessary for the success of the final link step. DEPLIBS allows you to characterize your program's dependencies more completely, so that when a library changes, *make* knows the program must be relinked.

make understands only filenames for purposes of dependency checking, so libraries must be assigned to DEPLIBS in pathname form, not −*l* form. The following doesn't work:

```
/* incorrect */
DEPLIBS = -lm
```

If you assign such a value to DEPLIBS, *make* complains when you use the resulting *Makefile*:

```
make: Fatal error: Don't know how to make target "-lm"
```

The default value of DEPLIBS refers to the Xlib, Xext, Xt, Xmu, and Xaw libraries. You should assign a different value to DEPLIBS if your program uses a different set of libraries. For instance, if your program uses no libraries at all, turn DEPLIBS off by assigning it an empty value:

```
DEPLIBS =
```

Actually, you can cheat and turn DEPLIBS off, even if your program does use libraries. If all the libraries are present, your program will still link correctly. (If the libraries are missing, you have more pressing concerns than writing an *Imakefile*!)

Now we know how library variables are used in general; let's look at some specific examples.

For a program that requires no libraries, the variables all have empty values:

```
LOCAL_LIBRARIES =
  SYS_LIBRARIES =
        DEPLIBS =
```

Since the first two variables aren't assigned any default value by the configuration files, the following is equivalent and simpler to write:

```
DEPLIBS =
```

For a program that does need libraries, we must consider three cases:

- Libraries built within the project
- System libraries
- X11 libraries

Within-Project Libraries

If a library is built within your project, you refer to it by pathname, usually relative to the project source tree root, which is specified by the *make* variable TOP. *imake* sets TOP for you when you build the *Makefile*. It provides a stable point of reference to use when specifying within-project paths, no matter what directory of your project you happen to be in.

Within-project library assignments are usually written using the *make* variable LOCAL_LIBRARIES. For example, if a program uses a library *libmylib.a* located in

the *lib* directory under the project root, specify it using the pathname
$(TOP)/*lib/libmylib.a*. Since pathnames are suitable for dependency lines, too,
specify the library the same way for dependency purposes and assign it to the
variable DEPLIBS. Thus, you set the variables like this:

```
LOCAL_LIBRARIES = $(TOP)/lib/libmylib.a
        DEPLIBS = $(TOP)/lib/libmylib.a
```

System Libraries

If you need a library that isn't built within your project, chances are it's a system
library accessed using *−l* syntax for linking purposes. This kind of library is typically assigned to the variable SYS_LIBRARIES. The math library is a good example.
If your program needs it, write this:

```
SYS_LIBRARIES = -lm
```

So far, so good. Now, how do you specify the library in dependency form for
DEPLIBS?

Answer: You don't, because DEPLIBS requires a pathname and *−lm* isn't one. You
could figure out where a given system library is located on your machine and
write its pathname into your *Imakefile*, but that's a system-specific value. (You
might know that the math library is in */usr/lib/libm.a* on your machine, but not all
machines are like yours. One system I've used has the math library in
/bsd43/usr/lib/libm.a.) In the absence of a portable mechanism for specifying the
locations of arbitrary system libraries, just leave them out of DEPLIBS:

```
SYS_LIBRARIES = -lm
        DEPLIBS =
```

This is a reasonable thing to do. System libraries rarely change, so not listing them
has minimal impact on the accuracy of dependency checking.

X11 Libraries

When you're building X11 programs, you'll need X11 libraries (Xlib at minimum,
possibly others). You can refer to these using literal values like -lX11 or -lXt for
linking, but the X11 configuration files provide a set of *make* variables for the
same purpose, as well as a set for use in dependencies. Table 6–1 lists the most
common ones; consult *Project.tmpl* for the full list.

Table 6–1: make Variables for X11 Libraries

X11 Library	Link Name	Dependency Name
Xlib	XLIB	DEPXLIB
Xmu	XMULIB	DEPXMULIB
X Toolkit	XTOOLLIB	DEPXTOOLLIB
Athena Widgets	XAWLIB	DEPXAWLIB
X Image Extension	XIELIB	DEPXIELIB
PHIGS	PHIGSLIB	DEPPHIGSLIB
PEX Library	PEXLIB	DEPPEXLIB

Suppose a program needs the Xlib and X Toolkit libraries. Consulting the table, we find that the names suitable for the linker are XLIB and XTOOLLIB. Similarly, DEP-XLIB and DEPXTOOLLIB are the names to use for dependency checking. So we write:

```
LOCAL_LIBRARIES = $(XTOOLLIB) $(XLIB)
        DEPLIBS = $(DEPXTOOLLIB) $(DEPXLIB)
```

The order is important here. The X Toolkit uses routines from Xlib, so Xt must precede Xlib in the link command. Otherwise, the linker doesn't know which Xlib routines to extract from the library and put into the executable, and you'll get "undefined symbol" errors.

Are X11 libraries local libraries or system libraries?

I assigned the link libraries to LOCAL_LIBRARIES in the preceding example. Actually, the X11 libraries are ambiguous, because they can be considered system libraries in some circumstances. If you're building an application within the source tree of the X11 distribution, you'll probably use versions of the libraries found within that tree. Those libraries are local to the distribution. If you're building an application outside the X11 source tree, you'll probably use versions of the X11 libraries installed under a public directory such as */usr/X11R6.1/lib* or */usr/lib*. Those libraries are system libraries.

In practice, this distinction isn't a problem. As long as you use the *make* variables to refer to X11 libraries, you can treat them either as local or system libraries and expect your program to link properly. Thus, these two sets of *make* variable assignments are equivalent:

```
LOCAL_LIBRARIES = $(XMULIB) $(XLIB)
   SYS_LIBRARIES =
LOCAL_LIBRARIES =
   SYS_LIBRARIES = $(XMULIB) $(XLIB)
```

If you're skeptical about this, take a look at the programs in the X11 *contrib* (user-contributed) distribution. They aren't built within the X11 source tree, but by and large their Imakefiles treat the X11 libraries as local libraries.

Athena client libraries

If a client program uses the Athena widgets, it uses Xaw, the Athena Widget library. Xaw in turn requires the Xlib, Xmu, and Xt libraries. You could write this in your *Imakefile*:

```
LOCAL_LIBRARIES = $(XAWLIB) $(XMULIB) $(XTOOLLIB) $(XLIB)
        DEPLIBS = $(DEPXAWLIB) $(DEPXMULIB) $(DEPXTOOLLIB) $(DEPXLIB)
```

However, it's a lot more convenient to use the *cpp* symbols XawClientLibs and XawClientDepLibs instead:

```
LOCAL_LIBRARIES = XawClientLibs
        DEPLIBS = XawClientDepLibs
```

The X11 configuration files define these two symbols as shorthand to achieve the same effect as the previous set of assignments. They're easier to write and they make sure the libraries are specified in the correct order for you.

The X extensions library

Xext, the X extensions library, contains routines for locally available extensions such as those for non-rectangular window shapes, double-buffering, and shared memory. If your program uses extensions, you don't need to write anything special in the *Imakefile* beyond including the Xlib variables XLIB and DEPXLIB in the link and dependency library lists. XLIB and DEPXLIB automatically include references to the extensions library.

Mixing Library Types

When you need several types of libraries (within-project, system, X11 libraries), specify the combination as the concatenation of the way you'd specify them individually. For a program that uses the local library $(TOP)/*lib/libmylib.a*, the X11 libraries Xlib and Xmu, and the system library *−lm*, set the variables like this:

```
LOCAL_LIBRARIES = $(TOP)/lib/libmylib.a $(XMULIB) $(XLIB)
   SYS_LIBRARIES = -lm
        DEPLIBS = $(TOP)/lib/libmylib.a $(DEPXMULIB) $(DEPXLIB)
```

Table 6-2 summarizes the use of link and dependency specifiers for different library types. *pathname* represents the path to a library starting from the project root. *libname* represents the basename of a system library.

Table 6–2: Forms of Link and Dependency Library Specifiers

Type of Library	Link Form	Dependency Form
Within project	`$(TOP)`/*pathname*	`$(TOP)`/*pathname*
System	`-l`*libname*	none
X11 library (e.g., Xlib)	`$(XLIB)`	`$(DEPXLIB)`
Athena client libraries	`XawClientLibs`	`XawClientDepLibs`

Multiple Programs

You cannot use `SimpleProgramTarget()` or `ComplexProgramTarget()` when you want to build more than one program in your *Imakefile*. To handle this, the X11 configuration files provide rules for building exactly two or three programs, and a rule for building an arbitrary number of programs.

Building Two or Three Programs

To build two or three programs in an *Imakefile*, use `ComplexProgramTarget_1()`, `ComplexProgramTarget_2()`, and `ComplexProgramTarget_3()`. The invocation sequence for each of the `ComplexProgramTarget_n()` rules is:

```
ComplexProgramTarget_n(prog,loclibs,syslibs)
```

prog is the name of your program. The other two arguments specify libraries needed to get *prog* to link correctly: *loclibs* is for libraries local to your project, and *syslibs* is for libraries provided by the system. They're similar to the `LOCAL_LIBRARIES` and `SYS_LIBRARIES` variables used with `ComplexProgram-Target()`. The difference is that you specify the values in the rule argument list rather than by setting *make* variables.

If you don't need libraries of a particular kind, pass `NullParameter` for *loclibs*, *syslibs*, or both.

Although you don't use `LOCAL_LIBRARIES`, `SYS_LIBRARIES`, or `DEPLIBS` with the `ComplexProgramTarget_n()` rules, you're expected to assign values to other *make* variables in the *Imakefile*:

- Set the variable `PROGRAMS` to the names of the programs you're building:

  ```
  PROGRAMS = prog1 prog2 prog3
  ```

  If you don't do this, *make all* and *make depend* won't work correctly.

- Set SRCS*n* and OBJS*n* to the source and object file lists for program *n*:

```
SRCS1 = file1a.c file1b.c
OBJS1 = file1a.o file1b.o

SRCS2 = file2a.c file2b.c file2c.c file2d.c
OBJS2 = file2a.o file2b.o file2c.o file2d.o

SRCS3 = file3a.c
OBJS3 = file3a.o
```

SRCS*n* is needed for depending and *lint*-ing the sources. OBJS*n* is needed for compiling and linking the program.

- DEPLIBS*n* names the libraries that program *n* depends on. The default value is the same as DEPLIBS, but you might wish to assign a different value. If a program uses no libraries, assign the empty value to DEPLIBS*n* to clear it. Otherwise, the value of DEPLIBS*n* should contain the dependency forms of the link libraries you use for the *loclibs* and *syslibs* arguments for program *n*. Suppose you're invoking ComplexProgramTarget_2() like this:

```
ComplexProgramTarget_2(prog2,$(TOP)/lib/libmylib.a $(XLIB),-lm)
```

Here, *loclibs* names $(TOP)/*lib/libmylib.a* and $(XLIB), and *syslibs* names -lm. To specify the value of DEPLIBS2, assign it the dependency forms of these three libraries: the reference to the local library *libmylib.a* is repeated without modification, XLIB becomes DEPXLIB, and *-lm* has no dependency form, so it's left out. Here's the result:

```
DEPLIBS2 = $(TOP)/lib/libmylib.a $(DEPXLIB)
```

An *Imakefile* using the ComplexProgramTarget_*n*() rules to build two programs, *prog1* and *prog2*, might look like this:

```
PROGRAMS = prog1 prog2
   SRCS1 = file1a.c file1b.c
   OBJS1 = file1a.o file1b.o
DEPLIBS1 = $(DEPXLIB)
   SRCS2 = file2a.c file2b.c file2c.c file2d.c
   OBJS2 = file2a.o file2b.o file2c.o file2d.o
DEPLIBS2 = $(DEPXTOOLLIB) $(DEPXLIB)
ComplexProgramTarget_1(prog1,$(XLIB),NullParameter)
ComplexProgramTarget_2(prog2,$(XTOOLLIB) $(XLIB),NullParameter)
```

To add a third program, *prog3*, append its name to PROGRAMS; set SRCS3, OBJS3, and DEPLIBS3; and invoke ComplexProgramTarget_3():

```
PROGRAMS = prog1 prog2 prog3
   SRCS1 = file1a.c file1b.c
   OBJS1 = file1a.o file1b.o
DEPLIBS1 = $(DEPXLIB)
```

```
    SRCS2 = file2a.c file2b.c file2c.c file2d.c
    OBJS2 = file2a.o file2b.o file2c.o file2d.o
 DEPLIBS2 = $(DEPXTOOLLIB) $(DEPXLIB)

    SRCS3 = file3a.c
    OBJS3 = file3a.o
 DEPLIBS3 = $(TOP)/lib/libutil.a $(DEPXLIB)

ComplexProgramTarget_1(prog1,$(XLIB),NullParameter)
ComplexProgramTarget_2(prog2,$(XTOOLLIB) $(XLIB),NullParameter)
ComplexProgramTarget_3(prog3,$(TOP)/lib/libutil.a $(XLIB),-lm)
```

If you want to add a fourth program, *prog4*, you, uh ... can't. Sorry. You have to rewrite your *Imakefile*. (See the discussion of `NormalProgramTarget()` in the next section. And try to anticipate whether or not you'll need to build more than three programs.)

The definitions of `ComplexProgramTarget_1()` and `ComplexProgramTarget_2()` are shown in the example below. `ComplexProgramTarget_3()` isn't shown; it's essentially identical to `ComplexProgramTarget_2()`.

```
/*
 * ComplexProgramTarget_1 - generate rules for compiling and linking the
 * program specified by $(OBJS1) and $(SRCS1), installing the program and its
 * man page, and generating dependencies for it and any programs described
 * by $(SRCS2) and $(SRCS3).  It should be used to build the primary
 * program in Imakefiles that describe multiple programs.
 */
#ifndef ComplexProgramTarget_1
#define ComplexProgramTarget_1(prog,locallib,syslib)                @@\
           OBJS = $(OBJS1) $(OBJS2) $(OBJS3)                        @@\
           SRCS = $(SRCS1) $(SRCS2) $(SRCS3)                        @@\
                                                                   @@\
AllTarget($(PROGRAMS))                                              @@\
                                                                   @@\
ProgramTargetHelper(prog,SRCS1,OBJS1,DEPLIBS1,locallib,syslib)      @@\
                                                                   @@\
DependTarget()                                                      @@\
LintTarget()                                                        @@\
                                                                   @@\
clean::                                                             @@\
    RemoveFiles($(PROGRAMS))
#endif /* ComplexProgramTarget_1 */

/*
 * ComplexProgramTarget_2 - generate rules for compiling and linking the
 * program specified by $(OBJS2) and $(SRCS2) and installing the program and
 * man page.  It should be used to build the second program in Imakefiles
 * describing more than one program.
 */
#ifndef ComplexProgramTarget_2
#define ComplexProgramTarget_2(prog,locallib,syslib)                @@\
ProgramTargetHelper(prog,SRCS2,OBJS2,DEPLIBS2,locallib,syslib)
#endif /* ComplexProgramTarget_2 */
```

Of the three rules, `ComplexProgramTarget_1()` does the most work. It does everything the other two rules do along with setting `SRCS` and `OBJS`, and producing `depend`, `lint`, and `clean` entries. Because of the way the rules work, these additional things need only be done once, not repeated three times.

I mentioned earlier that failure to set `PROGRAMS` causes two commands to work incorrectly:

```
% make all
% make clean
```

You can see why if you examine the definition of `ComplexProgramTarget_1()`. `PROGRAMS` is used to generate the `all` and `clean` entries. When you set `PROGRAMS` properly, the `all` entry causes your programs to be built and the `clean` entry removes the executables. But when you don't set `PROGRAMS`, its value is empty, and the two entries effectively end up looking like this in your *Makefile*:

```
all::
clean::
     $(RM)
```

As a result, neither entry does anything. Not quite the intended effect!

Building an Arbitrary Number of Programs

To build an arbitrary number of programs, invoke `NormalProgramTarget()` for each one:

```
NormalProgramTarget(prog,objs,deplibs,loclibs,syslibs)
```

You don't need to set any *make* variables to use `NormalProgramTarget()`. All the information it needs is passed in through the argument list. *prog* is the name of your program and *objs* is the set of object files from which it's built. *loclibs* and *syslibs* name the local and system link libraries your program needs. *deplibs* names those libraries in a form suitable for dependency checking.

Here's an *Imakefile* that uses `NormalProgramTarget()` to build four programs. (The *make* variables OBJS1 through OBJS4 are used to improve readability. You could put the object file lists directly into the rule invocations if you wanted to.)

```
OBJS1 = prog1a.o prog1b.o
OBJS2 = prog2a.o prog2b.o prog2c.o prog2d.o
OBJS3 = prog3a.o
OBJS4 = prog4a.o prog4b.o

NormalProgramTarget(prog1,$(OBJS1),$(DEPXLIB),$(XLIB),NullParameter)
NormalProgramTarget(prog2,$(OBJS2),$(DEPXLIB),$(XLIB),NullParameter)
NormalProgramTarget(prog3,$(OBJS3),$(DEPXLIB),$(XLIB),NullParameter)
NormalProgramTarget(prog4,$(OBJS4),$(DEPXLIB),$(XLIB),NullParameter)
```

This *Imakefile* is incomplete because it produces a *Makefile* without `all`, `install`, `depend`, or `lint` entries. To understand this, take a look at the definition of `NormalProgramTarget()`:

```
/*
 * NormalProgramTarget - generate rules to compile and link the indicated
 * program; since it does not use any default object files, it may be used for
 * multiple programs in the same Imakefile.
 */
#ifndef NormalProgramTarget
#define NormalProgramTarget(prog,objects,deplibs,locallibs,syslibs)  @@\
ProgramTargetName(prog): objects deplibs                            @@\
    RemoveTargetProgram($@)                                         @@\
    LinkRule($@,$(LDOPTIONS),objects,locallibs $(LDLIBS) syslibs)   @@\
                                                                   @@\
clean::                                                             @@\
    RemoveFile(ProgramTargetName(prog))
#endif /* NormalProgramTarget */
```

`NormalProgramTarget()` generates only two entries, a *prog* entry to build the executable program and a `clean` entry to remove it. This contrasts with the `ComplexProgramTarget_n()` rules, which epitomize the cradle-to-grave approach of producing entries for every target you need, and then some. `NormalProgram-Target()` is the entrepreneur's rule—it presumes you have more initiative. You must invoke the appropriate rules yourself if you want entries for any of the following targets:

`all`

> Invoke `AllTarget(prog)` before each invocation of `NormalProgram-Target(prog)`.

`install`

> Invoke an installation rule for each program you want installed. You have a choice of several installation rules; the simplest is `InstallProgram()`. This rule takes two arguments, the name of the program and the directory in which to install it:

```
InstallProgram(prog, dir)
```

`depend` and `lint`

> Invoke `DependTarget()` and `LintTarget()` once each per *Imakefile*. To use either of these rules you must set `SRCS` to the list of all source files used by all the programs in the *Imakefile*.

install.man

> If you provide any manual pages, you should invoke `InstallManPage()` for each one:

```
InstallManPage(prog,$(MANDIR))
```

> `MANDIR` is the manual page installation directory (the section 1 directory by default). Note that the rule takes the program name in the argument list, but the manual page itself should be named *prog.man*.

To fix the preceding *Imakefile* so it includes entries for the targets just described, write it like this:

```
SRCS1 = prog1a.c prog1b.c
OBJS1 = prog1a.o prog1b.o

SRCS2 = prog2a.c prog2b.c prog2c.c prog2d.c
OBJS2 = prog2a.o prog2b.o prog2c.o prog2d.o

SRCS3 = prog3a.c
OBJS3 = prog3a.o

SRCS4 = prog4a.c prog4b.c
OBJS4 = prog4a.o prog4b.o

 SRCS = $(SRCS1) $(SRCS2) $(SRCS3) $(SRCS4)

AllTarget(prog1)
NormalProgramTarget(prog1,$(OBJS1),$(DEPXLIB),$(XLIB),NullParameter)
InstallProgram(prog1,$(BINDIR))
InstallManPage(prog1,$(MANDIR))

AllTarget(prog2)
NormalProgramTarget(prog2,$(OBJS2),$(DEPXLIB),$(XLIB),NullParameter)
InstallProgram(prog2,$(BINDIR))
InstallManPage(prog2,$(MANDIR))

AllTarget(prog3)
NormalProgramTarget(prog3,$(OBJS3),$(DEPXLIB),$(XLIB),NullParameter)
InstallProgram(prog3,$(BINDIR))
InstallManPage(prog3,$(MANDIR))

AllTarget(prog4)
NormalProgramTarget(prog4,$(OBJS4),$(DEPXLIB),$(XLIB),NullParameter)
InstallProgram(prog4,$(BINDIR))
InstallManPage(prog4,$(MANDIR))

DependTarget()
LintTarget()
```

It's more work to write an *Imakefile* when you use `NormalProgramTarget()` than when you use the `ComplexProgramTarget_n()` rules. As compensation, `Normal-ProgramTarget()` gives you a broader range of choices in determining what ends up in the *Makefile*. It's also more general since you can use it to build any number of programs without a separate rule *n* for every program *n*.

linting Multiple Programs

The `ComplexProgramTarget_n()` rules automatically generate a `lint` target entry for you. `NormalProgramTarget()` does not, but you can invoke `LintTarget()` yourself to generate one. In both cases, you can use the `lint` entry to run your sources through the *lint* program. However, as noted in Chapter 2, you must interpret the output with some caution. *lint* expects to be fed the source files for a single program, but the `lint` entry passes the sources for all your programs. The result is output that contains spurious warnings, such as that *main()* is multiply defined.

In Chapter 12, *Writing Rule Macros*, we'll see an alternative way of generating `lint` entries that doesn't have this problem.

Organizing File Lists

The final *Imakefile* in the preceding section illustrates an important organizational technique: judicious use of *make* variables to improve the readability of the *Imakefile*. If we had written object file lists directly in the rule invocations, the invocations would be more difficult to read, particularly for targets built from lots of files. Instead of writing object file lists directly in invocations of `Normal-ProgramTarget()`, we assign them to variables and refer to the variables when we invoke the rules.

Similarly, variables make it easier to use `DependTarget()` and `LintTarget()`, which expect the *make* variable `SRCS` to name all source files used in the *Imakefile*. If you use a variable to specify the source list for each of your programs, you can set `SRCS` to their concatenation:

```
SRCS1 = prog1a.c prog1b.c
SRCS2 = prog2a.c prog2b.c prog2c.c prog2d.c
SRCS3 = prog3a.c
SRCS4 = prog4a.c prog4b.c
 SRCS = $(SRCS1) $(SRCS2) $(SRCS3) $(SRCS4)
```

Using variables for lists of source and object files adds more lines to the *Imakefile*. However, the resulting *Imakefile* is better structured, easier to read, and less prone to error:

- It's more obvious which files make up a given program because they're explicitly specified on their own line, not buried in an invocation of `Normal-ProgramTarget()`.

- When a new file is added to the source file list, it's harder to forget to add the corresponding object file to the object file list if the two lists are located together, because their contents are completely parallel:

  ```
  SRCS1 = prog1a.c prog1b.c
  OBJS1 = prog1a.o prog1b.o
  ```

  In the assignments above, it's not likely you'll add *prog1c.c* to SRCS1 but forget to add *prog1c.o* to OBJS1.

- When SRCS is defined as the concatenation of individual program source list variables, changes to an individual program's source list automatically propagate into SRCS, so that *make lint* and *make depend* continue to work properly without special attention.

Building Libraries

The X11 rules allow you to build normal, shared, profiled, or debugging libraries. I'll describe how to build normal libraries first, then the other kinds.

To create a normal library, use NormalLibraryTarget(), which takes two arguments: the basename of the library, and a list of the object files comprising it. For a library *libxyz.a*, the basename is *xyz*. Here's what an *Imakefile* for it might look like:

```
SRCS = a.c b.c c.c
OBJS = a.o b.o c.o

NormalLibraryObjectRule()
NormalLibraryTarget(xyz,$(OBJS))
InstallLibrary(xyz,$(USRLIBDIR))

DependTarget()
```

Notice that you don't use NormalLibraryTarget() in isolation:

- Invoke NormalLibraryObjectRule() before NormalLibraryTarget(), to provide some machinery telling *make* how to compile object files that are intended to be combined into libraries.

- Use InstallLibrary() to generate an install entry; NormalLibrary-Target() doesn't provide one.

- Invoke DependTarget() to produce a target entry for generating header file dependencies. This requires that you set SRCS.

NormalLibraryTarget() doesn't generate a clean entry. There is no need because the default clean entry provided by the configuration files automatically removes *.a* files.

Other Kinds of Libraries

When you want to compile shared, profiled, or debugging libraries in addition to or instead of a normal library, your *Imakefile* should look something like this:

```
#define DoNormalLib BoolVal
#define DoSharedLib BoolVal
#define DoDebugLib BoolVal
#define DoProfileLib BoolVal

#define LibName basename
#define SoRev revision-number-variable        (optional)

SRCS = file1.c file2.c file3.c ...
OBJS = file1.o file2.o file3.o ...

#include <Library.tmpl>

DependTarget()
```

The purpose of each section of the *Imakefile* is as follows:

- The first four lines define Boolean-valued macros that indicate what types of libraries you want to create. *BoolVal* is either YES or NO for each macro (it need not be the same on all four lines).

- The next two lines define macros that are used for constructing library names. LibName is the library basename. SoRev is used to refer to the revision number of your shared library. (The SoRev line is needed only if you're building a shared library, i.e., if DoSharedLib is YES.) Be careful how you define SoRev. Its value is not the revision number, but the name of a *make* variable that holds the revision number. This means you should have a line somewhere assigning the proper number to that variable. The revision-number variables for the X11 libraries are assigned values in *Project.tmpl*, but for a library of your own, you might want to assign the value right in your *Imakefile*. For example, for library *xyz*, revision 1.3, you could write something like this:

```
#define LibName xyz
SOREV = 1.3
#define SoRev SOREV
```

- SRCS and OBJS name the source and object files, just as for normal libraries.

- *Library.tmpl* is a special library template file, discussed in more detail below.

- DependTarget() produces a target entry for generating header file dependencies. It assumes that SRCS is set properly.

After you finish writing your *Imakefile*, build the *Makefile* from it, type *make*, and then sit back and watch the fireworks.

What Library.tmpl does for you

When *Library.tmpl* is processed during *Makefile* generation, it triggers a flurry of activity that sets up special definitions and rules that enable the proper kinds of object files to be built for the types of libraries you're building. Then, if you've defined LibName, it invokes those rules for you. Suppose your *Imakefile* defines as YES all four macros that determine what kinds of libraries to build. *Library.tmpl* generates the equivalent of the following lines for you:

```
LIBNAME = LibName
LibraryObjectRule()
SharedLibraryTarget($(LIBNAME),$(SoRev),$(OBJS),.,.)
InstallSharedLibrary($(LIBNAME),$(SoRev),$(SHLIBDIR))
UnsharedLibraryTarget($(LIBNAME),$(OBJS),unshared,..)
InstallLibrary($(LIBNAME),$(USRLIBDIR))
ProfiledLibraryTarget($(LIBNAME),$(OBJS))
InstallLibrary($(LIBNAME)_p,$(USRLIBDIR))
DebuggedLibraryTarget($(LIBNAME),$(OBJS))
InstallLibrary($(LIBNAME)_d,$(USRLIBDIR))
LintLibraryTarget($(LIBNAME),$(SRCS))
InstallLintLibrary($(LIBNAME),$(LINTLIBDIR))
NormalLintTarget($(SRCS))
```

LibraryObjectRule() handles the task of creating subdirectories named *unshared*, *profiled*, and *debugger*, to be used for compiling object files for normal, profiled, and debugging libraries. (Objects for the shared library are compiled in the current directory.) The remaining rule invocations generate target entries for building and installing each type of library, for building and installing a *lint* library, and for *lint*-ing the library source files. Note that the installation rules construct the library names for profiled and debugging libraries by appending _p and _d to $(LIBNAME).

The general strategy just described will give you a start at writing a library-building *Imakefile*. However, it's a good idea to examine some real-life Imakefiles as well. That will give you an idea of special cases that may arise and how to handle them. The Imakefiles used to build the X11 libraries are good examples; you can find them under the *xc/lib* directory in the X11 distribution.

If you have a desire to understand the underlying configuration file machinery, take a look at *Library.tmpl*. That way you can see for yourself just what's being taken care of for you. You might also study some of the platform-specific **Lib.rules* and **Lib.tmpl* files. (However, I recommend that you *not* start with the Linux rules file *lnxLib.rules*. The definition of SharedLibraryTarget() there is the most complicated rule I've ever seen.)

Building Libraries Under X11R5

If you're building a normal library using the configuration files from R5 rather than from R6.1, the procedure is the same as for R6.1.

For building shared, profiled, and debugging libraries, there are some significant differences. Your *Imakefile* should begin with this prologue:

```
#define DoNormalLib BoolVal
#define DoSharedLib BoolVal
#define DoDebugLib BoolVal
#define DoProfileLib BoolVal

#include <Library.tmpl>

SRCS = file1.c file2.c file3.c ...
OBJS = file1.o file2.o file3.o ...

LibraryObjectRule()
```

Superficially, this is similar to the *Imakefile* you'd write for R6.1, but *Library.tmpl* doesn't do as much work for you. So, following the prologue just shown, invoke rules for building each kind of library, surrounding each by the appropriate conditional construct. For normal, profiled, and debugging versions of a library named *xyz*, write this:

```
#if DoNormalLib
NormalLibraryTarget(xyz,$(OBJS))
InstallLibrary(xyz,$(USRLIBDIR))
#endif

#if DoProfileLib
ProfiledLibraryTarget(xyz,$(OBJS))
InstallLibrary(xyz_p,$(USRLIBDIR))
#endif

#if DoDebugLib
DebuggedLibraryTarget(xyz,$(OBJS))
InstallLibrary(xyz_d,$(USRLIBDIR))
#endif
```

Note that you must append _p and _d to the names of the profiled and debugging libraries.

For a shared library, you specify a revision number (denoted *rev* below) in addition to the library name. Also, the way you create a shared library depends on whether or not you're building a normal library:

```
#if DoSharedLib
#if DoNormalLib
SharedLibraryTarget(xyz,rev,$(OBJS),shared,..)
#else
SharedLibraryTarget(xyz,rev,$(OBJS),.,.)
#endif
```

```
InstallSharedLibrary(xyz,rev,$(USRLIBDIR))
#endif
```

The R5 convention when both normal and shared libraries are built is to compile the normal library objects in the current directory and the shared objects in a sub-directory named *shared*. This differs from the R6.1 convention of compiling shared objects in the current directory and the normal objects in an *unshared* subdirectory.

For some example R5 library-building Imakefiles, look under the *mit/lib* directory in the R5 distribution.

Building Other Types of Targets

This section describes how to compile individual object files with special flags. It also describes how to build other types of targets such as executable scripts and C++ programs, and how to force a target to be built when a rule doesn't generate an `all` entry for you.

Compiling Object Files Specially

Sometimes you need to compile a particular object file specially, e.g., to pass it special flags. To do this, invoke `SpecialCObjectRule()`. It takes three arguments:

```
SpecialCObjectRule(basename,depends,options)
```

This generates an entry to compile an object file from the source file *basename.c*. The *depends* argument names dependencies for the object file (other than the source file), and *options* names any special options needed to compile it.

For example, you might have a file *spawn.c* that contains code to spawn a new process using the *vfork()* system call if it's available and *fork()* otherwise. The X11 configuration files provide a macro `HasVFork` indicating the availability of *vfork()*, but you can't directly test `HasVFork` in your source file—the configuration files aren't accessed when your program is compiled. However, you can indirectly use `HasVFork` to pass a flag to the compiler, by putting the following in your *Imakefile*:

```
#if HasVFork
    VFORK_FLAGS = -DVFORK
#endif
SpecialCObjectRule(spawn,NullParameter,$(VFORK_FLAGS))
```

In the resulting *Makefile*, VFORK_FLAGS is –DVFORK if *vfork()* is available, and undefined (empty) otherwise. This allows you to test VFORK in *spawn.c* like this:

```
#ifndef VFORK
#define vfork() fork()  /* vfork() unavailable, use fork() */
#endif
```

Compiling object files specially under X11R5

In X11R5, SpecialCObjectRule() doesn't exist. Use SpecialObjectRule() instead. It takes three arguments:

```
SpecialObjectRule(obj,depends,options)
```

This generates an entry to compile *obj*. The *depends* argument names the source file used to compile *obj* and any other dependencies that *obj* may have. *options* names any special options needed to compile *obj*. For example, to compile *spawn.o* from *spawn.c*, you'd write this:

```
SpecialObjectRule(spawn.o,spawn.c,$(VFORK_FLAGS))
```

Although SpecialCObjectRule() and SpecialObjectRule() are similar, SpecialCObjectRule() is more general in that it doesn't assume the object file name has a *.o* extension. That means it can be used on systems that produce object files with a different extension (such as *.obj*).

Building Executable Scripts

We've focused thus far on building binary files, but the X11 configuration files provide support for building executable scripts, too. The CppScriptTarget() rule generates a target entry that takes a script template, runs it through *cpp* to perform parameterization, and makes the result executable.

Because the template passes through *cpp*, you can refer to *Makefile* variable values in it and they will appear in the resulting script. For example, if a script *myscript* needs to find X11 programs, you can make sure that BINDIR (the X11 binaries directory) is added to the PATH variable in the script by writing a line like this in the template *myscript.sh*:

```
PATH=$PATH:BINDIR
```

Then pass the value of the BINDIR *make* variable to CppScriptTarget() like this:

```
CppScriptTarget(myscript,myscript.sh,'-DBINDIR=$(BINDIR)',NullParameter)
```

The first two arguments are the names of the script and the template. The third argument lists any defines you want to pass to *cpp* when it processes the template (you can have multiple definitions if you like, separated by spaces). The final argument lists any dependencies that must be satisfied before *myscript* is built.

One thing to watch out for with CppScriptTarget() is that if you want lines in the script to begin with the # character, you should write them in the template beginning with XCOMM. If you write them with #, *cpp* will interpret them as preprocessing directives. CppScriptTarget() takes care of translating XCOMM to # after *cpp* has done its work.

Building C++ Programs

The X11 configuration files provide a set of C++ rules that are analogous to many of the C program-building rules we've already discussed in this chapter. The C++ rules are used under the same conditions as the corresponding C rules, except that you supply C++ rather than C source files. For instance, SimpleCplusplus-ProgramTarget() is used when you're building a single program from a single C++ source file. Table 6–3 shows the correspondences between several pairs of C and C++ rules.

Table 6–3: X11 Rules for Building C++ Programs

C Rule	C++ Rule
SimpleProgramTarget()	SimpleCplusplusProgramTarget()
ComplexProgramTarget()	ComplexCplusplusProgramTarget()
ComplexProgramTarget_1()	ComplexCplusplusProgramTarget_1()
ComplexProgramTarget_2()	ComplexCplusplusProgramTarget_2()
ComplexProgramTarget_3()	ComplexCplusplusProgramTarget_3()
NormalProgramTarget()	NormalCplusplusProgramTarget()

Forcing a Target To Be Built

To build all the targets named in an *Imakefile*, it's normally most convenient to be able to say simply *make* or *make all*. Unfortunately, if a rule doesn't generate an all entry for its target, you must name that target explicitly to cause it to be built. NormalProgramTarget() and CppScriptTarget() are instances of rules that generate no all entry. To remedy this and make it easier to build everything in a directory, invoke AllTarget() prior to the rule that builds your target.

Examples:

```
AllTarget(myprog)
NormalProgramTarget(myprog,myprog.o,$(DEPXLIB),$(XLIB),NullParameter)
AllTarget(myscript)
CppScriptTarget(myscript,myscript.sh,'-DBINDIR=$(BINDIR)',NullParameter)
```

Installing Files

Some rules, such as `ComplexProgramTarget()`, generate their own `install` entries. For those that do not, such as `NormalProgramTarget()` and `Normal-LibraryTarget()`, you need to invoke installation rules yourself. In general, they take this form:

> *InstallRuleName(what,where)*

what is the file you want to install; *where* is the destination directory in which to install it.

X11 has more than 25 rules for installing various kinds of targets. Many of them are for unusual cases; the list below describes rules for some of the more common target types. You don't need to check whether the installation directory exists—all the rules shown create the directory if it's missing by invoking `MakeDir()`.

`InstallProgram(`*prog,dir*`)`

> Generates an `install` entry to install the executable program *prog* into *dir/prog*. `InstallProgram()` can also be used to install executable scripts.

`InstallManPage(`*prog,dir*`)`

> Generates an `install.man` entry to install the manual page *prog.man* into *dir/prog*.`$(MANSUFFIX)`. The *dir* argument is normally `$(MANDIR)`, and `$(MANSUFFIX)` is n by default.

`InstallAppDefaults(`*prog*`)`

> Generates an `install` entry to install the application defaults file *prog.ad* into `$(XAPPLOADDIR)/`*prog*. Don't specify the *.ad* suffix when you invoke `InstallAppDefaults()`. This rule differs from the others in assuming a default installation directory XAPPLOADDIR, the value of which is set by the configuration files. Consequently, the rule only takes one argument.

`InstallLibrary(`*xyz,dir*`)`

> Generates an `install` entry to install the library *libxyz.a* into *dir/libxyz.a*.

`InstallNonExecFile(`*file,dir*`)`

> Generates an `install` entry to install *file* into *dir/file* as a read-only file.

Managing Multiple-Directory Projects

When a project has multiple directories, it's convenient to have *make* operate on the entire project tree (or on the entire subtree below your current position within the project) for commands such as these:

```
% make
% make Makefiles
% make clean
% make depend
% make install
```

The alternative to having *make* process the project tree for you is to move into each directory individually and run *make* yourself. Ugh. Fortunately, that's not necessary. The X11 configuration files provide rules you can invoke in your *Imakefile* to generate recursive target entries in your *Makefile*. This reduces to a relatively simple process the otherwise difficult project-management task of creating Makefiles that allow you to perform directory-traversing *make* operations throughout your entire project tree.

I'll show how to do this using the sample multiple-directory project organized as shown in Figure 6–1.

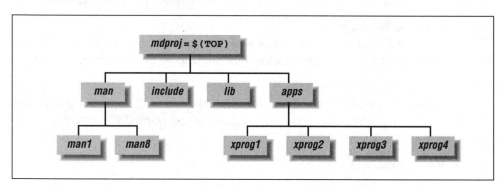

Figure 6–1: Sample multiple-directory project

First create a project directory tree and populate it with empty Imakefiles:

```
% mkdir mdproj
% cd mdproj
% mkdir man include lib apps \
    man/man1 man/man8 \
    apps/xprog1 apps/xprog2 apps/xprog3 apps/xprog4
% touch 'find . -type d -print | sed 's:$:/Imakefile:''
```

To be a good citizen in a multiple-directory project, each *Imakefile* needs certain minimal content. The nature of that content depends on whether or not the directory in which the *Imakefile* is located has subdirectories in which *make* should be run. I'll call a directory with subdirectories a branch directory, and a directory without subdirectories a leaf directory. The sample project contains three branch directories: $(TOP), *man*, and *apps*. The others are leaf directories.

In a branch directory, the *Imakefile* must trigger the recursive rules and specify which subdirectories they apply to. To do this, begin the *Imakefile* with the following three lines:

```
#define IHaveSubdirs
#define PassCDebugFlags
SUBDIRS = subdirectory-list
```

When the *Makefile* is built, the configuration files see that IHaveSubdirs is defined and they generate entries that perform recursive *make* operations. SUB-DIRS names the subdirectories those entries operate on, in the order you want them processed. (PassCDebugFlags is used for specifying debugging flags when you build your project; we'll discuss it shortly.)

In addition, you should invoke MakeSubdirs() and DependSubdirs() to generate recursive all and depend target entries, so the pattern for a minimal branch *Imakefile* looks like this:

```
#define IHaveSubdirs
#define PassCDebugFlags
SUBDIRS = subdirectory-list
MakeSubdirs($(SUBDIRS))
DependSubdirs($(SUBDIRS))
```

These two rules must be invoked because the X11 configuration files produce clean, install, includes, and Makefile entries automatically, but not all or depend entries. MakeSubdirs() should be invoked first, so that all becomes the default target.

For the sample project, create the branch directory Imakefiles according to the preceding pattern, using the values of SUBDIRS shown below.

$(TOP)/*Imakefile*:

```
SUBDIRS = man include lib apps
```

man/Imakefile:

```
SUBDIRS = man1 man8
```

apps/Imakefile:

```
SUBDIRS = xprog1 xprog2 xprog3 xprog4
```

We haven't written very much so far (the leaf directory Imakefiles are still empty). Nevertheless, we've already got enough to allow the Makefiles to be built. Execute the following commands in the project root directory. The first command boot-straps the root-level *Makefile* and the second causes *make* to traverse the rest of the project tree to create the other Makefiles:

```
% xmkmf
% make Makefiles
```

However, if you try *make all* after building the Makefiles, you'll find that the command works only partially. *make* descends properly into subdirectories, but when it reaches a leaf directory, it fails: none of the leaf directory Imakefiles contain an `all` target. (*make depend* fails for similar reasons.)

To fix this, each leaf *Imakefile* must produce at least an `all` entry and a `depend` entry. The minimum leaf *Imakefile* we can get away with is this:

```
all::
depend::
```

Put this minimal *Imakefile* in each of the sample project's leaf directories. Then build all subdirectory Makefiles:

```
% make Makefiles
```

Now *make all* and *make depend* will properly traverse the project tree.

The minimal leaf *Imakefile* shown here contains just enough to keep the `all` and `depend` *make* operations from generating errors. However, when you get around to building programs in a leaf directory, you should generate an `all` entry for each program by invoking `AllTarget()` or by using rules that invoke `All-Target()` themselves. Don't forget to set `SRCS` and invoke `DependTarget()` if your program building rules don't do so for you.

Restricting the Scope of Recursive Operations

If you want to perform a recursive *make* operation on some but not all subdirectories of your current directory, you can override any value that `SUBDIRS` might have in the *Makefile* by specifying a value directly on the *make* command line. For example, in the *apps* directory, this command installs only programs built in the *xprog1* and *xprog4* subdirectories:

```
% make install "SUBDIRS=xprog1 xprog4"
```

Adding a New Directory to an Existing Project

To add a new directory to an existing project, you must create it and put an *Imakefile* in it. Then, add the subdirectory's name to the value of `SUBDIRS` in the parent directory's *Imakefile*. Finally, rebuild the parent directory's *Makefile* so it knows about the new subdirectory, and use that *Makefile* to rebuild the subdirectory's *Makefile*:

```
% make Makefile
% make Makefiles "SUBDIRS=subdir"
```

Once this has been done, recursive operations invoked from the parent will include the new subdirectory.

Constraints on the Value of SUBDIRS

You cannot assign an empty value to SUBDIRS. Nor can SUBDIRS name the current directory or any directories above the current directory:

```
/* these are all incorrect */
SUBDIRS =
SUBDIRS = .
SUBDIRS = ..
```

If you assign SUBDIRS an empty value (perhaps thinking recursive operations will be null operations), you'll get syntax errors when you run *make*. If you assign the current or parent directory to SUBDIRS, *make* will either go into a loop, or crash and burn.

Specifying Debugging Flags

If you anticipate a need to specify debugging flags when you build a project, don't define PassCDebugFlags with an empty value in branch Imakefiles. Define it like this instead:

```
#define PassCDebugFlags 'CDEBUGFLAGS=$(CDEBUGFLAGS)'
```

Then you can specify debugging flags from the *make* command line:

```
% make "CDEBUGFLAGS=-g"
```

Combination Branch/Leaf Directories

A directory can be a branch directory and a leaf directory at the same time. That is, it can contain subdirectories, and you can also build targets in it. If you use a directory this way, though, it's difficult to process targets in just that directory without processing all the subdirectories, too.

Other Useful make Variables

DEFINES and INCLUDES are useful in Imakefiles for compiling programs, no matter which rules you're using:

- Use DEFINES to pass special −*D* or −*U* flags to the C compiler.
- Use INCLUDES to pass special −*I* flags to the C compiler.

These variables allow you to specify information on a per-*Imakefile* basis. Their values are incorporated into the value of the CFLAGS variable in *Imake.tmpl* and passed automatically to compilation commands and to invocations of *makedepend* and *lint*.

Since CFLAGS is given a value in *Imake.tmpl*, you should never set it in the *Imakefile*. Always use DEFINES and INCLUDES instead.

As a demonstration of how to use DEFINES and INCLUDES (as well as some of the other variables discussed earlier), suppose we have a project to build a program, *xblob*, composed of a root directory and three subdirectories (Figure 6–2).

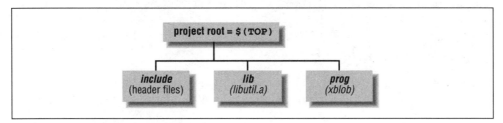

Figure 6–2: xblob project

We want to build *xblob* in the *prog* directory with the following considerations in mind:

- *xblob* is the only program in the *prog* directory.
- *xblob* is built from two source files: *main.c* and *funcs.c*.
- The *xblob* source files use the X11 double-buffer extension if possible, by bracketing sections of code as follows:

```
#ifdef DBE
    /* double-buffer code */
#endif
```

This means we should compile *xblob* with −DDBE when the extension is available.

- *xblob* source files include header files from the project's *include* directory.

- The *xblob* executable needs routines from the *util* library (found in the *lib* directory), Xlib, Xext, and the math library.

Given these conditions, how shall we write the *Imakefile* in the *prog* directory?

The two rules most suited for building a single program are `SimpleProgram-Target()` and `ComplexProgramTarget()`. We can't use `SimpleProgramTarget()` because that's only for programs built from a single source file. That leaves `ComplexProgramTarget()`.

Having decided which rule to use, we can set the relevant *make* variables in the *Imakefile* as follows:

- `DEFINES` is the natural way to specify the DBE flag. The X11 symbol `Extension-Defines` contains the appropriate defines for all the X extensions that are available. This includes `-DDBE` if the double-buffer extension is available, so we assign a value to `DEFINES` like this:

      DEFINES = ExtensionDefines

- We can use `INCLUDES` to pass directories in which to look for header files. `TOP` always indicates the project root directory, so we can refer to *include* as `$(TOP)`/*include* and set `INCLUDES` like this:

      INCLUDES = -I$(TOP)/include

- For `ComplexProgramTarget()`, use `LOCAL_LIBRARIES` and `SYS_LIBRARIES` to specify the link forms of any libraries needed. The *util* library is specified relative to `TOP`, Xlib is given by `XLIB`, and the math library is given as *−lm*:

      LOCAL_LIBRARIES = $(TOP)/lib/libutil.a $(XLIB)
        SYS_LIBRARIES = -lm

It's not necessary to list the Xext library explicitly because the value of `XLIB` automatically refers to it.

- Use `DEPLIBS` to specify the dependency forms of any libraries needed. The *util* library is specified relative to `TOP`, the dependency-checking form of Xlib is `DEPXLIB`, and the math library is a system library that has no dependency form, so we omit it:

      DEPLIBS = $(TOP)/lib/libutil.a $(DEPXLIB)

As with `XLIB`, `DEPXLIB` includes a reference to the Xext library automatically.

- `ComplexProgramTarget()` requires SRCS and OBJS to be set. It's straightforward to do so:

```
SRCS = main.c funcs.c
OBJS = main.o funcs.o
```

Putting all this together, we write the *Imakefile* to build *xblob* like so:

```
          DEFINES = ExtensionDefines
         INCLUDES = -I$(TOP)/include
  LOCAL_LIBRARIES = $(TOP)/lib/libutil.a $(XLIB)
    SYS_LIBRARIES = -lm
          DEPLIBS = $(TOP)/lib/libutil.a $(DEPXLIB)

             SRCS = main.c funcs.c
             OBJS = main.o funcs.o

ComplexProgramTarget(xblob)
```

Questions

These questions are intended to provoke further thought about how the X11 rules work, to illustrate some of their properties not discussed in the main chapter text, and to ask you how you might rewrite rules to fix problems.

They're not for beginners, so if you can't figure out the answers now and you don't understand the answers given, you might want to look at the questions again after reading Chapter 11, *Introduction to Configuration File Writing*, and Chapter 12, *Writing Rule Macros*.

Question 1: The `ComplexProgramTarget_n()` rules require you to set the *make* variable PROGRAMS because they don't do it themselves. Unfortunately, if you forget to set PROGRAMS, *make* doesn't do what you want for either of these commands:

```
% make all
% make clean
```

There are at least two ways to rewrite these rules to fix the problem. What are they?

Answer 1: The approach you take depends on whether or not you want to continue to use the PROGRAMS variable.

If you continue to use PROGRAMS, each rule can define a PROGRAM*n* variable and `ComplexProgramTarget_1()` can set PROGRAMS to the concatenation of the three PROGRAM*n* variables, in the same way that SRCS and OBJS are set to the concatenations of SRCS*n* and OBJS*n*. This way PROGRAMS is set automatically from the *prog* arguments you pass to the rules, and you don't have to assign it any value your-self:

```
#define ComplexProgramTarget_1(prog,loclibs,syslibs)              @@\
        PROGRAM1 = prog                                           @@\
        PROGRAMS = $(PROGRAM1) $(PROGRAM2) $(PROGRAM3)            @@\
            OBJS = $(OBJS1) $(OBJS2) $(OBJS3)                     @@\
            SRCS = $(SRCS1) $(SRCS2) $(SRCS3)                     @@\
    :
#endif /* ComplexProgramTarget_1 */

#define ComplexProgramTarget_2(prog,loclibs,syslibs)              @@\
        PROGRAM2 = prog                                           @@\
    :
#endif /* ComplexProgramTarget_2 */

#define ComplexProgramTarget_3(prog,loclibs,syslibs)              @@\
        PROGRAM3 = prog                                           @@\
    :
#endif /* ComplexProgramTarget_3 */
```

If you want to eliminate PROGRAMS entirely, the three rules each should be written to generate all and clean entries for their respective individual programs. The effect would be the same as setting PROGRAMS, but *make all* and *make clean* would work automatically without programmer intervention, and PROGRAMS becomes superfluous:

```
#define ComplexProgramTarget_1(prog,loclibs,syslibs)              @@\
            OBJS = $(OBJS1) $(OBJS2) $(OBJS3)                     @@\
            SRCS = $(SRCS1) $(SRCS2) $(SRCS3)                     @@\
AllTarget(prog)                                                   @@\
    :
clean::                                                           @@\
    RemoveFile(ProgramTargetName(prog))
#endif /* ComplexProgramTarget_1 */

#define ComplexProgramTarget_2(prog,loclibs,syslibs)              @@\
AllTarget(prog)                                                   @@\
    :
clean::                                                           @@\
    RemoveFile(ProgramTargetName(prog))
#endif

#define ComplexProgramTarget_3(prog,loclibs,syslibs)              @@\
AllTarget(prog)                                                   @@\
    :
clean::                                                           @@\
    RemoveFile(ProgramTargetName(prog))
#endif
```

Using either method, the ComplexProgramTarget_*n*() rules would be a little eas-ier to use because there'd be one less thing to remember.

Question 2: Will your rewritten `ComplexProgramTarget_n()` rules work with an *Imakefile* in which `PROGRAMS` does happen to be set properly? That is, are they backward compatible with the current implementation?

Answer 2: If your rewritten rules continue to use `PROGRAMS`, an *Imakefile* will work as long as the *Imakefile* assigns a value to `PROGRAMS` prior to the invocation of the `ComplexProgramTarget_1()` rule. Then the assignment in the rule will take priority.

If you rewrite the rules to make `PROGRAMS` irrelevant, they'll work no matter what the *Imakefile* does with `PROGRAMS`.

Question 3: Suppose you're building a single program consisting of multiple source files. Why might you choose to use `NormalProgramTarget()` instead of `ComplexProgramTarget()`?

Answer 3: You gain more control over what happens in the *Makefile*. For example, `ComplexProgramTarget()` decides for you that the installation directory is `BINDIR` (usually */usr/X11R6.1/bin* or */usr/bin/X11*). When you install the program, commands like the following are generated:

```
% make install
if [ -d /usr/X11R6.1/bin ]; then set +x; \
else (set -x; mkdirhier /usr/X11R6.1/bin); fi
install -c prog /usr/X11R6.1/bin/prog
```

If you want to change the installation directory, you have to reassign `BINDIR` in your *Imakefile*:

```
BINDIR = /usr/local/bin
```

However, if other variables in your *Makefile* depend on `BINDIR`, changing it might have unwanted side effects.

In this sense, `ComplexProgramTarget()` makes too many choices for you. `NormalProgramTarget()` puts the burden on you to invoke a rule to generate an `install` target, but then you can specify any installation directory you want.

Question 4: Suppose you're building three programs. Why might you choose to use three instances of `NormalProgramTarget()` rather than the `ComplexProgram-Target_n()` rules?

Answer 4: The `ComplexProgramTarget_n()` rules are easier to use if you're building just three programs. But if you decide to add another one, you have to rewrite most of your *Imakefile*. If you start with `NormalProgramTarget()`, you have to do more work to write your initial three-program *Imakefile*, but you can continue to use what you've already written in your *Imakefile* (rather than replace it) as you add more programs to it. Thus, `NormalProgramTarget()` might be a better choice if you're building three programs initially, but anticipate you'll build more than that eventually.

Another reason to use `NormalProgramTarget()` in preference to the `Complex-ProgramTarget_n()` rules is that the latter, like `ComplexProgramTarget()`, make many choices for you. Suppose you're building a pair of programs such as a server and a client of the server. `ComplexProgramTarget_1()` and `ComplexProgram-Target_2()` will want to install both programs in `BINDIR`, whereas you may want to put them in different locations, e.g., */usr/local/etc* and */usr/local/bin*. With `NormalProgramTarget()`, you can do that.

Question 5: Suppose you build *prog1*, *prog2*, and *prog3* using the `Complex-ProgramTarget_n()` rules. Later you decide *prog1* is useless, so you delete its name from the value of `PROGRAMS` and delete the `SRCS1` and `OBJS1` assignments and the invocation of `ComplexProgramTarget_1()` from your *Imakefile*. After rebuilding your *Makefile*, you discover some problems:

```
% make all
make: Fatal error: Don't know how to make target "all"
% make depend
make: Fatal error: Don't know how to make target "depend"
% make lint
make: Fatal error: Don't know how to make target "lint"
```

How do you explain this? What else do you need to change in your *Imakefile*?

Answer 5: `ComplexProgramTarget_1()` does more work than `ComplexProgram-Target_2()` or `ComplexProgramTarget_3()`. In particular, it sets the value of `SRCS` and generates `all`, `depend`, `lint`, and `clean` entries. By deleting the invocation of `ComplexProgramTarget_1()` from your *Imakefile*, you remove a number of useful things from the *Makefile*.

To fix the problem, you need to do some renaming in your *Imakefile*:

$$SRCS2 \rightarrow SRCS1$$
$$OBJS2 \rightarrow OBJS1$$

$$SRCS3 \rightarrow SRCS2$$
$$OBJS3 \rightarrow OBJS2$$

$$\text{ComplexProgramTarget\_2()} \rightarrow \text{ComplexProgramTarget\_1()}$$
$$\text{ComplexProgramTarget\_3()} \rightarrow \text{ComplexProgramTarget\_2()}$$

By the way, this illustrates another reason why you might prefer to use `Normal-ProgramTarget()` rather than `ComplexProgramTarget_n()` right from the start; it's not only easier to add new programs in your *Imakefile*, it's easier to get rid of them.

Question 6: The Motif rules file *Motif.rules* extends the X11 rules by adding `ComplexProgramTarget_n()` rules for *n* from 4 through 10. (They look essentially like `ComplexProgramTarget_3()` with instances of "3" changed to the appropriate number.) However, the Motif extension isn't quite correct: `SRCS` only knows about `SRCS1` through `SRCS3`, which means the `depend` and `lint` targets generated by `ComplexProgramTarget_1()` don't operate on the sources for programs 4 through 10. How would you fix this by rewriting the Motif rules?

Answer 6: One way is to reassign `SRCS`. `ComplexProgramTarget_1()` assigns `SRCS` like this:

```
SRCS = $(SRCS1) $(SRCS2) $(SRCS3)
```

`ComplexProgramTarget_4()` can include a reassignment that looks like this:

```
SRCS = $(SRCS1) $(SRCS2) $(SRCS3) $(SRCS4) $(SRCS5) \
       $(SRCS6) $(SRCS7) $(SRCS8) $(SRCS9) $(SRCS10)
```

The reassigned `SRCS` will take precedence over the initial assignment as long as the invocation of `ComplexProgramTarget_4()` in the *Imakefile* follows that of `ComplexProgramTarget_1()`.

Question 7: When you invoke `ComplexProgramTarget()`, `DEPLIBS` specifies libraries that the program depends on. That variable already has a default value assigned to it by the X11 configuration files, so if you assign a value to `DEPLIBS` in your *Imakefile*, the resulting *Makefile* has two `DEPLIBS` assignments (one provided by the X11 configuration files and one from your *Imakefile* later). If you want to check which value of `DEPLIBS` *make* actually uses, how do you make sure you find the correct assignment?

Answer 7: Multiple assignments to a given variable name are not a problem as far as *make* is concerned; it simply uses the last one. However, if you read the *Makefile* into an editor and simply start searching from the top downward for the variable's definition, you'll likely find the first assignment. Instead, start at the bottom of the file and search upward to find the last instance. Alternatively, use *make –p*, which prints out the variable values that *make* actually uses:

```
% make -p | grep DEPLIBS
DEPLIBS3= $(DEPLIBS)
DEPLIBS2= $(DEPLIBS)
DEPLIBS1= $(DEPLIBS)
DEPLIBS= $(DEPXAWLIB) $(DEPXMULIB) $(DEPXTOOLLIB) $(DEPXLIB)
```

The last line of the output is the one you're looking for.

Another approach to determining a variable's value is to use *msub*. Unlike *make* −*p*, this will show you the literal value of the variable, even if it's defined in terms of other variables:

```
% echo '$(DEPLIBS)' | msub
/usr/X11R6.1/lib/libXaw.a /usr/X11R6.1/lib/libXmu.a /usr/X11R6.1/lib/libXt.a
/usr/X11R6.1/lib/libXext.a /usr/X11R6.1/lib/libX11.a
```

Be sure to use single quotes rather than double quotes in the *echo* command; they prevent the shell from trying to interpret $ as beginning a shell variable reference.

Question 8: Why should you assign DEPLIBS an empty value to clear it if your program uses no libraries?

Answer 8: The default value of DEPLIBS refers to several X11 libraries. If you're not writing an X11 program, that's inaccurate, since it makes your program depend on libraries it really doesn't require. If you don't have those libraries installed on your machine, the dependencies fail and *make* refuses to link your program even if all of its object files have been compiled:

```
% make
make: Don't know how to make target "/usr/lib/libXaw.a". Stop.
```

Explicitly assigning an empty value to DEPLIBS eliminates the problem because then your program isn't dependent on the X11 libraries.

7

Imakefile Troubleshooting

Even if it can't go wrong, it will.
—Corollary to "Murphy's Law"

imake helps you create software that's portable to and easily configurable on a variety of machines—assuming your configuration files and Imakefiles are set up properly. However, when you make changes to those files, it's quite possible to introduce all sorts of errors. The result is Makefiles that are unusable.

Some errors have causes that are easy to determine. Others are more subtle. It may not be immediately obvious, for example, that the source of the following error is an extra space in the argument list of a rule invocation in your *Imakefile*:

```
make: Warning: Infinite loop: Target "lib" depends on itself
```

Compounding the difficulty of tracking down errors is the fact that the apparent location of a problem may not correspond to the location where it actually originates. An #endif that's missing from the early part of *Imake.tmpl* isn't detected until the end of the input stream—far away from the error.

The preceding counsel of despair notwithstanding, many of the problems you'll enounter are easily fixed, if you know what causes them. If you've read Chapter 6, *Writing Imakefiles*, you should be at a point where you can write Imakefiles. In this chapter I'll discuss problems likely to occur in them and possible solutions. (Problems can also occur in your configuration files, but we're not ready to tackle those yet. We've seen something of how configuration files work, but errors in those files are better discussed after we've dealt more fully with the issues involved in writing them. Thus, the second half of this topic is deferred until Chapter 14, *Troubleshooting Configuration Files*.)

This chapter often refers to the X11 configuration files, since those are the ones we've looked at most closely. If you're writing Imakefiles for use with another set of configuration files, there's no need to feel left out: you can make the mistakes described here just as easily, with equally lamentable results. Fortunately, no matter what files you use, the solutions are usually the same.

Diagnosing Errors

You'll discover on occasion, after you've rebuilt a *Makefile* and tried to use it, that it's unusable due to some mistake you made while editing the *Imakefile*. This phenomenon occurs less frequently as you gain experience with *imake*, but it never disappears entirely.

The error messages *make* produces can help you figure out where a problem occurs. Often *make* tells you which line of the *Makefile* it didn't like:

```
% make
make: line nnn: syntax error
```

Other times *make* lets you know which target it's having trouble with:

```
% make
make: don't know how to make target "target". Stop.
```

Either way, the information given helps narrow your focus when you search through the *Makefile* looking for the source of the problem. Locating the faulty part of the *Makefile* often allows you to relate the error back to the part of the *Imakefile* from which it's generated.

When *make* tells you there's an error on line *nnn*, you should view that as an approximation. The error might actually occur a line or two earlier, since *make* sometimes doesn't detect or announce an error until a bit later than its actual location. Also, the squawks emitted by *make* on your system might differ somewhat from those shown in this chapter; different versions of *make* sometimes produce different error messages for a given *Makefile* problem.

Disaster Recovery

When you find yourself faced with a *Makefile* that's been turned to rubble, you need to regenerate it—after fixing your *Imakefile*, naturally. Of course, since the *Makefile* has been destroyed you can no longer use it to rebuild itself. That is, the following command no longer works:

```
% make Makefile
```

You can run *imake* manually, but that's a last resort because of all the command-line options required. There are other alternatives:

- Use a bootstrapping program such as *xmkmf*. *xmkmf* works best in the root directory of a project. Fortunately, many projects consist of only one directory anyway.

- Use the general-purpose bootstrapper *imboot* developed in Chapter 10, *Coordinating Sets of Configuration Files*. *imboot* can be used anywhere in the project tree.

- Use the backup *Makefile* if you have one. Rules that generate a *Makefile* typically rename any existing *Makefile* to *Makefile.bak*, so even if you've just generated a *Makefile* that's garbage, you may have a backup that works. If so, save it and use it to generate a new *Makefile*:

  ```
  % mv Makefile.bak Makefile.sav
  % make -f Makefile.sav Makefile
  ```

- If the *Makefile* in the parent of your current directory works, change directory into the parent and use the Makefiles target entry. You can set SUBDIRS on the command line to limit the effect of the *make* command to the directory you're interested in:

  ```
  % make Makefiles "SUBDIRS=subdir"
  ```

  The command uses the parent *Makefile*'s knowledge about how to build child directory Makefiles.

Now that you know how to recover from disaster, let's have a look at some of the ways you can invite it to happen.

Whitespace Errors

There are several ways extraneous whitespace in an *Imakefile* can cause trouble.

make variable assignments in Imakefiles are often indented to make the = signs line up:

```
        DEPLIBS = XawClientDepLibs
LOCAL_LIBRARIES = XawClientLibs
           SRCS = xclock.c
           OBJS = xclock.o
```

This improves readability, but make sure you indent assignments using spaces; some versions of *make* report an error if you use tabs.

When you invoke a rule, an argument may contain spaces internally if it comprises a list of items such as filenames, libraries, or flags. However, you shouldn't put spaces at either end of the argument. This may take some getting used to if your

programming style for writing macro calls is to separate arguments by spaces like
this:

```
Macro(arg1, arg2, arg3)      /* incorrect */
```

For *imake*, you should invoke the macro like this:

```
Macro(arg1,arg2,arg3)        /* correct */
```

If you put extraneous spaces in an argument list, you'll often find that the invocation expands to a malformed *Makefile* entry, particularly if the rule constructs
tokens from its arguments. Consider the X11 rule `AliasedLibaryTarget()`, which
looks like this (I've deleted some lines that are irrelevant to the discussion):

```
#define AliasedLibraryTarget(libname,alias)                 @@\
  .
  .
LibraryTargetName(alias): LibraryTargetName(libname)        @@\
     RemoveFile($@)                                         @@\
     $(LN) LibraryTargetName(libname) $@                    @@\
  .
  .
```

The `LibraryTargetName()` rule is a macro that invokes `Concat()`, so `AliasedLi-
braryTarget()` is equivalent to the following:

```
#define AliasedLibraryTarget(libname,alias)                 @@\
  .
  .
Concat(lib,alias.a): Concat(lib,libname.a)                  @@\
     RemoveFile($@)                                         @@\
     $(LN) Concat(lib,libname.a) $@                         @@\
  .
  .
```

This rule expands to very different entries in the *Makefile*, depending on whether
or not spaces are included in the arguments.

`AliasedLibraryTarget(abc,xyz)` expands to this:

```
libxyz.a: libabc.a
    $(RM) $@
    $(LN) libabc.a $@
```

`AliasedLibraryTarget( abc, xyz)`, on the other hand, expands to this:

```
lib xyz.a: lib abc.a
    $(RM) $@
    $(LN) lib abc.a $@
```

The invocations are only slightly different, but the differences between the resulting *Makefile* entries are significant. The extra spaces in the second rule invocation
propagate directly into the rule expansion and are incorporated into the entry's
target name and dependency. Consequently, the entry appears to have two target

names and dependencies, and one of the names (lib) is dependent on itself! Thus, you have an entry with a dependency loop. This results in the "infinite loop" error message mentioned at the beginning of the chapter.

Whitespace at the end of a continuation line can cause problems as well. See the section "Continuation Line Problems" later in this chapter.

Misspelled Rules and Macros

Rule and macro names are case sensitive. If you spell a name with a letter in the wrong case, it's a spelling error.

Suppose you're using the X11 configuration files and you include the following line in an *Imakefile* you're using to build a library:

```
NormalLibraryObjectrule()
```

After you regenerate the *Makefile*, it's broken:

```
% make
make: Must be a separator on rules line nnn.   Stop.
```

You look at line *nnn* of your *Makefile*, only to find:

```
NormalLibraryObjectrule()
```

In other words, the rule wasn't expanded. This error is symptomatic of a spelling mistake (the rule name is actually NormalLibraryObjectRule, as you'll see if you look closely at *Imake.rules*). By misspelling a rule name, you effectively invoke a rule that doesn't exist. The result is macro expansion failure and typically an unusable *Makefile*.

The same phenomenon occurs with non-rule macros. Suppose you write the following in your *Imakefile* to indicate that your program uses the Athena Widget client libraries:

```
LOCAL_LIBRARIES = XawClientLibs
       DEPLIBS = XawClientDeplibs
```

You'd expect these to turn into properly expanded library lists in the *Makefile*:

```
LOCAL_LIBRARIES = $(XAWLIB) $(XMULIB) $(XTOOLLIB) $(XLIB)
       DEPLIBS = $(DEPXAWLIB) $(DEPXMULIB) $(DEPXTOOLLIB) $(DEPXLIB)
```

But to throw you into the slough of despond, *cpp* turns them into the following instead:

```
LOCAL_LIBRARIES = $(XAWLIB) $(XMULIB) $(XTOOLLIB) $(XLIB)
       DEPLIBS = XawClientDeplibs
```

This happens because `XawClientLibs` is spelled correctly in the *Imakefile*, but `XawClientDepLibs` is not. The resulting *Makefile* isn't syntactically malformed, but it won't work either:

```
% make
make:  Don't know how to make target "XawClientDeplibs".  Stop.
```

Recursive Rules and Spelling Errors

The final section of the X11 template *Imake.tmpl* generates several important recursive target entries for you automatically when `IHaveSubdirs` is defined. If you misspell that macro in your *Imakefile*, e.g., as `IHaveSubDirs`, the section of the template that generates those entries is not triggered and they'll be missing from your *Makefile*. The result is that operations such as *make Makefiles, make clean, make install,* etc., don't process subdirectories as they should.

Incorrect Library Dependency Specifications

Libraries on dependency lines must be specified using pathnames, not using −*l* linker syntax. If you see an error like this:

```
make: Fatal error: Don't know how to make target "-lX11"
```

you probably have a target entry that uses −*l* to list Xlib as a library dependency, such as:

```
prog:: prog.o -lX11
     $(CC) -o prog prog.o -lX11
```

This kind of error is sometimes difficult to relate back to its cause. You typically indicate a library by referring to a *make* variable rather than by writing it out literally. But error messages from *make* write out the literal value, not the variable name. Also, *imake* rules usually don't look much like the target entries they produce, so the part of the *Makefile* in which the error occurs may bear little resemblance to the part of the *Imakefile* from which it's generated.

The following rule invocation is syntactically legal but semantically incorrect because it generates a target entry with an −*l* name in the dependency list:

```
NormalProgramTarget(xprog,$(OBJS),$(XLIB),NullParameter,$(XLIB))
```

The error doesn't exactly leap off the page at you, does it? Hint: look at the third argument. For `NormalProgramTarget()` that argument indicates dependency libraries, but XLIB isn't a dependency symbol. The invocation should use DEPXLIB instead:

```
NormalProgramTarget(xprog,$(OBJS),$(DEPXLIB),NullParameter,$(XLIB))
```

The same considerations apply when you're assigning a value to DEPLIBS in your *Imakefile*. Make sure the values on the right-hand side of the assignment represent pathnames, not −*l* names:

```
/* these are correct */
DEPLIBS = $(DEPXTOOLLIB) $(DEPXLIB)
DEPLIBS = XawClientDepLibs

/* these are incorrect */
DEPLIBS = $(XTOOLLIB) $(XLIB)
DEPLIBS = XawClientLibs
```

Continuation Line Problems

Multiple-line *make* variable definitions need the "\" continuation character at the end of all lines but the last. It's easy to mess up and write an assignment like this in your *Imakefile*:

```
VAR = a b \
      c d \
      e f              ← Missing backslash
      g
```

When you use the resulting *Makefile*, you'll be rewarded for your efforts with a message like one of these:

```
make: line nnn: Unexpected end of line seen
make: line nnn: syntax error
```

Once you take a look at line *nnn* in the *Makefile*, you'll probably realize a backslash is missing.

Another related error is to put spaces after a backslash. If you do this, *make* won't consider the next line a continuation of the line with the backslash, and the variable value will be incomplete. You can find such lines with this command:

```
% grep '\\  *$' Imakefile
```

There are two spaces before the *, and you should use single quotes, not double quotes, to prevent the shell from interpreting the $ as the beginning of a variable reference.

Incorrect Value Assignments

cpp macros are given values using #define directives:

```
#define MacroName value
```

make variables are given values with assignment statements:

```
VARNAME = value
```

Don't reverse these forms or you won't get the right results. That is, don't use #define to set a *make* variable, and don't use = to define a macro value. One helpful rule of thumb is that macro names are ususally written in mixed case, whereas variable names are usually uppercase (e.g., LibDir is a macro and LIB-DIR is a variable). This guideline isn't infallible, but it's true far more often than not (notable exceptions are that TOPDIR, CURRENT_DIR, YES, and NO are macros, not variables).

Errors of Omission

If you use INCLUDES in an *Imakefile* to specify header file directories to be searched, don't leave out the *–I* before each directory. The following assignment isn't correct:

```
INCLUDES = $(TOP)/include
```

Write it like this instead:

```
INCLUDES = -I$(TOP)/include
```

Regenerating a *Makefile* has the side effect of wiping out header file dependencies, so remember to regenerate those too:

```
% make Makefile
% make depend
```

It's not actually an error to omit the second command, but if you do, you'll find that your programs aren't rebuilt properly after you modify header files.

Make sure you have a newline at the end of your *Imakefile*. Some versions of *cpp* generate an incorrect *Makefile* if you don't.

When you invoke a rule and one or more arguments are empty, be sure to specify that explicitly using NullParameter. If you just leave the arguments empty, some versions of *cpp* will complain when you build the *Makefile*:

```
% make Makefile
cpp: line n: Parameter holes filled with a null string
```

The message is harmless, but may alarm others who build your projects on their own machines. Using NullParameter makes the message go away, and others don't have to spend time figuring out whether it's something to worry about.

8

A Closer Look at Makefile Generation

Know thyself.
—Oracle of Delphi (Plutarch, *Morals*)

This chapter takes a detailed look at the *Makefile*-generation process. It focuses on the construction of *imake* commands, rather than on the function of individual configuration files. In particular, we'll examine how these two commands work:

```
% make Makefile
% make Makefiles
```

The first command causes the *Makefile* to regenerate itself, and the second builds the Makefiles in any subdirectories.

The `Makefile` and `Makefiles` target entries are available in the *Makefile* because the configuration files put them there. The entries help you produce new Makefiles by relieving you of the burden of typing *imake* commands manually, and they can be issued in any directory of your project, which lends consistency to the *Makefile*-generating process. (Both commands presuppose you have a *Makefile* in the first place, of course. You generate the initial *Makefile* from your *Imakefile* using a bootstrapper such as *xmkmf*.)

Being able to use Makefiles to rebuild themselves is something that normally proceeds without incident when we're using an existing set of configuration files. We tend to take that process for granted, but you should understand how the process works if you plan to write your own configuration files. Their usefulness will be severely compromised if they can't produce self-regenerating Makefiles.

What imake Needs To Know

imake needs two pieces of information to build a properly configured *Makefile*:

- It must know where the configuration files are located or it will fail to build any *Makefile* at all.

- It must know the location of the project root so that parameters defined relative to the root can be given their proper values.

Configuration File Location

The first thing *imake* needs to know is the location of the configuration file directory. If *confdir* denotes that directory, the *Makefile*-building command looks like this:

```
% imake -Iconfdir
```

When we're using configuration files installed in some public directory outside the project we're working on, *confdir* is normally specified using an absolute path. If the X11 configuration files are stored in */usr/X11R6.1/lib/X11/config*, for instance, the *imake* command to use them is:

```
% imake -I/usr/X11R6.1/lib/X11/config
```

When the configuration files are located within the project, *confdir* can be specified in either of two ways. To illustrate, suppose we have a project with the directory layout shown in Figure 8–1. The project is rooted at */usr/src/proj* and the configuration files are located in the *config* directory under the project root.[*]

For configuration files located inside the project tree, *confdir* can be specified using either an absolute path or a path relative to the current directory (Table 8–1).

---

[*] You can put the configuration files anywhere within the project you like. However, I strongly recommend that you always put within-project configuration files in a directory named *config* under the project root if you have any thought of making your files participate as good citizens in a world where multiple sets of configuration files are the norm (see Chapters 10, 15, and 16).

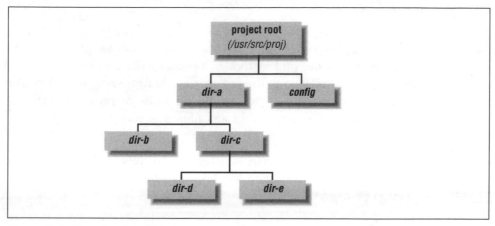

Figure 8-1: Sample project layout

Table 8-1: Specifying confdir for Within-Project Configuration Files

Location of Current Directory Within Project	*confdir* Specified As an Absolute Path	*confdir* Specified As a Relative Path
Project root	*/usr/src/proj/config*	*./config*
One level down	*/usr/src/proj/config*	*../config*
Two levels down	*/usr/src/proj/config*	*../../config*
Three levels down	*/usr/src/proj/config*	*../../../config*

When we use an absolute path, the value of *confdir* doesn't vary, so the command to build a *Makefile* is the same in any of the project's directories:

```
% imake -I/usr/src/proj/config
```

On the other hand, when we specify *confdir* relative to the current directory, its value changes as we change directories within the project. Thus, if we begin at the project root directory and descend through different levels of the project tree, the *imake* command varies accordingly:

```
% imake -I./config
% cd dir-a
% imake -I../config
% cd dir-c
% imake -I../../config
% cd dir-d
% imake -I../../../config
```

Project Root Location

Telling *imake* where the configuration files are located is sufficient to build a *Makefile*, but not necessarily sufficient to build a correctly configured one. *imake* also needs to know where the project root is, because configuration files often define parameters specified relative to the project root. For instance, we might use DOCSRC, LIBSRC, and INCLUDESRC to denote the locations of project directories that contain documentation, libraries, and header files. The project root is a convenient anchor point against which to specify such parameters.

Configuration files typically use the *make* variable TOP to signify the top (or root) of the project tree. That's why you often see lines like these when you examine Makefiles generated by *imake*:

```
       DOCSRC = $(TOP)/doc
       LIBSRC = $(TOP)/lib
   INCLUDESRC = $(TOP)/include
```

This notation is easy to grasp conceptually because it reflects how we think about the location of project directories in relation to the project root. The hard part is figuring out how to specify TOP. The obvious way to set its value is with an assignment statement in one of the configuration files, e.g., like this:

```
TOP = /usr/src/proj
```

But it's not as simple as that. Suppose our configuration files are publicly installed and are used to configure a variety of projects:

- We can't set TOP to an absolute path. Different projects have different root directories, and a fixed value of TOP cannot be correct for all of them simultaneously.

- If we specify TOP using a relative path instead, we get some consistency across projects. That is, TOP is always "." in the project root (no matter where the project is located), ".." in directories one level down, "../.." in directories two levels down, etc. However, by using relative paths, TOP becomes a dynamic quantity, and only fixed values can be specified in the configuration files.

If we're using configuration files located within the project tree, we still encounter problems:

- We can set TOP to the project root location using an absolute path because we need not be concerned with whether it's correct for any other project. But the value needs editing when the project is built on different machines, since other people will put the project tree wherever they like in their file systems.

We might even need to edit TOP ourselves, e.g., if we move a large project elsewhere on our own machine to put it on a file system with more free space.

- If we use relative values for TOP, again we run into the problem that TOP becomes a dynamic value.

The way around these difficulties is to set the value of TOP at *Makefile* generation time, i.e., when we run *imake*. Here the idiom of setting a *make* variable using an associated *cpp* macro is useful. Since it doesn't work to set TOP directly to a fixed value in the configuration files, we can set it to the value of a *cpp* macro instead and specify the macro value on the *imake* command line.

First, we set up (in *Imake.tmpl*) some machinery for TOP to get its value from a macro, TOPDIR:

```
#ifndef TOPDIR
#define TOPDIR .
#endif
TOP = TOPDIR
```

We give TOPDIR a default value of "." (the value that's correct in the project root). This value can be overridden by defining TOPDIR on the *imake* command line. Thus, we can set TOP on the fly to any value we like without editing the configuration files. The general form of the *imake* command now looks like this:

```
% imake -Iconfdir -DTOPDIR=topdir
```

As an example, suppose we're building Makefiles in the project shown in Figure 8–1, using relative paths for `confdir` and `topdir`. Starting in the project root and descending through the project tree, the *imake* commands are as follows:

```
% imake -I./config -DTOPDIR=.
% cd dir-a
% imake -I../config -DTOPDIR=..
% cd dir-c
% imake -I../../config -DTOPDIR=../..
% cd dir-d
% imake -I../../../config -DTOPDIR=../../..
```

In each case, *imake* can find the configuration files properly and can give TOP the correct value for the directory in which the *Makefile* is generated.

Now we know how to construct an *imake* command. Of course, our interest in knowing how to do this isn't for the purpose of being able to run *imake* manually. We want our Makefiles to generate the commands for us.

Running imake from a Makefile

Configuration files should provide a rule that expands to a `Makefile` target entry allowing us to use an existing *Makefile* to build a new one:

```
% make Makefile
```

The way configuration files write Makefiles with the ability to regenerate themselves is one of the areas of *imake* most shrouded in mystery—not quite deep magic from the dawn of time, but not obvious, either.

To work properly, the `Makefile` entry has to do the same things you do when you run *imake* manually. That is, it must generate an *imake* command that specifies the locations of the configuration file directory and the project root:

```
Makefile::
    imake -Iconfdir -DTOPDIR=topdir
```

This is slightly paradoxical. The configuration files generate the entry, but the entry refers to *confdir*, the location of those same files. For the value of *confdir* to be correct, the configuration files must possess self-knowledge of their own location. They cannot derive that knowledge on their own, so you must instill it yourself by informing them where they live. For instance, you could create in *Project.tmpl* a parameter IRULESRC that acts as a self-reference holding the name of the configuration file directory:

```
#ifndef IRuleSrc
#define IRuleSrc confdir
#endif

IRULESRC = IRuleSrc
```

Using `IRULESRC`, the `Makefile` entry becomes:

```
Makefile::
    imake -I$(IRULESRC) -DTOPDIR=topdir
```

The entry still needs to give a value to TOPDIR. Here we remember that the Makefile entry operates from within the context of a *Makefile*, and that the *Makefile* contains a parameter TOP indicating where the project root is. Thus, we can write the entry like this:

```
Makefile::
    imake -I$(IRULESRC) -DTOPDIR=$(TOP)
```

This is another paradox: TOP gets its value from TOPDIR when the *Makefile* is created, and TOPDIR gets its value from TOP when the *Makefile* itself creates a new *Makefile*. But how does this interplay of TOPDIR and TOP setting each other get started?

The cycle begins when you create the initial *Makefile*, e.g., with a bootstrapper. For example, if you're in the project root and the configuration files are located in *config*, the bootstrapper might generate an *imake* command something like this:

```
imake -I./config -DTOPDIR=.
```

This command defines the value of TOPDIR, which sets the value of TOP written into the the initial *Makefile*. Since that *Makefile* then knows the value of TOP, it can use that value to set TOPDIR when it rebuilds itself using the Makefile entry.

Where Are the Configuration Files?

I fudged on specifying a value when I wrote the preceding definition for IRule-Src. There are two cases. If your files are installed in some public directory, you'd use an absolute pathname:

```
#ifndef IRuleSrc
#define IRuleSrc /usr/local/lib/myconfdir
#endif
```

If the configuration files are installed within your project, you should specify a value relative to TOP so it will be correct no matter where the project is located:

```
#ifndef IRuleSrc
#define IRuleSrc $(TOP)/config
#endif
```

However, things can be more complicated: the files might be installed in both places. For instance, if you write configuration files for a particular project, it makes most sense to keep them in the project tree. If you later decide to configure other projects with them, you'd install them publicly as well, so those projects can access them.

To handle this, you specify both locations and choose one as circumstances warrant. X11 sets up its configuration files this way, selecting one location or the other based on whether or not the symbol UseInstalled is defined. For configuring X11 itself, UseInstalled is normally undefined, and the set of files within the project is selected. When X11 is installed, it copies the configuration files to a public location. Then other X-based projects outside the X11 source tree can select the public set of configuration files by defining UseInstalled when their Makefiles are built.

We can copy that idea. The following fragment (which you'd put in *Project.tmpl*) shows what you might write to indicate that a project has its own configuration files but also installs them publicly for use by other projects:

```
#ifndef ConfigDir
#define ConfigDir /usr/local/lib/myconfdir
#endif
#ifndef ConfigSrc
#define ConfigSrc $(TOP)/config
#endif
    CONFIGDIR = ConfigDir
    CONFIGSRC = ConfigSrc
#ifdef UseInstalled
    IRULESRC = $(CONFIGDIR)
#else
    IRULESRC = $(CONFIGSRC)
#endif
```

Now our `Makefile` entry can take two forms. If we're building a *Makefile* in the project to which the configuration files belong, we'd leave `UseInstalled` undefined and use the configuration files located in the project tree. The `Makefile` entry is therefore the same as before:

```
Makefile::
    imake -I$(IRULESRC) -DTOPDIR=$(TOP)
```

If we're building a *Makefile* for a project that's using the publicly installed files, `UseInstalled` must be defined:

```
Makefile::
    imake -DUseInstalled -I$(IRULESRC) -DTOPDIR=$(TOP)
```

The rule that generates these entries must itself adjust properly to whether `UseInstalled` is defined or not. A rule that does so is shown below:

```
#ifndef MakefileTarget
#ifdef UseInstalled
#define MakefileTarget()                          @@\
Makefile::                                        @@\
    imake -DUseInstalled -I$(IRULESRC) -DTOPDIR=$(TOP)
#else
#define MakefileTarget()                          @@\
Makefile::                                        @@\
    imake -I$(IRULESRC) -DTOPDIR=$(TOP)
#endif
#endif /* MakefileTarget */
```

This rule is quite simple and, as such, has some deficiencies that should be remedied. We won't do so here, but it's worth noting what they are:

- *imake* should be parameterized and the references to it replaced with $(IMAKE).

- The rule should save any existing *Makefile* by renaming it before running *imake*. In the event that something goes wrong, it's often useful to have the old *Makefile*. (See "Disaster Recovery" in Chapter 7, *Imakefile Troubleshooting*.)

Building Makefiles Recursively

It's a great convenience to be able to use a *Makefile* to rebuild itself, but we can go further and use it to build Makefiles in subdirectories, too. This process can be made recursive so as to build a whole project tree of Makefiles.

We do this by writing a Makefiles target entry for generating Makefiles in subdirectories of the current directory. Then, after building the *Makefile* in the project root, we can build the rest of the Makefiles in the project with:

```
% make Makefiles
```

For each subdirectory of the current directory, the Makefiles entry must generate commands to:

- Move into the subdirectory

- Run *imake* to generate the *Makefile* there

- Run *make Makefiles* using the new *Makefile*, in case the subdirectory has subdirectories of its own

In practice, the Makefiles entry must execute all three steps as part of the same command line, something like this:

```
cd subdir ; imake args ; make Makefiles
```

The commands must be combined onto a single line because *make* spawns a new shell for each command line in a *Makefile* entry. (If the commands were on separate lines, they'd be executed by separate shells. The effect of the *cd* command would not persist into the second and third commands, and they'd execute in the wrong directory.) The effect of the *cd* terminates when the command line finishes executing, so there's no need to *cd* back up out of the subdirectory.

Let's consider what arguments the Makefiles entry should pass to the *imake* command. We'll still need to specify the locations of the configuration directory and the project root, and we might need to define UseInstalled, too. (I assume in the following example that the location of the project root is specified as a relative path. If its location is specified as an absolute path, the following remarks still apply except that no path adjustment takes place.)

Specifying the location of the project root is a little tricky when a *Makefile* builds a *Makefile* in a subdirectory. The *Makefile* in the parent directory has to generate an *imake* command that executes in the subdirectory, where the path to the project root is different. We have to anticipate this and compensate in advance for the difference.

If the subdirectory is one level lower in the project tree than the parent, the relative location of the project root is one level higher. To adjust the value of TOPDIR so it's correct in the subdirectory, we prepend "../" to TOP:

```
-DTOPDIR=../$(TOP)
```

The adjustment value is "../../" for a subdirectory two levels lower than the parent, "../../../" for a subdirectory three levels lower, etc.

If we're using configuration files located within the project, we must also adjust how their location is specified, because it's defined in terms of TOP. (IRULESRC is defined as $(CONFIGSRC), which is defined as $(TOP)/*config*.) Thus the *imake* command that the *Makefile* in the parent directory creates to generate a *Makefile* in a subdirectory immediately below it looks like this:

```
imake -I../$(IRULESRC) -DTOPDIR=../$(TOP)
```

If we're using configuration files that are installed publicly, UseInstalled should be defined and the *imake* command looks like this:

```
imake -DUseInstalled -I$(IRULESRC) -DTOPDIR=../$(TOP)
```

In this case, the value of IRULESRC is an absolute pathname and doesn't need any adjustment.

Now we need to implement our knowledge as a rule that generates a Makefiles target entry. Such rules are typically somewhat difficult to write. The one shown below is an exceedingly stripped-down example.*

```
/*
 * MakefileSubdirs - generate entry to build Makefiles recursively
 */
#ifndef MakefileSubdirs
#define MakefileSubdirs(dirs)                                    @@\
Makefiles::                                                      @@\
    for i in dirs ; \                                           @@\
    do \                                                        @@\
```

---

* Even so, the rule uses some constructs that haven't been covered yet; for details, see the section "Shell Programming in Rules" in Chapter 13, *Configuration Problems and Solutions*.

```
        (cd $$i; imake -I$(IRULESRC) -DTOPDIR=../$(TOP); make Makefiles); \ @@\
    done
#endif /* MakefileSubdirs */
```

This rule is primitive, as recursive *Makefile*-generating rules go. And, like the
MakefileTarget() rule shown earlier, it has some deficiencies that we simply
note in passing:

- It adjusts TOP correctly only for subdirectories immediately below the current
  directory

- It doesn't handle the case when TOP is an absolute path

- It doesn't notice whether or not UseInstalled is defined

- It doesn't save existing Makefiles by renaming them before running *imake*

- It doesn't tell the user much about what it's doing or where it's executing

As you might guess, when these problems are addressed, rules to recursively generate Makefiles tend to become marvels of complexity, like Celtic knotwork.

Makefile Generation in X11

The X11 configuration files have their own versions of the MakefileTarget() and
MakefileSubdirs() rules to generate Makefile and Makefiles target entries.
Normally, you don't have to invoke either of these rules in your *Imakefile* because
the last section of *Imake.tmpl* automatically does so for you, in a sequence that
looks something like this:

```
MakefileTarget()

#ifdef IHaveSubdirs
MakefileSubdirs($(SUBDIRS))
#endif

#ifndef IHaveSubdirs
Makefiles::
#endif
```

The MakefileTarget() rule generates an entry containing an *imake* command
that looks like this:

```
$(IMAKE_CMD) -DTOPDIR=$(TOP) -DCURDIR=$(CURRENT_DIR)
```

The two −*D* arguments communicate information about the project tree. TOPDIR,
as already discussed, is the location of the project root, and the meaning of
−DTOPDIR=$(TOP) should be familiar. CURDIR and CURRENT_DIR specify the loca-
tion of the current directory within the project. They set each other reflexively, just
like TOPDIR and TOP. The X11 rules use CURRENT_DIR to generate messages
announcing to the user where in the project tree *make* happens to be executing.

This is useful feedback when you're watching the progress of a long recursive *make* operation, but has no functional significance for *Makefile* building.

The *imake* program and the location of the configuration files aren't named explicitly in the preceding command. They're specified in the value of IMAKE_CMD, which is defined in *Imake.tmpl* as follows:

```
#ifdef UseInstalled
    IRULESRC = $(CONFIGDIR)
    IMAKE_CMD = $(IMAKE) -DUseInstalled -I$(IRULESRC) $(IMAKE_DEFINES)
#else
    IRULESRC = $(CONFIGSRC)/cf
    IMAKE_CMD = $(IMAKE) -I$(IRULESRC) $(IMAKE_DEFINES)
#endif
```

IMAKE specifies the *imake* program and the *−I* argument indicates where the configuration files are.

Here's how IMAKE_CMD works:

- X11 can be configured using versions of the configuration files located either in a public directory (in $(CONFIGDIR)) or within the project tree ($(CONFIG-SRC)/*cf*). The location in which to look is determined based on whether or not the *cpp* symbol UseInstalled is defined. The default values of CONFIG-DIR and CONFIGSRC are */usr/X11R6.1/lib/X11/config* and $(TOP)/*config*; IRULESRC is set to the one that applies.

- In X11, UseInstalled determines not only where to look for the configuration files, but also where to look for *imake* itself. If UseInstalled is defined, IMAKE is simply *imake*, i.e., it's assumed to be somewhere in your search path. Otherwise, IMAKE is $(TOP)/*config/imake/imake*, i.e., it's found in the *config/imake* directory in the X11 source tree; this works because the source for *imake* is bundled into the X11 distribution to allow you to build X11 even if you don't already have *imake*.

- Since the value of IMAKE_CMD is selected based on whether UseInstalled is defined (or not), each value causes UseInstalled to be defined (or not) in future *imake* commands. The value selected if UseInstalled is defined makes sure it continues to be defined by passing -DUseInstalled to *imake*, whereas the value selected if UseInstalled isn't defined continues to leave it undefined.

- IMAKE_DEFINES allows arguments to be passed to the *imake* command from the *make* command line; it's usually empty and you can ignore it.

The X11 MakefileSubdirs() rule generates a recursive *Makefile*-generating target entry. Conceptually, MakefileSubdirs() is relatively straightforward. It takes a list of directories as its argument. For each one, it determines the correct path adjustment value for where to find *imake* and the configuration files if the ones located within the X11 source tree are being used, changes into the directory, executes IMAKE_CMD to create the *Makefile* there, and runs *make Makefiles* with the new *Makefile* in case the directory has any subdirectories of its own. The implementation is quite another matter, however. If you want the full story, take a look at the X11 *Imake.rules* for full details, but don't say you weren't warned.

9

A Configuration Starter Project

Well begun is half done.
—Aristotle, *Politics*

When you write configuration files, content depends on intent. If you want them to produce Makefiles for building programs, you write program-building rules and parameters. If you want them to produce Makefiles for document production, you write document-preparation rules and parameters. But regardless of any other intent you might have, one thing all configuration files should do is produce Makefiles that rebuild themselves properly. You want to be able to regenerate your Makefiles easily using these commands:

```
% make Makefile
% make Makefiles
```

Chapter 8, *A Closer Look at Makefile Generation*, discusses the mechanisms by which Makefiles rebuild themselves. This chapter shows how to make sure those mechanisms operate correctly when you copy an existing set of configuration files to create another.

We'll copy the X11 files to create a starter project, denoted as SP. You can use it as a basis for other projects that provide their configuration files within the project tree. Or, if you like, you can use it to develop files to be installed in a public directory so they can be shared by other projects that don't provide their own configuration files.

The differences between the X11 and SP files will be minimal. The purpose of the starter project isn't to develop new or different configuration functionality, but to illustrate the problems relating to *Makefile* generation that crop up when we copy a set of configuration files, and to show how to solve them. (In Chapters 11, *Introduction to Configuration File Writing*, and 12, *Writing Rule Macros*, we'll see how to modify the SP files further to change the functionality they provide.)

The SP files here are developed from the X11R6.1 configuration files. The procedure can be followed using the X11R5 files as well, although the particular changes needed are somewhat different. See "An X11R5 Starter Project" at the end of this chapter for more information.

If you want to compare the X11 files with the resulting SP files as you work through this chapter, retrieve the SP distribution (see Appendix A, *Obtaining Configuration Software*).

Creating the Starter Project

To create the starter project, we must first set up the directory structure and populate the project with configuration files. Let's assume initially that we'll be developing a project containing its own private configuration files. (Later in this chapter, we'll discuss the changes necessary to install the files publicly.)

Configuration files are important, but they aren't the reason a project exists—the programs it builds are. We can indicate the subservient role of the configuration files by isolating them in a *config* directory under the project root rather than cluttering up the root directory with them. Depending on whether or not a project builds everything in the project root, the project tree might look like one of those shown in Figure 9-1 or 9-2. However, when we consider only the configuration-related parts of the project trees that are common to both, they reduce to the one shown in Figure 9-3, and that's what we need to set up to create the starter project.

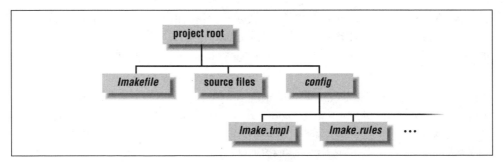

Figure 9-1: Project that builds programs in project root directory

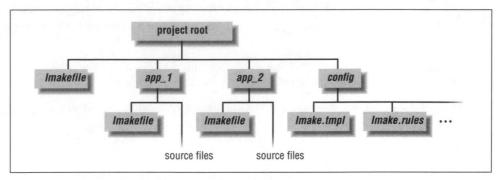

Figure 9–2: Project that builds programs in subdirectories

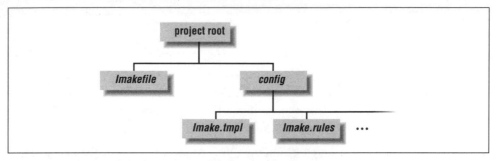

Figure 9–3: Minimal configuration-related parts of project tree

Figure 9–3 shows that we need a project root directory, as well as a *config* subdirectory to hold the configuration files. Create the initial project structure like this:

```
% mkdir SP
% cd SP
% mkdir config
```

Then populate the *config* directory with copies of the X11 configuration files:

```
% cp /usr/X11R6.1/lib/X11/config/* config
```

The X11 files may have been installed read-only. We'll need to modify our copies, so make them writable using one of the following commands:

```
% chmod 644 config/*        (or)
% chmod u+w config/*
```

We'll also need an *Imakefile* in the project root. Just create an empty one for the moment:

```
% cp /dev/null Imakefile
```

Now we have enough structure to try using the configuration files to generate a *Makefile*. For programs configured with the X11 files, we'd normally bootstrap a

Makefile with *xmkmf*. That doesn't work for the SP files because the command that *xmkmf* generates uses the original X11 files in */usr/X11R6.1/lib/X11/config*, not our copies:

```
% xmkmf
imake -DUseInstalled -I/usr/X11R6.1/lib/X11/config
```

However, we can mimic *xmkmf* by invoking *imake* manually and substituting the correct location of our files:

```
% imake -DUseInstalled -I./config
```

That command uses the starter project's configuration files, and sucessfully generates a *Makefile*. But the resulting *Makefile* doesn't regenerate itself properly:

```
% make Makefile
+ rm -f Makefile.bak
+ mv -f Makefile Makefile.bak
imake -DUseInstalled -I/usr/X11R6.1/lib/X11/config -DTOPDIR=. -DCURDIR=.
```

This happens because our files still expect to find themselves installed in */usr/X11R6.1/lib/X11/config*. Consequently, the Makefile target entry they generate looks in that directory for the configuration files, and the *Makefile* rebuilds itself using the original X11 files, not our copies.

Let's try bootstrapping and rebuilding the *Makefile* without defining Use-Installed:

```
% imake -I./config
% make Makefile
sh: ./config/imake: bad directory
*** Error code 1 (ignored)
+ rm -f Makefile.bak
+ mv -f Makefile Makefile.bak
./config/imake/imake -I./config/cf -DTOPDIR=. -DCURDIR=.
sh: ./config/imake/imake: not found
```

That doesn't work, either. When we build the *Makefile* without defining Use-Installed, the Makefile target entry looks for configuration files in the *config* directory, but also assumes that *imake* lives in the project tree. Our project contains only configuration files, so the attempt to use a within-project *imake* fails. (The same command sequence works in the X11 project tree because the X11 distribution does contain *imake* source code, in the *config/imake* directory under the project root.)

The preceding exercise illustrates the initial difficulties we face when we copy the X11 configuration files to create a new set:

- We need a bootstrapper that works with our files. *xmkmf* is unsuitable since it is intended for the X11 files.

- The `Makefile` target entry generated by the configuration files doesn't behave correctly. When `UseInstalled` isn't defined, the entry assumes *imake* is located within the project tree. When `UseInstalled` is defined, the entry looks in the wrong place for the configuration files. The files don't know their own location (i.e., their self-reference is incorrect).

We'll defer the bootstrapping problem until Chapter 10, *Coordinating Sets of Configuration Files*, and concentrate here on `UseInstalled` and the self-reference.

In X11, `UseInstalled` has two functions, both of which at the moment have been carried over without modification into the SP files.

First, the self-reference (the location where the configuration files look for themselves) is determined by `UseInstalled`. When `UseInstalled` isn't defined, the self-reference is *config/cf* under the project root; this allows X11 itself to be configured using the configuration files located in the X11 source tree. When `UseInstalled` is defined, the self-reference is */usr/X11R6.1/lib/X11/config*; this allows use of the files by other X-based software when the files are installed publicly.

This mechanism of determining the configuration file location based on `UseInstalled` is a useful thing to carry along into the starter project, to allow it to configure itself using the within-project files, and to optionally install the files for use by other projects. However, we need to change the value of the self-reference if we plan on installing the configuration files. When `UseInstalled` isn't defined, the self-reference is *config/cf*, whereas for the SP files it needs to be *config*. When `UseInstalled` is defined, the self-reference still points to the location of the installed X11 files. That isn't correct for the SP files, because we can't put them in the same place as the X11 files.

Second, X11 uses `UseInstalled` to determine where to find the configuration programs *imake*, *makedepend*, *mkdirhier*, and also *bsdinst* if you use it. They're expected to be installed in a public directory in your search path when `UseInstalled` is defined. But when `UseInstalled` is undefined, X11 expects to find the programs within the X11 source tree and builds them on the fly if necessary. That's useful in the sense that you can build X11 even if you didn't have the programs before. However, it does require that the source for the programs be bundled into the X11 distribution.

As a general practice, this second use of `UseInstalled` causes unnecessary redundancy: all projects configured along similar lines would need to include the programs within the project tree. One copy of the configuration programs is sufficient; we may as well install them once and be done with it. Then we can dissolve the connection between `UseInstalled` and the location of the programs. The changes needed to do this are shown in the following sections. They involve modifying files in the *config* directory so that *imake, makedepend, mkdirhier*, and *bsdinst* are always assumed to be installed publicly, not just when `UseInstalled` is defined.

Changes to Imake.tmpl

As originally written, `IMAKE_CMD` looks for the configuration files in *config/cf* under the project root if `UseInstalled` isn't defined. The starter project keeps those files in *config*, not *config/cf*, so the definition of `IMAKE_CMD` must change. The original definition looks like this:

```
#ifdef UseInstalled
        IRULESRC = $(CONFIGDIR)
        IMAKE_CMD = $(IMAKE) -DUseInstalled -I$(IRULESRC) $(IMAKE_DEFINES)
#else
        IRULESRC = $(CONFIGSRC)/cf
        IMAKE_CMD = $(IMAKE) -I$(IRULESRC) $(IMAKE_DEFINES)
#endif
```

Remove `/cf` from the end of the second definition of `IRULESRC` so the definition looks like this:

```
#ifdef UseInstalled
        IRULESRC = $(CONFIGDIR)
        IMAKE_CMD = $(IMAKE) -DUseInstalled -I$(IRULESRC) $(IMAKE_DEFINES)
#else
        IRULESRC = $(CONFIGSRC)
        IMAKE_CMD = $(IMAKE) -I$(IRULESRC) $(IMAKE_DEFINES)
#endif
```

The original *Imake.tmpl* also expects four of the programs we're interested in to be located in the project tree if `UseInstalled` is undefined:

```
#ifndef ImakeCmd
#ifdef UseInstalled
#define ImakeCmd imake
#else
#define ImakeCmd $(IMAKESRC)/imake
#endif
#endif

#ifndef DependCmd
#ifdef UseInstalled
#define DependCmd makedepend
#else
#define DependCmd $(DEPENDSRC)/makedepend
#endif
#endif

#ifndef MkdirHierCmd
#ifdef UseInstalled
#define MkdirHierCmd mkdirhier
#else
```

```
#define MkdirHierCmd $(SHELL) $(CONFIGSRC)/util/mkdirhier.sh
#endif
#endif

#ifndef InstallCmd
#if SystemV || SystemV4
#ifdef UseInstalled
#define InstallCmd bsdinst
#else
#define InstallCmd $(SHELL) $(CONFIGSRC)/util/bsdinst.sh
#endif
#else
#define InstallCmd install
#endif
#endif
```

Since we're going to assume these programs are installed publicly (i.e., in a directory that's in your search path), the definitions should be changed so they don't depend on UseInstalled:

```
#ifndef ImakeCmd
#define ImakeCmd imake
#endif

#ifndef DependCmd
#define DependCmd makedepend
#endif

#ifndef MkdirHierCmd
#define MkdirHierCmd mkdirhier
#endif

#ifndef InstallCmd
#if SystemV || SystemV4
#define InstallCmd bsdinst
#else
#define InstallCmd install
#endif
#endif
```

Changes to Imake.rules

The original X11 definitions of the ImakeDependency() and DependDependency() rules vary according to whether or not UseInstalled is defined. If it's not defined, the rules check whether *imake* and *makedepend* have been built within the project tree and try to build them if they haven't been. This must change, because we don't want to look for or build the programs in the SP project tree.

The cleanest thing to do is remove the definitions of ImakeDependency() and DependDependency() entirely. Then eliminate the line that invokes Imake-Dependency() from the definition of BuildMakefileTarget(), and eliminate the lines that invoke DependDependency() from the definitions of DependTarget() and DependTarget3().

In addition, it's necessary to change the definition of ImakeSubCmdHelper so it doesn't assume *imake* is in the project tree when UseInstalled is undefined.

Original:

```
#ifdef UseInstalled
#define ImakeSubCmdHelper $(IMAKE_CMD)
#else
#define ImakeSubCmdHelper $(IMAKEPREFIX)$(IMAKE) -I$(IMAKEPREFIX)$(IRULESRC) \
    $(IMAKE_DEFINES)
#endif
```

Change to:

```
#ifdef UseInstalled
#define ImakeSubCmdHelper $(IMAKE_CMD)
#else
#define ImakeSubCmdHelper $(IMAKE) -I$(IMAKEPREFIX)$(IRULESRC) $(IMAKE_DEFINES)
#endif
```

If you're using R6 files rather than R6.1 files, the change to ImakeSubCmdHelper is similar except that the definition uses $$imakeprefix instead of $(IMAKEPREFIX).

Testing the Starter Project

The changes made so far are sufficient to allow us to use the starter project to configure itself. Verify this as follows:

- Bootstrap the *Makefile* in the project root using the files in the *config* directory:

    ```
    % imake -I./config
    ```

- Make sure that the *Makefile* rebuilds itself using the same files:

    ```
    % make Makefile
    + rm -f Makefile.bak
    + mv Makefile Makefile.bak
    imake -I./config -DTOPDIR=. -DCURDIR=.
    ```

Now you can use the starter project as a basis for configuring other projects.

Using the Starter Project

Make a copy of the starter project and move into it. For instance, assuming the starter project is located under your current directory, you can do this:

```
% cp -r SP myproj
% cd myproj
```

If your *cp* has no *−r* (recursive copy) option, do this instead:

```
% mkdir myproj
% cd SP
% tar cf − . | ( cd ../myproj ; tar xf − )
% cd ../myproj
```

The *Imakefile* in the project root directory is empty, because that's all we needed for getting the starter project set up. Of course, a real project needs a more extensive *Imakefile*. If the project builds all its programs in the project root, put the information for building them into the *Imakefile*, perhaps using rules like `Simple-ProgramTarget()`, `ComplexProgramTarget()`, or `NormalProgramTarget()`. If the project builds programs in subdirectories, write the *Imakefile* in the project root directory to include subdirectory support as described in the section "Managing Multiple-Directory Projects" in Chapter 6, *Writing Imakefiles*.

Either way, once you've set up your project and written the *Imakefile* (or several Imakefiles, if you have subdirectories), run the following commands to verify that the project can configure itself:

```
% imake -I./config
% make Makefile
% make Makefiles          (If the project has subdirectories)
```

As you develop your project's programs, you'll get a better idea of their unique configuration requirements and you can further modify the configuration files accordingly. This may involve adding new parameters or rules, or perhaps deleting or modifying those already present. We'll take up these and other issues in Chapters 11 through 13, which discuss configuration file writing in more detail.

Installing Your Project's Configuration Files

By default, the starter project doesn't install the configuration files, and neither will any copy of it you're using. That's suitable if your project has unique configuration requirements and uses its own configuration files privately within the project tree. On the other hand, if you have related projects with similar configuration requirements, it might make sense to install the configuration files publicly so those other projects can use them.

To install the configuration files, three changes are necessary:

- **Change the project root *Imakefile* to allow recursive *make* operations**. This is necessary so that recursive *make* operations descend into the *config* directory.

  If the *Imakefile* in the project root already contains subdirectory support, add *config* to the value of `SUBDIRS`. Otherwise, put the following at the beginning of the *Imakefile*:

```
#define IHaveSubdirs
#define PassCDebugFlags

SUBDIRS = config

MakeSubdirs($(SUBDIRS))
DependSubdirs($(SUBDIRS))
```

- **Change the configuration file self-reference**. The self-reference specifies the configuration file installation directory. Move into the *config* directory and modify the value of ConfigDir in *Project.tmpl*. ConfigDir still points to */usr/X11R6.1/lib/X11/config*, so if you don't change it, installing the *myproj* configuration files will wipe out the X11 files. If you want to install the files into */usr/local/lib/config/myproj*, for example, the definition should look like this:

```
#ifndef ConfigDir
#define ConfigDir /usr/local/lib/config/myproj
#endif
```

- **Create an *Imakefile* in the *config* directory**. This is needed to direct installation of the configuration files. The *Imakefile* should look like this:

```
FILES = *.tmpl *.rules site.def *.cf *.bac

all::
depend::
InstallMultipleDestFlags(install,$(FILES),$(CONFIGDIR),$(INSTDATFLAGS))
```

InstallMultipleDestFlags() generates an install target entry to install the configuration files in CONFIGDIR. The empty all and depend entries are needed to suppress "don't know how to make target XXX" complaints that would otherwise result from the following commands:

```
% make all
% make depend
```

To verify these changes, rebuild the Makefiles by running the following commands in the project root:[*]

```
% make Makefile
+ rm -f Makefile.bak
+ mv Makefile Makefile.bak
imake -I./config -DTOPDIR=. -DCURDIR=.
% make Makefiles
making Makefiles in ./config...
```

---

[*] The output shown is what you should see if *config* is the only subdirectory of the project root. You'll see additional output if there are other subdirectories. Alternatively, use this command:

```
% make Makefiles "SUBDIRS=config"
```

That limits operation of the Makefiles target entry to the *config* directory.

Then change into the *config* directory and check where the *Makefile* thinks it should install the configuration files. Use *−n* so *make* announces its intentions without actually installing anything:

```
% cd config
% make -n install
if [ -d /usr/local/lib/config/myproj ]; then set +x; \
else (set -x; mkdirhier /usr/local/lib/config/myproj); fi
case '-bn' in *[i]*) set +e;; esac; \
for i in *.tmpl *.rules site.def *.cf *.bac; do \
(set -x; install -c -m 0444 $i /usr/local/lib/config/myproj); \
done
echo "install in . done"
```

The pathname of the intended installation directory (*/usr/local/lib/config/myproj*) should appear in the *make* command output. If it doesn't, check the value of ConfigDir in *Project.tmpl*. Otherwise you can run *make install* without the *−n* option, and the files will be installed in the right place.

An X11R5 Starter Project

If you prefer to create a starter project from the X11R5 configuration files rather than from the X11R6.1 files, the procedure is described below. The procedure is similar to the one discussed in the preceding sections. The primary differences are that the definitions of IMAKE_CMD, IMAKE, MAKEDEPEND, and MKDIRHIER are slightly different, and (for the last three) are located in *Project.tmpl* rather than in *Imake.tmpl*.

Create the initial project structure and populate it with copies of the X11R5 files:

```
% mkdir SP
% cd SP
% mkdir config
% cp /usr/lib/X11/config/* config
```

Make the files writable:

```
% chmod 644 config/*          (or)
% chmod u+w config/*
```

Create an empty *Imakefile* in the project root:

```
% cp /dev/null Imakefile
```

Changes to Imake.tmpl

As originally written, IMAKE_CMD looks for *imake* in the project tree if Use-
Installed isn't defined. If we assume *imake* is installed publicly, the definition of
IMAKE_CMD must change. The original definition looks like this:

```
#ifdef UseInstalled
    IRULESRC = $(CONFIGDIR)
    IMAKE_CMD = $(IMAKE)  DUseInstalled -I$(IRULESRC) $(IMAKE_DEFINES)
#else
    IRULESRC = $(CONFIGSRC)
    IMAKE_CMD = $(NEWTOP)$(IMAKE) -I$(NEWTOP)$(IRULESRC) $(IMAKE_DEFINES)
#endif
```

Remove the first $(NEWTOP) from the line preceding the #endif so the definition
looks like this:

```
#ifdef UseInstalled
    IRULESRC = $(CONFIGDIR)
    IMAKE_CMD = $(IMAKE) -DUseInstalled -I$(IRULESRC) $(IMAKE_DEFINES)
#else
    IRULESRC = $(CONFIGSRC)
    IMAKE_CMD = $(IMAKE) -I$(NEWTOP)$(IRULESRC) $(IMAKE_DEFINES)
#endif
```

InstallCmd needs to be changed for the same reason.

Original:

```
#ifndef InstallCmd
#if SystemV | SystemV4
#ifdef UseInstalled
#define InstallCmd $(BINDIR)/bsdinst
#else
#define InstallCmd $(SCRIPTSRC)/bsdinst.sh
#endif
#else
#define InstallCmd install
#endif
#endif
```

Change to:

```
#ifndef InstallCmd
#if SystemV || SystemV4
#define InstallCmd bsdinst
#else
#define InstallCmd install
#endif
#endif
```

Changes to Project.tmpl

The fragment of *Project.tmpl* that needs to be modified looks like this (the sections marked *other stuff* refer to some X-related parameters that are of no concern to us here):

```
#ifdef UseInstalled
        IMAKE = imake
       DEPEND = makedepend
    ...other stuff...
    MKDIRHIER = BourneShell $(BINDIR)/mkdirhier
#else
        IMAKE = $(IMAKESRC)/imake
       DEPEND = DependCmd
    ...other stuff...
    MKDIRHIER = BourneShell $(SCRIPTSRC)/mkdirhier.sh
#endif
```

As written above, the variables IMAKE, DEPEND, and MKDIRHIER are set to within-project paths when UseInstalled isn't defined. We need to change them so they do not depend on UseInstalled. Change the fragment (leaving the *other stuff* sections alone) so it looks like this:

```
        IMAKE = imake          /* assume publicly installed */
       DEPEND = makedepend     /* ditto */
    MKDIRHIER = mkdirhier      /* ditto */
#ifdef UseInstalled
    ...other stuff...
#else
    ...other stuff...
#endif
```

With this change, *imake*, *makedepend*, and *mkdirhier* will be assumed to be installed in a directory that's in your search path. Note that MKDIRHIER is revised so it does not depend on BINDIR, which allows you to change BINDIR without breaking the configuration files' ability to locate *mkdirhier*.

Changes to Imake.rules

The changes are the same as for the R6.1 files, except that there is no ImakeSubCmdHelper rule to modify.

Installing and Testing

The installation and testing procedures are the same as for the R6.1 files. Don't forget to change ConfigDir in *Project.tmpl* and to create the *Imakefile* in the *config* directory if you plan to install the files.

10

Coordinating Sets of Configuration Files

"Will you walk into my parlor?"
said the spider to the fly...
—Mary Howitt, *The Spider and the Fly*

Once upon a time, the only widely used *imake* configuration files around were the X11 files. Just about everything configured with *imake* used the same set of configuration files, and life was simple. But there's nothing to stop new sets of files from being developed. For instance, in Chapter 9, *A Configuration Starter Project*, we adapt the X11 configuration files into a starter project that can serve as a beginning point for developing your own configuration files. And we do just that in Chapter 11, *Introduction to Configuration File Writing*, and Chapter 12, *Writing Rule Macros*, where we use the starter project to illustrate the process that gives rise to a new set of files. Each time we go through this process, another set of configuration files springs into existence. In such a world, life becomes more complex. So, to avoid letting that complexity sneak up on us and catch us unawares, this chapter discusses the problems that arise from trying to coordinate multiple sets of configuration files and shows how to solve them.

The most obvious problem caused by the existence of multiple sets is location. We can't put different sets of files in the same place; they'll collide with each other and create a big mess. So we need to place them in different locations to ensure that this doesn't happen. Then, for any given set, we need to make its location known in two places:

- **In the configuration files themselves**. The files must know where they are so they can construct Makefiles that rebuild themselves with these commands:

    ```
    % make Makefile
    % make Makefiles
    ```

- **In the bootstrapper that uses the files**. The `Makefile` and `Makefiles` target entries only work when you already have a working *Makefile*. When you don't, you need a bootstrapper that knows where the configuration files are so it can tell *imake* where to find them.

With respect to the proper operation of the `Makefile` and `Makefiles` target entries, the existence of multiple sets of files doesn't in itself present any special difficulties. As long as each set correctly references its own location, Makefiles build themselves using the proper set.

What about bootstrapping with multiple sets? Here we have a problem: each set of files is located in a different place and must be used with a bootstrapper that knows the set's location. That's not a difficulty for any particular set of files, because we can write a bootstrapper that knows where they are. But the effect of that approach over the long haul is that we end up drowning in bootstrappers.

When you develop a set of configuration files, presumably you do so for specific and unique purposes and can make a good case for its existence. That's not true of bootstrappers. They all have essentially the same purpose (to spare you the burden of typing *imake* commands manually), so multiplying bootstrappers just creates litter. It would be better to have a single one that understands how to use different sets.

Designing a General-Purpose Bootstrapper

Let's consider how to avoid replicating bootstrappers by designing one that helps you work with multiple sets of configuration files easily. We'll call it *imboot*, a name that (unlike *xmkmf*) reflects its general-purpose nature in being tied to *imake* rather than to a particular project.[*]

---

[*] *imkmf* might have been a better name (it's more like *xmkmf*), but the Khoros project already used it.

From a user's point of view, selecting configuration files should be as simple as naming which set we want:

```
% imboot -c X11R6.1
% imboot -c SP
% etc.
```

From an implementer's point of view, things are less simple. It's easy enough to get the name of the configuration files from the command-line arguments, but what do we do with that name? A bootstrapper that works with any of several sets of files must know how to find each of them. This implies either that *imboot* knows explicitly where every set is located, or that we organize them according to some principle *imboot* can use to map names onto locations.

Both approaches have advantages and disadvantages. If we give *imboot* explicit knowledge about sets of files by hardwiring their locations into it, we have the luxury of putting them anywhere at all in the file system. For instance, in a shell script we could write a *case* statement with an entry for each set of files *imboot* should know about. The following example knows how to find the files for X11, OpenWindows, and the starter project:

```
case "$name" in
    X11R6.1)  dir=/usr/X11R6.1/lib/X11/config ;;
    OW)       dir=/usr/openwin/lib/config ;;
    SP)       dir=/usr/local/lib/config/SP ;;
    *)        echo "file set $name unknown" 1>&2
              exit 1
              ;;
esac
```

Unfortunately, with this approach, *imboot* is limited strictly to the files listed, and it must be modified every time we install another set. That makes it inherently non-portable since at any given site there will be an arbitrary number of paths to hardwire into it. You might have three sets of files; I might have eight.

If an organizing principle is used instead, we can figure out the location of any set of files from its name without explicitly coding the group's location into *imboot*. A reasonable way to do this is to exploit the natural hierarchical structure of the UNIX file system. We can provide a root directory for configuration files, */usr/local/lib/config*, under which we install sets of files.[*] Each set gets its own subdirectory, the name of which is the name the files are known by.

Designating a configuration root directory and installing sets of files under it allows *imboot* to find any set of files knowing just the name. This organization accommodates 200 sets just as well as it accommodates two, which makes *imboot*

---

[*] You can use a root directory other than */usr/local/lib/config*, as long as you do so consistently for all files installed on your machine.

implicitly extensible: no modifications to it are required when new files are installed.

Use of a configuration root also minimizes the machine dependencies in *imboot* itself. Only the path to the root need be parameterized, not the paths to some arbitrary number of sets of files.

The preceding discussion of the benefits of organizing files under the root directory */usr/local/lib/config* paints an idyllic picture, but there is a downside. Like any cooperative agreement, the organizational scheme must be adhered to by all participants (all sets of configuration files). The principle of arranging files by installing them all under the configuration root implicitly assumes we can put them all there. That assumption doesn't always hold, because some existing sets of files are not installed under */usr/local/lib/config*. For example, the X11 files are installed in */usr/X11R6.1/lib/X11/config*.

However, the reach of the configuration root directory often can be extended to files installed elsewhere by using symlinks. For the X11 files, we can do this with a single command:

```
% ln -s /usr/X11R6.1/lib/X11/config /usr/local/lib/config/X11R6.1
```

The symbolic link makes the configuration root appear to have a set of files named X11 under it and allows us to use them to bootstrap Makefiles like this:

```
% imboot -c X11R6.1
```

Essentially, *imboot* is the spider, */usr/local/lib/config* is the parlor, and the symlink lures the X11 flies into it.

A special class of configuration files not installed under the configuration root involves those not installed publicly at all, i.e., those that are stored in the source tree of a project that uses them privately. We could handle this with symlinks, but there's an easier way. We can consider private configuration files to be "nameless" and signify our desire to use them simply by the absence of any *-c name* option on the *imboot* command line. Of course, *imboot* needs to know where in the project to look for them. Examination of existing *imake*-configured projects suggests that the *config* directory under the project root is the closest thing to a convention available. (X11 is an important exception. From distribution R6 on, the configuration files are stored in *config/cf* rather than in *config*. In order to work with R6 and up, *imboot* first looks for a *config/cf* directory, then for a *config* directory.)

Implementing imboot

The information *imboot* needs is described in the list below. (The second and third points are based on the *Makefile*-generation issues discussed in Chapter 8, *A Closer Look at Makefile Generation*.)

- **The location of the configuration file directory.** *imboot* needs to tell *imake* where the configuration files are. By default, it assumes they're in either the *config/cf* or *config* directory under the project root. If a *-c name* option is present on the command line, *imboot* uses the directory */usr/local/lib/config/name* instead.

- **The location of the project root.** *imboot* needs to tell *imake* the location of the project root. *imboot* doesn't know where that is, though, so it must allow the location to be specified on the command line. We could decree that *imboot* can only be used in project root directories and that "." is therefore always the location of the root, but there is good reason to want to use *imboot* in arbitrary project directories. For example, you might generate a corrupt *Makefile* somewhere down inside a project tree and need to bootstrap a new one. Or you might want to write a recursive *Makefile*-generating rule that uses *imboot* rather than *imake*.

- **The location of the current directory within the project.** It can be useful for *imboot* to tell *imake* the location of the current directory within the project (recursive rules are often written to use that information to give feedback to the user as a progress indicator). Since *imboot* doesn't know the current directory, it must allow that location to be specified on the command line.

Putting this together, *imboot* allows a *-c name* option to specify the name of a set of configuration files and one or two other arguments specifying the locations of the project root and current directory. The syntax of *imboot* is:

```
imboot [ -c name ] [ topdir [ curdir ] ]
```

Other than the *-c* option, this syntax is similar to that of *xmkmf*.

imboot is easily implemented as a shell script:[*]

```
1: #!/bin/sh
2:
3: configrootdir=/usr/local/lib/config
4: configname=
5: topdir=.
6: curdir=.
7:
```

---

[*] This is a preliminary version that we'll replace with a more capable one in Chapter 15, *Designing Extensible Configuration Files*. But it will do for now.

```
 8: if [ $# -ge 2 -a "$1" = "-c" ]; then
 9:     configname="$2"
10:     shift;shift
11: fi
12:
13: if [ $# -gt 0 ]; then
14:     topdir="$1"
15:     shift
16: fi
17: if [ $# -gt 0 ]; then
18:     curdir="$1"
19: fi
20:
21: if [ "$configname" = "" ]; then
22:     useinstalled=
23:     if [ -d "$topdir/config/cf" ]; then
24:         configdir="-I$topdir/config/cf"
25:     else
26:         configdir="-I$topdir/config"
27:     fi
28: else
29:     useinstalled=-DUseInstalled
30:     configdir="-I$configrootdir/$configname"
31: fi
32:
33: if [ -f Makefile ]; then
34:     echo mv Makefile Makefile.bak
35:     mv Makefile Makefile.bak
36: fi
37:
38: echo imake $useinstalled $configdir -DTOPDIR=$topdir -DCURDIR=$curdir
39: imake $useinstalled $configdir -DTOPDIR=$topdir -DCURDIR=$curdir
```

The first line indicates that *imboot* is a Bourne shell script. (On systems that don't support the #! script-execution mechanism, change the first line to a colon.)

The next section of *imboot* sets up some default values (lines 3–6):

- The path to the configuration root directory.

- The default name of the configuration files, initially unknown.

- The default locations of the project root and current directory. By default we assume we're in the project root directory.

After setting up the initial values, *imboot* examines the command arguments (lines 8–19), first determining whether any set of configuration files was named on the command line, then using any remaining arguments to override the default project root and current directory locations.

Once the arguments have been collected from the command line, *imboot* determines how to construct the *imake* command (lines 21–31):

- If no set of configuration files was named, we leave UseInstalled undefined and use files from within the project. We look in *config/cf* if it exists under the project root, and in *config* otherwise. (Use of *config/cf* is a concession to X11, which, from R6 on, no longer keeps the configuration files in *config*.)

- If a set of files was named, we use the name to determine which publicly installed files to use. In this case, we define UseInstalled and look for the files under */usr/local/lib/config*.

The last section of *imboot* saves the current *Makefile* if it exists, then generates a new one (lines 33–39).

This version of *imboot* is simple, but functional. Now we need to consider how to write configuration files to cooperate with it, and how to achieve backward compatibility with configuration files that are already installed somewhere else.

Cooperating with imboot

imboot makes assumptions about the locations of the configuration files and about the meanings of UseInstalled, TOPDIR, and CURDIR. Obviously, this imposes some constraints on you as a configuration file writer. But if you keep the following guidelines in mind when you write your files, they'll be compatible with *imboot*, and you won't have to write your own bootstrapper:

- If you're going to use your files privately within a project, keep them in a directory named *config* under the project root.

- If you're going to install your files publicly, you need to do a couple of things. First, select a name for them. Remember that your files need to coexist with other sets of files. The potential exists for name clashing under */usr/local/lib/config*, so select a name you don't think anyone else will use. It's impossible to know in advance whether your name is sufficiently unique, of course, but names such as LOCAL or MYFILES are bound to be poor choices.

  Second, tell your files the name of the directory in which they'll be installed under the configuration root */usr/local/lib/config*, and install them there after you finish the other steps below. Essentially, this amounts to making sure the self-reference is correct. If the name of your set of files is XYZ, and the macro and variable you use to express the self-reference are ConfigDir and CONFIG-DIR, write the following in *Project.tmpl*:

```
#ifndef ConfigDir
#define ConfigDir /usr/local/lib/config/XYZ
```

```
#endif
CONFIGDIR = ConfigDir
```

For an instance of this technique, take a look at the starter project (SP) files.

- In your configuration files, use UseInstalled, TOPDIR, and CURDIR as follows:

  — Differentiate between installed and within-project versions of your configuration files based on whether or not UseInstalled is defined.

  — If you have parameters that signify the locations of the project root and current directory, set their values using the *cpp* macros TOPDIR and CURDIR. Here's an example showing how TOPDIR and CURDIR set the parameters TOP and CURRENT_DIR:

    ```
    #ifndef TOPDIR
    #define TOPDIR .
    #endif
    #ifndef CURDIR
    #define CURDIR .
    #endif
            TOP = TOPDIR
    CURRENT_DIR = CURDIR
    ```

    TOPDIR and CURDIR are normally defined on the *imake* command line, but you still need to specify a default value in the configuration files.

Extending imboot's Reach

In the previous section, we discussed how to design configuration files to take account of *imboot*'s assumptions. But preexisting configuration files don't necessarily conform to how *imboot* views the world. Khoros is an example of a project that is incompatible with *imboot* and cannot be used with it. Khoros stores configuration files in several directories, and doesn't use TOPDIR the way that *imboot* expects.

Nevertheless, some sets of files work just fine with *imboot* if you connect them to the configuration root */usr/local/lib/config*. There are two ways of doing this:

- **Use a symbolic link**. The first method is to put a symlink under the configuration root directory that points to the directory in which the files are installed. The symlink tells *imboot* how to find the files. For instance, if a set of files named ABC is installed in */path/to/ABC*, make a link to them like this:

  ```
  % ln -s /path/to/ABC /usr/local/lib/config/ABC
  ```

- **Copy the files and modify the self-reference**. The second method is to create a new directory under the configuration root and copy the files into it:

```
% cd /usr/local/lib/config
% mkdir ABC
% cp /path/to/ABC/* ABC
```

After you copy the files, you must also modify the self-reference. (The copies live in a different place than the originals, so they need to know where that is.) Tell the files their new location by modifying ConfigDir. Change into */usr/local/lib/config/ABC* and override the value of ConfigDir in *Project.tmpl* by defining it in *site.def* like this:

```
#ifndef ConfigDir
#define ConfigDir /usr/local/lib/config/ABC
#endif
```

Either method allows *imboot* to bootstrap Makefiles using the ABC files:

```
% imboot -c ABC
```

Which method is better? It depends. The symlink method is easier, certainly. If you don't expect to make any modifications to the configuration files, it may be the more suitable method. On the other hand, if you want to make changes to the files, it's better to use the copy-and-modify method. For example, working on copies is a good way to test the effect of changes to a set of production files without affecting people using the "real" files. Since the copies are independent of the original files, you can do whatever you want to them while leaving the originals alone. With a symlink, you're really modifying the files in the directory the symlink points to, i.e., the originals.

Now let's see how the symlink and copy-and-modify methods can be applied to some popular sets of configuration files to allow them to be used with *imboot*. As examples, we'll look at the files from X11, Motif, and OpenWindows.

Using imboot with X11

It's easy to use the X11 files with *imboot*. To use the symlink method, do this:

```
% ln -s /usr/X11R6.1/lib/X11/config /usr/local/lib/config/X11R6.1
```

To use the copy-and-modify method, create a directory under the configuration root and copy the X11 files into it:

```
% cd /usr/local/lib/config
% mkdir X11R6.1
% cp /usr/X11R6.1/lib/X11/config/* X11R6.1
```

Then modify the self-reference. Change into */usr/local/lib/config/X11R6.1* and define ConfigDir in *site.def* like this:

```
#ifndef ConfigDir
#define ConfigDir /usr/local/lib/config/X11R6.1
#endif
```

With either method, you can use *imboot* to bootstrap Makefiles using the X11 configuration files:

```
% imboot -c X11R6.1
```

The preceding discussion demonstrates that it's at least possible to use *imboot* with the X11 configuration files. It's reasonable to ask whether there are circumstances under which it's actually preferable to do so. After all, although the following two commands are equivalent, the first is certainly easier to type:

```
% xmkmf
% imboot -c X11R6.1
```

The answer is that *imboot* is indeed preferable, under at least two circumstances. The first occurs when you need to bootstrap an X-based *Makefile* and you're not in the root directory of your project. The second occurs when you need to manage multiple releases of X11 (for example, if you're migrating from R5 to R6 or to R6.1). The advantages of *imboot* in these situations are described below.

Bootstrapping in project subdirectories

xmkmf can bootstrap Makefiles within the X11 distribution, and it can also be used for other X-based projects. However, in projects located outside the X11 distribution, *xmkmf* generates partially misconfigured Makefiles in all directories but the project root. That's because *xmkmf* configures TOP to be "." (the current directory) by default. This is a problem if your Imakefiles refer to various project directories in terms of TOP, since "." is the correct value for TOP only in the project root.

You can try specifying the path to the project root on the *xmkmf* command line to make the value of TOP be correct. But the way *xmkmf* works is that if you tell it where the top of your project tree is, it assumes you also want to look for configuration files within the project. That makes sense in the context of configuring X11 itself, since you may not have installed its configuration files yet: by specifying the path to the project root, you also tell *xmkmf* how to find the configuration files located within the X11 distribution. However, when you have a project located outside the X11 distribution tree, looking in the project for configuration files doesn't work.

imboot doesn't behave the same way. It doesn't determine whether to use public or within-project configuration files based on the presence or absence of a project root argument. It makes that decision based on whether you specify a −*c* option. If you do, *imboot* uses public files; otherwise, it looks for the files within the project.

To see how *xmkmf* and *imboot* operate differently, suppose you're down one level in a multiple-directory project. In this case, ".." is the path to the project root. Attempts to use *xmkmf* to bootstrap the *Makefile* produce the following incorrect results:

```
% xmkmf
imake -DUseInstalled -I/usr/X11R6.1/lib/X11/config
% xmkmf ..
mv -f Makefile Makefile.bak
imake -I../config/cf -DTOPDIR=.. -DCURDIR=.
cpp: "Imakefile.c", line 3: error 4036: Can't open include file 'Imake.tmpl'.
```

The first command generates a *Makefile*, but incorrectly uses "." (the default value) as the value of TOP. The second command correctly uses ".." as the path to the top of the project, but incorrectly looks for configuration files within the project, and therefore fails to generate a *Makefile*.

With *imboot* there are no such problems since you can specify the project root and the configuration files independently:

```
% imboot -c X11R6.1 ..
mv Makefile Makefile.bak
imake -DUseInstalled -I/usr/local/lib/config/X11R6.1 -DTOPDIR=.. -DCURDIR=.
```

This command configures TOP correctly as ".." and it uses X11 configuration files that are installed publicly rather than trying to find them within the project.

Coordinating multiple X11 releases

imboot can be used to manage different releases of a project, which is important when you're migrating to a newer release. For example, X11 is at Release 6.1 as I write, but you might be at X11R5 and considering how to upgrade. The upgrade involves building and installing the R6.1 distribution itself, and you may also wish to verify that other X-based projects can be configured using the R6.1 files and run against the R6.1 server. You can cut over to the newer release when you're satisfied that everything works properly, but until then you have a transition period. A typical strategy for migrating between project releases is to maintain both releases online for a while.[*] That way you can test R6.1 but fall back to R5 as necessary if you run into problems.

---

* You probably don't want to wipe out your R5 installation by installing R6.1 right on top of it. It's more prudent to leave R5 in place and install R6.1 in a different location. You can accomplish this by defining ProjectRoot in *site.def*, e.g., as */usr/X11R6.1*. (If you don't define ProjectRoot, you'll install the R6.1 configuration files in */usr/lib/X11/config*, the default installation directory for R5.)

One difficulty of maintaining both R5 and R6.1 online is that it can be difficult to access the configuration files from each release. R5 *xmkmf* expects the original files to be located in $(TOP)/*config* within the R5 distribution and the installed files to be in */usr/lib/X11/config*. By contrast, R6.1 *xmkmf* expects the files to be located in $(TOP)/*config/cf* within the R6.1 distribution and installed in */usr/X11R6.1/lib/X11/config*. But since the bootstrappers from both distributions have the same name, *xmkmf*, it's not clear which set of files you'll get when you execute this command:

```
% xmkmf
```

imboot can help by giving you the ability to switch easily between the R5 and R6.1 configuration files however you like. And it's obvious with *imboot* which set of files you'll get, since you specify the set yourself using the −c option.

To use *imboot* this way, first you need to connect both the R5 and R6.1 files to the *imboot* configuration root directory */usr/local/lib/config*. The procedure for X11R6.1 was outlined earlier in this chapter.* For X11R5, the procedure is similar, except that the files will likely be installed in */usr/lib/X11/config*. To use a symlink, do this:

```
% ln -s /usr/lib/X11/config /usr/local/lib/config/X11R5
```

To copy the files, do this:

```
% cd /usr/local/lib/config
% mkdir X11R5
% cp /usr/lib/X11/config/* X11R5
```

Then change the self-reference in */usr/local/lib/config/X11R5* by defining Config-Dir in *site.def* as follows:

```
#ifndef ConfigDir
#define ConfigDir /usr/local/lib/config/X11R5
#endif
```

Once you have both sets of configuration files connected to the configuration root, use *imboot* −c to select the set of files you want. To configure a project with the R5 files, do this:

```
% imboot -c X11R5
```

---

* The procedure is the same if you have X11R6 except that you replace "X11R6.1" with "X11R6".

To reconfigure the project using the R6.1 files so you can test it against the R6.1 distribution, do this:

```
% imboot -c X11R6.1
```

Follow each *imboot* command with *make Makefiles* if the project has subdirectories.

Using imboot with Motif

Motif is closely related to X11, and in fact uses X11 configuration files. However, it has configuration requirements that go beyond what's provided by the X11 files. The additional configuration support is implemented in the Motif distribution by combining a set of X11 files with the Motif-specific configuration files *Motif.tmpl* and *Motif.rules*.

To bootstrap Makefiles for Motif-based projects using *imboot* and the configuration files distributed with Motif, use the procedure described below, which works for Motif versions 1.2 through 2.0. Motif currently expects to be used with X11R5, so I assume you have R5 header files and libraries installed.

The symlink method isn't suitable for integrating the configuration files supplied with the Motif distribution into the *imboot* configuration root directory */usr/local/lib/config*, because some modifications are necessary that are unlike any others we've made in this chapter. The copy-and-modify method is a better choice in this situation because it allows arbitrary modifications to be made without affecting the original files.

First, copy the files. If */path/to/Motif* is the pathname to the top of the Motif distribution, you can use these commands:

```
% cd /usr/local/lib/config
% mkdir Motif
% cp /path/to/Motif/config/* Motif
```

Then change directory into */usr/local/lib/config/Motif* and define `ConfigDir` in *site.def* like this:

```
#ifndef ConfigDir
#define ConfigDir /usr/local/lib/config/Motif
#endif
```

Now you must make a couple of additional modifications:

- If you want to use installed Motif header files and libraries, define the Use-InstalledMotif macro. Otherwise Makefiles will expect to find them in the Motif source tree. Put the following lines in *site.def*:

  ```
  #ifndef UseInstalledMotif
  #define UseInstalledMotif
  #endif
  ```

  In general, I recommend that you use installed Motif header files and libraries rather than relying on those files being available in the Motif source tree. If you run a *make clean* command in that tree, builds of your Motif-based projects will start failing.

- If your *Motif.tmpl* file contains the following construct (it's present from release 1.2.1 on), remove it:

  ```
  #if defined(UseInstalled) && !defined(UseInstalledMotif)
    IRULESRC = $(CONFIGSRC)
   IMAKE_CMD = $(IMAKE) -DUseInstalled -I$(NEWTOP)$(IRULESRC) $(IMAKE_DEFINES)
  #endif
  ```

  These lines reset IMAKE_CMD so that it sometimes looks in the Motif source tree for configuration files. That's not what you want when you're using files installed under the *imboot* configuration root.

After performing the preceding procedure, you can bootstrap Makefiles for Motif projects as follows:

```
% imboot -c Motif
```

As an alternative to using the full set of configuration files distributed with Motif, you can use just the Motif-specific files (*Motif.tmpl* and *Motif.rules*) and combine them with a set of X11 files that you provide. There are at least two circumstances under which this is an attractive option:

- You're already using a set of X11 files that you've modified to reflect local site-specific conventions. By reusing those files, you avoid having to make the same changes to the files provided with Motif.

- Since Motif as currently shipped is set up to be used with X11R5, its configuration files are R5-based. If you want to use Motif with R6 or R6.1, you must use different X11 files.

If you want to pursue the option of combining *Motif.tmpl* and *Motif.rules* with a different set of X11 files than those distributed with Motif, read the Motif configuration document listed in Appendix I, *Other Sources of Information*.

Using imboot with OpenWindows

Like Motif, OpenWindows is closely related to X11, uses configuration files based on X11, and has configuration requirements that go beyond those of X11. However, OpenWindows systems present a special difficulty in that you may need to fix the configuration support that Sun ships before you can use *imake* at all. That's a separate issue from the question of how to use the OpenWindows configuration files with *imboot*, and you must address it first.

Briefly, if you have a version of OpenWindows older than 3.3, your *imake* support probably needs to be modified. If you have OpenWindows version 3.3 or higher, your *imake* support should work reasonably well, although there are still some modifications you can make to improve it. A description of the problems present in various versions of OpenWindows, and how to deal with them, is given in Appendix J, *Using imake with OpenWindows.* I advise you to read that discussion and apply any modifications that may be needed on your system before you proceed further with this section.

Assuming your OpenWindows *imake* support is functional, you can integrate the configuration files into the *imboot* configuration root using either the symlink or copy-and-modify methods. To use a symlink, make a link under the configuration root */usr/local/lib/config* to the directory containing the OpenWindows configuration files:

```
% ln -s /usr/openwin/lib/config /usr/local/lib/config/OW
```

To copy the files instead, do this:

```
% cd /usr/local/lib/config
% mkdir OW
% cp /usr/openwin/lib/config/* OW
```

Then change directory into */usr/local/lib/config/OW* and define `ConfigDir` in *site.def* like this:

```
#ifndef ConfigDir
#define ConfigDir /usr/local/lib/config/OW
#endif
```

Now you can use *imboot* to bootstrap Makefiles using the OpenWindows configuration files:

```
% imboot -c OW
```

If you need to be able to switch between the OpenWindows and X11 configuration files, *imboot* makes it easy. Just use −*c* to select the set of configuration files you want. The OpenWindows version of *xmkmf* can select either set, too, but not so easily: to select the X11 files, you must unset the OPENWINHOME environment variable.* However, that's likely to cause other OpenWindows applications to fail. With *imboot* you don't have to take that risk since you can leave OPENWINHOME set to its usual value.

Using imboot in Makefiles

When you're developing a project, you can build the initial *Makefile* with *imboot* and use the *Makefile* to rebuild itself with *make Makefile* thereafter, as long as you remain on a single machine. When you move the project to another machine, the Makefile entry in the *Makefile* becomes invalid if it generates an *imake* command containing an explicit reference to the pathname of the configuration file directory on the original machine. That directory's location can vary among systems—e.g., it might be under */usr/local/lib/config* on one machine and under */var/lib/config* on another. Thus, in general you can't expect the Makefile entry in a *Makefile* created on one machine to work properly on another.

You can, of course, run the bootstrapper again on the second machine to regenerate the *Makefile* there. But another approach is to rewrite the rule that generates the *imake* command so that it generates an *imboot* command instead. With *imboot*, you don't supply the location of the configuration files. Instead, you supply their name and let *imboot* figure out where they are. Since the name remains constant from machine to machine, the *imboot* command can be invoked in a machine-independent manner.

The implication is that, although a *Makefile* built for one machine may be misconfigured in many or most respects for another machine, we can get it to do at least one thing reliably—generate an *imboot* command to rebuild itself so it *is* properly configured.

Before we can write a rule that invokes *imboot*, we need some parameters in the configuration files. *imboot* is a general-purpose program, so it's set up in *Imake.tmpl*, along with the command that invokes it:

```
#ifndef ImbootCmd
#define ImbootCmd imboot      /* assume it's publicly installed */
#endif
        IMBOOT = ImbootCmd
#ifdef UseInstalled
    IMBOOT_CMD = $(IMBOOT) -c $(CONFIGNAME)
#else
    IMBOOT_CMD = $(IMBOOT)
#endif
```

---

* OpenWindows *xmkmf* uses the configuration files located in $OPENWINHOME/*lib/config* if OPENWIN-HOME is set, and the X11 configuration files in */usr/lib/X11/config* otherwise.

The name of the configuration file set (CONFIGNAME) is specific to those files, so it goes in *Project.tmpl*. The name should be defined appropriately for your set of files. For a set named XYZ, the information looks like this:

```
#ifndef ConfigName
#define ConfigName XYZ
#endif
    CONFIGNAME = ConfigName
```

Now we need to rewrite the rule that generates the Makefile target entry. For the X11 or SP files, we can replace the definition of MakefileTarget() in *Imake.rules* with the one below:

```
#ifndef MakefileTarget
#define MakefileTarget()                          @@\
Makefile::                                        @@\
    $(IMBOOT_CMD) $(TOP) $(CURRENT_DIR)
#endif  /* MakefileTarget */
```

To use the rule, invoke MakefileTarget() in your *Imakefile*, and build the initial *Makefile* with *imboot*. Thereafter, you don't need to know anything but a couple of *make* commands to reconfigure the project on any machine on which *imboot* and the proper set of configuration files are installed. You can move the project to the other machine and rebuild the Makefiles like this:

```
% make Makefile
% make Makefiles                  (If the project has subdirectories)
```

Furthermore, if MakefileTarget() is invoked in the final section of *Imake.tmpl* (as it is in the X11 and SP files), the Makefile target entry will be included automatically in every *Makefile*. Then you don't have to invoke the rule in individual Imakefiles.

Introduction to Configuration File Writing

Simplify, simplify.
—Thoreau, *Walden*

When you develop a new set of configuration files, you have essentially two choices: write everything from scratch, or copy and modify existing files. We'll take the easier path and use the starter project developed in Chapter 9, *A Configuration Starter Project*, to create a new project containing configuration files; this will allow us to write Imakefiles for building and installing C programs and libraries of moderate complexity.

The purpose of this chapter isn't to create a set of super-whiz-bang configuration files. It's to demonstrate the process you go through to develop any set of files. Thus, I'll call this the demonstration project (DP).

Even when you begin with existing files, the process by which you modify one set of files to create another involves a sustained effort. This chapter discusses how to set up the DP files—how to decide what to keep, what to throw out, and what to add. Another important aspect of configuration file development is rule writing. That's a major topic in itself and is discussed separately in Chapter 12, *Writing Rule Macros*. For discussion of other miscellaneous issues that are involved in configuration file writing but aren't specifically related to the DP files, see Chapter 13, *Configuration Problems and Solutions*.

The DP distribution is available for examination (see Appendix A, *Obtaining Configuration Software*), and I recommend that you make use of it. The files in the DP distribution and the SP files from which they're derived differ extensively, and for some of the types of changes we'll be making, there is space here to show only representative examples. If you want to determine in detail the full scope of the modifications involved at each stage of the derivation, the distribution contains *diff* listings you can inspect.

Setting Up

Begin by making a copy of the starter project and moving into it. Assuming the starter project is located under your curent directory, do this:

```
% cp -r SP DP
% cd DP
```

If you expect to install the files for public use, do the following:

- Create a project root *Imakefile* like the following:

    ```
    #define IHaveSubdirs
    #define PassCDebugFlags

    SUBDIRS = config

    MakeSubdirs($(SUBDIRS))
    DependSubdirs($(SUBDIRS))
    ```

- Move into the *config* directory and create an *Imakefile*:

    ```
    FILES = *.tmpl *.rules site.def *.cf

    all::
    depend::

    InstallMultipleDestFlags(install,$(FILES),$(CONFIGDIR),$(INSTDATFLAGS))
    ```

- Edit *Project.tmpl* to change the value of ConfigDir from */usr/local/lib/config/SP* to */usr/local/lib/config/DP*.

- Move back up into the project root and verify that the DP project can build its own Makefiles and that it knows where to install the configuration files:

    ```
    % cd ..
    % imboot
    % make Makefiles
    % make -n install
    ```

    The output of the last command should confirm that */usr/local/lib/config/DP* will be used as the installation directory when you're ready to install the files. (To perform the installation later, you repeat the *make install* command, leaving off the *−n* option.)

Now we're ready to begin surgery.

When you create new configuration files by copying existing ones, there are only a few things you can do with their contents:

- **Delete information**. Information in the original files can be removed if it's superfluous to your requirements.

- **Retain information**. If a macro, rule, or parameter variable is useful to you, keep it instead of throwing it out.

- **Add information**. When the files don't provide the capabilities you need, extend them by adding new information.

The following sections show how to modify your configuration files in these ways and discuss the issues involved when you do so. As you read, make sure you're in the *config* directory, since that's where the files are located.

Deleting Information

We'll delete information first to make the configuration files easier to work with. To do this effectively, you need to understand your goals, so you know what result you're aiming for. You also need to understand the files you're modifying, so you can determine how the goals for which they were originally written overlap with your own and how they differ. That means you need to understand something about the X11 files, because the DP files are ultimately derived from the X11 files (Figure 11–1). If you're not familiar with the design and use of the X11 files, you should probably first take a look at Chapter 5, *The X11 Configuration Files*, and Chapter 6, *Writing Imakefiles*.

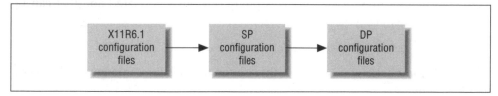

Figure 11–1: DP configuration file ancestry

Our goal is to be able to build and install moderately complex C programs and libraries. This isn't as ambitious a goal as being able to configure the X11 project. Consequently, our configuration files initially contain many symbols we don't need, and can thus remove to make the files simpler. The next section covers several areas we can whittle away at. These deal with support for C++ and FORTRAN programming, the X Window System, and shared libraries.

C++ *and FORTRAN Support*

The configuration files provide some support for C++ and FORTRAN programming. This information is found primarily in *Imake.tmpl* and *Imake.rules*, but also in some of the other **.tmpl* and **.cf* files. Since we're interested in C here, we can jettison the following C++ symbols:

Macros
   CCsuf and other macros with Cplusplus in their names

Variables
   Variables with CXX in their names

Rules
   Rules with Cplusplus in their names

The following FORTRAN symbols can also be removed:

Macros
   HasFortran, FortranCmd, FortranFlags, and FortranDebugFlags

Variables
   FC, FDEBUGFLAGS, and FCFLAGS

Rule
   NormalFortranObjectRule()

X11 *Support*

You'll find most of the X-specific symbols in *Project.tmpl*, *Imake.rules*, and the **.cf* files. One symbol in *Project.tmpl* that's pretty obviously X-related and that can be safely removed is ProjectX:

```
#define ProjectX  6   /* do *not* change this line */
```

Throw caution to the winds, ignore the admonition in the comment, and remove the definition.

Other discardable symbols pertain to:

X libraries
   XLIB, DEPXLIB, DebugLibX, etc.

The X11 server
   BuildServer, ConnectionFlags, SERVERSRC, etc.

X utilities and auxiliary programs
   BuildFontServer, InstallFSConfig, RGB, SetTtyGroup, etc.

X-related rules

ServerTarget(), FontTarget(), MakeFonts(), etc.

There are also some files that can be removed completely, such as *Threads.tmpl*, *Server.tmpl*, *xfree86.cf*, and *xf86.rules*.

These lists of symbols aren't exhaustive, as you'll discover when you start paring down the files. (Remember that you can retrieve the DP distribution and use the *diff* listings to determine the full extent of the changes at each step.)

Shared Library Support

Shared library development is a miasma we're going to avoid altogether, so we can delete symbols relating to it. Begin with the vendor files. Some of them contain #include directives that can be removed because they refer to files containing shared library rules. The files have names of the form **Lib.rules* and we can find the references to them like so:

```
% grep "include.*Lib\.rules" *.cf
FreeBSD.cf:#include <bsdLib.rules>
NetBSD.cf:#include <bsdLib.rules>
Oki.cf:#include <sv4Lib.rules>
fujitsu.cf:#include <sv4Lib.rules>
hp.cf:#include <hpLib.rules>
ibm.cf:#include <ibmLib.rules>
linux.cf:#include <lnxLib.rules>
moto.cf:#include <sv4Lib.rules>
nec.cf:#include <necLib.rules>
osf1.cf:#include <osfLib.rules>
sco.cf:#include <scoLib.rules>   /* minor changes to sv4Lib.rules */
sco.cf:#include <sv4Lib.rules>
sgi.cf:#include <sgiLib.rules>
sony.cf:#include <sv4Lib.rules>
sun.cf:#include <sunLib.rules>
svr4.cf:#include <sv4Lib.rules>
x386.cf:/* #include <sv3Lib.rules> */  /* not working yet */
x386.cf:#include <sv4Lib.rules>
```

The command output tells you which lines to remove from which files. For editing, you can grab all the affected files at once as follows:

```
% vi 'grep -l "include.*Lib\.rules" *.cf'
```

Each **Lib.rules* file defines symbols for building shared libraries and also defines ShLibIncludeFile as the name of a related **Lib.tmpl* file (e.g., *sunLib.rules* defines it as *sunLib.tmpl*). In turn, ShLibIncludeFile is referenced by the following section of *Project.tmpl*, which you should delete:

```
#ifndef ShLibIncludeFile
/* need this to make ANSI-style preprocessors happy */
#define ShLibIncludeFile <noop.rules>
#endif

#include ShLibIncludeFile
```

You can also remove the **Lib.rules* and **Lib.tmpl* files; they won't be needed:

```
% rm -f *Lib.rules *Lib.tmpl
```

Imake.tmpl, Imake.rules, Project.tmpl, Library.tmpl, and some vendor files contain symbols that relate to shared libraries and can be excised: HasSharedLibraries, SHAREDCODEDEF, SHLIBDEF, PositionIndependentCFFlags, etc. (Many shared library symbols, such as SharedLibX, are connected with X11 support, so they'll already have been removed.)

Imake.rules and some vendor files contain definitions for macros that generate references for shared library names and rules that generate shared library target entries: SharedLibReferences(), SharedDSLibReferences(), SharedLibrary-Target(), etc. These can all be deleted. (Don't remove UnsharedLib-References(), however.)

If you wish, you can apply a similar procedure to remove profiling and debugging library support.

Miscellaneous Symbol-Deleting Guidelines

Modifications to the configuration files should always be made in accordance with your goals. For example, since I'm not going to discuss shared libraries here, I deleted support for them so I could simplify the files. You might consider it crucial to be able to develop shared libraries. If so, by all means retain the information related to that kind of development. Similarly, if you're interested in writing C++ programs, don't delete the C++ information.

Wholesale deletion of information is the quickest way to reduce the complexity of the configuration files you're working with. However, you need to temper your zeal to simplify the files against the possibility of breaking them by going too far. Keep the following principles in mind as you brandish your scimitar—they'll help you avoid making deletions you'll regret and have to undo:

- If you don't understand what a symbol is used for, it's safer to leave it in than to remove it and possibly break your configuration files. Wait until you understand the symbol's use before deciding whether to delete it.

- If you do understand a symbol but you're not sure whether or not you'll need it, leave it in until you're sure you won't need it.

- If you remove a symbol, you must remove other symbols that depend on it. Stated another way, if you don't remove a symbol, you can't remove any symbols it depends on either. Consider the following definition from *Imake.tmpl*:

```
#ifndef StandardCppDefines
#define StandardCppDefines StandardDefines
#endif
```

  StandardCppDefines depends on StandardDefines, so if you were to remove StandardDefines, you'd also have to remove StandardCppDefines. Conversely, if you don't remove StandardCppDefines, you can't remove StandardDefines.

- When you're checking symbol dependencies, you may need to track down interactions involving *cpp* macros and *make* variables. Here's an example from *Imake.tmpl*:

```
#ifndef ManPath
#define ManPath ManDirectoryRoot
#endif
#ifndef ManSourcePath
#define ManSourcePath $(MANPATH)/man
#endif

MANPATH = ManPath
```

This tells us that ManSourcePath is defined in terms of MANPATH, which gets its value from ManPath, which in turn gets its value from ManDirectoryRoot. The chain of dependencies means that if we delete ManDirectoryRoot, we must also delete ManPath, MANPATH, and ManSourcePath as well.

As you're trying to decide what can and can't be removed from your configuration files, remember this: *grep* is your friend. You can use it to locate all instances of a symbol in the files, which will help you determine from context what the symbol is used for. *grep* can also help you trace through a symbol's interactions with other symbols.

A Shocking Fact

Strictly speaking, you don't need to remove extraneous information from the configuration files. In other words, you can completely skip all the instructions I've given so far about getting rid of stuff from the DP files! And, admittedly, it's easier to leave superfluous information alone than to take the trouble to remove it.

However, if you do that, your files will contain details that are irrelevant to your purposes and present simply because they were in the original files, not because they're related to your goals. This will be confusing later—to you after you've forgotten just why you left them in, and to others who'll be unsure why symbols with no apparent purpose are there. Remember: the more complex your files are, the harder they are to understand. If you can legitimately get rid of something (that is, you understand its purpose and know you don't need it), it's best to do so for simplicity's sake.

Retaining Information

We've removed a large portion of the original contents of our files, but there's still quite a bit left because they contain a lot of information we can keep for our own use. Some examples are:

- The definitions of YES and NO

- The vendor blocks

- The token-pasting rules Concat(), Concat3(), and Concat4()

- The BootstrapCFlags, OSMajorVersion, OSMinorVersion, and OSTeeny-Version macros

- The SystemV and SystemV4 macros used for determining system characteristics

- Rules, macros, and parameters for:

  — Building Makefiles: IMAKE, IMAKE_CMD, IMAKE_DEFINES, IRULESRC, CONFIGDIR, ConfigDir, CONFIGSRC, ConfigSrc, MakefileTarget(), etc.

  — Generating header file dependencies: UseCCMakeDepend, DEPEND, DependTarget(), DependTarget3(), etc.

  — Cleaning up: RmCmd, RM, RM_CMD, FilesToClean, ExtraFilesToClean, CleanTarget(), etc.

- The final section of *Imake.tmpl* (everything past the point where the *Imakefile* is included). This section invokes several common rules automatically so you don't have to.

- The rules that allow you to perform recursive *make* operations for managing multiple-directory projects. Most often these have names ending with Subdirs, such as CleanSubdirs(), InstallSubdirs(), and LintSubdirs().

Modifying Retained Information

Sometimes when we retain a construct we need to modify it slightly. `BinDir` is useful for specifying the program installation directory, but its original default value is */usr/X11R6.1/bin*, which is X specific:[*]

```
#ifndef BinDir
#ifdef ProjectRoot
#define BinDir Concat(ProjectRoot,/bin)
#else
#define BinDir /usr/bin/X11
#endif
#endif
```

If you want a more generic value like */usr/local/bin*, change the default to this:

```
#ifndef BinDir
#define BinDir /usr/local/bin
#endif
```

Simplifying Retained Information

Constructs in the original configuration files that are useful to you but unnecessarily complex can be retained but simplified. For example, the original definition of `UsrLibDir` looks like this (indentation added):

```
#ifndef UsrLibDir
#  ifdef ProjectRoot
#    define UsrLibDir Concat(ProjectRoot,/lib)
#    ifndef AlternateUsrLibDir
#      define AlternateUsrLibDir YES
#    endif
#  else
#    define UsrLibDir /usr/lib
#    ifndef AlternateUsrLibDir
#      define AlternateUsrLibDir NO
#    endif
#  endif
#else
#  ifndef AlternateUsrLibDir
#    define AlternateUsrLibDir YES
#  endif
#endif
```

---

[*] `ProjectRoot` is defined by default in *site.def* as */usr/X11R6.1*, so `BinDir` by default becomes */usr/X11R6.1/bin*. If `ProjectRoot` is left undefined, `BinDir` becomes */usr/bin/X11*.

If you don't have any use for specifying an alternate */usr/lib* directory, this can be simplified as follows:

```
#ifndef UsrLibDir
#define UsrLibDir /usr/lib
#endif
```

The final section of the template *Imake.tmpl* automatically invokes a number of helpful rules for you to generate some commonly used targets. Part of it that can be simplified looks like this:

```
#ifdef MakefileAdditions
MakefileAdditions()
#endif
```

If you search through the X11 distribution to determine how `MakefileAdditions` is used, you'll discover that it's not used at all. Since this symbol is employed nowhere in the X11 distribution, it's unlikely that we'll need it, either. We can dump the `MakefileAdditions` stuff completely.

Modifications like these are relatively minor, but their cumulative effect can make your configuration files significantly easier to understand.

Adding Information

We've removed several types of information from our configuration files, e.g., macros, parameter variables, and rule definitions. We've also removed part of the section of the template that invokes rules for us automatically. Thus, we've reduced the bulk of our original files considerably and simplified some of what remains.

Now it's time to start adding new information, which is essentially a reversal of the process of deleting it. Adding new macros and parameters is relatively simple; so is adding new rule invocations to the end of the template. Those subjects are discussed below. By contrast, rule writing is an extensive topic and is deferred until Chapter 12.

Adding Macros and Parameter Variables

As discussed in Chapter 3, *Understanding Configuration Files*, when you need a new parameter, you usually express it using the idiom of a *make* variable that's set to the value of a *cpp* macro. The macro should be given a default value in the same file as that in which the variable assignment occurs:

```
#ifndef MacroName
#define MacroName value
```

```
#endif
VARNAME = MacroName
```

Some parameter variables are given values entirely in terms of other variables, in which case there is no corresponding *cpp* macro. CFLAGS is one of these:

```
CFLAGS = $(CDEBUGFLAGS) $(CCOPTIONS) $(ALLDEFINES)
```

Conversely, some macros have no corresponding variable. These are usually used as Booleans (i.e., given a value of YES or NO) to indicate whether particular system facilities or characteristics are present, or whether or not to do something. For example, HasPutenv indicates whether the *putenv()* library function is available. RemoveTargetProgramByMoving indicates whether to rename *program* to *program˜* when a new version is built so the old version remains available (if not, the old version is simply overwritten).

Choosing Default Macro Values

When you create a new macro, you must provide a default value. Make sure it's the best value you can come up with for the largest number of cases, and that the value isn't "dangerous." The following sections describe how to do this.

Choose defaults as well as you can

The idiom of specifying parameter variables in terms of *cpp* macros allows parameter assignments to be placed in the template or project files along with default values that can be overridden. Vendor files specify macro values for a given platform that differ from the defaults. This idiom embodies the general principle of providing a reference or baseline configuration against which it's necessary only to specify variations.

There's a lesson in this for us as configuration file writers: the more accurate we can be about guessing appropriate default values in the template and project files, the less often we'll have to override them in the vendor files.

Suppose we're specifying a parameter for the flag that tells *lint* to create a *lint* library. We could write the following in *Imake.tmpl*:

```
#ifndef LintLibFlag
#define LintLibFlag -C
#endif

LINTLIBFLAG = LintLibFlag
```

Unfortunately, that's only correct for the BSD variant of *lint*. The System V variant requires *-o* instead of *-C*. If we use the default definition given above for the DP project, we'd need to override it in more than half of the more than 30 vendor files. That's a lot of overriding. If we choose *-o* as the default instead, the situation is only a little better.

The job can be made easier by using the SystemV and SystemV4 symbols to select the default value of LintLibFlag (and this is, in fact, exactly what the X11 configuration files do):

```
#ifndef LintLibFlag
#if SystemV || SystemV4
#define LintLibFlag -o
#else
#define LintLibFlag -C
#endif
#endif

LINTLIBFLAG = LintLibFlag
```

This does a better job of choosing the default and reduces to two the number of vendor files in which the default needs to be overridden.

Choose macro defaults conservatively

When you pick a default value for a macro that specifies how to do something, you often have to choose between two competing alternatives. For instance, there is code in the X Toolkit library that copies objects that can be larger than a byte and that can be located at arbitrary addresses. The library implements a method that's fast and efficient but depends on the CPU being able to access word and long word quantities that aren't necessarily aligned to word boundaries. Not all processors can do that, so the library also implements a byte-by-byte copy method that's slower but works on all machines.

When you provide two methods like this, you need a way to specify in the configuration files which one to use. In the case of the Xt library, the choice is between an efficient method that doesn't work on all processors and a universal method that runs more slowly. The X11 configuration files provide an UnalignedReferencesAllowed macro indicating whether the processor can perform word accesses at addresses not aligned to word boundaries. What should the default be?

Follow the principle of choosing a default that allows your programs to build and run on as many machines as possible. If an optimization is available to make a program run faster but it doesn't work universally, it's dangerous: allow it to be selected from the vendor file but don't make it the default. Err on the side of caution and choose the more conservative method that always works:

```
#ifndef UnalignedReferencesAllowed
#define UnalignedReferencesAllowed NO
#endif
```

Then, for any processor allowing arbitrary references, use the vendor file to indicate that the faster method can be used for better performance:

```
#ifndef UnalignedReferencesAllowed
#define UnalignedReferencesAllowed YES
#endif
```

You might wonder whether it really matters which default you choose. After all, when you develop your configuration files, you'll certainly make sure the default is overridden as necessary in all the vendor files. So it shouldn't make any difference whether or not you choose the more conservative value, right?

Wrong. You aren't necessarily the only person who'll use your configuration files. If others port your software to a machine on which it's never been built, they'll need to write a new vendor file. They won't understand your configuration files as well as you do, so minimize what someone must know about them by providing defaults that are as reasonable as possible. This way the software works with no modification, but effort spent in selecting optimizations pays a dividend.

In this context, a default value of NO for UnalignedReferencesAllowed is reasonable. The code will run on any system—more slowly than necessary on some systems, perhaps, but at least it won't crash mysteriously on others.

Sooner or later you'll write code that you know works on your own machines but won't work on certain other machines unless you plan for that in advance, i.e., unless you write it portably. It's tempting to just get the code to run locally. This mindset easily carries over into the design of configuration files: "This only needs to work at our site on our Alpha and our Ultra"; "We only have little-endian machines"; "Our machines are all BSD-based"; etc. For instance, if all your local machines can do unaligned word accesses, it's tempting to forget about making sure your copy routines work on machines that can't do such accesses. In that case, you might not even bother to create a macro like UnalignedReferences-Allowed for expressing the machine-dependency, even though it reduces the portability of your software if you don't.

If you can safely assume that your machines are going to run forever and you'll never get different ones, and you'll never get a new job somewhere else and want to take some of your software with you, and no one anywhere will ever want any of your programs, then fine. Go ahead and write your configuration files with limited portability in mind. Otherwise, design for a wide audience. If you assume someone else will be using your configuration files, it can make a lot of difference in your outlook on how generally you write them. This will help you write your configuration files so they won't require a lot of patching up later.

Subdirectory Support

In Chapter 6 we discussed how the X11 configuration files allow projects comprising multiple directories to be managed easily. This is done through the use of recursive rules (which the X11 files provide in abundance). The DP files ultimately derive from the X11 files, so the same rules are available to us. It's important to retain them[*] because recursive operations are one of the trickier things you can use *make* for, one of the most difficult to write *Makefile* entries for, and one of the easiest to get wrong. *imake* helps you with them two ways:

- *imake* lets you encapsulate recursive entries in the form of rule macros. Then you only need to figure out how to write each type of entry once. After that, you can propagate them into your Makefiles easily, simply by invoking them in your Imakefiles.

- Since *imake* provides a means for explicitly representing experience in configuring software, you can take advantage of someone else's hard-won knowledge by appropriating already-written rules from a set of configuration files in which the recursive rules are known to work. So usually you don't have to write the rules even once.

In addition to carrying over recursive rules from the X11 files to the DP files, we've also retained the final section of *Imake.tmpl*, which invokes a number of recursive rules for you to help automate their use. Thus, for rules such as `InstallSubdirs()` and `CleanSubdirs()`, it isn't necessary to explicitly invoke them in Imakefiles. Essentially, you get recursive `install` and `clean` targets (among others) for free.

However, there are certain useful targets not generated for you by the template, in particular `all` and `depend`. This means that unless you generate those targets yourself from within each *Imakefile* of a project, the *make all* and *make depend* commands won't work uniformly throughout the project tree.

This problem came up when we discussed multiple-directory projects in Chapter 6. There we saw that if a directory has subdirectories, we need to generate recursive `all` and `depend` entries to tell *make* to descend into the directories named by `SUBDIRS`. Since this is true whenever there are subdirectories, we may as well modify the final section of the template to invoke the proper rules for us automatically. Find the part of the template that looks like this:

```
#ifdef IHaveSubdirs
XCOMM ----------------------------------------------------------------------
XCOMM rules for building in SUBDIRS - do not edit
```

---

* Most of them, anyway. If you find some that are not useful for your purposes, you can delete them, of course.

Change it to this:

```
#ifdef IHaveSubdirs
XCOMM ------------------------------------------------------------------------
XCOMM rules for building in SUBDIRS

MakeSubdirs($(SUBDIRS))
DependSubdirs($(SUBDIRS))
```

This modification makes a DP *Imakefile* a little easier to write than the otherwise equivalent X11 *Imakefile*, because there are two fewer rules to invoke.

For a directory without subdirectories, it's less clear what to do about all and depend entries from within the template. We can't say with certainty what it will mean to carry out the all or depend operations for some arbitrary *Makefile*. On the other hand, entries for the all and depend operations still need to be present. Otherwise, when you try to perform those operations project-wide, they'll fail for any *Makefile* that doesn't support them. At the very least, empty all and depend entries need to be present.

Unfortunately, given our inability to predict the *Imakefile* writer's intentions, empty entries are also the most we can provide from within the template. Find the part of the template that applies when there aren't subdirectories:

```
XCOMM ------------------------------------------------------------------------
XCOMM empty rules for directories that do not have SUBDIRS - do not edit
```

Change it to this:

```
XCOMM ------------------------------------------------------------------------
XCOMM empty rules for directories that do not have SUBDIRS

all::
depend::
```

The only purpose of these entries is to prevent the all and depend operations from failing when *make* traverses the project tree. Nevertheless, these entries are empty and they don't cause any actual work to be done. In each *Imakefile*, you must still associate an all entry with each target you want built, and you must still invoke DependTarget() to generate header file dependencies if you're working with C source files.

12

Writing Rule Macros

If at first you don't succeed . . .
—Thomas Palmer, *Teacher's Manual*

In Chapter 11, *Introduction to Configuration File Writing*, we began to develop a new set of configuration files called the demonstration project (DP) files. We continue that process in this chapter, focusing primarily on how to write rule macros. Since the DP files are oriented toward building and installing C programs, we'll design a small set of program development rules. (The DP rules file *Imake.rules* already contains program-building rules, of course. I'm going to pretend they don't exist in order to show the process of developing a set of rules from beginning to end.)

In some cases, a configuration parameter or rule we create in this chapter has the same name as one that is already in the DP files. When this occurs, I'll say whether you can use the version already in the files, or whether you need to replace it with the version we develop here. For example, we write a rule All-Target(), but it's the same as the one that is already in the DP file *Imake.rules*, so you don't actually need to add anything to *Imake.rules*. On the other hand, we write a rule InstallManPage() that has a different definition than the original rule with that name in *Imake.rules*. In this case, you should replace the original version with the one we write.

Rule Syntax

The following list details the syntax used for writing rule macros:

- Define rules using the following form:

```
#define rule-name(rule-parameters)                    @@\
rule-body line 1                                        @@\
...                                                     @@\
rule-body line n-1                                      @@\
rule-body line n
```

  The first line specifies the invocation sequence, those following specify the body of the rule.

- Put @@\ at the end of all lines of a rule but the last.

- Indent lines in the rule definition body the way you want them indented in the *Makefile*. If the line you're writing will end up as a command line in a *Makefile* entry, it must be indented with a tab. If it's intended as a dependency line, don't indent it (make sure there are no leading spaces or tabs). If it's a *make* variable assignment, it can be indented, but use spaces, not tabs.

- Enclose every rule definition within #ifndef/#endif pairs so the rule can be overridden or replaced:

```
#ifndef rule-name
#define rule-name(rule-parameters)                    @@\
rule-body line 1                                        @@\
...                                                     @@\
rule-body line n-1                                      @@\
rule-body line n
#endif /* rule-name */
```

  For brevity, I omit the #ifndef/#endif pairs from all rules discussed in this chapter, but you should always include them in your own definitions.

- Don't put @@\ at the end of #ifndef or #endif lines.

Building the Basic Rule

Let's start by defining a rule BuildProgram() for building C programs. We'll write a simple version and go through several iterations of analyzing it, finding its limitations, and refining it. After you follow through this discussion, you'll have a better idea of what kind of functionality to design into your rules from the start instead of going through the revision process after you've already started using your rules in production.

As a first approximation, `BuildProgram()` can be defined like this:

```
#define BuildProgram(prog,objs)                              @@\
prog: objs                                                   @@\
    cc -o prog objs
```

This definition indicates the target you want built (prog) and the object files from which to build it (objs). `BuildProgram()` as given is sufficient for building simple targets, but since we're not at the end of the chapter yet, it would be best to identify several shortcomings so we have something to talk about:

- Parameterization is lacking. What if you want to use a different C compiler, such as *gcc*? You can edit the rule to change it, but then the rule isn't correct for anyone who wants to use *cc*. We should use $(CC) in the rule body instead of a literal cc. Then, in the other configuration files, we select the value of CC that's appropriate for the system on which the program is built.

- Generality is deficient. The rule can't build programs that require libraries or special linker flags, and it doesn't let us compensate for oddities such as broken "standard" libraries. For instance, some C libraries in early releases of Mips RISC/os are missing *vfprintf()*. Our rule cannot handle special cases like this.

- The rule doesn't work very hard; it produces only the final executable program. It could also generate entries for common useful operations such as a `clean` entry to remove the program after we've built and installed it.

We can address these issues one at a time through incremental revision.

Parameterizing the Rule

The definition of `BuildProgram()` will be more flexible if we refer to the C compiler using a parameter rather than by writing the name literally:

```
#define BuildProgram(prog,objs)                              @@\
prog: objs                                                   @@\
    $(CC) -o prog objs
```

The system parameters section of *Imake.tmpl* must support CC, so make sure the template contains the following:[*]

```
#ifndef CcCmd
#define CcCmd cc
#endif
CC = CcCmd
```

---

* You can use the CcCmd and CC that are already present in the DP *Imake.tmpl* file, although you'll notice the definition of CcCmd there is more complex than the one we're using here.

The usual idiom whereby the value of a *make* variable comes from a corresponding *cpp* macro is used here. The macro CcCmd sets the variable CC. A default value for CcCmd is supplied, but it can be overridden in *site.def* or *vendor.cf*. This allows you to select a different C compiler easily without changing any Imakefiles.

This simple change reflects an important principle: don't write literal names of tools, utilities, etc., into your rule definitions; parameterize them to make them flexible.

Link Libraries

To make BuildProgram() even more general by providing support for libraries, link flags, etc., we must be able to specify more information.

BuildProgram() doesn't let us say whether a program needs any libraries at link time. We could specify them by writing them literally into the rule definition. For instance, to link in the math and terminal capability libraries, we could change the rule to name them on the CC command line:

```
#define BuildProgram(prog,objs)                                          @@\
prog: objs                                                               @@\
    $(CC) -o prog objs -lm -ltermcap
```

This is the wrong way to make a change, because the rule really isn't any more general. The libraries are hardwired in, which isn't useful unless we'll always want exactly those two libraries every time the rule is used. (Not likely!) In general, there's no way to anticipate which libraries a given program will require, so we must let the *Imakefile* writer specify them. This can be done more than one way; I'll show two.

We could rewrite BuildProgram() to refer to a *make* variable BPLIBS to which the *Imakefile* writer can assign a value:

```
#define BuildProgram(prog,objs)                                          @@\
prog: objs                                                               @@\
    $(CC) -o prog objs $(BPLIBS)
```

To use the rule for a single program, you'd put something like this in your *Imakefile*:

```
BPLIBS = -lm -ltermcap
BuildProgram(myprog,myprog.o)
```

Now suppose you want to build a second program *myprog2* that needs the DBM and *termlib* libraries. To make sure each program links correctly, BPLIBS must name the libraries used by both programs:

```
BPLIBS = -lm -ltermcap -ldbm -ltermlib

BuildProgram(myprog,myprog.o)
BuildProgram(myprog2,myprog2.o)
```

As the number of targets you build grows, so does the list of libraries named by BPLIBS. That isn't a problem as far as *make* is concerned, because variables can have long definitions. However, the *Imakefile* becomes less informative because it isn't explicit anywhere which libraries are needed by which program. There is also the possibility of linker conflict: if two libraries happen to provide a function with the same name, you might not get the one you want. (This is not unlikely for the example just shown; the *termcap* and *termlib* libraries are quite similar in purpose.)

Alternatively, we can name libraries for a program by passing them as an argument to BuildProgram(). To do this, we must change its invocation sequence:

```
#define BuildProgram(prog,objs,libs)                                                @@\
prog: objs                                                                          @@\
    $(CC) -o prog objs libs
```

Now libraries can be given on a program-specific basis. That is, different libraries can be specified for each invocation of BuildProgram():

```
BuildProgram(myprog,myprog.o,-lm -ltermcap)
BuildProgram(myprog2,myprog2.o,-ldbm -ltermlib)
```

This approach makes explicit which libraries are needed for each program. It also eliminates the possibility of linker conflict because you pass to each invocation of BuildProgram() the libraries needed for building only one program.

Passing Information to Rules

We happen to be discussing libraries here, but the issue we're confronting is really more general: how can information be transmitted into a rule? As we've just seen, there's more than one way to do it, and each method has its own characteristics.

If you specify information as the value of a *make* variable in the rule definition, the value of the variable applies *Makefile*-wide to all entries produced by invocations of the rule. If you pass the information as an argument to a rule when you invoke it, the value of the argument applies only to entries generated by that one instance of the rule.

With respect to specifying libraries, these two approaches have different implications. If you name libraries using a *make* variable that the program-building rule refers to, all programs will be built using the same set of libraries. If you pass libraries as rule arguments, you have the flexibility to specify them independently for each program.

So, for libraries, which method is better? The choice depends on what you're trying to accomplish and which method's characteristics best match your goals. In the present case, BuildProgram() can be used to build multiple programs in the same *Imakefile*, and it's likely that different programs will use different libraries. Therefore, it's a better choice to pass libraries as a rule argument than to assign them to a *make* variable.

In general, *make* variables are not helpful for types of information that vary from target to target. When specifying such things as program names, object files, or libraries, rule arguments give you a degree of control that's difficult or impossible to achieve with a *make* variable.

On the other hand, *make* variables are a good choice when you want to specify values that should remain constant for multiple targets. For example, the preferred C compiler might vary from system to system or from project to project, but it's unlikely to vary from target to target within a project. It would just be a bother to the *Imakefile* writer if the compiler had to be named in every instance of program-building rules. The name is best expressed as a parameter that can be set once in the configuration files using a *make* variable.

Libraries as Dependencies

In the definition of BuildProgram(), the objs parameter is used in the program's dependency list and in the link command that creates the executable. However, the program is just as dependent on its libraries as on its object files. Why not write the rule so it tells *make* about this dependency, too? That's easy enough to do, by naming the libs parameter in the dependency list:

```
#define BuildProgram(prog,objs,libs)                              @@\
prog: objs libs                                                   @@\
    $(CC) -o prog objs libs
```

Unfortunately, this version of BuildProgram() doesn't work. If we invoke it like this:

```
BuildProgram(prog,prog.o,-lm)
```

we'll end up with this entry:

```
prog: prog.o -lm
    $(CC) -o prog prog.o -lm
```

−lm isn't a legal library specifier in a dependency list because *make* understands only filenames there. As discussed in Chapter 6, *Writing Imakefiles*, we need two

kinds of library specifiers. One kind names the libraries in a form suitable for linking (using either the −*l* form or pathnames). The other kind names them in a form suitable for dependencies (as pathnames). Thus BuildProgram() should be written like this:

```
#define BuildProgram(prog,objs,linklibs,deplibs)                    @@\
prog: objs deplibs                                                  @@\
    $(CC) -o prog objs linklibs
```

Our rule now handles many more cases and is much more versatile than it was initially. BuildProgram() is sufficiently general that we can use it to build many kinds of programs:

```
/* program with no libraries */
BuildProgram(prog1,prog1.o,NullParameter,NullParameter)

/* program with local libraries (built within the project) */
BuildProgram(prog2,prog2.o,libmylib.a,libmylib.a)

/* program with system libraries */
BuildProgram(prog3,prog3.o,-lndbm -lm,NullParameter)

/* program with local and system libraries */
BuildProgram(prog4,prog4.o,libmylib.a -lndbm -lm,libmylib.a)
```

Implications of Parameterization

Changing the literal cc to the *make* variable CC in the definition of Build-Program() is a form of parameterization that changes the implementation of the rule. The modification requires cooperation from other configuration files (*Imake.tmpl* must provide a default value of CC in this case), but the changes can be made by the configuration file writer without involving *Imakefile* writers.

Adding linklibs and deplibs to the definition of BuildProgram() is a form of parameterization that changes the way you use the rule. This kind of modification is not so benign as parameterizing the C compiler, because it affects *Imakefile* writers: changing a rule's invocation sequence immediately breaks every *Imakefile* that uses the rule! People who write Imakefiles using our configuration files are not likely to appreciate our indiscretion.

It's best to think through the ways in which you'll want to use a rule as well as you can while you're designing it and before you begin using it in production. While you're still in the process of developing a rule, you have the liberty to change it as you like. Once you start using it, your options become more limited. In the case of the BuildProgram() rule, if it had already been well known or widely used when we started thinking about adding library parameters, it probably would have been better to define a new rule than to break existing Imakefiles.

Special Linker Information

We still need a way to designate special linker information, such as loader prefix flags, compatibility libraries for deficient systems, and other miscellaneous low-level options that are sometimes necessary to make the linker behave itself. Before doing so, it's worthwhile to step back a little and reflect on what we've done so far. The original rule has been changed in two ways:

* Tools used in the rule body (e.g., the C compiler) have been parameterized to allow them to be selected on a system- or project-specific basis in the configuration files.

* Parameters have been added to the rule-calling sequence to allow information to be specified in rule invocations and substituted into the rule body on a target-specific basis.

Which of these two kinds of changes should we choose for specifying linker information? We could add parameters to the invocation sequence, but that's more appropriate for information that varies from program to program. Information needed to make the linker work properly tends to vary on a system or project basis. Therefore, instead of adding parameters to the calling sequence, we'll parameterize the rule body further:

```
#define BuildProgram(prog,objs,linklibs,deplibs)              @@\
prog: objs deplibs                                            @@\
    $(CC) -o prog objs $(LOADOPTS) linklibs $(LOADLIBS)
```

LOADOPTS and LOADLIBS can be defined appropriately in the configuration files as any extra flags and libraries the linker needs, respectively. The basic support for them goes in *Imake.tmpl*:

```
#ifndef LoadOpts
#define LoadOpts /* as nothing */
#endif
#ifndef LoadLibs
#define LoadLibs /* as nothing */
#endif
LOADOPTS = LoadOpts
LOADLIBS = LoadLibs
```

The default values for LOADOPTS and LOADLIBS assume no special flags or libraries are needed, but can be overridden in the vendor-specific file as necessary to adapt to particular systems. For instance, Mips RISC/os provides System V and BSD versions of system libraries, but fails to include *vfprintf()* in the BSD C library for releases of the OS prior to 4.50. That routine is found in either the *termcap* or *curses* libraries. We can use the vendor file *Mips.cf* to compensate for the deficiency like so:

```
#ifndef LoadLibs
#define LoadLibs -ltermcap
#endif
```

This works, but it's painting with a rather broad brush. We need the fix only when compiling under the BSD environment using early releases of the OS. Here's a more specific way to indicate when to use the library:

```
/*
 * vfprintf() is not in the BSD version of the C library in releases
 * of RISC/os prior to 4.50.  Link in -ltermcap to get it.
 */
#ifndef LoadLibs
#if !defined(SystemV) && !defined(SystemV4)
#if OSMajorVersion < 4 || (OSMajorVersion == 4 && OSMinorVersion < 50)
#define LoadLibs -ltermcap
#endif
#endif
#endif
```

If you were using *make* directly, a broken C library is the kind of shortcoming you typically would compensate for by editing the *Makefile*. That's ugly because you have to think about the machine dependency of whether extra libraries need to be linked into a program that calls *vfprintf()*.

With *imake* you don't concern yourself about the problem: it's handled in the vendor file and the solution is propagated into the *Makefile* automatically. The machine independence of the *Imakefile* is retained, and the burden on the programmer is lessened. The person who writes *Mips.cf* has to know about the problem with the C library, of course, but nobody else using the configuration files needs to. In effect, *Mips.cf* fixes a bug, silently. Programmers need not be aware of the special case the vendor file compensates for, and programs that use *vfprintf()* build correctly.

Thinking About Portability to Non-UNIX Systems

If you think your software might be used on non-UNIX systems, it's worth considering how to make your configuration setup work in such environments. For example, much of the X11 distribution can be built under Windows NT. We can take advantage of the X11 NT support and apply it to the development of our own rules so they'll work under NT, too.

One of the variations between UNIX and NT is that different naming conventions are used for object files, executables, and libraries. These conventions are summarized in Table 12–1.

Table 12–1: UNIX and Windows NT File-Naming Conventions

System Type	Object Files	Executables	Libraries
UNIX	*.o* suffix	no suffix	*lib* prefix, *.a* suffix
Windows NT	*.obj* suffix	*.exe* suffix	no prefix, *.lib* suffix

Later in this chapter we'll consider the issue of non-UNIX portability as it applies to library-building. For now, Table 12–1 illustrates two UNIX-specific aspects of how we build a program with `BuildProgram()` currently: we've been specifying object files with a *.o* suffix when invoking the rule, and, for the final executable, the rule definition generates a target name with no suffix.

To generalize the object file suffix, we can use a macro `Osuf` that is defined by default as o in *Imake.tmpl*:[*]

```
#ifndef Osuf
#define Osuf o
#endif
```

The suffix definition can be overridden for Windows NT like this:

```
#define Osuf obj
```

Then, instead of invoking `BuildProgram()` like this:

```
BuildProgram(myprog,myprog.o,NullParameter,NullParameter)
```

we'd invoke it like this:

```
BuildProgram(myprog,myprog.Osuf,NullParameter,NullParameter)
```

With that change, the resulting *Makefile* will contain the correct form of the object file name for either type of system (*myprog.o* for UNIX, *myprog.obj* for NT).

We must also generalize the executable name, since NT executables are named with a *.exe* suffix. At present, our `BuildProgram()` rule builds executables that would need renaming after being built. That is, we'd need to do this:

```
% make myprog
% mv myprog myprog.exe
```

We can avoid this work by writing our rule to generate a properly named target instead. The X11 configuration files do this using a `ProgramTargetName()` rule to

---

[*] You can use the `Osuf` that is already present in the DP *Imake.tmpl* file.

generate the executable name in the target entry. We can use this rule in Build-
Program():

```
#define BuildProgram(prog,objs,linklibs,deplibs)                    @@\
ProgramTargetName(prog): objs deplibs                               @@\
    $(CC) -o ProgramTargetName(prog) objs $(LOADOPTS) linklibs $(LOADLIBS)
```

How does ProgramTargetName() work? For the default case, the rule simply produces the name as given:

```
#ifndef ProgramTargetName
#define ProgramTargetName(target)target
#endif
```

For Windows NT, the rule is overridden appropriately to add a *.exe* suffix:

```
#define ProgramTargetName(target)target.exe
```

After building the *Makefile* using the revised BuildProgram(), you'd build a program under UNIX like this:

```
% make myprog
```

Under Windows NT, you'd do this instead:

```
% make myprog.exe
```

Generalizing the way the object and executable filenames are constructed allows
programs to be built on more systems. We'll use a similar technique later in the
chapter when we consider how to write rules to build libraries.

Making the Rule Work Harder

At this point, BuildProgram() is a reasonably capable rule. On a system- or project-wide basis, we can choose the C compiler and be flexible about special
options needed at link time by providing that information in the configuration
files. On a per-invocation basis, BuildProgram() allows us to specify the object
files and libraries needed to produce the final executable.

The primary purpose of BuildProgram() is to build programs. That has now been
accomplished, but we can flesh out the rule a bit to do more for us. How much?
That depends on how all-encompassing we want the rule to be. For our discussion, we'll extend BuildProgram() to generate entries for clean, all, and lint
targets.

The clean Target

BuildProgram() builds a program, so it might as well help us clean up afterward too, by generating a clean entry. (Logically, after you build your program, you'd install it, but we'll discuss installation rules later in their own section.) In order to avoid writing the name of the file-removing program literally into the rule, parameterization support is needed in the template *Imake.tmpl*:[*]

```
#ifndef RmCmd
#define RmCmd rm -f
#endif

RM = RmCmd
```

As usual, the default parameter value can be overridden in the vendor file by providing a different definition of RmCmd. For example, it's defined as del for Windows NT.

We must also consider what it is that should be "cleaned." For programs, this generally means removing the final executable image and the object files created from its source files. The last section of *Imake.tmpl* automatically provides a default clean entry that removes object files, so the entry generated by BuildProgram() need only remove the final executable:

```
#define BuildProgram(prog,objs,linklibs,deplibs)                      @@\
ProgramTargetName(prog): objs deplibs                                 @@\
    $(CC) -o ProgramTargetName(prog) objs $(LOADOPTS) linklibs $(LOADLIBS)  @@\
clean::                                                               @@\
    $(RM) ProgramTargetName(prog)
```

The clean entry is written with a double colon instead of a single colon, because the clean target name might be associated with multiple entries (one for each invocation of BuildProgram() in the *Imakefile* and one for the default clean entry provided by *Imake.tmpl*). The double colon ensures that *make* generates and executes an RM command for each clean entry, instead of quitting with "inconsistent entry," "target conflict," or "too many rules for target" errors. Thus, we can remove debris for every program built by the *Makefile* by saying:

% **make clean**

Note that the clean entry is written at the end of the definition of Build-Program(). If you put it at the beginning, clean becomes the default target for your *Makefile*, and *make* with no arguments doesn't build your program, as you'd normally want—it removes it!

The result of adding a clean entry to BuildProgram() is a more functional *Makefile* with no change to the *Imakefile*. We can take advantage of the modified rule

---

[*] You can use the RmCmd and RM that are already present in the DP *Imake.tmpl* file.

simply by rebuilding the *Makefile*. That's certainly preferable to editing Makefiles manually to add `clean` entries.

Since a `clean` entry is a generally useful thing, it's worthwhile to put one in other target-building rules we write, too. But let's think ahead a little bit. The path we're now traveling is to write the entry literally into the rule definition. If we do this for each rule that generates a `clean` entry, we might have problems later. Suppose we decide to change the form of our `clean` entries; having written them literally into rule definitions, we'd have to edit each of them individually.

We can improve our rules and solve this problem with a level of indirection, that is, by defining another rule and invoking it to generate the `clean` entry. `Clean-Target()` is a reasonable name for the rule, but a rule with that name already exists in the rules file and has a different purpose (it generates the generic `clean` entry). We'll call our new rule `StuffToClean()` instead. It looks like this:

```
#define StuffToClean(stuff)                                         @@\
clean::                                                             @@\
    $(RM) stuff
```

It's easy to revise `BuildProgram()` to use `StuffToClean()`:

```
#define BuildProgram(prog,objs,linklibs,deplibs)                    @@\
ProgramTargetName(prog): objs deplibs                               @@\
    $(CC) -o ProgramTargetName(prog) objs $(LOADOPTS) linklibs $(LOADLIBS)  @@\
StuffToClean(ProgramTargetName(prog))
```

By using `StuffToClean()`, we can make changes to or fix bugs in `clean` entries simply by changing the definition of `StuffToClean()` —a single modification. It's unnecessary to change every rule that uses it.

This flexibility can help you achieve portability more easily. Suppose you find that `StuffToClean()` doesn't work on a particular platform (this isn't likely to happen for such a simple rule, but humor me for this example). You can provide a working version of `StuffToClean()` in the vendor file for that platform. By doing so, you fix `BuildProgram()` and any other rules that invoke `StuffToClean()`. If you had written `clean` entries literally into those rules, you'd have to redefine every one of them in the vendor file.

Another reason to write the file-removal entry as a separate rule is that you can invoke it on its own to easily generate additional `clean` entries. Suppose you have an *Imakefile* into which you've written a `test` entry that runs a program to generate some test output:

```
BuildProgram(myprog,myprog.Osuf,NullParameter,NullParameter)

test:: ProgramTargetName(myprog)
    ProgramTargetName(myprog) > myprog.out
```

StuffToClean() is useful for removing any kind of debris, not just executables, so it can help you clean up the test output. Just add a line to your *Imakefile*:

```
BuildProgram(myprog,myprog.Osuf,NullParameter,NullParameter)

test:: ProgramTargetName(myprog)
    ProgramTargetName(myprog) > myprog.out

StuffToClean(myprog.out)
```

The all Target

If an *Imakefile* contains a single invocation of BuildProgram(), the *Makefile* will contain an entry to build the program and a clean entry to clean it up. Since the program-building entry is first, it's the default target, and *make* with no arguments builds it. If the *Imakefile* contains several invocations of BuildProgram(), the *Makefile* will contain several program-building entries and several clean entries. Now what's the default target? It's still the program-building entry for the first program, so if we say:

```
% make
```

only the first program is built. Not very useful.

Neither is this:

```
% make all
make: Fatal error: Don't know how to make target "all"
```

The error occurs because there's no all target in the *Imakefile*.

make all should certainly build all the programs, and if we can just say *make* with no arguments to cause the same thing to happen, so much the better. Currently, that's not what happens, which is troublesome:

- BuildProgram() builds Makefiles that do not behave the way we'd expect and therefore surprise the person using them.

- BuildProgram() builds Makefiles that are hard to use. To build all the targets, each one must be named explicitly on the command line.

We could "fix" the problem by writing an all entry at the top of our *Imakefile*:

```
all::   ProgramTargetName(program1) \
        ProgramTargetName(program2) \
        ProgramTargetName(program3) \
        ...
```

This indeed causes *make* or *make all* to build all the programs, but we have to change the all entry every time we add or delete an invocation of Build-Program() from the *Imakefile*. That's a poor solution—we're forcing the *Imakefile* writer to work around problems that really should be handled in the configuration files.

An alternative that involves no *Imakefile* editing is to modify `BuildProgram()` to produce an `all` entry. First we define a rule `AllTarget()` to generate the entry:[*]

```
#define AllTarget(target)                                              @@\
all:: target
```

Then we invoke `AllTarget()` from within `BuildProgram()`:

```
#define BuildProgram(prog,objs,linklibs,deplibs)                       @@\
AllTarget(ProgramTargetName(prog))                                     @@\
ProgramTargetName(prog): objs deplibs                                  @@\
    $(CC) -o ProgramTargetName(prog) objs $(LOADOPTS) linklibs $(LOADLIBS)   @@\
StuffToClean(ProgramTargetName(prog))
```

Since the `all` target might be associated with multiple entries, `AllTarget()` uses a double colon on the dependency line. Also, `AllTarget()` appears at the beginning of `BuildProgram()`, so that an `all` entry appears first in the *Makefile*. Thus, `all` becomes the default target.

Once again, a simple change to `BuildProgram()` results in a more functional *Makefile* without changing the *Imakefile*. The modification is minor but its effect is significant:

- Our Imakefiles produce Makefiles that don't surprise people who use them. `BuildProgram()` causes *make all* to behave as we'd normally expect—it builds all the programs.

- Our Imakefiles produce Makefiles that are easier to use. Since `all` is the default target, *make* with no arguments is shorthand for *make all*. (We can still build individual programs by naming them on the *make* command line, of course.)

The lint Target

Many programmers use *lint* to check their source files for problems, so let's consider how we might extend `BuildProgram()` to help us use it. We can guess that `BuildProgram()` should look something like this:

```
#define BuildProgram(prog,objs,linklibs,deplibs)                       @@\
AllTarget(ProgramTargetName(prog))                                     @@\
ProgramTargetName(prog): objs deplibs                                  @@\
    $(CC) -o ProgramTargetName(prog) objs $(LOADOPTS) linklibs $(LOADLIBS)   @@\
StuffToClean(ProgramTargetName(prog))                                  @@\
LintSources(arguments)
```

---

[*] You can use the `AllTarget()` that is already present in the DP *Imake.rules* file.

But what arguments should we pass to `LintSources()`?

If `BuildProgramTarget()` generates a `lint` target entry, then the command:

```
% make lint
```

should generate one *lint* command for each program built by the *Makefile*. Each command passes the source files for one program to *lint*. (This contrasts with *makedepend*, to which you pass all sources for all programs in the *Makefile* simultaneously.) For example, if we have two programs, *prog1* and *prog2*, this is what should happen:

```
% make lint
lint lint-flags prog1-sources
lint lint-flags prog2-sources
```

Unfortunately, *lint* needs to know the set of source files used to build a program, but that information isn't available from within `BuildProgram()` at present. If `LintSources()` is invoked from within `BuildProgram()`, the latter must be changed to accept the target program source list as one of its own parameters, otherwise it can't pass the list to `LintSources()`. This change makes `Build-Program()` more complicated to invoke.

Another possibility to consider is whether `BuildProgram()` is really the correct place to generate a `lint` entry after all. We can invoke `LintSources()` independently of `BuildProgram()` if we want. If we make that choice, we don't need to change the latter at all, although we do end up with longer Imakefiles.

I'll come down on the side of adding the parameter to `BuildProgram()` and not having to remember to invoke `LintSources()` explicitly:

```
#define BuildProgram(prog,srcs,objs,linklibs,deplibs)               @@\
AllTarget(ProgramTargetName(prog))                                  @@\
ProgramTargetName(prog): objs deplibs                               @@\
    $(CC) -o ProgramTargetName(prog) objs $(LOADOPTS) linklibs $(LOADLIBS)  @@\
StuffToClean(ProgramTargetName(prog))                               @@\
LintSources(srcs)
```

`LintSources()` might look something like this:

```
#define LintSources(srcs)                                           @@\
lint::                                                              @@\
    $(LINT) $(LINTFLAGS) srcs $(LINTLIBS)
```

A double colon is in order because the `lint` target can be associated with multiple entries. The rule uses three *make* variable parameters, LINT, LINTFLAGS, and LINTLIBS. LINT names the *lint* program itself. LINTFLAGS specifies any flags needed to get *lint* to run properly. (This will include any *lint*-specific options as well as any flags we'd normally pass to the C compiler, such as defines and include directories. The *lint*-specific options can be specified using a variable

LINTOPTS; the other flags are already available in CFLAGS.) LINTLIBS names any special *lint* libraries needed for source checking that aren't in the default set of libraries. Each *lint*-related parameter needs to be defined appropriately in *Imake.tmpl*:[*]

```
#ifndef LintCmd
#define LintCmd lint
#endif
#ifndef LintOpts
#if SystemV || SystemV4
#define LintOpts -bh
#else
#define LintOpts -axz
#endif
#endif
#ifndef LintLibs
#define LintLibs /* as nothing */
#endif

      LINT = LintCmd
  LINTOPTS = LintOpts
 LINTFLAGS = $(LINTOPTS) $(CFLAGS)
  LINTLIBS = LintLibs
```

Refining the Scope of a Target

If you issue the following command, the source for every program in the *Imakefile* is checked by *lint*:

```
% make lint
```

That's okay when you haven't checked anything yet. But suppose you've already run *lint* on your sources and cleaned up any problems it reports. If you make some further changes to the source for a single program, you'll want to re-*lint* only that program. It's certainly overkill to *lint* every other program again, too. Unfortunately, the "granularity" of the lint target is insufficient to provide single-program *lint* operations.

We can modify the LintSources() rule to handle that by telling it the name of the program being *lint*'ed:

```
#define LintSources(prog,srcs)                                    @@\
lint:: lint.prog                                                  @@\
lint.prog:                                                        @@\
    $(LINT) $(LINTFLAGS) srcs $(LINTLIBS)
```

---

[*] You can use the LintCmd, LINT, LintOpts, and LINTOPTS that are already present in the DP *Imake.tmpl* file. Replace the definition of LINTFLAGS. LintLibs and LINTLIBS are not present; add them.

We also need to tell BuildProgram() to pass the program name to the instance of LintSources() it contains, since the latter rule's invocation sequence has changed:

```
#define BuildProgram(prog,srcs,objs,linklibs,deplibs)              @@\
AllTarget(ProgramTargetName(prog))                                 @@\
ProgramTargetName(prog): objs deplibs                              @@\
    $(CC) -o ProgramTargetName(prog) objs $(LOADOPTS) linklibs $(LOADLIBS) @@\
StuffToClean(ProgramTargetName(prog))                              @@\
LintSources(ProgramTargetName(prog),srcs)
```

The change to LintSources() interposes another target into the rule so you can say:

> % **make lint.***program*

to *lint* an individual program.[*] As before, you can still *lint* everything with:

> % **make lint**

These changes give us the flexibility to apply *lint* very specifically. Again, we achieve a more effective *Makefile* with some thought about how to design rule macros.

Documenting Rules

When you write a rule, you should think about documenting it so people who don't know how to read rule definitions can still look through the rules file to find out something about how the rule works. A comment for BuildProgram() is shown below. The comment is longer than the rule, but it will be appreciated by the uninitiated:

```
/*
 * BuildProgram() generates entries to build, remove, and
 * lint a single program.  May be invoked multiple times
 * in the same Imakefile.
 *
 * Arguments:
 * prog         program name
 * srcs         program's source files
 * objs         program's object files
 * linklibs     libraries needed to link program
 * deplibs      libraries to check as dependencies
 *              (must be given as pathnames)
```

---

[*] Under Windows NT, you'd say:

> % **make lint.***program***.exe**

since you're running *lint* on the sources for an executable *program.exe*.

```
 *
 *   Targets produced:
 *   all          build prog (and all others in Imakefile)
 *   prog         build prog only
 *   clean        remove all programs in Imakefile
 *   lint         lint all programs in Imakefile
 *   lint.prog    lint prog only
 */
```

Building Libraries

Program libraries are useful as repositories of commonly used functions that we wish to share among multiple executables. To write a rule for a library, we need to know, at minimum, the list of object files and the library's name. We could refer to a library as, for example, *libxyz.a*, but it's easier to write *xyz* and let the rule create the full name for itself using the Concat() token-pasting rule:

```
Concat(lib,xyz.a)
```

In fact, since we may need to refer to library names in multiple places, we can define a rule to generate the name for us:[*]

```
#ifndef LibraryTargetName
#define LibraryTargetName(name)Concat(lib,name.a)
#endif
```

Another reason to use a rule to construct the name is that, like ProgramTarget-Name(), it can be redefined if necessary on a vendor-specific basis for systems that have a different form of library name. For instance, under Windows NT, the *xyz* library would be named *xyz.lib*, so the rule can be redefined like this:

```
#define LibraryTargetName(name)name.lib
```

The rule that actually builds the library should generate an entry that takes the list of object files, mashes them together to create the library, and (on systems supporting it) runs the library through *ranlib*.[†] For good measure, the rule can also generate all and clean entries:

```
#define BuildLibrary(name,objlist)                          @@\
AllTarget(LibraryTargetName(name))                          @@\
LibraryTargetName(name): objlist                            @@\
    $(RM) $@                                                @@\
    $(AR) $@ objlist                                        @@\
    RanLibrary($@)                                          @@\
StuffToClean(LibraryTargetName(name))
```

---

[*] You can use the LibaryTargetName() rule that is already present in the DP *Imake.rules* file.

[†] *ranlib* creates a table of contents in the library so the linker can be more efficient.

This definition is similar to the X11 rule `NormalLibraryTarget()`. Build-
Library() refers to the archiving program using the variable AR and uses the
RanLibrary() rule to invoke the *ranlib* program if it's available. RanLibrary()
looks like this:[*]

```
#if DoRanlibCmd
#define RanLibrary(args) $(RANLIB) args
#else
#define RanLibrary(args) $(__NULLCMD__)
#endif
```

DoRanlibCmd is YES if *ranlib* is available on your system, NO otherwise. RANLIB is
the name of the *ranlib* program.

We need support for AR, RANLIB, and DoRanlibCmd. The default values of each
can be specified in *Imake.tmpl*:[†]

```
#ifndef DoRanlibCmd
#if SystemV || SystemV4
#define DoRanlibCmd NO
#else
#define DoRanlibCmd YES
#endif
#endif

#ifndef ArCmd
#if SystemV4
#define ArCmd ar cq
#else
#define ArCmd ar clq
#endif
#endif

#ifndef RanlibCmd
#define RanlibCmd ranlib
#endif

        AR = ArCmd
#if DoRanlibCmd
    RANLIB = RanlibCmd
#endif
```

These values can be overridden in vendor files. In particular, DoRanlibCmd should
be defined as YES in the vendor file for any system that supports *ranlib*.

Using BuildLibrary(), an *Imakefile* to build *libxyz.a* from files *a.c*, *b.c*, and *c.c*
might look like this:

---

* You can use the RanLibrary() rule that is already present in the DP *Imake.rules* file.

† You can use the AR, RanlibCmd, RANLIB, and DoRanlibCmd symbols that are already present in the
DP *Imake.tmpl* file. Replace the definition of ArCmd.

```
SRCS = a.c    b.c    c.c
OBJS = a.Osuf b.Osuf c.Osuf

BuildLibrary(xyz,$(OBJS))

DependTarget()
```

Note that the object filenames are specified using `Osuf` to accommodate systems that use an object file suffix other than *.o*.

Installation Rules

We have not yet thought about how to install anything—a grievous oversight, since unless we install our software, it's of dubious utility. This section describes how to write installation rules, as well as the parameter macro and variable support that undergirds them.

Several parameter and rule names used in this section are used in the DP files already. In most cases, the existing versions conflict with those we create here. To eliminate these conflicts in one fell swoop, remove the `Inst*Flags` macros, the `INST*FLAGS` variables, and all the installation rules except `InstallSubdirs()`, `InstallManSubdirs()`, and the `InstallMultiple*()` and `InstallLinkKit*()` rules.*

For installing files, the obvious choice is the *install* program. However, there are System V and BSD variants of *install*, and they behave quite differently. For instance, the BSD variant interprets *−s* as "strip the installed image," whereas for the System V variant, *−s* means "operate in silent mode."

The X11 configuration files handle this problem by assuming a BSD *install* is available and providing compatibility scripts *bsdinst* and *install.sh* for systems without one. These scripts emulate BSD *install* behavior so we don't have to cope with the differences between the way the BSD and System V versions of *install* work. *bsdinst* is used more often, but *install.sh* works better on some systems.

I'm going to assume a BSD *install* is available, just as the X11 files do. Installing is such a common operation that if you don't have a BSD *install*, you should install *bsdinst* or *install.sh* in a public directory so it can be assumed available just like *imake*, *makedepend*, and *mkdirhier*. See Appendix B, *Installing Configuration Software*, if you need a compatibility script and don't have one.

---

* The *DP.tar.Z* distribution listed in Appendix A, *Obtaining Configuration Software*, includes a patch you can use to remove existing installation support.

We can select the appropriate default value of the INSTALL parameter in *Imake.tmpl* based on what we know about the system type:[*]

```
#ifndef InstallCmd
#if SystemV || SystemV4
#define InstallCmd bsdinst
#else
#define InstallCmd install
#endif
#endif

INSTALL = InstallCmd
```

If this default doesn't happen to be correct for your system, override it in the vendor file (e.g., if you have a System V machine, but also have a BSD *install* available).

The simplest useful *install* command looks like this and installs the given file into the given directory:

```
% install -c file dir
```

The −*c* (copy) option is used commonly because without it *install* removes the original file. (It takes up more room to keep the original files around, but if a multiple-directory installation operation fails in the middle, you don't have to rebuild everything up to that point.) However, if for some reason you wanted to override this behavior, it would be easier to do so were −*c* expressed as a parameter. Also, some systems don't support −*c*. So we'll parameterize this option, to allow it to be overridden:

```
#ifndef InstCopy
#define InstCopy -c
#endif

INSTCOPY = InstCopy
```

Now we can instantiate the *install* command in a rule this way:

```
#define InstallTarget(file,dir)                                 @@\
install:: file                                                  @@\
        $(INSTALL) $(INSTCOPY) file dir/file
```

Unfortunately, if dir doesn't exist, we might run into a problem. Suppose you invoke the rule as:

```
InstallTarget(xyz,/usr/lib/abc)
```

This indicates you want *xyz* installed as */usr/lib/abc/xyz*. But if */usr/lib* doesn't exist, *install* may fail. Therefore, it's best to make sure the installation directory

---

[*] You can use the InstallCmd and INSTALL that are already present in the DP *Imake.tmpl* file.

exists first. To accomplish this, we can do the same thing the X11 installation rules do, which is to invoke the rule `MakeDir()` to create the directory if it's missing:[*]

```
/* if [ -d ] or [ ! -d ] causes make to fail, define this as - */
#ifndef DirFailPrefix
#define DirFailPrefix
#endif

#define MakeDir(dir) DirFailPrefix@if [ -d dir ]; then set +x; \          @@\
    else (set -x; $(MKDIRHIER) dir); fi
```

Define `DirFailPrefix` as "-" in your vendor file if your system doesn't perform the -d test properly.

Now we can rewrite `InstallTarget()` to use `MakeDir()`:

```
#define InstallTarget(file,dir)                                         @@\
install:: file                                                          @@\
    MakeDir(dir)                                                        @@\
    $(INSTALL) $(INSTCOPY) file dir/file
```

Note that the body of `MakeDir()` begins on the first line of the rule definition, and that we invoke it indented in the body of another rule, rather than left-justified. These are exceptions to the usual way rules are defined and used. In general, you begin the body of a rule on the `#define` line when the purpose of the rule is to generate commands in the command section of a target entry and not to generate an entire entry.

`InstallTarget()` could use some improvement, given that it doesn't allow us to specify user and group ownership, file mode, or whether to strip the installed image. The way we indicate these things boils down to a choice between the usual two alternatives:

- If we specify a flag by means of a *make* variable used in the rule body, the flag applies to all targets installed by the rule. This is a good choice if we want the flag to be the same for every target we install.

- If we specify a flag by means of an argument passed to the rule when we invoke it, we can vary the flag on a per-target basis. This is a good choice if the flag differs for different targets.

The most general approach is to write a rule that supplies no flags itself but expects them all to be passed as arguments when the rule is invoked:

```
#define InstallTarget(file,dir,flags)                                   @@\
install:: file                                                          @@\
    MakeDir(dir)                                                        @@\
    $(INSTALL) $(INSTCOPY) flags file dir/file
```

---

[*] You can use the `DirFailPrefix` and `MakeDir()` that are already present in the DP *Imake.rules* file.

You might use the rule like this:

```
InstallTarget(prog,$(BINDIR),-s -m 0755)
InstallTarget(prog.help,$(USRLIBDIR),-m 0444)
InstallTarget(progd,$(ETCDIR),-s -m 4755 -o root)
```

This is the most flexible way to write an installation rule because it affords the caller complete control over the installation flags. Of course, the caller also has the full burden of specifying them, so that's a mixed blessing.

We usually install files according to certain patterns, so in most cases we can make some good guesses about the proper flags for a particular type of target. Therefore, it makes sense to define other higher-level "convenience" rules that invoke InstallTarget() but provide best-guess flags according to the target type. Then we'd have a selection of rules to choose from to get the flags we want without specifying them all ourselves.

For instance, a rule to install binary executables is likely to install them with mode 0755 and to strip the image. Installed manual pages need to be readable by everybody, but there's no need for them to be writable; the appropriate mode is 0444. We can write rules InstallProgram() and InstallManPage() to handle these cases:

```
#define InstallProgram(file,dir)                                    @@\
InstallTarget(ProgramTargetName(file),dir,-s -m 0755)

#define InstallManPage(file,dir)                                    @@\
InstallTarget(file,dir,-m 0444)
```

However, it's better not to write installation options literally into rules. For instance, if we don't want to strip installed programs, a literal −s in the rule is inconvenient. To change it, we'd have to put an override rule in *site.def*. If instead we use a variable INSTSTRIP, we can define it either as −s or as the empty value, which gives us an easy way to modify the behavior of InstallProgram() without changing the rule itself.

Specifying installation options using parameters gives us a consistent symbolic means of referring to them in rules and in Imakefiles, and allows us to change them more easily in the configuration files (and therefore project-wide in Makefiles). Table 12−2 shows some installation parameters I find useful; your own set may be larger or smaller, depending on your requirements.

Table 12–2: A Set of Installation Parameters

Installation Parameters	Description
INSTSTRIP	Flag for stripping executable binaries
INSTPROGMODE	Mode for executable binaries
INSTSCRIPTMODE	Mode for executable scripts
INSTLIBMODE	Mode for libraries
INSTDATMODE	Mode for data (read-only) files
INSTMANMODE	Mode for manual pages
INSTOWNER	Owner of installed files
INSTGROUP	Group of installed files

We can parameterize the strip flag as follows:

```
#ifndef InstStrip
#define InstStrip -s
#endif

INSTSTRIP = InstStrip
```

This way, installed binary images are stripped by default, which uses less disk space. If you don't want them stripped (e.g., for debugging), you simply give `InstStrip` an empty value in *site.def*:

```
#ifndef InstStrip
#define InstStrip /**/
#endif
```

For most of the other parameters, reasonable defaults are easy to choose:

```
#ifndef InstProgMode
#define InstProgMode -m 0755
#endif
#ifndef InstScriptMode
#define InstScriptMode -m 0755
#endif
#ifndef InstLibMode
#define InstLibMode -m 0444
#endif
#ifndef InstDatMode
#define InstDatMode -m 0444
#endif
#ifndef InstManMode
#define InstManMode -m 0444
#endif

  INSTPROGMODE = InstProgMode
INSTSCRIPTMODE = InstScriptMode
   INSTLIBMODE = InstLibMode
   INSTDATMODE = InstDatMode
   INSTMANMODE = InstManMode
```

The owner and group flags are different; we leave them empty, because there isn't any good way to guess defaults:

```
#ifndef InstOwner
#define InstOwner /* as nothing */
#endif
#ifndef InstGroup
#define InstGroup /* as nothing */
#endif

INSTOWNER = InstOwner
INSTGROUP = InstGroup
```

You can override `InstOwner` and `InstGroup` in the vendor or site file if you want to install targets using an owner or group ID that differs from whatever defaults your *install* program uses:

```
#ifndef InstOwner
#define InstOwner -o username
#endif
#ifndef InstGroup
#define InstGroup -g groupname
#endif
```

Now that we have our individual installation flags parameterized, we can define some additional parameters that give us useful combinations of flags:

```
   INSTPROGFLAGS = $(INSTOWNER) $(INSTGROUP) $(INSTSTRIP) $(INSTPROGMODE)
 INSTSCRIPTFLAGS = $(INSTOWNER) $(INSTGROUP) $(INSTSCRIPTMODE)
    INSTLIBFLAGS = $(INSTOWNER) $(INSTGROUP) $(INSTLIBMODE)
    INSTDATFLAGS = $(INSTOWNER) $(INSTGROUP) $(INSTDATMODE)
    INSTMANFLAGS = $(INSTOWNER) $(INSTGROUP) $(INSTMANMODE)
```

We can rewrite the convenience rules in terms of these combination flag parameters to eliminate references to literal flags:

```
#define InstallProgram(file,dir)                                        @@\
InstallTarget(ProgramTargetName(file),dir,$(INSTPROGFLAGS))
```

```
#define InstallManPage(file,dir)                                        @@\
InstallTarget(file,dir,$(INSTMANFLAGS))
```

Other convenience rules might look like this:

```
#define InstallScript(file,dir)                                         @@\
InstallTarget(file,dir,$(INSTSCRIPTFLAGS))
```

```
#define InstallData(file,dir)                                           @@\
InstallTarget(file,dir,$(INSTDATFLAGS))
```

Library installation presents a special problem because we not only need to install the library image, but to run *ranlib* again if it's available:

```
#define InstallLibrary(name,dir)                                    @@\
InstallTarget(LibraryTargetName(name),dir,$(INSTLIBFLAGS))          @@\
install:: LibraryTargetName(name)                                   @@\
    RanLibrary(dir/LibraryTargetName(name))
```

For targets that require special treatment, bypass the convenience rules and invoke `InstallTarget()` directly. For instance, to install a setuid-*root* program, the owner and mode must be indicated specially:

```
SETUIDFLAGS = -o root $(INSTGROUP) $(INSTSTRIP) -m 04755

InstallTarget(ProgramTargetName(file),dir,$(SETUIDFLAGS))
```

Installing on Non-UNIX Systems

Installing files on non-UNIX systems presents an interesting challenge. Taking Windows NT as an example, we can identify several issues that must be addressed:

- There is no BSD *install* command and *bsdinst* doesn't work because shell scripts don't work under NT. We can use *copy* instead.

- *copy* doesn't understand any of the usual *install* flags, so the parameters controlling them must all be redefined.

- Under UNIX, the installation destination name is specified as a pathname that contains / as the pathname separator character. Under NT, \ is the pathname separator.

- Rules like `InstallScript()` have little meaning because shell scripts don't work under NT.

Let's tackle these issues one at a time.

The usual installation program, *install*, isn't available under Windows NT. The usual alternative, *bsdinst*, can't be used either, because it's a shell script and doesn't work under NT. We can redefine `InstallCmd` in *Win32.cf* to use the *copy* command instead:

```
#define InstallCmd copy
```

Also, the installation-related parameters associated with *install* have no meaning for *copy*, so we must redefine each of them as nothing:

```
#define InstCopy /* as nothing */
#define InstStrip /* as nothing */
#define InstProgMode /* as nothing */
#define InstScriptMode /* as nothing */
#define InstLibMode /* as nothing */
#define InstDatMode /* as nothing */
#define InstManMode /* as nothing */
#define InstOwner /* as nothing */
#define InstGroup /* as nothing */
```

The changes just shown allow us to replace *install* and its flags with *copy* in Make-files generated under Windows NT, but they do not change the pathname of the installed file. That's a problem, because NT uses \ as the pathname separator character rather than / as UNIX uses. Fortunately, all of our installation rules invoke InstallTarget(), so if we can fix that rule for NT, most of our other rules will be fixed as well. (Exceptions are InstallLibrary() and InstallScript(), which we'll deal with shortly.)

Currently the InstallTarget() rule looks like this:

```
#define InstallTarget(file,dir,flags)                           @@\
install:: file                                                   @@\
    MakeDir(dir)                                                  @@\
        $(INSTALL) $(INSTCOPY) flags file dir/file
```

If we assume that the dir value will be passed appropriately using \ rather than /, the simplest way to change the rule is to override it in *Win32.rules* and change the literal / to \ (note that the \ is doubled):

```
#define InstallTarget(file,dir,flags)                           @@\
install:: file                                                   @@\
    MakeDir(dir)                                                  @@\
        $(INSTALL) $(INSTCOPY) flags file dir\\file
```

This works if installation rules are invoked with dir values that have been properly parameterized for NT. However, it doesn't work if a literal pathname using / is specified, and we can't assume that *Imakefile* writers will never do that. We can handle this problem by modifying the rule to perform /-to-\ mapping in the pathname:

```
#define InstallTarget(file,dir,flags)                           @@\
XVARdef0 = dir                                                   @@\
install:: file                                                   @@\
    MakeDir($(XVARuse0:/=\))                                      @@\
        $(INSTALL) $(INSTCOPY) flags file $(XVARuse0:/=\)\\file
```

XVARdef and XVARuse provide a special mechanism for generating and referring to unique *make* variable names in rules. When XVARdef*n* occurs in a rule, it is replaced by a unique *make* variable name. (*n* can be a digit from 0 to 9, so you can have up to 10 such variables in a rule.) Any reference of the form XVARuse*n* later in the rule is replaced by a reference to the corresponding variable. This mechanism is used to generate different variables for each invocation of the rule.[*]

The $(XVARuse0:/=\) construct in the definition of InstallTarget() just shown is a variable reference that takes the value of the variable XVARuse0 and changes

---

[*] Processing of XVARdef and XVARuse is performed by *imake* as part of the postprocessing it does on *cpp* output. Currently, *imake* does this only under Windows NT. If you need to generate unique variable names for another type of system, you must modify the source for *imake* and recompile it.

each instance of / to \ to produce an NT-style pathname. That way, if a dir value like */a/b/c* is passed to InstallTarget(), it is turned into \a\b\c when the *copy* command is executed.

The preceding changes suffice to fix InstallTarget() and most of our other installation rules. InstallLibrary() is an exception. It invokes Install-Target(), but also contains a *ranlib* command that refers to the installation directory and uses the pathname separator. An approach similar to the one we just used for InstallTarget() can be used to modify InstallLibrary():

```
#define InstallLibrary(name,dir)                                    @@\
XVARdef1 = dir                                                      @@\
InstallTarget(LibraryTargetName(name),dir,$(INSTLIBFLAGS))          @@\
install:: LibraryTargetName(name)                                  @@\
    RanLibrary($(XVARuse1:/=\)\\LibraryTargetName(name))
```

XVARdef1 and XVARuse1 are used here (rather than XVARdef0 and XVARuse0) because InstallLibrary() invokes InstallTarget(), which already uses XVARdef0 and XVARuse0.

Another exception is InstallScript(), which becomes meaningless under Windows NT because shell scripts do not work. There isn't much recourse here except to redefine the rule to do nothing:

```
#define InstallScript(file,dir)                                     @@\
install:: file                                                      @@\
    @echo sorry, file cannot be installed
```

Should BuildProgram() Generate an install Target?

We could make BuildProgram() more comprehensive by changing it to invoke an installation rule. Do we want to do this, or invoke the installation rule separately?

If we change BuildProgram() to install the program, we need to either add installation-related parameters to its invocation sequence or assume defaults for them. BuildProgram() already has several parameters; it's unclear that adding more is a good idea. If instead we assume default installation parameters, we'll actually limit the usefulness of BuildProgram(). For example, if we assume an installation mode of 0755, the rule can't be used with setuid programs.

Neither alternative warrants changing BuildProgram(); it's best to leave it alone and to invoke the appropriate installation rule separately. If you expect to install

several programs exactly the same way, you can always define another rule that
invokes `BuildProgram()` as well as an installation rule:

```
#define BuildAndInstallProgram(prog,srcs,objs,linklibs,deplibs)      @@\
BuildProgram(prog,srcs,objs,linklibs,deplibs)                        @@\
InstallProgram(prog,$(BINDIR))
```

Refining the Scope of Installation Rules

If you say:

```
% make install
```

all targets in the *Makefile* are installed. That's okay for the initial installation
because you want to install everything. But if you rebuild a single target later, do
you want to install everything else along with it? No. We encountered this same
kind of problem earlier with `LintSources()`, where *make lint* caused all programs in the *Makefile* to be run though *lint*, even if we wanted only to *lint* a single program.

We handled that difficulty by revising `LintSources()` to allow single-target `lint`
granularity. We can do the same thing to `install` rules to allow installing at the
individual target level without losing the general install-everything-in-sight result of
make install. When you see the following in an installation rule:

```
install:: target                                                     @@\
```

change it to this:

```
install:: install.target                                             @@\
install.target: target                                               @@\
```

Then, after regenerating the *Makefile*, you can say either of the following:

```
% make install.program          Install program only
% make install                  Install everything
```

13

Configuration Problems and Solutions

You know how hard it is to get hammers these days.
—Betty MacDonald, *Mrs. Piggle-Wiggle*

Chapter 11, *Introduction to Configuration File Writing*, and Chapter 12, *Writing Rule Macros*, discuss general configuration file writing techniques in the context of modifying the starter project (SP) files to create a "product," i.e., the demonstration project (DP) files.

This chapter takes a different approach. Instead of focusing on a particular set of configuration files, we discuss several miscellaneous configuration problems, to show how *imake* helps you solve them. Because this is a problem-oriented rather than product-oriented approach, the discussion is by necessity something of a collection of odds and ends.

Describing Project Layout

In a multiple-directory project it's common for an *Imakefile* in one directory to refer to files or directories located elsewhere in the project tree. Figure 13–1 shows a simple project with a root directory and subdirectories for header files, library source files, and application source files. In the context of program development, the *Imakefile* in the *lib* directory will likely refer to the *include* header file directory, and the *Imakefile* in the *app* directory will likely refer to both the *include* and *lib* directories.

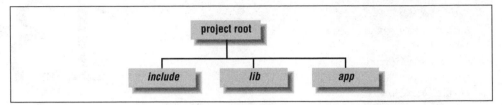

Figure 13-1: Simple project tree

One way of referring to directories is to write out pathnames literally in your Imakefiles. You can use either relative or absolute paths. If you use relative paths, the path to a given directory varies depending on your location within the project tree. Table 13-1 illustrates this variation, showing how paths to the header file and library directories change by location within the project. Because the pathnames vary, you have to be careful to write them correctly each time you use them. Moreover, if you rearrange the project layout, as sometimes occurs during the development process, you must revise all the references to reflect the changes.

Table 13-1: Directory Locations Expressed Using Relative Pathnames

From...	Path to *include*	Path to *lib*
project root	./include	./lib
lib	../include	.
app	../include	../lib

You can write the directory references as absolute pathnames instead, but then you get pathname variation from machine to machine. If the project is installed at */usr/src/proj* on one machine and */usr/local/src/proj* on another, all the paths must be edited when the project is moved from one machine to the other.

imake allows you to use symbolic references and to propagate symbol values throughout your project, so you might as well take advantage of those capabilities. As an alternative to writing out directory references literally, we can define parameters and refer to those instead. It's most convenient to specify project directory parameters in terms of TOP, the project root location. Thus, for the header file and library directories, you'd define parameters in *Project.tmpl* like this:

```
#ifndef IncludeSrc
#define IncludeSrc $(TOP)/include
#endif
#ifndef LibSrc
#define LibSrc $(TOP)/lib
#endif
INCLUDESRC = IncludeSrc
    LIBSRC = LibSrc
```

This has two distinct advantages over literal paths:

- TOP specifies the location of the top of the project tree. *imake* ensures that TOP is correct no matter what the current directory is, so parameters defined relative to TOP (such as INCLUDESRC and LIBSRC) are automatically defined correctly in every *Makefile*. This gives you a consistent way of referring to the header file and library directories (compare Tables 13–1 and 13–2).

Table 13–2: Directory Locations Expressed Using Parameters

From...	Path to *include*	Path to *lib*
project root	$(INCLUDESRC)	$(LIBSRC)
lib	$(INCLUDESRC)	$(LIBSRC)
app	$(INCLUDESRC)	$(LIBSRC)

- Parameters make it easy to change directory references, e.g., to reconfigure your project after rearranging the source tree. Simply modify the parameter values in the configuration files to reflect layout changes, and rebuild your Makefiles to propagate the new values thoughout the project.

Specifying Library Names

Suppose you've written a library of useful functions that you build as *libuseful.a* in the *lib* directory of your project. You could refer to this library in the project's Imakefiles by writing out the pathname literally, but that is subject to the problems discussed in the previous section: the path to the library directory varies by location within the project (or from machine to machine), and the path references must be revised if you rearrange the project. An additional consideration is that if the library really is so wonderful, you'll likely decide to use it in other projects, too. If you do, you might split it out into a separate project and install it as a system library for general use. When you do that, however, references to the library from within the original project change (from pathname form to *–luseful*) and must be revised.

We can solve the problem using parameters instead of literal values. When *libuseful.a* is built within your project, define parameters for it in *Project.tmpl* like this:

```
#ifndef UsefulLib
#define UsefulLib $(TOP)/lib/LibraryTargetName(useful)
#endif
#ifndef DepUsefulLib
#define DepUsefulLib $(TOP)/lib/LibraryTargetName(useful)
#endif
    USEFULLIB = UsefulLib
```

```
DEPUSEFULLIB = DepUsefulLib
```

Then you refer to the library in your project's Imakefiles using these parameters. For example:

```
BuildProgram(prog,$(SRCS),$(OBJS),$(USEFULLIB),$(DEPUSEFULLIB))
```

If you split out *libuseful.a* into its own project and make it a system library later, the only change you need to make to the original project is to change the values of UsefulLib and DepUsefulLib in the configuration files:

```
#ifndef UsefulLib
#define UsefulLib -luseful
#endif
#ifndef DepUsefulLib
#define DepUsefulLib /**/
#endif
    USEFULLIB = UsefulLib
 DEPUSEFULLIB = DepUsefulLib
```

Then rebuild your Makefiles. No other changes are needed. You still refer to the library the same way in the Imakefiles ($(USEFULLIB), $(DEPUSEFULLIB)), even though the library now comes from a different source. This illustrates how parameters promote nomenclatural stability: the underlying details of library specification are buried in the configuration files so you can write Imakefiles in a consistent way.

Handling Newly Discovered Nonportabilities

Suppose you've written a project containing programs that create temporary files. You've ported the project to four different systems. On all of them */tmp* is the preferred temporary file directory, so you've done the expedient thing and written "/tmp" into your programs. Then you port the project to a fifth system and find that the temporary file directory is */var/tmp*. You've discovered a nonportability.

You might try to view this fly in the ointment as an opportunity to improve your code rather than as an annoyance, but regardless of the nature of your disposition, the system variation you've identified needs to be parameterized. TMPDIR will do for a parameter name, and we can set its value in *Project.tmpl* using the macro TmpDir.

What should the default value be? Here we use our porting experience to make a decision. The temporary file directory was the same on all systems except the most recent, so the default should be the value we've been using all along:

```
#ifndef TmpDir
#define TmpDir /tmp
#endif

TMPDIR = TmpDir
```

The default needs only to be overridden (as */var/tmp*) in the vendor file associated with the system we've most recently ported to. No overriding is necessary in the four original vendor files.

Each time you discover you've written a nonportable construct, fix it and add the discovery to your repertoire of experience. If possible, codify your knowledge by adding a mechanism to ensure portability to your configuration files (in the present case, we added the parameter TMPDIR). Instantiating your knowledge reduces your work in the future by helping to automate or formalize a configuration task. It also helps others, since the nonportability is made explicit in your configuration files (and so is the solution). This gives others who use and/or study your files the benefit of your experience and increases their awareness of portability issues that may affect their own projects.

Of course, we must still fix the source code of the programs that referred directly to */tmp*, so we need a mechanism to transmit the value of TMPDIR to the programs that need it. That's discussed later in the section "Configuring Source Files."

Conditionals in Imakefiles

It's a given that you'll use *cpp* conditionals in your configuration files, but less widely appreciated that conditionals can be used in Imakefiles, too. I'll show three applications of this fact:

* Selecting targets to build
* Selecting files or directories to process
* Selecting flags for commands

Selecting Targets To Build

You can use *cpp* conditionals in an *Imakefile* to select which programs to build. Suppose you have a project for a client-server application, and you want to build different programs depending on whether the machine is a client machine and/or server machine. If the macros ClientHost and ServerHost are defined as YES or NO, you can write the *Imakefile* like this:

```
#if ClientHost
CSRCS = client.c
COBJS = client.o

BuildProgram(client,$(CSRCS),$(COBJS),NullParameter,NullParameter)
InstallProgram(client,$(BINDIR))
```

```
#endif
#if ServerHost
SSRCS = server.c
SOBJS = server.o
BuildProgram(server,$(SSRCS),$(SOBJS),NullParameter,NullParameter)
InstallProgram(server,$(ETCDIR))
#endif
  SRCS = $(CSRCS) $(SSRCS)
DependTarget()
```

The defaults for ClientHost and ServerHost can be placed in *Project.tmpl* and overidden appropriately on a per-machine basis in *site.def.*

Note that if both ClientHost and ServerHost are NO, nothing is built. If you consider that an error (as well you might), you can put the following at the beginning of the *Imakefile*:

```
#if !ClientHost && !ServerHost
all::
    @echo "Neither a client nor a server be?"
    @echo "Please define ClientHost and/or ServerHost as YES."
#endif
```

If both symbols are NO when the *Makefile* is generated, *make* alerts you to the problem at build time.

Selecting Files or Directories To Process

imake is designed to allow you to write machine-independent target description files, but sometimes you really do need to know the kind of machine on which you're running. In such cases, it's helpful to exploit *imake*'s knowledge about your system.

Suppose you're writing a project that shares some of its source among all platforms on which the project is built, but also contains a significant amount of platform-dependent source. You can put the machine-independent source in one subdirectory, *mi*, and partition the machine-dependent source for each platform into separate subdirectories.

When you build the project, the code in *mi* is used on all platforms, so that directory should always be processed. But only one of the machine-dependent directories should be processed. How do you tell which one? *imake* helps us here. The system type is determined by the vendor blocks in the configuration files when *imake* runs, and each vendor block defines a unique architecture symbol like UltrixArchitecture or SunArchitecture. You can test those symbols using conditionals in the *Imakefile* to select the proper machine-dependent directory.

If you've ported the project to Sun, HP, SGI, and DEC machines, for example, you can write the *Imakefile* as shown in Figure 13–2. The figure illustrates how the *Imakefile* selects the proper parts of the project tree for processing. *mi* is always included in the value of SUBDIRS, regardless of architecture. The directory named by MD_DIR is machine-dependent; the architecture symbols are used to determine its value. This organization helps you modularize your project to keep its complexity manageable: to port the program to a new system, add a new directory containing code for that system and add a new selector block to the project root *Imakefile*.

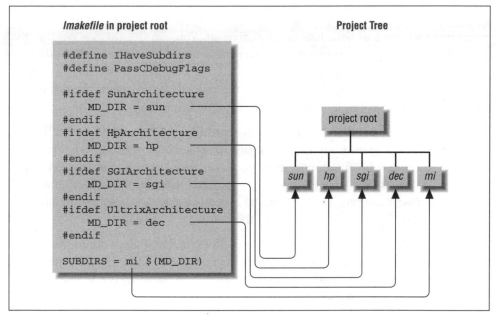

Figure 13–2: Directory-selecting Imakefile

If the amount of machine-dependent code is not extensive, it may make more sense to keep it all in a single directory and select individual files rather than directories. Suppose you're writing a program that processes CPU load information. This involves yanking CPU time information out of the running kernel. Unfortunately, the system interface to get that information varies widely among versions of UNIX and is highly machine-dependent. Table 13–3 shows some of the differences for several types of systems.

Table 13-3: System CPU Time Interface Differences

System Dependency	SunOS 5.x	HP-UX 9.x	IRIX 5.x	Ultrix 4.x
UNIX image name	not needed	*/hp-ux*	*/unix*	*/vmunix*
CPU time symbol name	*cpu*	*cp_time*	*sysinfo*	*_ccpu*
function to read namelist	*kvm_nlist()*	*nlist()*	*nlist()*	*nlist()*
function to read CPU time	*kvm_read()*	*read()*	*sysmp()*	*read()*
number of CPU states	5	9	6	4
link libraries	*-lkvm -lelf*	none	*-lmld*	none

All these differences add up to a fun time when you're trying to write a portable program. You can tear your hair out and give up. You can decide to scrap the goal of portability and make your program run on a single kind of machine. You can litter its source code with an ugly rat's nest of #ifdefs that test for machine type. Or you can let *imake* help you determine the machine type, again by making use of the architecture symbols defined in the configuration files.

One way to attack the difficulty is to wedge a level of abstraction between the system calls and the main body of your program. Instead of writing your main program to know about different system interfaces, you define specifications for a standard interface. For example, you can declare that the "CPU load interface" consists of two functions: InitCPULoad(), to do any system-specific initialization necessary, and GetCPULoad(), to return the current CPU load.

Then, for each system you support, you write a machine-dependent source file implementing this standard interface. Each file performs all the gyrations necessary to wrest the desired information from one particular system type and maps it onto a form suitable for the standard interface.

In the *Imakefile*, use the architecture-indicator symbols defined by the vendor blocks in the configuration files to select the machine-dependent file. The *Imakefile* below generates a *Makefile* that compiles the program from *main.c* and the appropriate machine-dependent file, and links in any special libraries needed:

```
#ifdef SunArchitecture
    CPU_SRC = cpu-sunos.c
    CPU_OBJ = cpu-sunos.o
    CPU_LIB = -lkvm -lelf
#endif
#ifdef HPArchitecture
    CPU_SRC = cpu-hpux.c
    CPU_OBJ = cpu-hpux.o
    CPU_LIB =
#endif
#ifdef SGIArchitecture
    CPU_SRC = cpu-irix.c
```

```
        CPU_OBJ = cpu-irix.o
        CPU_LIB = -lmld
#endif
#ifdef UltrixArchitecture
        CPU_SRC = cpu-ultrix.c
        CPU_OBJ = cpu-ultrix.o
        CPU_LIB =
#endif
          SRCS = main.c $(CPU_SRC)
          OBJS = main.o $(CPU_OBJ)
BuildProgram(prog,$(SRCS),$(OBJS),$(CPU_LIB),NullParameter)
```

Selecting Flags for Commands

The X11, SP, and DP files each allow you to pass special definitions to compile commands in a given directory by assigning a value to DEFINES in the *Imakefile*.

You can set DEFINES unconditionally:

```
    DEFINES = -Dflag
```

Or, if you need to pass a flag only when some condition holds, you can make the assignment conditional:

```
#if condition
    DEFINES = -Dflag
#endif
```

When you have several conditional flags, setting DEFINES becomes trickier. Suppose you have two conditional flags. You could set DEFINES by testing each combination of conditions:

```
#if condition_1
#  if condition_2
    DEFINES = -Dflag_1 -Dflag_2
#  else
    DEFINES = -Dflag_1
#  endif
#else
#  if condition_2
    DEFINES = -Dflag_2
#  else
    DEFINES =
#  endif
#endif
```

The trouble with this approach is that the number of tests grows exponentially as the number of conditions increases: for n conditions, the number of tests is 2^n, which quickly becomes unmanageable.

A better way to attack the complexity that arises from multiple conditions is to test each one independently, record the result in an auxiliary *make* variable, and concatenate the results after all the tests are performed. Then the number of tests equals the number of conditions.

Suppose you have four conditional flags. To check every combination of conditions you'd need 16 tests. Instead, to keep the number of tests at four, do the following:

```
#if condition_1
    AUXDEF_1 - -Dflag_1
#endif
#if condition_2
    AUXDEF_2 = -Dflag_2
#endif
#if condition_3
    AUXDEF_3 = -Dflag_3
#endif
#if condition_4
    AUXDEF_4 = -Dflag_4
#endif
        DEFINES = $(AUXDEF_1) $(AUXDEF_2) $(AUXDEF_3) $(AUXDEF_4)
```

Each `AUXDEF_n` variable records the result of a test. If condition n holds, the variable is set to –D*flag_n*, otherwise it's empty.[*] Then `DEFINES` is set to the concatenation of the auxiliary variables. Using this technique, the number of tests for n conditions is n rather than 2^n.

Configuring Source Files

imake characteristically generates Makefiles that contain values for each of your configuration parameters, represented by *make* variables. These variables are available at your fingertips for generating commands from within *Makefile* target entries. But sometimes you need the values of those variables in files other than a *Makefile*:

- A C program or shell script creates temporary files. How do the programs know where your system's temporary file directory is?

- A project installs a server program and a file that the server reads when it starts up. How does the server know where its startup file is?

- A help file needs editing to reflect local convention for the email address to which help requests can be sent. How can that be done automatically?

- A program needs to know whether or not it can use shared memory. How can it tell?

---

[*] That is, the variable is not assigned any value and is therefore implicitly empty.

All these questions can be answered if we can find a way to get values of our configuration parameters into the source files we want to configure.

Let's say our files need to know the pathname of the system directory used for temporary files. We can define the parameter in *Project.tmpl*:

```
#ifndef TmpDir
#define TmpDir /tmp
#endif
TMPDIR = TmpDir
```

Makefiles generated using the configuration files will have a line in them like this:

```
TMPDIR = /tmp
```

The value of `TmpDir` can be overridden as necessary in the vendor or site file, e.g., as */usr/tmp, /var/tmp*, etc., and Makefiles are affected accordingly.

We can get this parameter value into our source files several ways. For a single C source file *src.c*, pass the value to the compile operation using `SpecialCObject-Rule()`, a rule discussed in Chapter 6, *Writing Imakefiles*:

```
SpecialCObjectRule(src,NullParameter,'-DTMPDIR="$(TMPDIR)"')
```

This passes a definition for the macro `TMPDIR` to the command that compiles *src.c*. The value of the macro `TMPDIR` is the value of the variable `TMPDIR` from the *Makefile*. You might use its value in *src.c* like this:

```
char *tmpDir = TMPDIR;
```

If you want to provide a "best guess" default value in *src.c* (e.g., so it can be compiled by hand), write this instead:

```
#ifndef TMPDIR
#define TMPDIR "/usr/tmp"
#endif
char *tmpDir = TMPDIR;
```

The same technique can be used to compile a server program that needs to know where its startup file is. Assuming that `ETCDIR` is defined in the configuration files somewhere, you can write the *Imakefile* like this:

```
SERVCONFFILE = $(ETCDIR)/myserv.conf
        SRCS = myserv.c
        OBJS = myserv.o
BuildProgram(myserv,$(SRCS),$(OBJS),NullParameter,NullParameter)
InstallProgram(myserv,$(ETCDIR))
SpecialCObjectRule(myserv,NullParameter,'-DSERVCONFFILE="$(SERVCONFFILE)"')
InstallData(myserv.conf,$(ETCDIR))
```

In *myserv.c*, you might access the startup file name like this:

```
if ((f = fopen (SERVCONFFILE, "r")) == (FILE *) NULL) ...
```

When you need to send a parameter value into several or all C source files in a directory, `SpecialCObjectRule()` isn't very convenient since you must invoke it once for every file you want to compile specially. Instead, include the parameter in the value of `DEFINES`, which is passed to every compile command. For the previous examples, instead of invoking `SpecialCObjectRule()`, we could assign values to `DEFINES` like this:

```
DEFINES = '-DTMPDIR="$(TMPDIR)"'
DEFINES = '-DSERVCONFFILE="$(SERVCONFFILE)"'
```

`SpecialCObjectRule()` and `DEFINES` are appropriate only for C source files. If you need to configure executable scripts, the X11 rule `CppScriptTarget()` might be helpful. To use it, create a template file containing references to the parameters you're interested in. `CppScriptTarget()` generates an entry that runs the template through *cpp* to perform parameter value substitution and writes the output to the destination file. For instance, if we want to generate a shell script that needs to know the value of `TMPDIR`, we could write it as a template *script.sh* and put a line like this in it:

```
tmpdir=TMPDIR
```

To produce the script from the template, invoke `CppScriptTarget()` in the *Imakefile*:

```
CppScriptTarget(script,script.sh,'-DTMPDIR=$(TMPDIR)',NullParameter)
```

The script generated by the resulting *Makefile* target entry will have a line in it like this:

```
tmpdir=/tmp
```

You can refer to the directory in the script using variable references of the form `$tmpdir` or `${tmpdir}`.

A related rule is `CppFileTarget()`, which is like `CppScriptTarget()` except that the target isn't made executable.

Configuring Source Files with msub

You can specify more than one `-D` option in the last argument to `Special-CObjectRule()` or in the third argument to `CppScriptTarget()` or `CppFile-Target()`, but it doesn't take very many definitions before invocations of these rules become long and unwieldy. Both rules also require that you specify a definition for every parameter you want to substitute into the template.

An alternative is to use *msub*, a program designed specifically to yank parameter values out of Makefiles and substitute them into templates to produce properly configured destination files.* It reads a *Makefile* and determines the values of all the parameters named in it, then reads a template file and replaces parameter references in it with the corresponding parameter values. You refer to parameter variables in *msub* templates the same way as in a *Makefile*, i.e., as $(var) or ${var}. No prior arrangement is necessary to use a particular *make* variable. All of them are available on demand, so you need not list the variables you want in rule invocations.

Suppose a program uses a help file that indicates the local email address to which questions about the program may be sent. The address can be parameterized and given a default value in *Project.tmpl*:

```
#ifndef EMailHelpAddr
#define EMailHelpAddr help@my.host.edu
#endif

EMAILHELPADDR = EMailHelpAddr
```

This address is likely to vary from machine to machine, but the default can be overridden in *site.def* as necessary.

To use the email parameter, write the help file as an *msub* template *helpfile.msub* that contains the following:

```
  :
  :
If you have questions, send an electronic mail message
to $(EMAILHELPADDR).
  :
  :
```

To generate the help file manually, use this command:

```
% msub helpfile.msub > helpfile
```

msub looks in the *Makefile*, finds that EMAILHELPADDR has the value help@my.host.edu, and substitutes that value into the template. The result, *helpfile*, looks like this:

```
  :
  :
If you have questions, send an electronic mail message
to help@my.host.edu.
  :
  :
```

---

* *msub* is available as part of the *itools* distribution. See Appendix A, *Obtaining Configuration Software*.

To use *msub* with *imake*, we need a rule to produce a target entry. Here's a simple one:

```
#define MsubTarget(dest,src)                        @@\
AllTarget(dest)             ,                        @@\
dest: src                                           @@\
    $(MSUB) src > dest                              @@\
StuffToClean(dest)
```

This rule refers to MSUB, which we define either in the system description section of *Imake.tmpl* or in *Project.tmpl*:

```
#ifndef MsubCmd
#define MsubCmd msub
#endif

MSUB = MsubCmd
```

A target description for *helpfile* in an *Imakefile* looks like this:

```
MsubTarget(helpfile,helpfile.msub)
```

msub can also be used to produce other kinds of targets, such as executable scripts. A rule for doing this is shown below. It's similar to MsubTarget(), but it makes the target executable:

```
#define MsubScriptTarget(dest,src)                  @@\
AllTarget(dest)                                     @@\
dest: src                                           @@\
    $(MSUB) src > dest                              @@\
    chmod a+x dest                                  @@\
StuffToClean(dest)
```

Use the rule as follows. Suppose you want to write a script that formats and prints manual pages. You can write a template *prman.msub* that looks like this:

```
#!$(SHELL)
$(TROFF) $(MANMACROS) $1 | $(PRINTER)
```

The target description for *prman* in an *Imakefile* looks like this:

```
MsubScriptTarget(prman,prman.msub)
```

After generating the *Makefile* you can produce the executable script *prman*:

```
% make prman
msub prman.msub > prman
chmod a+x prman
```

What does *prman* look like? It depends on your *Makefile*. If the *Makefile* contains the following parameter assignments:

```
     TROFF = $(BINDIR)/pstroff
 MANMACROS = -man
   PRINTER = $(LPR) -P$(PSPRINTER)
       LPR = lpr
 PSPRINTER = laser1
    BINDIR = /usr/bin
     SHELL = /bin/sh
```

then *prman* will look like this:

```
#!/bin/sh
/usr/bin/pstroff -man $1 | lpr -Plaser1
```

Note that *msub* unwinds embedded variable references, e.g., TROFF is defined as $(BINDIR)/*pstroff*, but, given that BINDIR is */usr/bin*, the value that's substituted into the template for TROFF is */usr/bin/pstroff*.

When *msub* is used to produce input files for script processors that allow variable references of the form ${*var*} or $(*var*), an ambiguity arises. For instance, *msub* and *sh* both recognize ${*var*} as a variable reference, so in an *msub* template does ${*var*} refer to a shell variable that you want *msub* to leave alone, or to a *make* variable for which you want *msub* to substitute the variable's value?

To avoid the ambiguity, you can make use of the fact that the shell recognizes $var and *msub* doesn't, whereas *msub* recognizes $(*var*) and the shell doesn't.

It's also possible to eliminate the ambiguity. You can tell *msub* to recognize variable reference delimiters other than $(...) and ${...} using the *+R* and *−R* options. For example, to use @< and >@ to refer to variables that you want *msub* to recognize, invoke *msub* like this:

```
% msub +R"@<" -R">@" template > output
```

You must quote the delimiters in this case because < and > are special to the shell.

An example of a script template that uses these delimiters follows:

```
#!@<SHELL>@
TMPFILE=@<TMPDIR>@/xxx$$
command1 $* > ${TMPFILE}
command2 < ${TMPFILE}
@<RM>@ ${TMPFILE}
```

When *msub* is told to recognize only @< and @>, the references to ${TMPFILE} in the template are unambiguous and will pass untouched into the final script.

The MsubScriptTarget() rule shown earlier doesn't allow any means of passing the +*R* and −*R* options to *msub*, so we need a rule with a little more flexibility:

```
#define MsubScriptTargetWithFlags(dest,src,flags)     @@\
AllTarget(dest)                                       @@\
dest: src                                             @@\
    $(MSUB) flags src > dest                          @@\
    chmod a+x dest                                    @@\
StuffToClean(dest)
```

Now we can write target descriptions like this:

```
MsubScriptTargetWithFlags(script,script.msub,+R"@<" -R">@")
```

Configuring Macro Values into Source Files

The methods we've discussed for configuring source files are all predicated on the use of parameters that are available as *make* variables. Sometimes it's necessary to configure files based on the values of *cpp* macros instead. For instance, if you're writing a program that uses shared memory when it's available and a fallback method otherwise, you can express the system's shared memory capability using a macro:

```
#ifndef HasShm
#if SystemV || SystemV4
#define HasShm YES
#else
#define HasShm NO
#endif
#endif
```

However, you can't test HasShm in C source files because it's available only when the *Makefile* is generated, not when you run *make* to compile your program. But you can transmit the macro value to compiler commands by assigning it to a macro the compiler does have access to.

To do so for an individual file, use SpecialCObjectRule():

```
SpecialCObjectRule(src,NullParameter,-DHASSHM=HasShm)
```

To pass the value to all compiler commands, use DEFINES:

```
DEFINES = -DHASSHM=HasShm
```

Either way, the effect is to define HASSHM at compile time as either YES or NO (i.e., as either 1 or 0). Within C source files, test HASSHM to determine availability of shared memory:

```
#if HASSHM
    /* shared memory is available */
#else
    /* shared memory is not available */
#endif
```

Configuring Header Files

If a programming project uses several configuration parameters in several C source files, it's tedious to write out the parameters in invocations of SpecialCObject-Rule() or in definitions of DEFINES, especially if you need to do so in multiple Imakefiles. It would be much easier if any source file that needed access to any of the parameter values could simply #include a header file.

We can accomplish that by generating just such a header file *conf.h* from an *msub* template *conf.h.msub*. Suppose we want the template file to contain the parameters we've discussed in the previous examples (temporary file directory, server startup file pathname, email address, shared memory availability). TMPDIR, SERVCONFFILE, and EMAILHELPADDR can be taken directly from the *Makefile* by *msub*, since they're *make* variables. However, the availablility of shared memory is determined by a macro HasShm, not by a variable which is accessible to *msub*. We need to get around this by inventing a *make* variable that corresponds to HasShm so *msub* can get at it:

```
HASSHM = HasShm
```

Now we can write *conf.msub* like this:

```
/* configuration parameter header file */

#define tmpDir          "${TMPDIR}"
#define servConfFile    "${SERVCONFFILE}"
#define emailHelpAddr   "${EMAILHELPADDR}"
#define HASSHM          ${HASSHM}
```

To produce the header file *conf.h*, invoke MsubTarget() in the *Imakefile*:

```
MsubTarget(conf.h,conf.msub)
depend:: conf.h
```

The depend entry is necessary because source files may depend on *conf.h*, and we must ensure *conf.h* exists before header file dependencies are generated. The depend line should precede the invocation of DependTarget() in the *Imakefile*, so that *make depend* causes *conf.h* to be generated before *makedepend* is executted.

Using make Suffix Rules

In addition to explicit rules for building targets, *make* supports the concept of implicit rules to determine how to produce one type of file from another (e.g., how to derive object files from C source files, C source files from *lex* files, object files from FORTRAN source files). These rules are called suffix rules because they're driven by filename suffixes (.c, .o, .l, .f, etc.). This section describes how to usc *imake* to take advantage of them.

An example suffix rule (for deriving a .o file from a .c file) follows. It specifies the source and target suffixes, as well as the command to execute to produce the target file from the source file. ($< signifies the file from which the target is built):

```
.c.o:
    $(CC) $(CFLAGS) -c $<
```

make has a set of built-in (default) suffix rules used to produce targets provided there are no explicit instructions otherwise. For those occasions when the built-in rules are inadequate, you can modify *make*'s behavior several ways. Some examples of what you can do are:

- Tell *make* to compile certain object files specially, but all others using the default rule. This is done by overriding the default suffix rules for particular targets without changing the default rules.

- Tell *make* to compile all object files a certain way. This is done by redefining a suffix rule to change the way all object files are produced.

- Invent new suffix rules to define new target types. For instance, you can tell *make* how to process *.abc* files to produce *.xyz* targets.

Suppose you're compiling a set of .c source files to produce a set of .o object files. By default, *make* uses its built-in rule describing the .c → .o transformation. To override use of that rule for a particular target, use the *Makefile* to explicitly associate the target with the commands that produce it. For example, to turn on debugging code with *−DDEBUG* for a target you can use an entry like this:

```
file.o: file.c
    $(CC) $(CFLAGS) -DDEBUG -c file.c
```

The entry tells *make* to ignore the implicit built-in rule for *file.o*; the built-in rule continues to be used to compile other object files.

You can override the default for any number of individual targets:

```
file1.o: file1.c
    $(CC) $(CFLAGS) -DDEBUG -c file1.c
file2.o: file2.c
    $(CC) $(CFLAGS) -DDEBUG -c file2.c
```

```
file3.o: file3.c
    $(CC) $(CFLAGS) -DDEBUG -c file3.c
```

However, you can achieve the same result more easily with *imake* by writing a rule macro and placing it in *Imake.rules*:

```
/* compile obj from src with debugging code enabled */
#define
DebugCompile(obj,src)                                          @@\
obj: src                                                       @@\
    $(CC) $(CFLAGS) -DDEBUG -c src
```

Then we invoke `DebugCompile()` in the *Imakefile* once for each object file to be compiled specially:

```
DebugCompile(file1.o,file1.c)
DebugCompile(file2.o,file2.c)
DebugCompile(file3.o,file3.c)
```

This allows us to write more concise target descriptions. Using the resulting *Makefile*, *make* compiles *file1.o*, *file2.o*, and *file3.o* specially; other object files are still compiled normally.

If you want to compile every object in the *Imakefile* specially, you can invoke `DebugCompile()` for each one, but it's easier and more efficient to redefine the suffix rule itself:

```
.c.o:
    $(CC) $(CFLAGS) -DDEBUG -c $<
```

What you do with the rule depends on the extent to which you want it to propagate into your Makefiles:

- You can place the suffix rule directly in the *Imakefile*:

  ```
  .c.o:
      $(CC) $(CFLAGS) -DDEBUG -c $<
  ⋮
  other target descriptions
  ⋮
  ```

  This is suitable when you want the rule to apply to a single *Makefile*. However, to make the rule apply to several Makefiles throughout your project, you'd have to write it into all the corresponding Imakefiles. That's a lot of work to begin with, and if you want to change the suffix rule later, you're faced with several tedious and repetitive edits.

- You can place the suffix rule directly in *Imake.rules*:

```
.c.o:
    $(CC) $(CFLAGS) -DDEBUG -c $<
:
other rule definitions
:
```

This method is suitable when you want to override the default suffix rule project-wide. Since *Imake.rules* is used to generate all your Makefiles, centralizing the rule definition into *Imake.rules* propagates it into every *Makefile* automatically. It's unnecessary to write the rule into every *Imakefile*. This method also makes the rule easy to change; just edit *Imake.rules* and run *imake* to regenerate your Makefiles with the new definition.

However, since the method propagates the suffix rule indiscriminately into every *Makefile*, it doesn't give you much help if you want the rule to apply only to certain Makefiles.

- You can place the suffix rule in *Imake.rules* as a rule macro instead of writing it directly:

```
#define DebugCompileRule()                        @@\
.c.o:                                             @@\
    $(CC) $(CFLAGS) -DDEBUG -c $<
:
other rule definitions
:
```

In this case, you invoke the macro (once) in each *Imakefile* to which you want the suffix rule to apply:

```
DebugCompileRule()
:
other target descriptions
:
```

Again the definition is centralized in *Imake.rules*, so it's written only once and it's easy to change. In addition, you have complete control over propagation of the suffix rule: if you invoke DebugCompileRule() in the *Imakefile*, the modified suffix rule applies to the corresponding *Makefile*; if you don't invoke it, the default suffix rule applies.

Defining New Target Types

You can define a new target type by writing an appropriate suffix rule. To do so, write the rule and use the methods just described to propagate it into your Makefiles. The only difference is that in addition to providing a definition for the suffix rule, you must also supply a `.SUFFIXES` line to inform *make* of the new suffixes.

For example, suppose you have a project that runs *.abc* files through a filter to produce *.xyz* files. You might write a suffix rule like this (`$@` signifies the target to be built):

```
.SUFFIXES: .abc .xyz
.abc.xyz:
    filter $< > $@
```

As before, you can put this suffix rule in an *Imakefile* to propagate it into an individual *Makefile*, or in *Imake.rules* to propagate it into all Makefiles. Or, if you want the rule to apply selectively only to certain Makefiles, write it as a rule macro:

```
#define AbcXyzSuffixRule ()                   @@\
.SUFFIXES: .abc .xyz                          @@\
.abc.xyz:                                     @@\
    filter $< > $@
```

Then invoke `AbcXyzSuffixRule()` once in each *Imakefile* to which you want the suffix rule to apply.

Shell Programming in Rules

This section discusses some ways to use shell programming constructs in *imake* rules. It's sometimes necessary to use these constructs to circumvent some of *make*'s limitations. For example, *make* support for programming facilities such as conditionals or loops is meager, but you can get around this with a little creative use of the shell in *Makefile* entries.

Multiple-Line Constructs

The shell allows you to write command sequences that execute over the course of several lines. Here's an example:

```
set +x
for i in a b c; do
    echo $i
done
```

Multiple-line sequences like this that you might put in a shell script don't work the same way in a *Makefile* target entry. We must make several changes:

- *make* and the shell both treat $ specially, so $i is not sufficient to indicate a shell variable reference. To tell *make* to pass a $ to the shell, you must double it as $$ in the *Makefile*.

- *make* spawns a new shell for each command line of a *Makefile* entry. This causes two problems:

  — Shell flag and variable settings don't carry over from one line to another. The effect of *set +x* vanishes as soon as the *set* command finishes executing. Similarly, the shell variable i only retains its value through the end of the line on which it's set; by the time the *echo* command is executed, the variable has no value.

  — You lose the continuity necessary for multiple-line statements. A *for* loop only makes sense when executed by a single shell. In the previous entry, the loop is executed by multiple shells, the continuity is lost, and you get syntax errors.

  Both problems can be corrected by treating multiple-line constructs as a single command line. To do this, introduce semicolons between commands and backslash continuation characters at the ends of lines as necessary.

When we double the $-signs and add semicolons and backslashes, the target entry looks like this:

```
target:
    set +x;                 \
    for i in a b c; do  \
        echo $$i;           \
    done
```

To convert a multiple-line construct in a *Makefile* entry that contains multiple-line constructs for use as an *imake* rule, we add the usual @@\ *imake* continuation sequence at the ends of rule lines. Thus, the preceding target entry looks like this in a rule definition:

```
#define SomeRule()                          @@\
target:                                     @@\
    set +x;                 \               @@\
    for i in a b c; do  \                   @@\
        echo $$i;           \               @@\
    done
```

The syntax is ugly, but constructs like this are indispensable for carrying out complex tasks such as multiple-file or recursive operations.

Directory Changes

Sometimes it's necessary to write a rule that changes directory, e.g., to process files in subdirectories. You can use *cd* in a target entry, but the commands to which the *cd* applies must be part of the same command line so they're all executed by the same shell:

```
#define SomeRule(dir)                    @@\
target:                                  @@\
    cd dir;          \                   @@\
    command1;        \                   @@\
    command2
```

A complication is that if a *cd* should apply to only some of the commands on a command line, its effect must be isolated. For example, a loop that processes sub-directories might need to change into each subdirectory, run some commands, then return to the parent directory before the next pass through the loop. Restoration of the parent directory can be accomplished by executing the *cd* and the commands associated with it in a subshell. This is done by surrounding them with parentheses:

```
#define SomeRule(dirs)                   @@\
target::                                 @@\
    for i in dirs; do        \           @@\
        (cd $$i; commands);  \           @@\
    done
```

It is incorrect to *cd* into a directory and then *cd* back up. If a subdirectory is a symlink, the second *cd* command won't change back into the original parent directory. So *do not* write the rule like this:

```
#define IncorrectRule(dirs)              @@\
target::                                 @@\
    for i in dirs; do          \         @@\
        cd $$i; commands; cd ..;  \      @@\
    done
```

Command Echoing

make normally echoes commands before it executes them; an @-prefix on a command suppresses echoing. However, in a multiple-command sequence, you can't use @ as a prefix on any but the first command since *make* doesn't recognize @ in the middle of command lines. If you want to suppress echoing of some commands within a sequence but not others, use @ at the beginning of the sequence and adopt one of the following approaches:

- Use *echo* explicitly to echo those commands you deem important to announce:

```
#define SomeRule(args)                          @@\
target:                                         @@\
    @for a in args;                    \        @@\
    do                                 \        @@\
        echo "command 1";              \        @@\
        command 1;                     \        @@\
        command 2;                     \        @@\
    done
```

- Use *set* *−x* to invoke the shell's own echoing facilities. It's also useful to enclose within parentheses the commands you want echoed so that echoing terminates when the subshell finishes:

```
#define SomeRule(args)                          @@\
target:                                         @@\
    @for a in args;                    \        @@\
    do                                 \        @@\
        (set -x; command 1);           \        @@\
        command 2;                     \        @@\
    done
```

Error Processing in Rules

make normally quits when a command terminates in error, but you can specify *−i* on the command line to tell *make* to ignore errors and continue processing. A related flag is *−k*. When a target depends on multiple prerequisites, *−k* tells *make* to build as many prerequisites as possible, even if the attempts to build some of them fail.

The *−i* and *−k* flags both cause *make* to execute commands more aggressively than usual in the face of error. However, a command line in a target entry that consists of multiple commands can subvert the intent of these options: if any command in the line fails, the shell exits early without executing the rest of the line. If you want all commands to execute in partially failed multiple-command lines, too, you can use *set* *+e* to turn off the shell's early termination behavior.

Within a target entry, you can use the following construct to execute *set* *+e* conditionally according to the presence or absence of *−i*:

```
case '${MFLAGS}' in *[i]*) set +e;; esac
```

Use the construct by prepending it to the command sequence to which it should apply. Here's an example (a rule that installs several files one at a time):

```
#define InstallFiles(files,dir,flags)                     @@\
install:: files                                           @@\
    MakeDir(dir)                                          @@\
    @case '${MFLAGS}' in *[i]*) set +e;; esac;        \   @@\
    for i in files; do                                \   @@\
        (set -x; $(INSTALL) $(INSTCOPY) flags $$i dir); \ @@\
    done
```

In a recursive rule you may want to test for both −*i* and −*k*. This example runs *make clean* in each of a set of directories:

```
#define RecursiveClean(dirs)                            @@\
clean::                                                 @@\
    @case '${MFLAGS}' in *[ik]*) set +e;; esac;    \    @@\
    for i in dirs ;                                \    @@\
    do                                             \    @@\
        (cd $$i;                                   \    @@\
        echo "cleaning in $(CURRENT_DIR)/$$i...";  \    @@\
        $(MAKE) $(MFLAGS) clean);                  \    @@\
    done
```

Writing a World Target

The commands to build a project from start to finish might look something like this:

```
% make Makefile
% make Makefiles
% make clean
% make depend
% make
```

It's convenient to have a World target in the project root *Makefile* that allows you to do the same thing with one command:

```
% make World
```

The easiest way to write a World target entry in the *Makefile* is to concatenate the commands you run by hand:

```
World:
    $(MAKE) $(MFLAGS) Makefile
    $(MAKE) $(MFLAGS) Makefiles
    $(MAKE) $(MFLAGS) clean
    $(MAKE) $(MFLAGS) depend
    $(MAKE) $(MFLAGS)
```

World entries tend to vary from project to project, so it may not be worthwhile to write a rule to generate them. Just put the World entry directly in the *Imakefile*.

Note that when you move the project to another machine, you'll likely need to bootstrap the top-level *Makefile* before the World operation can be performed. Be sure to include instructions in your documentation. (No manual bootstrapping should be necessary if you write the rule that generates your Makefile target so that it uses *imboot* rather than invoking *imake* directly. See Chapter 10, *Coordinating Sets of Configuration Files*, for further details on how to do this.)

14

Troubleshooting Configuration Files

Double, double, toil and trouble;
Fire burn and cauldron bubble.
—Shakespeare, *Macbeth*

This chapter describes how to court disaster as you write or otherwise modify configuration files, i.e., various ways you can break them. You should also read Chapter 7, *Imakefile Troubleshooting*, because many of the problems that occur in Imakefiles can occur in configuration files as well.

Rule Syntax Errors

Suppose you have a rule that looks like this:

```
#define RuleName(param1,param2)        @@\
line a                                 @@\
line b                                 @@\
line c
```

If you edit this rule's definition, several mistakes are particularly easy to make:

- Inserting a line with no @@\ at the end into the middle of the rule:

```
#define RuleName(param1,param2)        @@\
line a                                 @@\
new line                                        ← error, missing @@\
line b                                 @@\
line c
```

  Result: the new definition won't include line b or line c.

- Adding a line at the end of the rule and forgetting to add @@\ to the end of the preceding line:

```
#define RuleName(param1,param2)        @@\
line a                                 @@\
line b                                 @@\
line c                                          ← error, missing @@\
new line
```

  Result: the new definition won't include `new line`.

- Deleting the last line of the rule and forgetting to drop the @@\ from the end of the preceding line:

```
#define RuleName(param1,param2)        @@\
line a                                 @@\
line b                                 @@\    ← error, extraneous @@\
```

  Result: the new definition will, but shouldn't, include the line following `line b`, whatever it might be.

Beware of making any of these errors—and suspect one of them immediately if you edit a rule and your Makefiles are broken after you rebuild them.

It's prudent while modifying configuration files to periodically run *make Makefile* twice in a row as a sanity check on your modifications. The first time builds a *Makefile* that incorporates the changes you've made; the second time helps verify that the new *Makefile* is still usable.

Whitespace Problems

Rules should be defined with no space between the rule name and the parameter list:

```
/* correct */
#define Rule(paramlist) ...
/* incorrect */
#define Rule (paramlist) ...
```

In the second case, *cpp* defines `Rule` as a parameterless macro with value (`paramlist`). If you invoke `Rule()` in an *Imakefile*, it causes two errors. First, when you generate the *Makefile*, you get an "argument mismatch" error from *cpp*. Second, when you use the *Makefile*, you discover it's malformed:

```
make: line nnn: syntax error
```

At line *nnn* of the *Makefile*, you'll find (`paramlist`), because `Rule()` won't have been expanded as you wanted. Get rid of the extraneous space and all will be well.

Malformed Conditionals

Some *cpp* macros are used in Boolean fashion and are defined as either YES or NO. Others are "existence" macros; they're "turned off" by being left undefined and "turned on" by being defined. These two types of macros are defined and tested differently, as summarized in Table 14-1.

Table 14-1: Use of Boolean and Existence Macros

Macro Type	How To Define	How To Test
Boolean	#define *MacroName* YES #define *MacroName* NO	#if *MacroName* #if !*MacroName*
Existence	#define *MacroName*	#ifdef *MacroName* #ifndef *MacroName*

Failure to distinguish the way each type of macro is used leads to problems:

- **Failure to test Boolean macros properly.** If a macro has a value of YES or NO and you test it with #ifdef, the test always succeeds since the macro is defined in either case. Use #if instead.

- **Failure to test existence macros properly.** An existence macro is defined with an empty value:

  ```
  #define MacroName /* as nothing */
  ```

  Suppose you test it like this:

  ```
  #if MacroName
  ```

  When *MacroName* is replaced by its value (i.e., nothing), the test turns into this:

  ```
  #if
  ```

  Since that's not a legal conditional, *cpp* complains about it:

  ```
  cpp: line nnn: syntax error
  ```

  Use #ifdef and #ifndef to test existence macros.

- **Overriding a macro with a value of the wrong type.** Suppose a macro is defined as a YES/NO Boolean in the template or project file, and you override the default in the site file by defining it as an existence macro:

  ```
  #define MacroName /* as nothing */
  ```

Your definition takes precedence, but now tests of the macro in the configuration files won't work correctly because you've given *MacroName* the wrong type of value.

Similarly, if a macro is normally defined as an existence value, and you override the default by defining it as though it were a Boolean (e.g., by giving it the value NO), you'll sabotage your configuration files. The following test succeeds, even if *MacroName*'s value is NO:

```
#ifdef MacroName
```

Misuse of Boolean and existence macros is easy to fall into, unfortunately. For instance, Motif 2.0 is normally used with X11R5, but the Motif 2.0 release notes suggest that if you want to try using Motif with X11R6, you should put the following in *site.def*:

```
#define UsingR6Source YES
#if defined(UsingR6Source)
#define XTop     top_of_X11r6_source_tree/xc
#else
#define XTop     top_of_X11r5_source_tree
#endif
```

The definition of UsingR6Source as YES implies that the macro is a Boolean, and thus that defining it as NO would have some effect. But that's not the case. UsingR6Source is tested only to see whether or not it's defined, not what its value is.

Along similar lines, OpenWindows 3.3 ships with a *site.def* file containing this line:

```
#define UseInstalled YES
```

However, UseInstalled is an existence macro, not a Boolean macro. The definition is incorrect, just like the definition of UsingR6Source above. In this case, the definition is not only incorrect, it results in error messages, manifest by the appearance of "macro redefined" messages when you execute *make Makefile*. This occurs because Makefiles generated from the OpenWindows configuration files produce an *imake* command that passes -DUseInstalled on the command line. That (correct) existence definition conflicts with the (incorrect) Boolean definition in *site.def*, and *cpp* complains about it. The fix for this problem is described in Appendix J, *Using imake with OpenWindows*.

Unbalanced Conditionals

Conditional constructs begin with #if, #ifdef, or #ifndef, and end with #endif. If you're missing either the beginning or the end, *cpp* complains:

```
cpp: If-less endif            (Beginning of conditional missing)
cpp: missing endif            (End of conditional missing)
```

These errors usually occur if you forget to do the whole job when you're adding or removing a conditional construct. They're sometimes pernicious and difficult to diagnose, since *cpp* may not alert you until it's far away from the source of the problem. (For instance, *cpp* doesn't detect or announce a missing #endif until it sees "end of file" on the input stream.) Another reason a missing beginning or ending might be hard to spot, even if you have some idea where the problem might be, is that it can be embedded in a morass of other conditionals. The following construct (modified from part of X11's *Imake.tmpl*) illustrates this. Do you see the problem?

```
#ifndef UsrLibDir
#ifdef ProjectRoot
#define UsrLibDir Concat(ProjectRoot,/lib)
#ifndef AlternateUsrLibDir
#define AlternateUsrLibDir YES
#endif
#else
#define UsrLibDir /usr/lib
#ifndef AlternateUsrLibDir
#define AlternateUsrLibDir NO
#endif
#else
#ifndef AlternateUsrLibDir
#define AlternateUsrLibDir YES
#endif
#endif
```

The error is a missing #endif after the tenth line.

Before resigning yourself to some careful detective work, you might try using *imdent*, a utility that shows *cpp* conditional levels by adding indentation based on #if (#ifdef, #ifndef) nesting.[*] *imdent* often gives a strong visual clue as to the location of imbalances. (For example, it helped me catch errors several times while I was working on the DP files in Chapter 11, *Introduction to Configuration File Writing*.)

Missing Default Values

When a *make* variable is assigned the value of a *cpp* macro, the macro must be defined prior to the variable assignment. Otherwise the *make* variable is set to the literal macro name.

---

[*] *imdent* is available as part of the *itools* distribution. See Appendix A, *Obtaining Configuration Software*.

Suppose you create a parameter for the *awk* program so you can refer to it symbolically. To do this, you put a new parameter assignment in your configuration files:

```
AWK = AwkCmd
```

After you regenerate the *Makefile*, you set about building a target that's produced using *awk*:

```
% make awk-thing
AwkCmd file > output
sh: AwkCmd: not found
*** Error code 1
make: Fatal error: Command failed for target "awk-thing"
```

When you look through your *Makefile*, you find that the parameter assignment is exactly as you specified in the configuration files:

```
AWK = AwkCmd
```

No macro substitution occurred for AwkCmd. That's because you forgot to provide a default value for it. Without it, *cpp* thinks AwkCmd is a literal value, not a macro name. You need to provide a default:

```
#ifndef AwkCmd
#define AwkCmd awk
#endif

AWK = AwkCmd
```

Then after you rebuild the *Makefile*, AWK will be defined as awk and *awk-thing* will build properly:

```
% make awk-thing
awk file > output
```

Incorrect Version Number Tests

Vendor files often select parameter values depending on the version of the operating system (e.g., to compensate for deficiencies of older releases or to take advantage of new facilities in more recent releases). It's easy to write these so they appear correct but aren't quite. For instance, you might write the following, intending to distinguish releases 4.3 and up of an operating system from earlier releases:

```
#if OSMajorVersion >= 4 && OSMinorVersion >= 3
    /* 4.3 and up-specific stuff here */
#endif
```

The test is correct for releases 4.3, 4.4, 4.5, etc. But if the version ever reaches 5.0, the OSMinorVersion clause of the test fails. Write the test like this instead:

```
#if OSMajorVersion > 4 || (OSMajorVersion == 4 && OSMinorVersion >= 3)
    /* 4.3 and up-specific stuff here */
#endif
```

Missing Template

If the self-reference in your configuration files is incorrect, you'll end up with mis-configured rules for generating Makefile target entries. The result is that *imake* commands generated by them won't specify the correct location of the configuration directory. This causes the *Makefile*-generation process to fail at a very early stage because the template cannot be found. You'll see the following error from *cpp*:

```
Can't find include file Imake.tmpl
```

See Chapter 8, *A Closer Look at Makefile Generation*, for instructions on making sure the self-reference is correct.

Another possibility is that you're using software from a vendor that ships a broken bootstrapper and/or *imake*. You may have better luck if you install configuration software from a standard distribution (see Appendix B, *Installing Configuration Software*).

Nonportable cpp or make Constructs

Configuration files should be written assuming as little as possible about *cpp* because use of nonuniversal extensions reduces portability of those files. For instance, the following construct might work fine on your system:

```
#if Something
    /* stuff */
#elif SomethingElse
    /* more stuff */
#else
    /* yet more stuff */
#endif
```

However, many *cpp*s don't recognize #elif. It's mandated by the ANSI standard, but that's certainly no guarantee of portability—your *cpp* may not be ANSI conformant. Other directives to avoid are #import and #pragma. Using them reduces the portability of your configuration files.

Don't put comment text after #else or #endif narratives without protecting it in C comment markers. Older versions of *cpp* allow such comments, but the ANSI standard forbids them:

```
#endif end of test            Incorrect
#endif /* end of test */      Correct
```

Just as you shouldn't write nonportable *cpp* constructs in your configuration files, those files shouldn't generate *Makefile* constructs that rely on extensions made to different versions of *make*. Doing so reduces the portability of the *Makefile* produced by your configuration files. The VPATH variable, the use of null suffixes in suffix rules, and dependencies that specify individual files within a library are some examples of enhancements you should avoid.

Errors of Omission

Make sure you have a newline at the end of your configuration files. Some versions of *cpp* generate an incorrect *Makefile* if you don't.

15

Designing Extensible Configuration Files

Various authors have tackled bits and pieces of imake, but they fail to separate the tool's general use from the eccentricities of its employment in the distribution of the X Window System.

—Oram and Talbott, *Managing Projects with make*

To use *imake* to configure a project, we need a set of configuration files to use for building the Makefiles. However, it's a good idea to avoid writing new configuration files for every project. Developing software that way makes the *imake* cure worse than the nonportability disease.

One way to minimize the cost of configuring new projects is to reuse the configuration files from an existing project. This chapter is the first of three that cover the design and use of general-purpose configuration files that can be used again and again to configure multiple, possibly unrelated projects. It presents the necessary background and discusses implementation problems. Chapter 16, *Creating Extensible Configuration Files*, presents the implementation in cookbook form as a procedure you can apply to a set of existing configuration files to convert them for multiple-project use. Chapter 17, *Using Extensible Configuration Files*, shows how to use the files once you've created them.

Reusing Configuration Files

We don't rewrite *imake* when we start a new project, so why should we create new configuration files? Why not just reuse existing files over and over? Those are reasonable questions—but just what does it mean to "reuse" configuration files?

Reusability is related to portability and thus far we've discussed portability as it applies to software projects. But portability and reusability are somewhat different for configuration files.

Software is written to run on a system. If it's portable, the software can be reused without a lot of rewriting to run on different systems. Configuration files, on the other hand, are written to configure a software project. If they're portable, the files can be reused without a lot of rewriting to configure different projects.

It's clear that *imake* has been used successfully to achieve software portability. X11 is evidence of that—it runs on zillions of systems. It's not so clear whether configuration files themselves are so portable. This is reflected in our language: we speak of "the X11 configuration files," "the Khoros files," etc., identifying them according to the project for which they were designed and revealing our expectation that they will be put to a particular use.

The issues pertaining to this project specificity that we'll examine here are:

- Can we use configuration files written specifically for a given project to configure a different project?

- Are there difficulties we're likely to encounter in doing so? If there are, what alternatives are available?

We'll consider these questions in relation to the X11 configuration files. X11 has been widely and successfully deployed. The fact that it runs on so many different systems attests to the portability of the X11 software, the success of *imake* in configuring it, and how well suited the X11 files are to configuring the X11 distribution. The X11 configuration files are sufficiently well written that if any set of files might be expected to be reusable, they're it.

Are the X11 Configuration Files Reusable?

We can determine whether the X11 files are usable for projects other than X11 itself by inspecting existing software. For instance, the *contrib* software adjunct to the X11 core distribution and the Usenet newsgroup *comp.sources.x* are both sources of projects configured using the X11 files. This shows that the X11 files can indeed configure other programs—quite a few of them, in fact! But these projects do not tell us much about how generally the X11 files can be applied. After all, *contrib* and *comp.sources.x* projects are closely related to X11 itself, and they use the same sort of information: X libraries, X header files, X toolkits, X utilities, X this, X that.

If instead we want to configure a project that isn't based on X11 and hence doesn't use the same configuration information, we begin to run into difficulties. These arise principally from two somewhat contradictory properties of the X11 configuration files:

- **Too much information.** The X11 files contain a striking amount of information that will be irrelevant to our project—this is extra bulk and complexity that we could do without.[*] Parameters used to specify the names and locations of X libraries, header files, and utility programs are of no use to non-X programs. For instance, it's not likely we'll have a use for the particular bit of information shown below, assuming we even know what it refers to:

  ```
  #ifndef DefaultRGBDatabase
  #define DefaultRGBDatabase $(LIBDIR)/rgb
  #endif
  ```

- **Too little information.** The X11 files are tuned to X11 and not to our project, so we may need configuration information that's missing from them. If we need to find header files located in a nonstandard place, we must specify where they are. If we need to build a type of target not covered by the X11 rules, we need to define a new rule. If the project is built using programs not used to build X, we need to specify configuration parameters for those programs and any options they might take.

These two properties of the X11 files mean that they may not be the best match for the requirements of our project. Can we adapt them for our purposes? In theory we could go into */usr/X11R6.1/lib/X11/config* and modify the X11 files directly, but in practice we're not supposed to do that. (Witness the "Don't modify these files!" warnings they contain.) Of course, no one could stop us if we really wanted to make changes, but the warnings aren't there for nothing. In a very real sense the X11 files are "owned" by the X11 project: making arbitrary changes to them is definitely the wrong way to adapt them for other projects.

Why? For one thing, you can't simplify the X11 configuration files by deleting information your project doesn't need, since you can't just decide *ex cathedra* that information is superfluous to your project and that you'll therefore remove it. If you do, you'll break existing X-based projects. It isn't especially safe to add anything to the files, either. You'd better understand them pretty thoroughly before

---

[*] And the amount of information isn't likely to decrease any time soon, if the historical evidence means anything. The number of configuration parameters has increased steadily from R1 through R6.1.

you put anything else in them, or again you run the risk of breaking existing X11 projects. Also, you must check any new symbols you define to be sure they really are new, and it isn't sufficient to check only the configuration files—you also need to check every *Imakefile* in the entire X11 distribution. For example, if you were thinking about using the symbol OtherSources, be aware that although it isn't used anywhere in the installed configuration files, it is used under the server part of the source tree. You don't want to define it and possibly mess up server config-uration, do you? The phrase "fraught with peril" comes to mind and takes on a new and frightening immediacy in this context.

Instead of modifying the configuration files, you could try adding information to the *Imakefile*. When you need to access header files found in a nonstandard place, you can tell the C compiler where to look by adding a line like this:

```
INCLUDES = -I/extra/include/dir/path
```

Similarly, to add special symbol definitions, a line like this will do:

```
DEFINES = -Ddef1 -Ddef2 ...
```

The degree to which this kind of tweaking is reasonable depends on how exten-sive it needs to be. If you only have to add information to a single *Imakefile*, it's probably acceptable. But if your project spans multiple directories and you need to add a nontrivial amount of project-specific configuration information to each *Imakefile*, this process becomes ugly, tedious, and error prone very quickly. The misery associated with this kind of exercise is one of the things *imake* is supposed to help us avoid! We begin to suspect that the *i* in *imake* stands not for "include," as we were taught in the days of our youth, but for "invidious."

The feasibility of using the X11 configuration files for a new project is a direct function of the degree to which the project's configuration requirements are a sub-set of the requirements of X. If you have a project not related to X, you can proba-bly *force* the X11 files to work, given enough effort and ingenuity, but you'll feel like Procrustes, trying to shoehorn configuration information into a framework not meant for it.

I'm not trying to pick on the X11 files. They are very good indeed at the task for which they were designed. They're simply not generally applicable outside of the X11 world. Besides, limitations on reusability aren't inherent to X11 only: any set of files designed specifically for a particular project will be useful for that project and other closely related ones, but often unsuitable otherwise.

This phenomenon of configuration file project specificity reveals something of a paradox. *imake* helps us widen our view of software development beyond the limited scope of a single system or platform. But in our effort to write source code to run on a wide variety of machines, we can become so focused on the requirements of our project that our configuration files become very special-purpose and oriented only toward that particular project. As our code is freed from the confines of a single platform, our configuration files become bound to a single project. And if we can't take a set of files developed for one project and easily configure another project with them, they're not very reusable. *imake* helps us write portable code that can easily be moved around to various systems, but it doesn't in itself help us to write portable configuration files.

I'm not saying configuration files should automatically be considered deficient if they're not reusable. That may not have been the goal in writing them. If they were designed only to make a single project portable to different systems, and they alleviate the need to do a lot of ugly reconfiguring by hand when the project is moved around from machine to machine, then they achieve their purpose. What I'm suggesting is that our purpose can be more far-reaching: our overall effort can be reduced by minimizing the work involved when we're configuring several projects rather than just one. When we have that goal in mind, configuration files oriented toward a particular project are limiting.

Methods of Reusing Configuration Files

This section discusses how to develop configuration files that can be shared among (and thus be portable between) several projects, even if those projects aren't necessarily strongly related. I'll show three ways of attempting to do this. The first two fail to achieve the goal of providing general-purpose configuration files, but in doing so illustrate design traps to avoid and point the way to a third method that's not subject to the same pitfalls.

Method 1: Copy and Modify Existing Configuration Files

One way to reuse configuration files is to keep a set of prototypes. These could be the X11 files, the SP files, the DP files, whatever. When we start a new project, we create a *config* directory under its top-level directory, copy the prototypes there, and modify the copies appropriately. For example, to use the X11 files as the prototypes, we'd start by doing something like this:

```
% mkdir myproject
% cd myproject
% mkdir config
% cp /usr/X11R6.1/lib/X11/config/* config
```

Most of the X-specific stuff is in *Project.tmpl*, so it might be sufficient to plug in a different version of that file. For other projects, changes to more of the files might be needed:

```
% cd config
% vi Imake.tmpl Project.tmpl site.def ...
```

Since we're working with copies, not the original files "owned" by X11, we're not constrained to leaving them alone. This affords complete control over a project's configuration and allows us to make any kind of change we wish. We can hack out what we don't need and add in whatever we like.

The primary drawback of this approach is that we may end up with many sets of configuration files. It's possible to switch between multiple sets of files easily (see Chapter 10, *Coordinating Sets of Configuration Files*), but whether they can be maintained easily is another matter. The sets of files share a common "ancestor" (the prototype files), but as projects develop, the files used to configure them develop, too, and each set of files begins to take on individual characteristics. In effect, they form separate lineages on a family tree.

The resulting proliferation of file sets, each slightly different from the others, creates maintenance difficulties. Suppose you discover a bug in one of your rules. Was the bug present in the prototype files? If so, you need to fix the prototypes and then go look through each project using them to see if its configuration files have the same bug. If instead it's a bug you introduced during a modification to one of the copies of the prototypes, you need to look through each project in which you may have made a similar modification. Your labors begin to bear a striking resemblance to the task confronting Heracles at the Augean stables. Do you really want to maintain independent sets of configuration files for each project this way? What a headache!*

imake is supposed to reduce, not multiply, software maintenance chores, so this result is discouraging, and suggests that the copy-and-modify approach might be suitable on a limited basis for a small number of projects, but not for long-term software development involving a significant number of projects. The method doesn't really solve the problem of reusing files, either—they're not really being shared among projects, simply replicated. What have we actually gained? Yet more

---

* Worse than a headache, really. Eventually you reach the point where you lie awake at night with thoughts of all those sets of files running through your head. They begin to take on a life of their own, clamoring incessantly for your attention, raising a racket, preying on your insecurities, cackling hideously: "Have you changed *that* set of files, but not changed *me*? You know I'll exact revenge on you sooner or later if you haven't!" *O cruel files—A pox! A pox on imake!* you cry, exhausted and weary, wracked with doubt and uncertainty. The next day, seeking less stressful work, you quit your job to become a flight controller.

sets of single-project files. So the copy-and-modify method merely perpetuates the syndrome of project-specific configuration files.

Method 2: Share Comprehensive Configuration Files

Instead of copying configuration files for each new project, we could try to create a single set of files that will do everything and use it for all our projects. That is, for each configuration situation that arises, we put into the files the information necessary to handle it—the "everything but the kitchen sink" method. This minimizes the number of files that have to be maintained, unlike the copy-and-modify method, and there's no problem of sets of files getting out of sync with each other, since there's only one set. The disadvantages are that files constructed along these lines become unstable and tend inevitably to greater and greater complexity:

- Instability occurs because do-everything files must continually be changed to accommodate special requirements of new projects they're called on to configure. Any set of configuration files changes somewhat over time, but the kitchen-sink method accelerates the process.

- Complexity increases as we find new configuration situations that need to be incorporated into the files as new parameters. A library here, a header file there, a new rule or two, and soon we find ourselves overwhelmed—led by our method into a slow death of asphyxiation from information overload. The investment necessary to "speak *imake*" fluently becomes greatly increased. The creator of such files might understand them, but it will be difficult for anyone else to.

Backward compatibility can be difficult to maintain in the face of instability and increasing complexity. Suppose you develop projects A, B, C, etc., making changes to the configuration files to handle the requirements of each project as you go along. Several months (and projects) later, you decide to return to project A to do some further work on it. You'd better hope none of the changes you've made to the configuration files are incompatible with the way they worked when you originally developed the project. There's an irony here: the files can't get out of sync with themselves, but they might get out of sync with the projects they're supposed to configure!

Consider also what happens if other people at a different site decide to use your configuration files as a basis for their own work. Modifications they make to the files will be independent of your own changes, effectively resulting in a new set of files floating around, despite the effort to keep the number of sets at one. These multiple sets will exhibit the same kinds of divergence that plagued the copy-and-modify method. The lesson suggested by this observation is that multiplication of file sets is something we simply can't prevent entirely. Instead of trying to prohibit replication and divergence, we should simply try to minimize the need for that to happen, whenever possible, and provide a mechanism for managing its occurrence in an orderly fashion otherwise.

We already have the mechanism for managing several sets of configuration files. In Chapter 10 I discussed how to coordinate multiple sets as they spring up. I said there that the method for doing so accommodates 200 sets just as well as it accommodates two. Nevertheless, I take it as a given that two sets are preferable to 200. To help keep the number of sets to a minimum, we must reduce the need to develop new sets, and we haven't achieved that yet.

Method 3: Share Extensible Configuration Files

The basic problem of the copy-and-modify method is that the number of configuration files we need to maintain is a function of the number of projects—one set for each project. The result is a spreading contagion of configuration files as we create new projects. The kitchen sink method attempts to solve this problem by combining all sets into one and sharing it among all projects. But because they have to do everything, the files quickly become complex, and unstable due to frequent change.

These are not trivial problems, but we can discover something about how to avoid them if we simply step back, forget about *imake* for the moment, and consider the nature of our work.

Suppose you develop several projects (by any method), then stop to reflect on how you went about it. You'll recognize that you use certain habits, and you diverge from your habits:

- You use habits because projects are not all completely different and they share some common elements: if you're building C programs, you use the same C compiler most of the time; you usually install public programs in the same directory; you put frequently used functions in a library rather than multiply instances of identical source code; you use the same set of formatting tools to process documentation.

- You diverge from your habits because, although projects have similarities, they're not completely similar: one project requires ANSI C rather than K&R C; another builds a program that must be linked in a special way; another requires a nonstandard installation directory.

Projects are neither completely different nor completely similar, and you work accordingly. You take the requirements presented to you by the projects you work on and adapt to them.

Now let's come back to *imake*. Can these observations be applied to the problem of designing reusable configuration files? Yes—if we change our thinking a bit.

imake is usually used to express the requirements of a project so it can be adapted to multiple platforms. The question we need to ask is whether we can use *imake* to reflect our development patterns and help us apply them to multiple projects. This is a change of focus.

Rather than designing configuration files specifically for a particular project, consider several projects you've worked on and the patterns you recognize to be typical of your efforts as you've gone about developing them. Each project can be characterized in terms of how much it has in common with other projects, and how much it requires its own unique (project-specific) treatment. For configuration files to facilitate this kind of characterization and allow us to avoid the problems of the copy-and-modify and kitchen sink methods, they need to be designed with certain goals in mind:

- **Minimize the number of files to be maintained.** We should recognize patterns by identifying common elements in configuration requirements of different projects and in the way we develop them. This redundancy and overlap should be used to form a baseline level of configuration functionality. The files providing this functionality should be shared among projects rather than replicated unnecessarily for each project.

- **Extensibility.** We must be able to address the special configuration needs of individual projects. When a project's requirements differ from the baseline, we must be able to override a general pattern with a more specific one or to specify something entirely new instead. This will reduce the need to multiply sets of files unnecessarily. If a project can supply its own extensions to a baseline configuration, there is less incentive for developers to go off and write a whole new set of files.

- **Simplicity.** Complexity increases when we try to specify too much in configuration files, as with the kitchen sink method. Therefore, information that's specific to individual projects should be separated from information that's shared among multiple projects.

These goals can be met using a two-directory strategy. First, we provide a public directory containing standard (baseline) configuration files. This is a public directory; its files are shared among the set of projects that use them. Next, we allow each project to designate a directory in which it provides configuration information that applies only to itself. Files in this directory are private, or project specific. Finally, we tell *imake* to give files in the project-specific directory precedence over those in the public directory, thus allowing private information to override shared information.

Implementing Extensible Configuration Files

It's anathema to write configuration files from scratch, so we'll implement the two-directory strategy—how else?—by starting with an existing set and modifying it to create reusable files. We'll begin with the starter project (SP) files created in Chapter 9, *A Configuration Starter Project*, and turn them into a project containing extensible-architecture (EA) files. If you want to see the configuration files we'll end up with, so you can follow along in them while reading this discussion, retrieve the EA distribution (see Appendix A, *Obtaining Configuration Software*). For the remainder of the present chapter, we'll focus on architecture design and the problem of *Makefile* generation. Chapter 16 shows the conversion process from start to finish in recipe form.

There are a number of aspects to the conversion process, but there are three principal things we must do if we're to have any hope of making things work:

- Modify the architecture of the template file *Imake.tmpl* and modify the vendor block file *Imake.cf* to allow coordination of access to shared and project-specific information.

- Decide where to put the directories containing the shared and project-specific configuration files.

- Make sure we have a bootstrapper and *Makefile*-building commands that know about the shared and project-specific configuration file directories.

Step 1: Modify Imake.tmpl and Imake.cf

The SP files we're using here were developed from the X11 files, and both sets have the same basic architecture (Figure 15–1). Recall that `MacroIncludeFile` refers to the vendor-specific file and `INCLUDE_IMAKEFILE` refers to the *Imakefile*.

To allow a project to specify its own unique requirements, the template must refer to additional files that the project can supply. The modified *Imake.tmpl* is shown in Figure 15–2, with new files shown in boldface.

The modified architecture has the following characteristics:

- The template refers to *vendor.cf* (via `MacroIncludeFile`), *site.def*, *Imake.rules*, and *Project.tmpl*. These are shared files that describe the baseline configuration; they're taken from the public directory. The template now also refers to project-specific files *vendor.p-cf* (via `ProjectMacroIncludeFile`), *site.p-def*, *Imake.p-rules*, and *Project.p-tmpl*, which are taken from a project's private directory. (*Project.tmpl* now applies to multiple projects, but we leave the name alone for compatibility with existing files.)

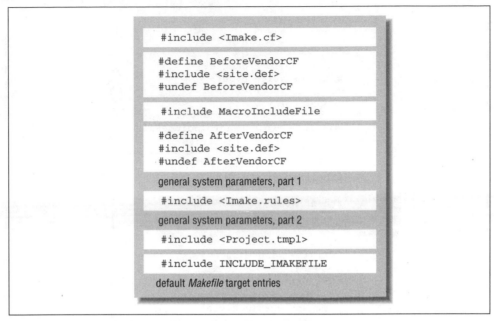

Figure 15–1: X11R6.1/SP template architecture

- Each project-specific file is included immediately before the shared file to which it's related (*site.p-def* before *site.def*, etc.), so that private information takes precedence over public information.

- The vendor blocks in *Imake.cf* define the name of the vendor file. Since there's a project-specific vendor file in the architecture now, each vendor block must be modified to define the name of that file. For instance, the modifications to the HP vendor block look like this:

Original vendor block:

```
#ifdef hpux
# define MacroIncludeFile <hp.cf>
# define MacroFile hp.cf
# undef hpux
# define HPArchitecture
#endif /* hpux */
```

Modified vendor block (new lines are shown in boldface):

```
#ifdef hpux
# define ProjectMacroIncludeFile <hp.p-cf>
# define ProjectMacroFile hp.p-cf
# define MacroIncludeFile <hp.cf>
# define MacroFile hp.cf
# undef hpux
```

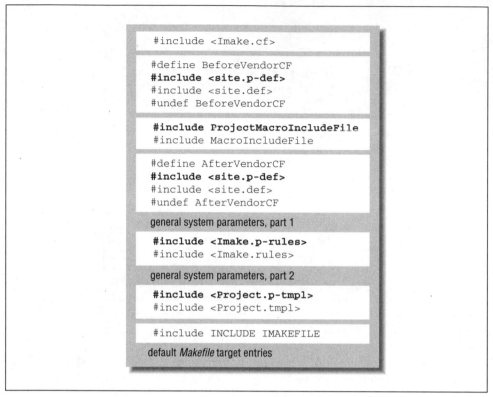

```
#include <Imake.cf>

#define BeforeVendorCF
#include <site.p-def>
#include <site.def>
#undef BeforeVendorCF

#include ProjectMacroIncludeFile
#include MacroIncludeFile

#define AfterVendorCF
#include <site.p-def>
#include <site.def>
#undef AfterVendorCF
```
general system parameters, part 1
```
#include <Imake.p-rules>
#include <Imake.rules>
```
general system parameters, part 2
```
#include <Project.p-tmpl>
#include <Project.tmpl>
```
```
#include INCLUDE IMAKEFILE
```
default *Makefile* target entries

Figure 15–2: Extensible-architecture (EA) template

```
# define HPArchitecture
#endif /* hpux */
```

By expressing a project's individual requirements in the project-specific files, developers have latitude to override or extend the contents of the shared files. Since each project has its own private configuration directory, it can tailor files in that directory to its own requirements without regard to those of any other project, and without need to have any changes made to the shared files.

But what if a project doesn't need any project-specific information? In that case, the shared files are entirely sufficient. This presents us with a dilemma. We don't want to require a project to supply private files if it has no need for them, but they do need to be somewhere, or *cpp* will issue rude "file not found" file-inclusion errors.

One simple solution is to create dummy versions of the project-specific files and put them in the shared configuration directory. The dummy files should be empty—all we care about is that they exist, to keep *cpp* happy when a project doesn't provide its own versions. The contents of the shared directory therefore consist of two kinds of files:

Shared baseline files:

```
site.def
Imake.rules
Project.tmpl
generic.cf, hp.cf, ...
```

Dummy project-specific files:

```
site.p-def
Imake.p-rules
Project.p-tmpl
generic.p-cf, hp.p-cf, ...
```

The following examples illustrate how the EA files provide an additional degree of flexibility and extensibility compared to the standard X11/SP architecture:

- **Greater flexibility in specifying parameter values**. Sites often have a directory for locally installed programs, but the location of that directory is quite likely to vary from site to site, and sometimes from project to project at a given site. The value of a parameter that names that directory is therefore likely to vary also. The way to handle this is with the shared files *Project.tmpl* and *site.def*, and the project-specific file *site.p-def*. *Project.tmpl* should contain a *cpp* macro BinDir that supplies a best-guess value for the installation directory, and that sets the *make* variable BINDIR to that macro:

  ```
  #ifndef BinDir
  #define BinDir /usr/local/bin
  #endif
  BINDIR = BinDir
  ```

  When you install the shared configuration files on a given machine, you check whether the default value in *Project.tmpl* is appropriate for local convention. If not, you supply the correct value in *site.def*. For instance, if programs are installed in */var/local/bin* instead of */usr/local/bin*, *site.def* should contain the following definition to override the default:

  ```
  #ifndef BinDir
  #define BinDir /var/local/bin
  #endif
  ```

  Projects that want programs installed in the "usual" directory simply refer to BINDIR in their Imakefiles; the site default is sufficient and need not be overridden. To use an alternate directory for a particular project instead, you specify an override value for BinDir in *site.p-def*. For example, if I'm developing a project which builds programs for my own use only, and I want to install them in my own *bin* directory, I create a version of *site.p-def* in the project's private directory and specify the value of BinDir there:

```
#ifndef BinDir
#define BinDir /u/dubois/bin
#endif
```

This overrides the default value in the shared configuration files and allows my project to put programs where it wants without requiring any changes to the shared files and without infringing on the configuration requirements of any other projects.

- **Extensibility of the baseline configuration.** Project-specific files may be used to specify configuration parameters or rule macros not appearing at all in the shared files. For instance, if you want to install some of a project's programs in BINDIR, and others in a private directory, you can write *Project.p-tmpl* to provide a new parameter PROJBINDIR for the latter purpose. In this case, you're not just overriding the value of an existing parameter, you're inventing a new one. This requires that you provide a *make* variable to hold the parameter value in addition to the *cpp* macro specifying the default value:

```
#ifndef ProjBinDir
#define ProjBinDir /usr/myproject/bin
#endif

PROJBINDIR = ProjBinDir
```

If you override the default value of this new parameter in *site.p-def*, you do so by supplying the macro definition only (not another *make* variable assignment).

The extensible architecture has a few drawbacks: *Imake.tmpl* is more complex because it references more files; each vendor block in *Imake.cf* must be modified; and the shared directory must be populated with dummy *vendor.p-cf*, *site.p-def*, *Imake.p-rules*, and *Project.p-tmpl* files. But *Imake.tmpl* and *Imake.cf* need only be modified once to add the extra #include directives and to change the vendor blocks, and it's easy to create the dummy files since they're all empty:

```
% touch Imake.p-rules
% touch Project.p-tmpl
% touch site.p-def
% touch generic.p-cf
% touch hp.p-cf
% ...
```

Step 2: Determine Configuration File Directory Locations

If we're going to use public configuration files in a shared directory and private files in a project-specific directory, where exactly should those directories be located? The organizational principles adopted to arrange configuration file directories in Chapter 10 are directly applicable here:

- Project-specific configuration files are in a directory *config* under the project root.

- Publicly installed configuration files are in a directory under the configuration root */usr/local/lib/config*.

These principles were originally developed to handle projects configured with either private or public files, and to select files from one directory or the other. The extensible architecture allows us to configure projects with private and public files, selecting files from each directory as we please. The simplest thing to do is adapt these organizational principles to use the within-project and public directories conjunctively rather than disjunctively. That is, we look under the project root as well as under the configuration root.

Step 3: Modify Makefile-Building Commands

We need to figure out how to construct *imake* commands that use the extensible files and the project-specific files. If the EA files weren't extensible, we'd only look in one directory for them, and the *imake* command to build a *Makefile* would look something like this:

```
% imake -DUseInstalled -I/usr/local/lib/config/EA -DTOPDIR=.
```

But since we need to tell *imake* to look in a project's private configuration file directory as well as in the shared directory, the *imake* command is slightly more complex. The private directory is always *config* under the project root, and the public directory is *EA* under the configuration root */usr/local/lib/config*. We have to search the project-specific directory first so that files in the project's private directory take precedence. This prevents the dummy versions in the public directory from overriding them.

In the root directory of a project we build the *Makefile* like this:

```
% imake -DUseInstalled -I./config -I/usr/local/lib/config/EA -DTOPDIR=.
```

The general command to build the *Makefile* in an arbitrary directory of a project configured with the EA files looks like this, where `topdir` denotes the location of the project root:

```
% imake -DUseInstalled -Itopdir/config -I/usr/local/lib/config/EA -DTOPDIR=topdir
```

It's a nuisance to type such long commands manually, though. *imboot* and the `Makefile` and `Makefiles` target entries should generate *imake* commands for us. *imboot* is discussed in Chapter 10 and the *Makefile*-generating target entries are discussed in Chapter 8, *A Closer Look at Makefile Generation*. However, none of the *Makefile*-building methods described in those chapters work with the extensible architecture because they all assume the configuration files are found in a single directory. We need to adapt our methods to construct *imake* commands appropriately for a two-directory architecture.

Bootstrapping a Makefile

As developed in Chapter 10, *imboot* passed to *imake* either the directory *config* under the project root or, if a *−c name* argument was given, the directory */usr/local/lib/config/name*. Now we want to be able to tell it to pass both. This can be done by using *−C* instead of *−c* and defining *−C name* to mean that the project-specific directory should be used in addition to the public directory */usr/local/lib/config/name*.

This EA-compatible version of *imboot* differs from the one developed in Chapter 10 only in that if we use *−C* instead of *−c*, it looks in the private and public directories, not just in the public directory.[*] To use it in a project root directory, bootstrap the *Makefile* like this:

```
% imboot -C EA
```

Otherwise, specify the location of the project root:

```
% imboot -C EA topdir
```

Makefile generation revisited

We can bootstrap a *Makefile* with *imboot*, but we also need to make sure that we can use an existing *Makefile* to rebuild itself or Makefiles in subdirectories with these commands:

```
% make Makefile
% make Makefiles
```

---

[*] I don't show the listing of the new version of *imboot* here. You can examine it by retrieving the *itools* distribution in which it is included. See Appendix A for more information.

The rules that generate the Makefile and Makefiles entries are Makefile-Target() and MakefileSubdirs(), but all they do is supply the correct values of TOPDIR and CURDIR to the *imake* command specified by the IMAKE_CMD variable. Thus, we need to change IMAKE_CMD to understand the extensible architecture.

Here's the definition of IMAKE_CMD from the starter project *Imake.tmpl*:

```
#ifdef UseInstalled
    IRULESRC = $(CONFIGDIR)
    IMAKE_CMD = $(IMAKE) -DUseInstalled -I$(IRULESRC) $(IMAKE_DEFINES)
#else
    IRULESRC = $(CONFIGSRC)
    IMAKE_CMD = $(IMAKE) -I$(IRULESRC) $(IMAKE_DEFINES)
#endif
```

Here, IMAKE_CMD specifies only one directory in which to look for configuration files. We must change it for the EA files to look in two directories. Before we do that, though, some additional parameters will be helpful:

CONFIGROOTDIR

The root directory for installed configuration files. It should be a full (absolute) pathname. The most sensible value is the pathname to the *imboot* configuration root directory.

CONFIGNAME

The name of the configuration file set. This is the name of the directory under CONFIGROOTDIR that holds the shared configuration files.

PUBCONFIGDIR

The full pathname of the directory that holds the shared files. Its value is constructed from CONFIGROOTDIR and CONFIGNAME.

PRIVCONFIGDIR

The private, project-specific configuration directory. It's located within the project tree and thus is defined relative to the top of the tree.

The values of these variables are specified using the usual macro/variable idiom:

```
#ifndef ConfigRootDir
#define ConfigRootDir /usr/local/lib/config
#endif

#ifndef ConfigName
#define ConfigName EA
#endif

#ifndef PubConfigDir
#define PubConfigDir $(CONFIGROOTDIR)/$(CONFIGNAME)
#endif

#ifndef PrivConfigDir
#define PrivConfigDir $(TOP)/config
#endif
```

```
 CONFIGROOTDIR = ConfigRootDir
    CONFIGNAME = ConfigName
  PUBCONFIGDIR = PubConfigDir
 PRIVCONFIGDIR = PrivConfigDir
```

With the preceding parameter support in *Project.tmpl*, IMAKE_CMD becomes:

```
#ifdef UseInstalled
    IMAKE_CMD = $(IMAKE) -DUseInstalled \
                -I$(PRIVCONFIGDIR) -I$(PUBCONFIGDIR) \
                $(IMAKE_DEFINES)
#else
    IMAKE_CMD = $(IMAKE) \
                -I$(PRIVCONFIGDIR) -I$(PUBCONFIGDIR) \
                $(IMAKE_DEFINES)
#endif
```

In addition, the ImakeSubCmdHelper macro in *Imake.rules* should be changed, from this:

```
#ifdef UseInstalled
#define ImakeSubCmdHelper $(IMAKE_CMD)
#else
#define ImakeSubCmdHelper $(IMAKE) -I$(IMAKEPREFIX)$(IRULESRC) $(IMAKE_DEFINES)
#endif
```

To this:

```
#ifdef UseInstalled
#define ImakeSubCmdHelper $(IMAKE_CMD)
#else
#define ImakeSubCmdHelper $(IMAKE) \
                -I$(IMAKEPREFIX)$(PRIVCONFIGDIR) -I$(PUBCONFIGDIR) \
                $(IMAKE_DEFINES)
#endif
```

Note that these changes make IRULESRC, CONFIGDIR, and CONFIGSRC obsolete.

Does This Architecture Really Work?

Now we need to ask an important question: do the architectural changes just described in fact satisfy the three goals listed earlier in this chapter? Let's revisit each goal in turn.

- **Minimize the number of files to be maintained**. Compared to the X11 template, the multiple-project version of *Imake.tmpl* references more configuration files. So at first glace, it appears we've increased the number of files to be maintained. However, when we're developing multiple projects, the total number of configuration files involved is much lower than if individual projects each have their own complete set. By recognizing patterns in our project development habits and in the configuration requirements of our projects, we can factor out common information and centralize it in the shared files *Imake.tmpl*, *vendor.cf*, *site.def*, *Imake.rules*, and *Project.tmpl*. Since these files are located in the public directory, multiple projects may use them cooperatively. We don't need a full set for each project, thus avoiding the problem of the copy-and-modify method where we end up with a huge mess of configuration files multiplying without limit.

- **Extensibility.** The shared files describe a standard baseline configuration held in common by all projects that use them. A project can extend or override information in the shared files if necessary, using project-specific files *vendor.p-cf*, *site.p-def*, *Imake.p-rules*, and *Project.p-tmpl* in a private configuration directory. But a project isn't forced to provide private files if the shared files are sufficient for its needs. Private override files need be supplied only to the extent that a project's requirements differ from the baseline. Dummy versions of the project-specific files are provided in the shared directory for files for which no override is necessary.

  By providing for private configuration files, the extensible architecture gives us the flexibility to make changes to the configuration of one project without affecting other projects. The architecture also promotes stability of the shared files, because the need to modify them is minimized by private override files. This differs from the kitchen sink approach, where the files are modified each time we make any change to the configuration requirements for any project.

  By designing configuration files so they can be shared by (i.e., be portable between) different projects, it's less work to begin a new project. The ability to use private files to extend a set of shared files means you don't need to find a set of shared files that supplies every last detail of your configuration requirements—just one that handles a reasonable subset of them. That way, you're more likely to be able to build on an existing set of files and less likely to need to write a new set.

- **Simplicity.** The architecture provides a means for gathering common elements of the configuration requirements of a group of projects, while splitting out project-specific elements. This allows us to make the shared files simpler, since project-specific information can be kept out of them. They're also more accessible to people who didn't write them since simpler files are easier to understand and use. This contrasts with the tendency toward unbounded complexity that characterizes files constructed by the kitchen sink method.

This configuration architecture satisfies the design goals by exploiting redundancy among project configurations while allowing project-specific information to be specified in a way that doesn't affect other projects. Furthermore, using the arrangement discussed in Chapter 10, multiple sets of configuration files can peacefully coexist on a single machine.

16

Creating Extensible Configuration Files

> *Q.E.D.*
> —Euclid, *Elements*

The reason for writing extensible configuration files is simple: to avoid work! Extensible files can easily be used and extended by multiple, possibly unrelated projects. This allows us to avoid much of the cost of setting up new projects. There is, of course, the question of how to get extensible files in the first place. The answer is to create them by modifying a set of project-specific files. After all, we certainly don't want to expend any more effort than necessary. By taking advantage of existing work, we don't have to write the files from scratch.

As in Chapter 15, *Designing Extensible Configuration Files*, we'll use the starter project (SP) files to produce a set of extensible-architecture (EA) files. By necessity, the discussion repeats certain points from that chapter, but the emphasis is different. Chapter 15 focuses on general background information. This chapter is more pragmatic and "recipe-oriented." It provides step-by-step guidelines for converting project-specific configuration files to be extensible.

Preliminaries

I'll assume that the general-purpose *Makefile*-bootstrapper *imboot* is available on your machine, and develop the extensible files in accordance with its organizational conventions. Specifically, *imboot* uses a configuration root directory under which all directories used to hold shared configuration files are located. I'll assume the configuration root is */usr/local/lib/config* in this discussion; modify the instructions below appropriately if the pathname is different on your machine.

Setting Up

There are a few things we need to do to get ready to create extensible configuration files:

1. Select a name for your configuration files. Ultimately, the files will be installed in a directory with that name under the configuration root, and projects that use your shared files will expect to find them there. Since that directory needs to coexist with others, you should try to select a unique name.

   For this discussion, we'll use the name EA; the installation directory is therefore */usr/local/lib/config/EA*.

2. Create a "configuration project directory" in which to work. For example, if the starter project is located under your current directory, do this to make a copy of it:

   ```
   % cp -r SP EA
   ```

   You could just create the installation directory */usr/local/lib/config/EA*, install the configuration files into it, and do all your work right there, but I recommend against it. Any improvements you make to files in the public directory are immediately available to any project that uses them, but so are any bugs.[*] It's better to use a separate development directory in which to work. That way you can work on your files and install them only after you've tested them to be sure any changes you make are correct, without inflicting the results of your experiments on other people.

Modifying the Architecture

Now we can convert the configuration files so they're extensible:

1. Make sure you're in the directory containing the configuration files:

   ```
   % cd EA/config
   ```

2. Examine the template to see where it references other configuration files. For each instance of an #include directive, precede it with an #include for a related project-specific file. This process was described for the starter project files in Chapter 15. You should end up with a template that looks like the one shown in Figure 16–1 (the new files are shown in boldface).

---

[*] Not that you'd ever introduce a bug, of course.

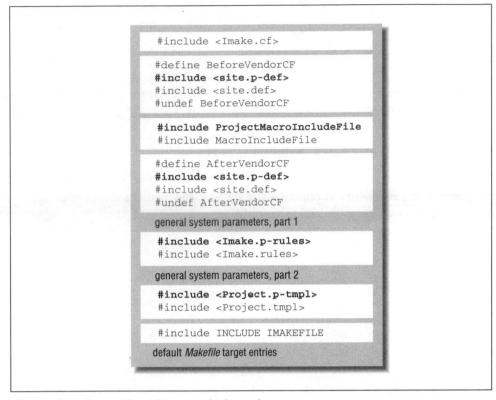

Figure 16–1: Extensible-architecture (EA) template

3. Change the vendor blocks in the template so each one defines symbols for the project-specific vendor files. If a vendor block looks like this:

```
#ifdef trigger
# define MacroIncludeFile <vendor.cf>
# define MacroFile vendor.cf
# undef trigger
# define VendorArchitecture
#endif
```

Change it to this (new lines are shown in boldface):

```
#ifdef trigger
# define ProjectMacroIncludeFile <vendor.p-cf>
# define ProjectMacroFile vendor.p-cf
# define MacroIncludeFile <vendor.cf>
# define MacroFile vendor.cf
# undef trigger
# define VendorArchitecture
#endif
```

4. Create dummy project-specific files:

```
% touch site.p-def
% touch Imake.p-rules
% touch Project.p-tmpl
% touch 'ls *.cf|sed 's/\.cf$/.p-cf/''
```

The last command creates an empty *vendor.p-cf* file for each *vendor.cf* file.
(Or just create all the *vendor.p-cf* files manually.)

Making the Files Self-Aware

1. Add the following to *Project.tmpl* to indicate the name of the configuration
   files, the path to the configuration root, and the path to the public (shared)
   configuration directory used to hold the files:

```
#ifndef ConfigName
#define ConfigName EA
#endif
#ifndef ConfigRootDir
#define ConfigRootDir /usr/local/lib/config
#endif
#ifndef PubConfigDir
#define PubConfigDir $(CONFIGROOTDIR)/$(CONFIGNAME)
#endif
    CONFIGNAME = ConfigName
CONFIGROOTDIR = ConfigRootDir
  PUBCONFIGDIR = PubConfigDir
```

Make sure the value of the configuration root `ConfigRootDir` is the same as
the value that *imboot* uses.

2. In *Project.tmpl*, indicate the location of the project-specific configuration directory. This is where *imake* will look for any private configuration files a project
   might supply. *imboot* assumes they're in *config* under the project root; I recommend using the same value in the absence of a compelling reason to do
   otherwise:

```
#ifndef
#define PrivConfigDir $(TOP)/config
#endif

PRIVCONFIGDIR = PrivConfigDir
```

3. In *Imake.tmpl*, change `IMAKE_CMD` to reference two configuration directories
   instead of just one. This command must refer to `PUBCONFIGDIR` and `PRIVCON-`
   `FIGDIR`, the public and private directory parameters you just created. The
   modification to `IMAKE_CMD` is as follows.

Original:

```
#ifdef UseInstalled
    IRULESRC = $(CONFIGDIR)
   IMAKE_CMD = $(IMAKE) -DUseInstalled -I$(IRULESRC) $(IMAKE_DEFINES)
#else
    IRULESRC = $(CONFIGSRC)
   IMAKE_CMD = $(IMAKE) -I$(IRULESRC) $(IMAKE_DEFINES)
#endif
```

Change to:

```
#ifdef UseInstalled
    IMAKE_CMD = $(IMAKE) -DUseInstalled \
                -I$(PRIVCONFIGDIR) -I$(PUBCONFIGDIR) \
                $(IMAKE_DEFINES)
#else
    IMAKE_CMD = $(IMAKE) \
                -I$(PRIVCONFIGDIR) -I$(PUBCONFIGDIR) \
                $(IMAKE_DEFINES)
#endif
```

In addition, the `ImakeSubCmdHelper` macro in *Imake.rules* should be changed, from this:

```
#ifdef UseInstalled
#define ImakeSubCmdHelper $(IMAKE_CMD)
#else
#define ImakeSubCmdHelper $(IMAKE) -I$(IMAKEPREFIX)$(IRULESRC) $(IMAKE_DEFINES)
#endif
```

To this:

```
#ifdef UseInstalled
#define ImakeSubCmdHelper $(IMAKE_CMD)
#else
#define ImakeSubCmdHelper $(IMAKE) \
                -I$(IMAKEPREFIX)$(PRIVCONFIGDIR) -I$(PUBCONFIGDIR) \
                $(IMAKE_DEFINES)
#endif
```

As discussed in Chapter 15, these modifications make `IRULESRC` obsolete.

4. By default, the starter project doesn't install the configuration files anywhere, nor do any copies of it. The EA project is just such a copy, so, because we're developing public files that must be installed to be useful, we must add installation support.

— Create an *Imakefile* in the EA project root that looks like this:

```
#define IHaveSubdirs
#define PassCDebugFlags

SUBDIRS = config
```

```
MakeSubdirs($(SUBDIRS))
DependSubdirs($(SUBDIRS))
```

— Create an *Imakefile* in the *config* directory:

```
FILES = *.tmpl *.p-tmpl *.rules *.p-rules \
        site.def site.p-def *.cf *.p-cf

all::
depend::

InstallMultipleDestFlags(install,$(FILES),$(PUBCONFIGDIR),$(INSTDATFLAGS))
```

Generalizing File Contents

Look for extraneous symbols that can be dropped, such as parameters specific to the project for which the files were originally designed, and for which you don't anticipate any use in a more general-purpose setting. Remove these symbols to reduce noise and simplify your files.

When you delete a symbol from configuration files, exercise caution (and *grep*) to make sure the symbol isn't used somewhere else in the configuration files. If you're not confident you understand the configuration files, it's better to leave a symbol in than to remove it and suffer the potential consequences.

The choice of what to delete depends on your goals. For instance, the EA files trace their ancestry through the SP files to the X11 files, and still contain all the X11 parameters. If you want to use the EA files to configure X-based projects more easily (e.g., to allow projects to supply additional parameters in the private project-specific files), you wouldn't remove any X11 parameters. On the other hand, you'd treat the files quite differently if you want to use them for projects unrelated to X11; in that case, you'd excise X-specific symbols. (The latter course is the one we took in Chapter 11, *Introduction to Configuration File Writing*, when we developed the DP files.)

After you've removed irrelevant configuration information, generalize all constructs that are written in such a way that you can't override them easily. These come in two forms: *cpp* macro definitions that aren't enclosed within #ifndef/#endif, and *make* variables that are set to literal values rather than to *cpp* macros or other *make* variables.

• Look for *cpp* symbol definitions that aren't enclosed within #ifndef/#endif blocks. These are a problem since you might want to override them in project-specific files. Vendor files are common offenders in this regard; they usually appear so early in the sequence of files referenced by the template that configuration file writers often assume that any macros defined in the vendor file will not have already been defined. That assumption is invalid in an environment where *vendor.p-cf* is included before *vendor.cf*. For example, *moto.cf* defines a couple of search path macros:

```
#define DefaultUserPath :/bin:/usr/bin:$(BINDIR)
#define DefaultSystemPath /etc:/bin:/usr/bin:$(BINDIR)
```

Definitions like this cause trouble in a multiple-project environment; a project built on a Motorola system that wanted to change these paths in a project-specific *moto.p-cf* would be out of luck. The definitions should be rewritten as follows so they can be overridden as necessary:

```
#ifndef DefaultUserPath
#define DefaultUserPath :/bin:/usr/bin:$(BINDIR)
#endif
#ifndef DefaultSystemPath
#define DefaultSystemPath /etc:/bin:/usr/bin:$(BINDIR)
#endif
```

cpp macro definitions in configuration files should always be written so they can be overridden. This includes definitions you think will never need to be changed because they occur in files processed early in the configuration process. Somewhere down the road you might modify your configuration file architecture and have a need to override things in ways you don't now anticipate.

• Look for *make* variables (parameters) that are assigned literal or partly literal values. Directly assigning parameters like this works in a single-project environment, but not in a shared environment where different projects might want to give different values to a given parameter. We need to make sure parameters get their values from *cpp* macros that can be overridden or from other *make* variables.

For example, due to their X11 heritage, the EA configuration files contain several *SRC variables in *Project.tmpl*:

```
      LIBSRC = $(TOP)/lib
  INCLUDESRC = $(TOP)/X11
      DOCSRC = $(TOP)/doc
```

These are used to designate various parts of the X11 distribution within the project tree. Since the layout of the X11 project doesn't change from system to system, the X11 configuration files don't provide any way of overriding the locations of these directories. This causes a problem in the context of extensible configuration files. You want the variables to reflect the structure of the project you're configuring, not that of the X11 tree. To work in a multi-project environment where projects organize their directories differently, assignments like those just shown must be rewritten so they can be overridden.

Usually, this is fairly easy. For example, instead of directly setting DOCSRC to $(TOP)/*doc*, introduce a macro DocSrc and use $(TOP)/*doc* for its default value. Then set DOCSRC to DocSrc:

```
#ifndef DocSrc
#define DocSrc $(TOP)/doc
#endif

DOCSRC = DocSrc
```

Individual projects can redefine DocSrc as necessary in *Project.p-tmpl*.

It's less clear how to change INCLUDESRC, because $(TOP)/*X11* is not an especially good general-purpose default value. Here you need to be guided by your own experience. I tend to use a directory named *h* near the top of the project tree to hold project-specific header files. You might use a different name, such as *include*. Select a default that reflects your habits:

```
#ifndef IncludeSrc
#define IncludeSrc $(TOP)/include
#endif

INCLUDESRC = IncludeSrc
```

The important thing is that whether you choose $(TOP)/*h*, $(TOP)/*include*, or something else entirely, individual projects can override the default by providing the appropriate value in their own *Project.p-tmpl*.

- Not all parameter assignments need to be modified so they can be overridden, as the following example shows. VAR1 and VAR2 are already written entirely in terms of macros that can be overridden. VAR3 is not, but it needs no rewriting since you can change its value by overriding Macro1, Macro2, or Macro3:

```
#ifndef Macro1
#define Macro1 value1
#endif
#ifndef Macro2
#define Macro2 value2
#endif
#ifndef Macro3
#define Macro3 value3
#endif

VAR1 = Macro1
VAR2 = Macro2
VAR3 = $(VAR1) $(VAR2)/Macro3
```

In general, if a parameter is assigned a value entirely in terms of *make* variables and/or *cpp* macros, you need not rewrite it: if part or all of a parameter's value is literal, you do.

Installing the Files

We can configure the Makefiles for the EA project itself by executing the following commands in the EA root directory:

```
% imboot
% make Makefiles
```

The *make* command generates an *imake* command that looks for configuration files in $(TOP)/*config* as well as in */usr/local/lib/config/EA*. (Subtle point: There won't be anything in the latter directory until the files are installed. But that doesn't matter because $(TOP)/*config* contains all the files we need. That's where the files to be installed in */usr/local/lib/config/EA* come from, after all!)

After building the Makefiles, change into the *config* directory and verify that the *Makefile* there will install the configuration files in the right place:

```
% cd config
% make -n install
if [ -d /usr/local/lib/config/EA ]; then set +x; \
else (set -x; mkdirhier /usr/local/lib/config/EA); fi
for flag in bn ''; do \
case "$flag" in *=*) ;; *[i]*) set +e;; esac; done; \
for i in *.tmpl *.p-tmpl *.rules *.p-rules site.def site.p-def *.cf *.p-cf; do \
(set -x; install -c -m 0444 $i /usr/local/lib/config/EA); \
done
echo "install in config done"
```

The *-n* option is used so we can see what *make* will do. If the output seems okay (look for */usr/local/lib/config/EA* as the installation directory), repeat the command without the *-n* to actually perform the installation.

We're finished. Quite Easily Done.

17

Using Extensible Configuration Files

Let us, then, be up and doing.
—Longfellow, *A Psalm of Life*

In Chapter 16, *Creating Extensible Configuration Files*, we convert a group of project-specific configuration files to produce extensible-architecture (EA) files that can be shared among and extended by multiple projects. Here we discuss how to take advantage of the flexibility extensible files provide when you configure projects with them. First, I'll describe how to set up such a project and the principles by which you use the project's private configuration files to override or extend the information in the shared files. Then I'll present some examples which will show you how to put those principles to work in practice.

Starting Your Project

Before you can do anything else, you need to set up some minimal project structure. You can create a blank "skeleton" project as follows:

% **mkdir myproj**	Create project directory
% **cd myproj**	Move into it
% **mkdir config**	Create directory for private configuration information
% **cp /dev/null Imakefile**	Create *Imakefile*
% **imboot -C EA**	Create initial *Makefile* from *Imakefile*

Once you have a blank project, you can elaborate it by creating the rest of the project tree, other Imakefiles, and your source files.

If the project root is your only source directory, there isn't much project tree to create. Otherwise, you'll be dealing with the greater complexity of a multiple-directory project. (For general information on managing multiple-directory projects, see Chapter 6, *Writing Imakefiles*, and Chapter 11, *Introduction to Configuration File Writing*.) At the very least, the root *Imakefile* must define IHaveSubdirs and PassCDebugFlags and assign a value to SUBDIRS:

```
#define IHaveSubdirs
#define PassCDebugFlags
SUBDIRS = subdirectory-list
```

The *config* directory need not be listed in the value of SUBDIRS, since operations such as clean and install don't need to be done there. *config* is used only as a repository for project-specific configuration information. You provide this information when you create private configuration files *vendor.p-cf*, *site.p-def*, *Imake.p-rules*, or *Project.p-tmpl*.

Override and Extension Principles

When you configure a project using extensible files, you use a set of shared files installed in a public directory, and optionally some project-specific files stored in the private *config* directory under the project root. The private configuration files serve to override the values of parameters that are present in the shared files, and to extend the shared files by defining new parameters that aren't present in them. Three principles govern the specifics of what you put in the private files:

- If a parameter is present in the shared files and its specified value is appropriate for your project, you need not put any information for that parameter in the private files.

- If a parameter is present in the shared files but its value isn't appropriate for your project, override the value in the private files.

- If you need a parameter that isn't present at all in the shared files, create a new parameter in the private files.

These principles can be applied in various ways, as illustrated by the examples in the following sections.

Project Layout

In Chapter 13, *Configuration Problems and Solutions*, we discussed how to specify the layout of your project using parameter variables in *Project.tmpl*. Some advantages of using variables instead of literal pathnames are:

- You can refer to project directories in terms of TOP (the location of the project root) and let *imake* figure out the value of TOP that's correct in each directory.

- You can refer to directories in a consistent symbolic way.

- You can rearrange the project easily, since you only need change the variable values once in the configuration files and then rebuild the Makefiles. It's unnecessary to edit each *Imakefile* that refers to directories that have moved.

Perhaps you tend to use a similar layout over and over. In that case, you can leave the layout specification in the shared *Project.tmpl* to exploit the redundancy between projects. The specification can be considered a prototype, but one you have the flexibility to modify as necessary. This allows you to take advantage of common structural elements among projects, yet still be able to specify differences between them.

If your typical layout is that shown in Figure 17–1, specify it like this in *Project.tmpl*:

```
#ifndef IncludeSrc
#define IncludeSrc $(TOP)/include
#endif
#ifndef LibSrc
#define LibSrc $(TOP)/lib
#endif
#ifndef ApplSrc
#define ApplSrc $(TOP)/appl
#endif
#ifndef ManSrc
#define ManSrc $(TOP)/man
#endif
#ifndef DocSrc
#define DocSrc $(TOP)/doc
#endif

INCLUDESRC = IncludeSrc
    LIBSRC = LibSrc
   APPLSRC = ApplSrc
    MANSRC = ManSrc
    DOCSRC = DocSrc
```

When a project conforms to the prototype, it's unnecessary to specify any layout information for it in the project's private configuration files. When a project differs, use *Project.p-tmpl* to say how. Suppose a project uses *h* rather than *include* for its header file directory and has an *examples* directory not appearing at all in the prototype layout (Figure 17–2).

Specify how this layout differs from the prototype in *Project.p-tmpl* as follows:

```
#ifndef IncludeSrc
#define IncludeSrc $(TOP)/h
#endif
```

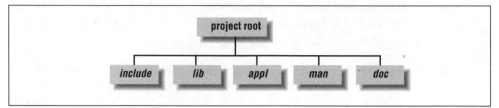

Figure 17–1: Prototype project layout

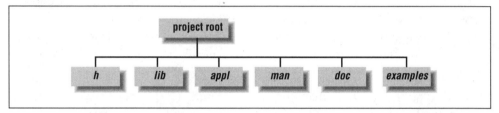

Figure 17–2: Project with layout differing from prototype

```
#ifndef ExampleSrc
#define ExampleSrc $(TOP)/examples
#endif

EXAMPLESRC = ExampleSrc
```

There is already a parameter for the header file directory location in the shared files, so we only need to override the value of IncludeSrc. For the *examples* directory, there is no parameter, so we must provide not only the macro definition but the variable assignment.

But what if *Project.tmpl* is shared by different projects that don't have similar layouts, i.e., ones that do not have the same set of directories, or do not arrange them the same way? The values of the layout parameters vary from project to project—variation that's hard to deal with if you put the parameters in a single file shared among several projects.

You can handle this problem easily using extensible configuration files. One way is to move the layout specification from the shared files to the private files. That is, instead of putting the layout parameters in the shared *Project.tmpl*, put them in the private *Project.p-tmpl* of the project to which they apply. This works well if your projects tend to have unique layouts.[*]

---

* TOP should always remain in the shared files; the fact that it names the top of the project tree must be invariant across all projects.

Installation Directories

Specifying installation directories is the inverse of specifying project layout: you're indicating where files should go rather than where they come from. However, the principles by which you specify the parameters are the same.

If you tend to use a particular installation directory frequently, you can provide the usual value as a parameter BINDIR set from the macro BinDir in the shared configuration files. If all of a project's files are installed in BINDIR and the value of BINDIR supplied in the shared configuration files is appropriate, you don't specify anything in the project's private files. If the value of BINDIR is incorrect for a project, override it by defining the macro BinDir in *Project.p-tmpl*. If a project's files are not all installed in a single directory, create new parameters. For example, if you want to install some files in */usr/local/etc* and others in a library directory */usr/local/lib/mylib*, put this in *Project.p-tmpl*:

```
#ifndef EtcDir
#define EtcDir /usr/local/etc
#endif
#ifndef ProjLibDir
#define ProjLibDir /usr/local/lib/mylib
#endif
    ETCDIR = EtcDir
PROJLIBDIR = ProjLibDir
```

Then refer to ETCDIR and PROJLIBDIR when you invoke installation rules.

Project-Specific Rules

The extension and override principles apply to rules, too. If a rule in the shared file *Imake.rules* is suitable, use it as is. If a rule in *Imake.rules* isn't suitable, override it in *Imake.p-rules* with a different version. And if you need a rule for your project that's not present in the shared rules file, define it in *Imake.p-rules*.

Libraries

Use the shared files to define parameters for libraries you tend to use commonly in project after project. Thus, if you use the math library a lot and you want to refer to it symbolically, put this in *Project.tmpl*:

```
#ifndef MathLib
#define MathLib -lm
#endif

MATHLIB = MathLib
```

Use the private file *Project.p-tmpl* to define parameters for libraries you don't use commonly, but need for a given project. These are usually libraries that are built within and used by only that project, or system libraries used on a more specialized basis only by a few projects:

```
/* within-project library */
#ifndef ProjLib
#define ProjLib $(TOP)/lib/libproj.a
#endif

/* rarely used system library */
#ifndef RareLib
#define RareLib -lrare
#endif

PROJLIB = ProjLib
RARELIB = RareLib
```

System Characteristics

In Chapter 11 we discussed the mechanism of using *cpp* macros to indicate the presence or absence of system features. Typically you define defaults for these macros in the template or project files, and override them as necessary on a platform-specific basis in the vendor files.

You can write your configuration files to provide symbols for any system feature you want: HasVFork, HasShm, HasMmap, HasBlueEyes, etc. The danger when you're writing configuration files shared among many different projects is that each project's need for particular feature symbols contributes additional complexity to the files. You can end up with quite a large set of symbols if the configuration file architecture doesn't provide any way of keeping less commonly used symbols out of the shared files.

We can better partition these symbols using an extensible configuration file architecture. Because the shared files hold symbols for the most commonly needed features only, those symbols are centralized instead of being unnecessarily duplicated in the private files of several individual projects. Conversely, infrequently used feature symbols are defined in the private configuration files of specific projects, which reduces clutter in the shared files. Table 17–1 summarizes where you define the default and override values for symbols, depending on how extensively you need to refer to them.

Table 17–1: Defining Feature Symbol Default and Override Values

Feature Symbol Type	Define Default In...	Override Default In...
Commonly used	*Imake.tmpl* or *Project.tmpl*	*vendor.cf*
Infrequently used	*Project.p-tmpl*	*vendor.p-cf*

The Site-Specific File

The site-specific file *site.def* in the X11 files (and in the SP, DP, and EA files) is split into two sections that are selected depending on which of the two macros `BeforeVendorCF` and `AfterVendorCF` is defined. If your configuration files use a shared *site.def* that follows the same pattern, any private *site.p-def* in a project's *config* directory should follow it, too. Site-specific definitions should be placed in the appropriate half of *site.p-def*:

```
#ifdef BeforeVendorCF
    /* site-specific definitions needed by vendor files go here */
#endif
#ifdef AfterVendorCF
    /* other site-specific definitions go here */
#endif
```

If a project has already been installed and you want to do some further work on it but leave the original installation alone, you can use *site.p-def* to help build a parallel project release. Specify a set of alternate installation directories in *site.p-def* (e.g., directories under your own account) and install everything into them. When you're satisfied with your modifications, remove the alternate definitions from *site.p-def*, reconfigure and rebuild the project, and reinstall it into the real destination directories.

Experimenting with Configuration Files

The extensible architecture allows you to test the effect of modifying information in the shared files without actually making any changes to those files, by copying information from them into private configuration files of a test project. For example, if you want to try out different versions of a rule that's in *Imake.rules*, copy the rule into your project's *Imake.p-rules* file. By modifying the copy, you can see how your changes work without disturbing the shared files or other projects that use the shared files. If you decide the modified version is an improvement worth installing, put it back into *Imake.rules*.

Distributing Software Configured with Extensible Files

When you distribute a project configured with extensible files, you should include any private configuration files in the project distribution. Of course, the project is dependent on the shared configuration files, too, so the shared files need to be made available as well. In the documentation for your project, you should note its dependency on the shared configuration files and indicate how to get them.

Creating a New Set of Extensible Files

The nature of extensible configuration files is such that you can develop an arbitrary number of projects with them, even if the files don't exactly match the configuration requirements of any particular project. This reduces the need to create new sets of configuration files. Nevertheless, at some point you might find you need to develop some projects with requirements significantly different from those addressed by configuration files you've been writing.

For instance, you may have a set of extensible files oriented toward program development. If you need to develop projects oriented toward database management, for example, you'll be producing different kinds of targets (report generators, canned queries, etc.). You may well decide to write another set of shared configuration files for use with this group of projects.

To create a new set of extensible configuration files, use the following procedure:

- Select a name for your files and copy an existing set of extensible files. If the EA project is located under your current directory, create a copy of it like this:

    ```
    % cp -r EA NEW-EA
    ```

- Change the self-reference by editing *config/Project.tmpl* to indicate the name of the new set of files:

    ```
    #ifndef ConfigName
    #define ConfigName NEW-EA
    #endif
    ```

- Make any other modifications you need. The specifics of this step vary according to the purposes you have in mind for the new files, of course.

- In the NEW-EA project root, build the Makefiles and install the configuration files:

    ```
    % imboot
    % make Makefiles
    % make -n install
    ```

    In the last command, we use *−n* to see where *make* thinks it should install the files. If the directory is correct in the output, repeat the command without the *−n*.

Now you can develop projects using the NEW-EA files. Bootstrap the Makefiles in such projects like this:

```
% imboot -C NEW-EA
% make Makefiles
```

18

Using imake on Non-UNIX Systems

Like oil and water...

imake was originally written for use with UNIX and is used most widely in that environment. Nevertheless, efforts have been made, with varying degrees of success, to use *imake* under other systems such as Windows NT, OS/2, AmigaOS, and VMS. This chapter describes some of the issues involved in supporting *imake* on systems that aren't UNIX-based. We've already touched on this subject elsewhere, e.g., in Chapter 12, *Writing Rule Macros*, where we discussed some of the considerations that go into designing rules to work under Windows NT.

This chapter goes into less detail on particular problems and takes a broader approach. That means it doesn't necessarily give you specific answers to questions about specific systems; rather, it points out problem areas that are likely to be the source of difficulties you'll need to deal with. This should be useful if you're actively engaged in porting *imake* to a system on which it's not currently supported or simply assessing whether the attempt would be feasible.

imake porting difficulties tend to fall into two categories:

- **What programs are needed and how must they be modified?** The primary tools are *cpp*, *make*, and *imake*; this chapter provides some pointers for getting them to run on non-UNIX systems. Also, your development efforts will be easier if you can get secondary tools such as *makedepend* and *Makefile* bootstrappers to function properly.

- **What changes are necessary in configuration files and Imakefiles?** The chapter discusses where UNIXcentric constructions tend to crop up and how you might generalize them or work around them.

Keep in mind that you might be able to avoid doing the work yourself (or at least some of it) if someone else has already made the attempt. Look around on the Net to find existing work you can use as a guide (e.g., post questions on Usenet or the *imake-talk* mailing list,[*] or use your Web browser's search capabilities). Study examples from systems most like yours to see how others who've preceded you have dealt with problems similar to those you face. Look at existing configuration files. Support for Windows NT is included in the X11R6.1 configuration files. Information about files for other systems is available at:

```
http://www.primate.wisc.edu/software/imake-stuff/OS
ftp://ftp.primate.wisc.edu/software/imake-stuff/OS
```

If you work only with UNIX and your involvement with *imake* is limited to writing Imakefiles, it's still a good idea to read this chapter. Suppose you make your work available in source form. Even if you aren't interested in porting your work to non-UNIX systems, others may be and there are some simple things you can do to make your Imakefiles easier to use on those systems.

Primary Tools

As we've discussed throughout this handbook, the three principal programs you need when you use *imake* are *cpp*, *make*, and *imake* itself. It's important to determine whether or not you can get these to run on your system, because absence of any one of them pretty well prevents being able to use Imakefiles to configure software. In general, since *cpp* and *make* are more commonly used than *imake* and have been ported to many systems already, it's likely that you'll be able to find working versions of them more easily than *imake*.

cpp and make

Assuming you have a C compiler,[†] it's likely you also have *cpp* or can make the C compiler itself act like *cpp*. However, if your *cpp* seems unsuitable for use with *imake*, public implementations are available as described in Appendix A, *Obtaining Configuration Software*. You may be able to modify one of them as necessary to meet the requirements of your system.

If you have no *make* program, your best bet is likely to be *gmake*, the GNU Project's free *make* program. The source is available at *prep.ai.mit.edu* (in the */pub/gnu* directory) or at one of its mirror sites.

---

* See Appendix I, *Other Sources of Information.*

† I assume this because unless you have a C compiler, you won't be able to build *imake* and you'll be dead in the water right from the start.

Another possibility if you have no *make* program is that you have another program with a similar purpose, such as *mms* on VMS. If so, you may be able to write configuration files or adapt existing ones to generate suitable target entries for that program. This would allow you to develop projects that can be configured using *imake*, although there are likely to be some tradeoffs.

On the positive side, being able to use Imakefiles means you can write target descriptions more concisely. Also, you can modify the form of target entries easily by redefining a rule in your configuration files and rebuilding the Makefiles, rather than by editing individual Makefiles.

On the other hand, since you'll be writing entries for a different target description language than the one *make* understands, you'll almost certainly need to provide an extensive set of parameter and rule redefinitions. The different target description language will likely be reflected in your Imakefiles as well. This means they may not be very portable to systems that use *make*. For example, under VMS *mms*, file lists have commas between elements:

```
SRCS = file1.c,    file2.c,    file3.c
OBJS = file1.Osuf, file2.Osuf, file3.Osuf
```

This differs from *make*. You might be able to make the file list descriptions more portable by writing something like the following:

```
#ifdef VMSArchitecture
SRCS = file1.c,    filc2.c,    file3.c
OBJS = file1.Osuf, file2.Osuf, file3.Osuf
#else
SRCS = file1.c    file2.c    file3.c
OBJS = file1.Osuf file2.Osuf file3.Osuf
#endif
```

But this takes care of just one difference between *make* and *mms*. Attempting to account for more of them runs the risk of making it harder to write a portable *Imakefile* than it would be to write different Makefiles yourself.

What all this means is that use of an alternate *make* program with *imake* may make it easier to configure projects on a particular type of system, but it may not help much if you want to achieve portability to other systems. Consider carefully the costs and benefits of using *imake* under such circumstances. It may be that the potential benefits justify the *imake* porting effort in terms of the goals you want to achieve. Then again, you may decide it simply isn't worth it.

Note that the use of VMS in the preceding discussion isn't meant to imply that it's out of the question to try to port *imake* to VMS. In fact, an implementation for use with *mms* already exists.

imake

The source for *imake* is freely available, so you can make whatever modifications to it that you find necessary. Familiarize yourself with the general issues involved in building *imake* on systems to which it has already been ported by reading Appendix B, *Installing Configuration Software*. This background will help you begin assessing what you'll need to do to port *imake* to a new system. Other issues you may need to consider are listed below:

- How does your system indicate line endings? Originally *imake* looked for line-feeds, the conventional line-ending character under UNIX. Later it was modified to look for carriage return/linefeed pairs under Windows NT. If your system uses a different convention (e.g., a carriage return with no linefeed), you might need to teach *imake* about it.

- You must be able to create a subprocess and capture its termination status. This is needed so *imake* can run *cpp*.

- Signal handling varies quite a bit between systems. You'll need to select one of the methods available in the *imake* source, or write your own.

- MAGIC_MAKE_VARS can be defined in *imakemdep.h* to allow for dynamic creation (via XVARDEF and XVARUSE) of *make* variables that are unique to a given target entry. MAGIC_MAKE_VARS is defined for Windows NT; if you need a similar capability, be sure to define it for your system as well.

Secondary Tools

This section describes some tools that aren't quite as important as *cpp*, *make*, and *imake*, but that make life easier if you can use them or find equivalents.

makedepend

makedepend generates header file dependencies for your *Makefile* when you run *make depend*. Some of the issues involved in porting *imake* apply to *makedepend* as well, such as signal handling. Also, if your system uses an object file suffix other than *.o*, you should use the *−osuf* option to pass the correct suffix value to *makedepend*.

Bootstrappers

When you write an *Imakefile*, a bootstrapper program such as *xmkmf* or *imboot* is typically used to create your initial *Makefile* so you don't have to invoke *imake* manually. However, UNIX bootstrappers tend to be written as shell scripts. Unless your system supports *sh* or equivalent, you'll need to rewrite them. For example, you might do this in REXX for OS/2, or perhaps in Perl on systems that support it.

Imakefiles

Imakefiles are typically highly portable and system independent within the UNIX domain, but problems arise when you move outside of UNIX. This section describes a few simple principles that help make Imakefiles reasonably portable to non-UNIX systems.

Imakefiles make little or no reference to the commands used to build targets, which is one reason they're more portable than Makefiles. On the other hand, Imakefiles always refer to the files from which those targets are created. This is a problem because file-naming conventions vary among systems, as illustrated in Table 18–1. If you refer to target names literally, they'll be incorrect on systems that use different naming conventions than those you had in mind when you wrote your *Imakefile*.

Table 18–1: Sample File-Naming Conventions

Type of File	UNIX	Windows NT, OS/2
Executable	no suffix	*.exe* suffix
Object file	*.o* suffix	*.obj* suffix
Library	*lib* prefix, *.a* suffix	no prefix, *.lib* suffix

The way around these variations is to use target name generator macros, if any are provided by your configuration files. Table 18–2 compares the use of literal target names with the corresponding X11 macros that work more generally. The macros are preferable to literal target names since they produce correct names on more systems.

Table 18–2: Methods of Writing Target Names

Type of File	Nonportable Literal Name	Portable Generated Name
Executable	*name*	`ProgramTargetName(`*name*`)`
Object file	*name*`.o`	*name*`.Osuf`
Library	`Concat(lib,`*name*`,.a)`	`LibraryTargetName(`*name*`)`
C++ source file	*name*`.cc`, *name*`.C`, etc.	*name*`.CCsuf`

When you need to compile a single C source file specially and you're using the X11 configuration files, you can choose either `SpecialCObjectRule()` or `SpecialObjectRule()`. The former is preferable because you supply only the file's basename and the rule provides the proper object file suffix automatically for you.

For occasions when there is no way around referring to system-dependent files or flags in an *Imakefile*, use architecture-indicator macros to section off such references. These macros have names like `Win32Architecture` or `Linux-Architecture`. Examples that show how to use this technique may be found in the section "Conditionals in Imakefiles," in Chapter 13, *Configuration Problems and Solutions*.

Configuration Files

In general, most configuration files remain unchanged when you adapt them to a new system, with the following exceptions:

- You must write a vendor block and add it to the vendor block section (e.g., for X11R6.1, you add the block to the *Imake.cf* file).

- You must write a new vendor file. This is likely to be one of the most difficult parts of any *imake* porting effort. The vendor file is where you specify those things that differ from the configuration information defaults. The more your system differs from UNIX, the more system-specific information you must provide.

Appendix B describes how to write a vendor block. Likely trouble spots to watch out for when you're writing your vendor file are discussed below.

You'll need to provide appropriate definitions for programs and flags where the default values are incorrect for your system. For instance, if you have no *install* program, you'll need to redefine `InstallCmd` as well as the associated `Inst*Flags` macros.

Your configuration files should provide macros that can generate appropriate forms of target names, given a target basename. This allows *Imakefile* writers to use them, and you should use them in your own rules. Table 18–2 lists some of the macros available in the X11 configuration files. If you're using other files that don't provide similar macros, it would be a good idea to define some.

In addition to providing definitions of target name macros that are appropriate for Windows NT, *Win32.rules* goes to some lengths to handle Imakefiles that have already been written using UNIX filenames. This is done using `XVARDEF` and `XVARUSE` to do on-the-fly translation of *.o* to *.obj* in filenames, translation of the pathname separator character from / to \, etc. The same technique may be useful on other systems as well. Note that to do this, you need a *make* program that's capable of performing such translations, such as *nmake* under Windows NT or OS/2.

Rules that rely on shell programming constructs are likely to cause problems on systems with no *sh* or equivalent. Unfortunately, this affects whole classes of rules, such as those that generate recursive target entries. Unless you can work around this problem, you'll have a difficult time providing decent support for multiple-directory projects. You may also have difficulty with rules that use < and > syntax to perform UNIX-style input and output redirection.

Epilogue

If you port *imake* to a new system and you are willing to let others benefit from your labors, I'd be interested in hearing from you. Please write to me at *dubois@primate.wisc.edu*.

Obtaining Configuration Software

This appendix describes how to obtain the software discussed in this book. Most distributions are provided as *tar* files that have been compressed with *gzip* or *compress*. These are indicated by filename suffixes of *.gz* and *.Z*, respectively. The distributions are listed below.

imake configuration tools (*itools.tar.gz, itools.tar.Z*)

> The configuration software described in this book. The distribution contains *imake, xmkmf, imboot, makedepend, mkdirhier, msub, bsdinst, install.sh, imdent*, the X11 configuration files, and some other miscellaneous utilities. Instructions for building and installing this distribution are given in Appendix B, *Installing Configuration Software*.

TOUR configuration files (*TOUR.tar.gz, TOUR.tar.Z*)

> The examples in Chapter 2, *A Tour of imake*, are based on the X11 configuration files. The TOUR distribution contains an alternate set of configuration files that can be used for working through the examples. The TOUR files are similar to the X11 files, but they're simpler and easier to understand.

Starter project configuration files (*SP.tar.gz, SP.tar.Z*)

> The starter project files described in Chapter 9, *A Configuration Starter Project*.

Demonstration project configuration files (*DP.tar.gz, DP.tar.Z*)

> The demonstration project files developed in Chapter 11, *Introduction to Configuration File Writing*, and Chapter 12, *Writing Rule Macros*.

Extensible-architecture configuration files (*EA.tar.gz, EA.tar.Z*)

> The configuration files implementing the extensible architecture described in Chapter 15, *Designing Extensible Configuration Files*, and Chapter 16, *Creating Extensible Configuration Files*.

der Mouse *cpp* (*mouse-cpp.tar.gz, mouse-cpp.tar.Z*)

> A public implementation of *cpp* by der Mouse. You might find it useful if your C preprocessor doesn't work with *imake*.

DECUS *cpp* (*DECUS-cpp.tar.gz, DECUS-cpp.tar.Z*)

> Another public implementation of *cpp*.

This handbook's configuration files (*bookcf.tar.gz, bookcf.tar.Z*)

> The configuration files used in connection with the writing of *Software Portability with imake*.

Errata sheet (*Errata*)

> Last and, I hope, least, the current list of known errors in this book.

Obtaining the Distributions

The software is available electronically via World Wide Web, FTP, or FTPMAIL. Use a Web browser or FTP if you are directly on the Internet. Use FTPMAIL if you are not on the Internet but can exchange electronic mail with Internet sites.

After you obtain a distribution, you need to unpack it. To uncompress and extract files from a distribution that has been compressed with *gzip* (e.g., *itools.tar.gz*), use this command:

```
% gunzip < itools.tar.gz | tar xf -
```

Or, on System V systems:

```
% gunzip < itools.tar.gz | tar xof -
```

For a distribution that has been compressed with *compress* (e.g., *itools.tar.Z*), use this command instead:

```
% zcat itools.tar.Z | tar xf -
```

Or, on System V systems:

```
% zcat itools.tar.Z | tar xof -
```

If *zcat* is not available on your system, use separate *uncompress* and *tar* commands:

```
% uncompress itools.tar.Z
% tar xf itools.tar
```

Or, on System V systems:

```
% uncompress itools.tar.Z
% tar xof itools.tar
```

World Wide Web

To use the World Wide Web, you need a machine with direct access to the Internet. The software may be obtained with a Web browser using the following URL:

```
http://www.primate.wisc.edu/software/imake-book
```

This will take you to an index page containing links to the available distributions. Select the link corresponding to the distribution in which you're interested.

FTP

To use FTP, you need a machine with direct access to the Internet. The software may be obtained from any of the hosts below. The last host is likely to have the most up-to-date distributions.

Machine	Directory
ftp.uu.net	*/published/oreilly/nutshell/imake*
ftp.ora.com	*/pub/examples/nutshell/imake*
ftp.primate.wisc.edu	*/pub/imake-book*

A sample session is shown, with what you should type in **boldface**:

```
% ftp ftp.uu.net
Connected to ftp.uu.net.
220 FTP server (Version 6.21 Tue Mar 12 22:09:55 EST 1996) ready.
Name (ftp.uu.net:dubois): anonymous
331 Guest login OK, send domain style e-mail address as password.
Password: dubois@ora.com          (Use your user name and host here)
230 Guest login OK, access restrictions apply.
ftp> cd /published/oreilly/nutshell/imake
250 CWD command successful.
ftp> binary          (Very important! You must specify binary transfer for compressed files.)
200 Type set to I.
ftp> get itools.tar.gz
200 PORT command successful.
150 Opening BINARY mode data connection for itools.tar.gz.
226 Transfer complete.
ftp> quit
221 Goodbye.
%
```

FTPMAIL

FTPMAIL is a mail server available to anyone who can exchange electronic mail with Internet sites. This includes most workstations that have an email connection to the outside world, and CompuServe users. You do not need to be directly on the Internet. Here's how to do it.

You send mail to *ftpmail@decwrl.dec.com*. In the message body, give the name of the anonymous FTP host and the FTP commands you want to run. The server will run anonymous FTP for you and mail the files back to you. To get a complete help file, send a message with no subject and the single word "help" in the body. The following is an example mail session that should get you a listing of the files in the selected directory and the file *itools.tar.gz*. The listing is useful in case there are other files you may be interested in.

```
% mail ftpmail@decwrl.dec.com
Subject:
reply dubois@ora.com                    (where you want files mailed)
connect ftp.uu.net
cd /published/oreilly/nutshell/imake
dir
binary
uuencode                                (or btoa if you have it)
get itools.tar.gz
quit
.                                       (or CONTROL-D)
%
```

A signature at the end of the message is acceptable as long as it appears after "quit."

All retrieved files will be split into 60KB chunks and mailed to you. You then remove the mail headers and concatenate them into one file, and then *uudecode* or *atob* it.

B

Installing Configuration Software

This appendix describes how to build and install *imake* and related configuration software if you do not already have it on your machine. The software (referred to here as "the distribution") is available as *itools.tar.gz* or *itools.tar.Z* from the archive sites listed in Appendix A, *Obtaining Configuration Software*.

The essential programs you will need for working your way through this book are:

imake   *Makefile* generator

xmkmf   Bootstrapper that uses the X11 configuration files

imboot   General purpose bootstrapper

makedepend   Header file dependency generator

mkdirhier   Directory creation tool

Some of these may be new to you, particularly if you are looking at this appendix without reading the rest of the book first. *imake*, of course, is discussed throughout the book. *xmkmf*, *makedepend*, and *mkdirhier* are discussed in Chapter 2, *A Tour of imake*. *imboot* is discussed in Chapter 10, *Coordinating Sets of Configuration Files*, and Chapter 15, *Designing Extensible Configuration Files*.

The distribution also includes the X11 configuration files and some miscellaneous programs like *msub* and *imdent*.

Most of the distribution is based on the current release of X11 (X11R6.1, public patch 1 at the time of writing), but some programs are not part of the standard X11 distribution, e.g., *imboot*, *msub*, and *imdent*.

Distribution Layout

The software is distributed as a *gziped* or *compressed* *tar* file *itools.tar.gz* or *itools.tar.Z*. Retrieve the distribution and unpack it according to the instructions in Appendix A. This will create an *itools* directory and several subdirectories. You should then familiarize yourself with the distribution's structure and contents. Move into the distribution root so you can look around:

```
% cd itools
```

The distribution root directory contains an *include* subdirectory in which some header files needed to compile *imake* and *makedepend* are located. The *itools* directory also contains a *config* subdirectory under which the rest of the configuration software is located. *config* is divided into the following subdirectories:

cf   The X11 configuration files.

imake   The source for *imake*.

makedepend   Source for the C version of *makedepend*. Several programs go by this name; the version included here is intended for use with *imake* and is written by Todd Brunhoff, *imake*'s author.

util   Source for *xmkmf, mkdirhier, bsdinst, install.sh, lndir, mkshadow,* and some other miscellaneous scripts, such as *which* and a script version of *makedepend* (if you can't get the C version to work).

extras   Source for *imboot, msub,* and *imdent*.

misc   Miscellaneous bits and pieces: portions of the X11 Release Notes that pertain to *imake*; any errors that have been found in this appendix since publication; troubleshooting information too detailed or specialized to be included in this appendix; reader-contributed notes about porting *imake* to systems not covered by the distribution, etc.

Finding out What You Already Have

Survey the landscape of your system, since some or all of the software you need may already be present on your machine. For instance, if you are using a workstation running X11, there is a good chance the configuration files and some of the programs are already installed, because X11 itself is configured with *imake*.

To find programs, use the *which* command. It will tell you either where a program is located, or, if it couldn't find it, which directories it looked in (usually the directories named in your PATH variable). In the following example, *which* tells you that *imake* is installed in */usr/local/bin*:

```
% which imake
/usr/local/bin/imake
```

On the other hand, if *which* can't find *imake*, you'll get a result like this:

```
% which imake
no imake in . /usr/local/bin /usr/bin/X11 /usr/ucb /bin /usr/bin
```

If you don't have *which*, you can use either of the scripts *which.sh* or *which.csh* supplied in the *util* directory. If *which* doesn't find *imake*, try looking in */usr/local/bin, /usr/bin, /usr/bin/X11*, or in any */usr/X11Rn/bin* directory you may have. You can also look in */var/X11Rn/bin, /opt/X11Rn/bin*, or */local/X11Rn/bin*. If you have OpenWindows, look for */usr/ openwin/bin*.

In many instances, if you discover that a program included in the distribution is already installed, you don't need to install it. However, you should make exceptions when you have out-of-date or broken versions of programs:

* Use the X11R6.1 version of *imake* if you have an earlier version.

* The current versions of *makedepend* and *xmkmf* each understand a *−a* option. Older versions (distributed prior to X11R5) do not. The current version of *makedepend* also has improved parsing of *cpp* preprocessor conditional directives, which results in more accurate results than with earlier versions. Install the versions in the distribution to update your system.

* The versions of *imake* and *xmkmf* distributed with Sun systems are nonstandard and modified specially for use with OpenWindows. If the pathnames for your versions of *imake* and *xmkmf* have *openwin* in them (e.g., */usr/openwin/bin/imake*), you may be better off installing the standard X11 versions because the OpenWindows versions do not work very well to configure non-OpenWindows software. See Appendix J, *Using imake with OpenWindows*, for further discussion of this issue.

In addition to the programs, you need a copy of the X11 configuration files, because many examples throughout this book assume they are available to play with. The default location for the X11 files is usually */usr/X11R6.1/lib/X11/config, /usr/X11R6/lib/X11/config*, or */usr/lib/X11/config* for X11R6.1, X11R6, or X11R5. If you can't find the X11 files but you have *xmkmf* installed, look at it to see where it expects to find the files.

Preparing To Install the Distribution

The first thing you should do is read through the *README* file in the *itools* directory. Then, before building the distribution, you must decide where you will install the software to avoid misconfiguring the programs. Some installation locations are built in. The defaults are:

/usr/X11R6.1/bin	Location of programs
/usr/X11R6.1/lib/X11/config	Location of the X11 configuration files
/usr/local/lib/config	Location of the *imboot* configuration root directory

You can change the default installation locations if you like. If you do, then whenever you see the defaults in examples elsewhere in this book, you must substitute the locations you have chosen.

Suppose you want to install programs in */usr/local/bin* and the X11 configuration files in */var/X11R6.1/lib/X11/config*, and that you want to use */var/lib/config* for the *imboot* configuration root. Make the changes as follows:

- To change the program installation directory, add the following to the second half of *config/cf/site.def*:

  ```
  #ifndef BinDir
  #define BinDir /usr/local/bin
  #endif
  ```

- To change the X11 configuration file installation directory, add the following to the second half of *config/cf/site.def*:

  ```
  #ifndef ConfigDir
  #define ConfigDir /var/X11R6.1/lib/X11/config
  #endif
  ```

- To change the configuration root directory used by *imboot*, edit this line in *config/extras/Imakefile*:

  ```
  CONFIGROOTDIR = /usr/local/lib/config
  ```

  Change it to this:

  ```
  CONFIGROOTDIR = /var/lib/config
  ```

The *imdent* script is built assuming that *perl* is installed as */usr/local/bin/perl* on your system. If that is incorrect, edit the *Imakefile* in *config/extras* to have the correct value for PERLPATH.

Installing with Limited Privileges

If you have insufficient privileges to install software on your machine wherever you like, try to convince a sympathetic site administrator to install files that need to go in system directories.[*] If that is not possible, install everything under your own account (use the instructions just given for changing the default locations). If the path to your home directory is */u/you*, I suggest the following installation directories:

/u/you/bin	Location of programs
/u/you/lib/config/X11R6.1	Location of the X11 configuration files
/u/you/lib/config	Location of the *imboot* configuration root directory

Building the Distribution—Quick Instructions

This section contains quick instructions for building the distribution. If they don't work, read the section "Building the Distribution—Detailed Instructions."

Change into the *config/cf* directory and look around; you'll see the configuration files listed below:

```
% cd config/cf
% ls
Amoeba.cf      Server.tmpl    hp.cf          necLib.rules   site.def
DGUX.cf        Threads.tmpl   hpLib.rules    necLib.tmpl    site.sample
FreeBSD.cf     Win32.cf       hpLib.tmpl     noop.rules     sony.cf
Imake.cf       Win32.rules    ibm.cf         oldlib.rules   sun.cf
Imake.rules    WinLib.tmpl    ibmLib.rules   osf1.cf        sunLib.rules
Imake.tmpl     apollo.cf      ibmLib.tmpl    osfLib.rules   sunLib.tmpl
Imakefile      bsd.cf         linux.cf       osfLib.tmpl    sv4Lib.rules
Library.tmpl   bsdLib.rules   lnxLib.rules   pegasus.cf     sv4Lib.tmpl
Makefile       bsdLib.tmpl    lnxLib.tmpl    sco.cf         svr4.cf
Mips.cf        bsdi.cf        luna.cf        scoLib.rules   ultrix.cf
NetBSD.cf      convex.cf      macII.cf       sequent.cf     usl.cf
Oki.cf         cray.cf        moto.cf        sgi.cf         x386.cf
Project.tmpl   fujitsu.cf     ncr.cf         sgiLib.rules   xf86.rules
README         generic.cf     nec.cf         sgiLib.tmpl    xfree86.cf
```

Find a vendor-specific configuration file that applies to your machine. This will be one of the files named with a *.cf* suffix. For Sun machines, use *sun.cf*, for Silicon Graphics machines, use *sgi.cf*, etc. If you find no vendor file for your system, you may need to write one using the detailed instructions. (First look in the *config/misc* directory, though. It contains instructions for some systems that aren't supported in the standard X11 distribution.)

---

[*] Yes, I know that "sympathetic site administrator" is oxymoronic.

Find the definitions of OSMajorVersion, OSMinorVersion, and OSTeenyVersion in your vendor file. They represent the major, minor, and subminor release numbers for your operating system. Check that they are correct, and change them if they are not. Suppose *linux.cf* specifies Linux 1.2.11:

```
#ifndef OSMajorVersion
#define OSMajorVersion       1
#endif
#ifndef OSMinorVersion
#define OSMinorVersion       2
#endif
#ifndef OSTeenyVersion
#define OSTeenyVersion       11
#endif
```

If you're running Linux 1.2.8, the major and minor numbers are correct, but you must change the subminor number to 8:

```
#ifndef OSTeenyVersion
#define OSTeenyVersion       8
#endif
```

If your OS release is defined only by major and minor numbers, your vendor file may not contain any definition for OSTeenyVersion.

Look over *site.def* to see whether you want to change anything. In particular, to use *gcc* (version 2.x.x) as your C compiler, define HasGcc2 as YES by uncommenting the #define that is already there.

The distribution should build on many systems at this point. In the distribution root (the *itools* directory) execute the following command:

```
% make World >& world.log
```

The command just shown uses *csh* redirection. If you are using a shell from the Bourne shell family (*sh*, *ksh*, *bash*), use this command instead:

```
$ make World > world.log 2>&1
```

For Windows NT, use this command:

```
nmake World.Win32 > world.log
```

When the command terminates, look through *world.log* to see whether or not the World operation completed without error. If everything looks okay, go to the next section, "Installing the Software." Otherwise you may need to specify BOOTSTRAP-CFLAGS. Look in Table B–1 and find the bootstrap flags for your system. If the value is *varies*, several values are possible and you must examine the vendor file and figure out which value is appropriate for your machine. If your system is not listed, the distribution hasn't been ported to it and you need to use the detailed instructions.

Table B-1: Bootstrap Flags for Various Systems

Vendor File	Bootstrap Flags	Remark
Amoeba.cf	-DAMOEBA -DCROSS_i80386 -DCROSS_COMPILE	For i80386 architecture
	-DAMOEBA -DCROSS_mc68000 -DCROSS_COMPILE	For Sun 3 architecture
	-DAMOEBA -DCROSS_sparc -DCROSS_COMPILE	For SPARC architecture
DGUX.cf	-DDGUX	
FreeBSD.cf	-D__FreeBSD__	
Mips.cf	-DMips	
NetBSD.cf	-D__NetBSD__	
Oki.cf	-DOki	
Win32.cf	-DWIN32	
apollo.cf	-Dapollo	
bsd.cf	-DNOSTDHDRS	
bsdi.cf	-D__bsdi__	
convex.cf	-D__convex__ -tm c1	
cray.cf	-DCRAY	possibly -D_CRAY?
fujitsu.cf	-D__uxp__	For SPARC architecture
	-D__sxg__	For mc68000 architecture
hp.cf	-Dhpux	
ibm.cf	*varies*	Will include -Dibm
linux.cf	-Dlinux	
luna.cf	-Dluna	
macII.cf	-DmacII	
moto.cf	-DMOTOROLA -DSVR4	If SVR4 conformant
	-DMOTOROLA -DSYSV	If not SVR4 conformant
ncr.cf	-DNCR	
nec.cf	-DNEC	
osf1.cf	-D__osf__	
pegasus.cf	-DM4310 -DUTEK	
sco.cf	*none*	
sequent.cf	-Dsequent	For Dynix 3
	-D_SEQUENT_	For Dynix Ptx
sgi.cf	-DSYSV	For IRIX 3.x, 4.x
	-DSVR4	For IRIX 5.x and up
sony.cf	-Dsony	
sun.cf	-Dsun -DNOSTDHDRS	For SunOS before 4.1
	-Dsun	For SunOS 4.1 up to 5.0
	-Dsun -DSVR4	For SunOS 5.0 and up
svr4.cf	-DSVR4 -Di386	For i386 architecture
	-DSVR4	For non-i386 architecture
ultrix.cf	-Dultrix	
usl.cf	-DUSL	
x386.cf	*varies*	Will include -DSYSV386

You should also look in the *config/misc* directory to see if there are any files pertaining to your system. Some patches to make the distribution build on older releases of OSes are contained there, and you may need to apply one of them.

In the distribution root, execute the following command, replacing *flags* with the appropriate bootstrap flags for your system:

```
% make World BOOTSTRAPCFLAGS="flags" >& world.log
```

Examples:

```
% make World BOOTSTRAPCFLAGS="-Dsun -DSVR4" >& world.log
% make World BOOTSTRAPCFLAGS="-Dhpux" >& world.log
```

When the command terminates, look through *world.log* to see whether or not the World operation completed without error. If it failed, use the detailed instructions. Otherwise, go ahead and install the software.

Installing the Software

If you want to install everything, use the following command in the distribution root directory (you may need to be *root* to do this):

```
% make install
```

Otherwise, change into individual directories under the *config* directory and install only those files in which you are interested. The instructions below show how to do this; leave out the parts for the files you don't want to install.

* In *cf*, install the X11 configuration files:

  ```
  % make install.cffiles
  ```

* In *imake*, install *imake*:

  ```
  % make install.imake
  ```

  Do not install *ccimake*; it is only needed for compiling *imake*.

* In *makedepend*, if you built the compiled version of *makedepend* (the default on most systems), install it:

  ```
  % make install.makedepend
  ```

  If you did not build the compiled version, the script version will be installed from the *util* directory.

- In *util*, install various scripts:

  ```
  % make install.xmkmf
  % make install.mkdirhier
  ```

  If you have a System V version of *install* instead of a BSD-compatible one, the distribution contains two scripts *bsdinst* and *install.sh* that you can use instead. Some systems use one, others use the other. You can tell which one to install by watching what commands *make* has been executing as you've been installing the software above:

  ```
  % make install.bsdinst        (or)
  % make install.install.sh
  ```

  If you built the script version of *makedepend*, install it:

  ```
  % make install.makedepend
  ```

- In *extras*, install *imboot*, *msub*, and *imdent*:

  ```
  % make install.imboot
  % make install.msub
  % make install.imdent
  ```

Building the Distribution—Detailed Instructions

This section contains detailed instructions for building *imake*. You're probably reading it either because *imake* hasn't been ported to your type of system, or because you just tried the quick instructions and they didn't work on your machine. In the first case, you need to modify your copy of the distribution according to the following instructions. In the second case, you should look for discrepancies between how the distribution expects your system to be set up and how it actually is set up. Make sure you've read through the quick instructions first because they contain information you will need here. You might also find it helpful to read Chapter 3, *Understanding Configuration Files*, to get some idea of how *imake* works. That will help you understand the result you're trying to produce.

If you're porting *imake* to a system on which it's not currently supported, use one of the following locators to see if there's any information for your type of system:

```
http://www.primate.wisc.edu/software/imake-stuff/OS
ftp://ftp.primate.wisc.edu/software/imake-stuff/OS
```

If you're not running UNIX, you should also read Chapter 18, *Using imake on Non-UNIX Systems*.

When *imake* runs, it invokes *cpp* to process the configuration files. Default values for most configuration parameters are defined in *Imake.tmpl*, *Project.tmpl*, etc.

Also included among the configuration files are many vendor files, each of which contains parameter values that override any defaults that are inappropriate for a particular vendor's systems. Since there are several different vendor files from which to choose, *cpp* has to figure out which is the right one for the machine you are actually using. *cpp* does this by checking various symbols known to identify different types of systems. The one that is defined determines the current system type.

The symbol that identifies your system can come from a couple of sources. Some vendors ship a *cpp* that predefines a symbol unique to that vendor's systems. For instance, on Ultrix, *cpp* predefines `ultrix`, which makes it easy to ascertain the system type:

```
#ifdef ultrix
    /* it's Ultrix, all right... */
#endif
```

Unfortunately, some vendor-supplied symbols aren't useful for system identification because they are ambiguous (or have become so). For instance, at one time (in the days of X11R3) the `mips` symbol unambiguously indicated a true Mips Computers, Inc. machine, but the symbol later became ambiguous when several other OS's written to run on Mips processors also defined `mips` (Ultrix, NEWS OS, IRIX, etc.). In the absence of a unique predefined vendor symbol, it is necessary to make up an identifier symbol and to tell *imake* to define it when starting up *cpp*. Thus, to signify true Mips machines, the "artificial" symbol `Mips` is now used.

It might even be that your preprocessor predefines no useful system-indicating symbols at all. ANSI C takes a dim view of most predefined symbols, so ANSI *cpp*s tend to provide few symbols that can be used to determine the system type. Here, too, you invent an identifier symbol and make sure *imake* defines it so *cpp* can determine which vendor file to use.

Thus, to port *imake* to your machine, you must satisfy three requirements:

1. The configuration files must contain a block of code that "recognizes" your system type and selects the correct vendor file. The block is called the vendor block and the system-identifier symbol that activates it is called the trigger symbol. In the X11 configuration files, the vendor blocks are located in the *Imake.cf* file.

2. You need a vendor file that describes your system and contains any information needed to override default values of parameters specified in the other configuration files.

3. *imake* must make sure the trigger symbol is defined when *cpp* starts up if *cpp* doesn't predefine it.

We'll discuss how to meet these requirements by porting *imake* to systems built by the hypothetical vendor Brand XYZ, as well as what to look for if *imake* has already been ported to your type of system but you can't get it to work on your machine.

Writing the Vendor Block

The vendor block for your system goes in the *Imake.cf* file and is activated by the trigger symbol. You should examine that file for examples of how to write a vendor block. The Linux block is relatively simple:

```
#ifdef linux
# define MacroIncludeFile <linux.cf>
# define MacroFile linux.cf
# undef linux
# define LinuxArchitecture
# define i386Architecture
# undef i386
#endif /* linux */
```

The SunOS block is more complex:

```
#ifdef sun
# define MacroIncludeFile <sun.cf>
# define MacroFile sun.cf
# ifdef SVR4
#   undef SVR4
#   define SVR4Architecture
# endif
# ifdef sparc
#   undef sparc
# define SparcArchitecture
# endif
# ifdef mc68000
#   undef mc68000
# define Sun3Architecture
# endif
# ifdef i386
#   undef i386
#   define i386Architecture
# endif
# undef sun
# define SunArchitecture
#endif /* sun */
```

The first line of each block tests the trigger symbol. If it is undefined, the block is skipped. Otherwise, the block does three things:

1. It defines the name of the vendor file. The name is defined two different ways because it is used in different contexts later.

2. It undefines the trigger symbol and any other OS- or processor-specific symbols that *cpp* might have predefined.

3. It defines a vendor-specific OS architecture symbol. If the OS runs on more than one type of processor, a processor-specific architecture symbol is usually defined, too (e.g., SparcArchitecture, Sun3Architecture, and i386-Architecture in the SunOS vendor block). Architecture symbols are useful in Imakefiles when it is necessary to know the OS or hardware type.

Following this model, you can write the vendor block for Brand XYZ systems using brandxyz as the trigger symbol and BrandXYZArchitecture as the architecture symbol:

```
#ifdef brandxyz
# define MacroIncludeFile <brandxyz.cf>
# define MacroFile brandxyz.cf
# undef brandxyz
# define BrandXYZArchitecture
#endif
```

After you write the vendor block, document the trigger symbol that identifies your system type by putting a definition for BootstrapCFlags in your vendor file. The following line goes in *brandxyz.cf*:

```
#define BootstrapCFlags -Dbrandxyz
```

Writing the Vendor File

For a new port of *imake*, you have to write the vendor file from scratch. For Brand XYZ systems, we'll write a file *brandxyz.cf*. If there is already a vendor file for your system type, you need to fix the vendor file you do have.

There are a few symbols you must define in the vendor file:

* Define the major and minor release numbers for your operating system, and, if necessary, the subminor number. For instance, if your OS is at release 3.4.1, write this:

```
#ifndef OSMajorVersion
#define OSMajorVersion 3
#endif
#ifndef OSMinorVersion
#define OSMinorVersion 4
#endif
#ifndef OSTeenyVersion
#define OSTeenyVersion 1
#endif
```

The OS numbers are used when you need to select parameter values that vary for different releases of the system. Define them even if you don't use them anywhere else in the vendor file, because *Imakefile* writers sometimes need to know the release numbers.

- If your system is based on System V Release 2 or 3, define SystemV:

    ```
    #define SystemV YES
    ```

    If your system is based on System V Release 4, define SystemV4:

    ```
    #define SystemV4 YES
    ```

    If your system isn't based on System V, don't define either symbol.

The remaining contents of the vendor file are largely determined according to whether or not the default parameter values provided in the template and project files are appropriate for your system. Provide override values in the vendor file for those that are not.

To some extent, you find out which defaults to override by trial and error: write a minimal vendor file containing only the symbols described above, then try to build the distribution. If the build fails because a parameter value is incorrect, put the correct value in the vendor file and try again. However, you can minimize trial and error by taking advantage of the experience of those who've gone before you. Existing vendor files serve as a guide to help you figure out what should go in your own vendor file by giving you some idea of the parameters most likely to need special treatment. If any existing files are for operating systems that are similar to yours, your vendor file is likely to be similar to those files.

You now have the vendor block and the vendor file written; all you need is *imake*.

Configuring *imake*

The source for *imake* is in the *imake* directory. *imake* is compiled using a minimal hand-written file *Makefile.ini*. (You want the *Makefile.ini* that is in the *imake* directory, not the one in the distribution root directory.) If you see a *Makefile* in the *imake* directory, ignore it, as it was not configured on your machine.

Makefile.ini builds *imake* in two steps because some systems require special flags to ensure proper compilation of all but the most trivial programs. *imake* isn't especially complex, but it isn't trivial, either, so a small helper program *ccimake* is compiled first. *ccimake* is designed to be simple enough to compile with no special treatment, and it figures out any extra flags needed to get *imake* to compile without error on your platform. Those flags are added to the *imake*-building command.

To build *ccimake* and *imake*, you'll run the following *make* command (but don't run it yet; we won't be ready for a few pages):

```
% make -f Makefile.ini BOOTSTRAPCFLAGS="flags"
cc -o ccimake -O -I../../include ccimake.c
cc -c -O -I../../include './ccimake' imake.c
cc -o imake imake.o
```

The trigger is specified in the value of BOOTSTRAPCFLAGS. For existing ports, determine *flags* from Table B–1. For new ports, use *–Dtrigger* (e.g., *–Dbrandxyz* for Brand XYZ systems).[*]

Makefile.ini incorporates the value of BOOTSTRAPCFLAGS into CFLAGS and generates the three commands just shown. The first compiles *ccimake*. The second invokes *ccimake* and includes the result in the arguments passed to the command that compiles *imake.o*. The third produces the *imake* executable.

The trigger symbol passed in through BOOTSTRAPCFLAGS is used to determine the platform type, but in different ways for each program. The key to understanding trigger use is *imakemdep.h* in the *config/imake* directory. This header file is included by the source for *ccimake* and *imake* and has one part for each. (It is also used by *makedepend* and has a third part for that program; we'll get to that shortly.)

The contents of *imakemdep.h* are organized like this:

```
#ifdef CCIMAKE
        /* part 1 (for ccimake) */
#else
# ifndef MAKEDEPEND
        /* part 2 (for imake) */
# else
        /* part 3 (for makedepend) */
# endif
#endif
```

The source for *ccimake* defines CCIMAKE before including *imakemdep.h*, so that part 1 is processed. *makedepend* source defines MAKEDEPEND, so that part 3 is processed. *imake* source doesn't define either symbol, so part 2 is processed.

For a new port of *imake*, you must add the proper information for your system to each part of *imakemdep.h*. For existing ports you need to verify that the information already there is correct, and fix it if it isn't. The following discussion shows how to set up each part of *imakemdep.h*.

---

[*] If your *cpp* predefines the trigger, BOOTSTRAPCFLAGS can be empty:

```
% make -f Makefile.ini BOOTSTRAPCFLAGS=""
```

However, it doesn't hurt to specify the trigger explicitly.

imakemdep.h — Part 1 (for ccimake)

The first part of *imakemdep.h* consists of a bunch of #ifdef/#endif blocks. Each of them defines imake_ccflags as a string containing the flags needed to get *imake* to compile on a particular platform. The proper definition is selected according to the trigger symbol that is defined when *ccimake* is compiled.

Some flags commonly specified in the definition of imake_ccflags are -DSYSV (System V Release 2 or 3), -DSVR4 (System V Release 4), or -DUSG to indicate USG systems. For instance, if Brand XYZ systems are based on System V Release 4, specify the following:

```
#ifdef brandxyz
#define imake_ccflags "-DSVR4"
#endif
```

You might need more than one flag (see the hpux block for a particularly unpleasant example). Note that all flags are specified in a single string.

If no special flags are necessary to compile *imake*, there need not be any block for your system, and imake_ccflags is given a default definition (currently -O).

If you don't know whether or not *ccimake* needs to produce any special flags, experiment by trying to compile *imake* by hand. Once you figure out how to do it, make your knowledge explicit by defining imake_ccflags appropriately in *imakemdep.h*.

imakemdep.h — Part 2 (for imake)

The second part of *imakemdep.h* contains four sections. Each of them poses a question:

- Do you have a working *dup2()* system call? If not, define a work-around for it.

- Does your *cpp* collapse tabs in macro expansions? If not, define FIX-UP_CPP_WHITESPACE or your Makefiles will not have tabs where necessary and the @@\ sequences will not be stripped out properly.

- Do you want to use the default preprocessor */lib/cpp*? If not, choose an alternate by defining DEFAULT_CPP. The value of DEFAULT_CPP must be a full pathname and only a pathname (no arguments). You can specify an alternate preprocessor at *imake* runtime by setting the IMAKECPP environment variable, but it is better to compile it in using DEFAULT_CPP so *imake* knows the correct value automatically. This may sound nonportable, and it is. But that's okay, because on the particular machine where you're building *imake*, you want it to know exactly where *cpp* is so you don't have to tell it.

- Are there arguments you want *imake* to pass to *cpp* automatically? This section initializes a string array cpp_argv[] with those arguments. The most important entry is a definition for the trigger symbol used to select the correct vendor block in *Imake.tmpl*, but other entries may be necessary, too.

Of the four sections of *imakemdep.h* that apply to *imake*, the one that sets up the string array cpp_argv[] is the most complex. It contains a set of #ifdef/#endif blocks that adds entries to the array. The most common construction looks like this:

```
#ifdef trigger
    "-Dtrigger",
#endif
```

If *trigger* is defined when *imake* is compiled, it causes a definition of itself to be passed to *cpp* when *imake* executes. (If your *cpp* predefines the trigger, you may not see an instance of this construction for your system, but there is no harm in adding one explicitly.)

For Brand XYZ systems, add the following entry to cpp_argv[]:

```
#ifdef brandxyz
    "-Dbrandxyz",
#endif
```

This causes *imake* to pass *–Dbrandxyz* to *cpp*, allowing *cpp* to select the Brand XYZ vendor block as it processes the configuration files.

If you need to pass more than one argument to *cpp*, add the definitions for each argument as separate strings:

```
#ifdef brandxyz
    "-Dbrandxyz",
    "-DSVR4",
#endif
```

imakemdep.h — Part 3 (for makedepend)

The third part of *imakemdep.h* applies to the compiled version of *makedepend*. (This has nothing to do with compiling *imake*, but since we're talking about *imakemdep.h*, we might as well cover it here.)

This part of *imakemdep.h* puts entries in the predefs[] string array based on which of various system- and compiler-related definitions are predefined by *cpp*. *makedepend* uses this information to be smart about which header files to pay attention to when it generates header file dependencies. Consider the following C program fragment:

```
#ifdef ultrix
#include "headera.h"
#else
#include "headerb.h"
#endif
```

makedepend knows to generate a dependency for *headera.h* and not *headerb.h* if `ultrix` is defined, and the other way around if it is undefined; a dumb dependency generator has to assume dependencies on both files in either case.

For existing ports, you can leave this part of *imakemdep.h* alone. For a new port, add symbols appropriate for your system if they are not already listed among the `predefs[]` initializers. First, find the lines that end the `predefs[]` initialization:

```
/* add any additional symbols before this line */
{NULL, NULL}
```

Then add new entries before those lines for any symbols predefined by your *cpp*:

```
#ifdef sym1
    {"sym1", "1"},
#endif
#ifdef sym2
    {"sym2", "1"},
#endif
    /* add any additional symbols before this line */
    {NULL, NULL}
```

Building imake

You're ready to build *imake*. This should be simple if you have set up the vendor block, vendor file, and *imakemdep.h* correctly. First remove the remains of any previous failed build attempts:

```
% make -f Makefile.ini clean
rm -f ccimake imake.o imake
rm -f *.CKP *.ln *.BAK *.bak *.o core errs ,* *~ *.a tags TAGS make.log \#*
```

Then build *ccimake* and *imake*, substituting the bootstrap flags for your system into the following command:

```
% make -f Makefile.ini BOOTSTRAPCFLAGS="flags"
```

For Brand XYZ, the command looks like this:

```
% make -f Makefile.ini BOOTSTRAPCFLAGS="-Dbrandxyz"
making imake with BOOTSTRAPCFLAGS=-Dbrandxyz
cc -o ccimake -Dbrandxyz -O -I../../include ccimake.c
cc -c -Dbrandxyz -O -I../../include './ccimake' imake.c
cc -o imake imake.o
```

After you build *imake*, test whether it is configured correctly, using *imake*'s −*v* option to tell it to echo the *cpp* command it executes. The normal input and output files are of no interest here, so we use *−T/dev/null* and *−f/dev/null* to provide an empty input template and target description file, and *−s/dev/null* to throw away the output:

```
% imake -v -T/dev/null -f/dev/null -s/dev/null
cpp -I. -Uunix -Dbrandxyz Imakefile.c
```

If you see a definition for your trigger symbol in the *cpp* command echoed by *imake* (*−Dbrandxyz* in the example above), *imake* is properly configured. If you don't see the definition, *imake* should still be okay if *cpp* predefines the trigger. Use the following command to check whether that is so (assuming the preprocessor *imake* uses is */lib/cpp*):

```
% echo "trigger" | /lib/cpp
```

If the trigger doesn't appear in the output or turns into "1", *cpp* predefines it. If you see the trigger string literally in the output, *cpp* doesn't predefine it, and you need to reconfigure *imake* to pass *−Dtrigger* to *cpp* explicitly.

Building the Rest of the Distribution

Now that you have the configuration files properly set up to build *imake*, you should be able to execute the `World` operation. In the distribution root directory, run this command:

```
% make World BOOTSTRAPCFLAGS="flags" >& world.log
```

This will rebuild *imake* and also build the rest of the distribution. After it finishes, see the section "Installing the Software" for installation instructions.

If you can build *imake* but *make World* still fails, try building the distribution in stages to get an idea of where the problem lies. First, build the Makefiles from the distribution root:

```
% ./config/imake/imake -I./config/cf
% make Makefiles
```

If that works, try the following:

```
% make clean
% make depend
% make
```

If *make depend* fails while trying to compile *makedepend*, skip it and try the step following it. You can go back later and try to figure out why *makedepend* doesn't build.

If you can't get any of this to work, read *misc/Porting* to see if it contains any helpful advice.

C

Configuration Programs: A Quick Reference

This appendix briefly documents the programs *imake*, *imboot*, *imdent*, *make-depend*, *mkdirbier*, *msub*, and *xmkmf*. The information here is similar, but not identical, to what may be found in the manual pages for these programs. Generally the descriptions here are more condensed, e.g., to eliminate mention of obscure or rarely used options.

Several of the manual pages on which this appendix is based were written by Todd Brunhoff and Jim Fulton.

Name

imake – generate a *Makefile* from an *Imakefile* and a set of configuration files

Synopsis

imake [*options*]

Description

imake generates a *Makefile* by running *cpp* to process an *Imakefile* and a set of configuration files. One of the configuration files is a template that directs the order in which the files are processed. The template tells *cpp* to read other configuration files containing machine- and site-dependent configuration parameters, rules for generating *Makefile* target entries, and, finally, the *Imakefile*. The *Imakefile* contains descriptions of targets to be built, written as calls to *cpp* macros. *imake* takes care of expanding the macros into the corresponding *Makefile* target entries. The entries are properly configured for the current machine using the machine dependencies specified in the configuration files. This allows machine-specific information (such as compiler options, alternate command names, and special *make* rules) to be kept separate from the descriptions of the various items to be built.

imake also replaces any occurrences of the word XCOMM with the character # to permit placing comments in the *Makefile* without causing "invalid directive" errors from the preprocessor.

Some complex *imake* macros require generated *make* variables local to each invocation of the macro, often because their value depends on parameters passed to the macro. Such variables can be created by using an *imake* variable of the form XVARdef*n*, where *n* is a single digit. A unique *make* variable will be substituted. Later occurrences of the variable XVARuse*n* will be replaced by the variable created by the corresponding XVARdef*n*.

Options

imake understands the following options:

–D*name*, –D*name*=*value*, –I*dir*

> These options are passed directly to *cpp*. The –D options are typically used to set directory-specific variables, such as TOPDIR and CURDIR to indicate the top of the project and the current directory within the project. The –I option is used to indicate where to find the configuration files.

–Ttemplate   This option specifies the name of the template. The default is *Imake.tmpl.*

–ffilename   This option specifies the name of the per-directory target-description file. The default is *Imakefile.*

–Cfilename   This option specifies the name of the .c file that is constructed in the current directory. The default is *Imakefile.c.*

–sfilename   This option specifies the name of the output file. The default is *Makefile.*

–e   This option tells *imake* to execute the generated *Makefile*. The default is not to do so.

–v   This option tells *imake* to print the *cpp* command line that it is using to generate the *Makefile*.

Environment Variables

imake uses the following environment variables if they are defined. Their use is not recommended, as they introduce dependencies that are not readily apparent when *imake* is run:

IMAKEINCLUDE

This variable may be defined as a *–Idir* argument to indicate the directory in which to look for configuration files, e.g., *–I/usr/include/local.* Actually, any *cpp* arguments are allowed in IMAKEINCLUDE, but the first one must begin with *–I* (e.g., *–I.*) or *imake* will reject it.

IMAKECPP

By default, *imake* uses */lib/cpp* as the preprocessor program. IMAKECPP may be defined to specify the path of an alternate preprocessor, e.g., */usr/local/cpp.*

IMAKEMAKE

By default, *imake* uses whatever *make* program is found first in your search path. IMAKEMAKE may be defined to specify the path of an alternative *make*, e.g., */bin/s5make.* IMAKEMAKE has no effect unless *–e* is specified on the *imake* command line.

Name

imboot – bootstrap a *Makefile* from an *Imakefile*

Synopsis

imboot [*options*] [*topdir* [*curdir*]]

Description

imboot is a general-purpose *imake* bootstrapper for generating a *Makefile* from an *Imakefile*. By default, *imboot* looks for configuration files in a private project-specific directory (i.e., located within the current project's source tree). The *-c* (or *-C*) option may be given to tell *imboot* to use a set of publicly installed configuration files instead of (or in addition to) any files in the project's private directory.

The private configuration file directory, if used, is taken to be *config* or *config/cf* at the top of the project source tree. *config* is the usual location, but by looking in *config/cf* as well, *imboot* works within the X11R6 or X11R6.1 source trees. The public configuration file directory will be one of those located under */usr/local/lib/config*. The name of the directory is specified by the *-c* and *-C* options.

The *topdir* argument specifies the location of the project root. The default value is "." and thus may be omitted if the current directory is the project root. Otherwise it may be specified as an absolute pathname or as a path relative to the current directory. *curdir*, if given, specifies the name of the current directory, relative to the project root. *curdir* is usually omitted.

Options

imboot understands the following options:

-c name   Use the named set of public configuration files instead of the files in the project's private configuration file directory.

-C name   Use the named set of public configuration files in addition to the files in the project's private configuration file directory. *imboot* tells *imake* to look in the private directory under the project root before looking in the public directory when searching for configuration files. The intent is to support an extensible configuration file architecture such that the public files define a baseline configuration that individual projects can extend or override by providing project-specific information in files in their private configuration file directory.

Name

imdent – indent *cpp* directives to show nesting level

Synopsis

```
imdent [ options ] [ file ] ...
```

Description

imdent reads the named input files, or the standard input if no files are named, and adds indentation to *cpp* directives based on the nesting level of conditional directives. This shows the nesting visually as an aid to finding malformed conditional constructs, and can be helpful when debugging *imake* configuration files.

Example: given the following input:

```
#ifndef LintLibFlag
#if SystemV || SystemV4
#define LintLibFlag -o
#else
#define LintLibFlag -C
#endif
#endif
```

imdent produces the following output:

```
#ifndef LintLibFlag
#   if SystemV || SystemV4
#     define LintLibFlag -o
#   else
#     define LintLibFlag -C
#   endif
#endif
```

Option

imdent understands the following option:

−n   Specify indentation increment per nesting level. *n* is a number. The default is 2 spaces. *−0* removes all indentation.

Name

makedepend – create header file dependencies in Makefiles

Synopsis

makedepend [*options*] *file* ...

Description

Every file that a source file references via an #include directive is what *makedepend* calls a "dependency." For example, if the source file *main.c* includes *defs.h*, which in turn includes *conf.h*, then the object file *main.o* depends on both *def.h* and *conf.h*. This is expressed in a *Makefile* as:

```
main.o: defs.h conf.h
```

makedepend reads the named input source files in sequence and parses them to process #include, #define, #undef, #ifdef, #ifndef, #endif, #if, and #else directives so that it can tell which #include directives would be used in a compilation. Any #include directives can reference files having other #include directives, and parsing occurs in those files as well. *makedepend* determines the dependencies and writes them to the *Makefile* so that *make* knows which object files must be recompiled when a dependency has changed.

makedepend first searches the *Makefile* for the line:

```
# DO NOT DELETE
```

If *makedepend* finds this line, it deletes everything following it to the end of the *Makefile* and writes the dependencies after it. If it doesn't find the line, *makedepend* appends it to the end of the *Makefile* before writing the dependencies.

By default, *makedepend* writes its output to *makefile* if it exists, or to *Makefile* if it does not. An alternate *Makefile* may be specified with the –*f* option.

To use *makedepend* with *imake*, set the variable SRCS to the names of the source files to be checked and invoke DependTarget() in the *Imakefile*:

```
SRCS = main.c aux.c funcs.c io.c
DependTarget()
```

After generating the *Makefile*, generate dependencies by typing *make depend*.

Options

makedepend ignores any option it does not understand so that you may use the same arguments you would use for *cc*. *makedepend* understands the following options:

-Dname=value, *-Dname*
> Define *name* with the given value (first form) or with value 1 (second form).

-Idir
> By default, *makedepend* searches only */usr/include* to find files named on #include directives. This option tells *makedepend* to prepend *dir* to the list of directories it searches.

-a
> Append dependencies to any that already exist in the *Makefile* instead of replacing them.

-ffilename
> Write dependencies to *filename* instead of to *makefile* or to *Makefile*.

-oobjsuffix
> Object file suffix. Some systems may have object files whose suffix is something other than *.o*. This option allows you to specify another suffix, such as *.b* with *-o.b*, *.obj* with *-o.obj*, and so forth.

-pobjprefix
> Object file prefix. The prefix is prepended to the name of the object file. This is usually used to designate a different directory for the object file. The default is the empty string.

-- options --
> When *makedepend* encounters a double hyphen (*--*) in the argument list, any unrecognized argument following it is silently ignored; a second double hyphen terminates this special treatment. In this way, *makedepend* can be made to safely ignore esoteric compiler arguments. All options that *makedepend* recognizes that appear between the pair of double hyphens are processed normally.

Name

mkdirhier – make a directory hierarchy

Synopsis

mkdirhier *dir*

Description

mkdirhier creates the specified directory and any missing parent directories. Suppose you execute the following command:

  % **mkdirhier /usr/local/lib/myproj**

If any of the directories */usr*, */usr/local*, or */usr/local/lib* do not exist, *mkdirhier* creates them before creating */usr/local/lib/myproj*. This differs from *mkdir*, which fails if any parent directories are missing.

Name

msub – substitute *make* variables into a template to produce a parameterized file

Synopsis

msub [*options*] [*file*] ...

Description

msub allows targets to be produced easily from templates that contain references to the variables found in a *Makefile*.

First *msub* reads the *Makefile* in the current directory to find all variable definition lines of the form "*var* = *value*" (*value* can be empty). Then it reads any files named on the command line (or the standard input if none), searches through them for references to the *Makefile* variables, and replaces the references with the corresponding variable values. References to undefined variables are replaced by the empty string. The result is written to the standard output.

Options

msub understands the following options:

–f file   By default, variable values are extracted from *Makefile* (or *makefile* if *Makefile* is missing) in the current directory. If the *–f* option is given, variable values are extracted from *file* instead.

+Rstr, *–Rstr*   The default variable reference indicators within templates are the same as those used by *make*, i.e., $(and), and ${ and }. These can be changed with the *+R* and *–R* options, which must be specified in pairs. *+R* specifies the string that initiates a variable reference and *–R* specifies the string that terminates it. Multiple pairs of *+R/–R* options may be given if you want *msub* to recognize more than one set of reference indicators.

–e   Environment variable values override assignments within Makefiles. Normally assignments within Makefiles override environment variables.

variable=value

     Variable definition. This definition overrides any regular definition for the specified variable within the *Makefile* itself or in the environment.

Name

xmkmf – bootstrap a *Makefile* from an *Imakefile*

Synopsis

xmkmf [*options*] [*topdir* [*curdir*]]

Description

When invoked with no arguments in a directory containing an *Imakefile, xmkmf* runs *imake* with arguments appropriate to use the publicly installed X11 configuration files to generate a *Makefile.*

If you specify a *topdir* argument to indicate the root directory of your project, *xmkmf* does not use the installed configuration files. Instead, it looks for the files in the *config/cf* directory under the project root.

curdir may be specified as a relative pathname from the top of the build tree to the current directory. *curdir* is usually omitted.

Option

xmkmf understands the following option:

−*a*   The command *xmkmf −a* is equivalent to the following command
                     sequence:

```
% xmkmf
% make Makefiles
% make includes
% make depend
```

D

Generating Makefiles: A Quick Reference

The command you use to build a *Makefile* from an *Imakefile* depends on the configuration files you're using and where they're located:

- Bootstrap a *Makefile* using the X11 configuration files:

      % xmkmf

- Bootstrap a *Makefile* using configuration files stored in the *config* directory under the project root:

      % imboot [topdir]

  topdir is the path from your current directory to the project root directory; it's optional if you're in the root.

- Bootstrap a *Makefile* using installed configuration files named *name*:

      % imboot -c name [topdir]

- Bootstrap a *Makefile* using installed extensible configuration files named *name*:

      % imboot -C name [topdir]

- Rebuild a *Makefile* using an existing *Makefile* built by any of the above methods:

      % make Makefile

- Build Makefiles in subdirectories (you must build the *Makefile* in the current directory first):

      % make Makefiles

- Build Makefiles only in subdirectories *a*, *b*, and *c*:

    ```
    % make Makefiles "SUBDIRS=a b c"
    ```

- Append header file dependencies to the *Makefile*:

    ```
    % make depend
    ```

    This should be done after any bootstrapping command, *make Makefile*, or *make Makefiles*.

Whenever you modify an *Imakefile*, rebuild the *Makefile* so your changes take effect. Also, when you first install a project on your machine, rebuild its Makefiles to configure them properly.

For background information on the *Makefile*-generation process, see Chapter 8, *A Closer Look at Makefile Generation*; Chapter 10, *Coordinating Sets of Configuration Files*; and Chapter 15, *Designing Extensible Configuration Files*.

Writing Imakefiles: A Quick Reference

This appendix discusses rule invocation etiquette and some X11 rules commonly used to write Imakefiles.

- To invoke a rule, you simply name it and pass any arguments necessary:

  ```
  RuleName(arguments)
  ```

- Some rules have no arguments, some have one, some have many:

  ```
  DependTarget()
  SimpleProgramTarget(myprog)
  CppScriptTarget(script,script.cpp,'-DLIBDIR="$(LIBDIR)"',Makefile)
  ```

- Don't put any spaces before or after arguments, or the rule may not expand properly in the *Makefile*:

  ```
  InstallLibrary( mylib,$(USRLIBDIR))       /* incorrect */
  InstallLibrary(mylib ,$(USRLIBDIR))       /* incorrect */
  InstallLibrary( mylib , $(USRLIBDIR) )    /* VERY incorrect */
  InstallLibrary(mylib,$(USRLIBDIR))        /* correct */
  ```

- However, an argument may contain spaces internally when it comprises a list of items such as filenames, libraries, or flags:

  ```
  NormalLibraryTarget(mylib,a.o b.o c.o)
  ComplexProgramTarget_1(myprog,$(XMULIB) $(XLIB),-ly -lm)
  SpecialObjectRule(file.o,file.c,-DFLAG1 -DFLAG2)
  ```

- Specify empty arguments using a macro defined as nothing. The X11 configuration files (from R5 on) provide `NullParameter` for this purpose:

  ```
  ComplexProgramTarget_1(myprog,NullParameter,NullParameter)
  ```

Subdirectory Support

To write an *Imakefile* that generates target entries for processing subdirectories, begin with the following three lines:

```
#define IHaveSubdirs
#define PassCDebugFlags
SUBDIRS = subdirectory-list
```

The value assigned to SUBDIRS consists of the names of the subdirectories in which you want *make* to run, in the order you want them processed.

The presence of the IHaveSubdirs, PassCDebugFlags, and SUBDIRS lines tells the configuration files to generate certain default target entries for processing subdirectories recursively. The particular set of entries depends on the configuration files you're using:

- The X11 files generate install, install.man, clean, tags, Makefiles, and includes entries. They don't automatically generate recursive all or depend target entries; to get those entries, you must invoke MakeSubdirs() and DependSubdirs() yourself:

  ```
  #define IHaveSubdirs
  #define PassCDebugFlags
  SUBDIRS = subdirectory-list

  MakeSubdirs($(SUBDIRS))
  DependSubdirs($(SUBDIRS))
  ```

- The DP configuration files developed in Chapters 11 and 12 generate recursive all and depend entries for you automatically, so you don't need to invoke MakeSubdirs() or DependSubdirs().

To determine what entries your configuration files generate for you, check the final section of the template file *Imake.tmpl*.

If you want to pass debugging flags to *make* operations in subdirectories, don't give PassCDebugFlags an empty value; define it like this instead:

```
#define PassCDebugFlags 'CDEBUGFLAGS=$(CDEBUGFLAGS)'
```

Then you can specify debugging flags from the *make* command line, e.g.:

```
% make "CDEBUGFLAGS=-g"
```

For more information on writing Imakefiles that cause *make* operations to be performed in subdirectories, see Chapter 6, *Writing Imakefiles*, and Chapter 11, *Introduction to Configuration File Writing*.

Rule Descriptions

The following pages provide brief descriptions of some commonly used X11 rules. If you're using different configuration files, they might contain similar rules. For more information, see Chapter 5, *The X11 Configuration Files*, and Chapter 6.

Name

SimpleProgramTarget()

Synopsis

Build a single program from a single source file.

Syntax

SimpleProgramTarget(*prog*)

prog is the name of the program.

Description

SimpleProgramTarget() is the simplest program-building rule:

- You tell it only the name of your program, which must consist of a single source file *prog.c.*

- SimpleProgramTarget() generates a target entry *prog* for building your program, as well as all, install, install.man, depend, lint, and clean entries.

- If you need to link libraries into your program, you set certain *make* variables in the *Imakefile.* Use LOCAL_LIBRARIES for local libraries or X11 libraries. Specify local libraries built within the project using pathnames. Specify X11 libraries using the variables XLIB, XMULIB, XTOOLLIB, etc. Use SYS_LIBRARIES for system link libraries, specified using −l*name* syntax.

- To indicate libraries for dependency checking, assign a value to the variable DEPLIBS. (Asssign the empty value if there are no dependency libraries.) Dependency libraries must be given in pathname form. Specify local within-project libraries just as for LOCAL_LIBRARIES. Specify X11 libraries using the variables DEPXLIB, DEPXMULIB, DEPXTOOLLIB, etc. But don't specify system libraries, since, in general, there's no portable pathname form for them.

Example

```
LOCAL_LIBRARIES = $(TOP)/lib/libmylib.a $(XMULIB) $(XLIB)
  SYS_LIBRARIES = -lm
        DEPLIBS = $(TOP)/lib/libmylib.a $(DEPXMULIB) $(DEPXLIB)
SimpleProgramTarget(myprog)
```

Caveat

SimpleProgramTarget() can be invoked only once per *Imakefile.*

Name

ComplexProgramTarget()

Synopsis

Build a single program from multiple source files.

Syntax

ComplexProgramTarget(*prog*)

prog is the name of the program.

Description

ComplexProgramTarget() is much like SimpleProgramTarget(), but the program can be built from an arbitrary number of files:

- ComplexProgramTarget() makes no assumptions about the names of the files, so you must set the *make* variables SRCS and OBJS to the names of the source files and object files.

- ComplexProgramTarget() generates the same target entries as SimpleProgramTarget().

- Libraries are specified the same way for ComplexProgramTarget() as for SimpleProgramTarget().

Example

```
          SRCS = myproga.c myprogb.c myprogc.c
          OBJS = myproga.o myprogb.o myprogc.o
LOCAL_LIBRARIES = $(XLIB)
  SYS_LIBRARIES =
        DEPLIBS = $(DEPXLIB)
ComplexProgramTarget(myprog)
```

Caveat

ComplexProgramTarget() can be invoked only once per *Imakefile*.

Name

```
ComplexProgramTarget_1()
ComplexProgramTarget_2()
ComplexProgramTarget_3()
```

Synopsis

Build two or three programs; each may consist of multiple source files.

Syntax

```
ComplexProgramTarget_1(prog, loclibs, syslibs)
ComplexProgramTarget_2(prog, loclibs, syslibs)
ComplexProgramTarget_3(prog, loclibs, syslibs)
```

prog is the name of the program; *loclibs* and *syslibs* name local and system link libraries. *loclibs* and *syslibs* are analogous to LOCAL_LIBRARIES and SYS_LIBRARIES, except that you specify them as rule arguments rather than as *make* variables.

Description

To use any of the ComplexProgramTarget_*n*() rules:

- Set the *make* variable PROGRAMS to the names of the programs you wish to build.

- Set the variables SRCS*n* and OBJS*n* to the source and object files for program *n* and invoke the corresponding rule.

- To specify dependency libraries for program *n*, assign a value to DEPLIBS*n* (asssign the empty value if there are no dependency libraries).

- The ComplexProgramTarget_*n*() rules generate a target entry for each program to be built, as well as all, install, install.man, depend, lint, and clean entries.

Example

```
PROGRAMS = prog1 prog2 prog3
   SRCS1 = prog1a.c prog1b.c
   OBJS1 = prog1a.o prog1b.o
DEPLIBS1 = $(DEPXLIB)

   SRCS2 = prog2a.c
   OBJS2 = prog2a.o
DEPLIBS2 =

   SRCS3 = prog3a.c prog3b.c prog3c.c
   OBJS3 = prog3a.o prog3b.o prog3c.o
```

```
DEPLIBS3 = $(DEPXTOOLLIB) $(DEPXLIB)
ComplexProgramTarget_1(prog1,$(XLIB),NullParameter)
ComplexProgramTarget_2(prog2,NullParameter,-lm)
ComplexProgramTarget_3(prog3,$(XTOOLLIB) $(XLIB),NullParameter)
```

Caveats

Each rule can be invoked only once in an *Imakefile*. The second and third rules cannot be invoked without the first.

Name

```
NormalProgramTarget()
```

Synopsis

Build an arbitrary number of programs.

Syntax

```
NormalProgramTarget(prog,objs,deplibs,loclibs,syslibs)
```

prog is the name of the program; *objs* names the object files from which to build the program; *deplibs* names the dependency libraries; *loclibs* and *syslibs* name the local and system link libraries.

Description

`NormalProgramTarget()` provides a general-purpose interface for program building:

- You can invoke `NormalProgramTarget()` any number of times in an *Imakefile* to build any number of programs.

- However, `NormalProgramTarget()` generates only two entries (a *prog* entry to build the program, and a `clean` entry to remove it), so you must invoke additional rules to generate `all`, `install`, `install.man`, `depend`, or `lint` entries. Thus, each use of `NormalProgramTarget()` is normally preceded by `AllTarget()` to generate an `all` entry and followed by installation rules to generate `install` and `install.man` entries.

- In addition, to generate `depend` and `lint` entries, set `SRCS` to the names of all the source files for all the programs and invoke `DependTarget()` and `LintTarget()` once each at the end of the *Imakefile*.

Example

```
SRCS1 = prog1a.c prog1b.c
OBJS1 = prog1a.o prog1b.o

SRCS2 = prog2a.c prog2b.c prog2c.c prog2d.c
OBJS2 = prog2a.o prog2b.o prog2c.o prog2d.o
  ⋮
SRCSn = progna.c prognb.c
OBJSn = progna.o prognb.o
 SRCS = $(SRCS1) $(SRCS2) ... $(SRCSn)
AllTarget(prog1)
NormalProgramTarget(prog1,$(OBJS1),$(DEPXLIB),$(XLIB),NullParameter)
InstallProgram(prog1,$(BINDIR))
```

```
InstallManPage(prog1,$(MANDIR))

AllTarget(prog2)
NormalProgramTarget(prog2,$(OBJS2),$(DEPXLIB),$(XLIB),-lm)
InstallProgram(prog2,$(BINDIR))
InstallManPage(prog2,$(MANDIR))
    .
    .
    .
AllTarget(progn)
NormalProgramTarget(progn,$(OBJSn),$(DEPXLIB),$(XLIB),-ly)
InstallProgram(progn,$(BINDIR))
InstallManPage(progn,$(MANDIR))

DependTarget()
LintTarget()
```

The second argument to `InstallProgram()` and `InstallManPage()` is the installation directory for the program and manual page. The first argument to `Install-ManPage()` is the name of the program to which the page applies, but the manual page file itself should be named *prog.man*.

Name

NormalLibraryTarget()

Synopsis

Build a library.

Syntax

NormalLibraryTarget(*name*, *objs*)

name is the basename of the library (e.g., for *libmylib.a*, *name* should be mylib); *objs* names the object files from which to build the library.

Description

NormalLibraryTarget() builds a library:

- You should precede it with an invocation of NormalLibraryObjectRule() so the configuration files can set up some additional library-building machinery.

- For a library with basename mylib, NormalLibraryTarget() generates a libmylib.a target entry and an all entry.

- NormalLibraryTarget() doesn't generate depend or lint targets, so you should also set SRCS to the names of the library source files and invoke DependTarget() and LintTarget().

- If you intend to install the library, invoke InstallLibrary() to generate an install entry.

- No explicit clean entry is necessary; the X11 configuration files provide a default clean entry that removes *.a* files.

Example

```
SRCS = file1.c file2.c file3.c ... filen.c
OBJS = file1.o file2.o file3.o ... filen.o

NormalLibraryObjectRule()
NormalLibraryTarget(mylib,$(OBJS))
InstallLibrary(mylib,$(USRLIBDIR))

DependTarget()
LintTarget()
```

The second argument to InstallLibrary() is the installation directory.

Caveat

Building shared, profiled, or debugging libraries is more complicated. See Chapter 6 for more details.

F

Writing Configuration Files: A Quick Reference

Detailed guidelines for developing configuration files are given in Chapter 11, *Introduction to Configuration File Writing*; Chapter 12, *Writing Rule Macros*; and Chapter 13, *Configuration Problems and Solutions*. If you're writing a set of extensible configuration files, see also Chapter 16, *Creating Extensible Configuration Files*.

Here are some general principles for creating configuration files:

- To avoid writing everything from scratch, copy an existing set of files. For instance, you can start with the starter project (SP) files discussed in Chapter 9, *A Configuration Starter Project*, or the extensible-architecture (EA) files discussed in Chapter 16, depending on whether you want nonextensible or extensible files.

- Simplify the files you're starting with by deleting information from them that's superfluous to your configuration requirements. But make sure you understand the purpose of the symbols you remove so you know you really can get rid of them, and don't remove a symbol if other symbols you retain depend on it.

- Add configuration information you need that wasn't in the original configuration files.

- If you intend to install the configuration files publicly, tell them where they will live by modifying their self-reference. Do this by changing the value of ConfigDir in *Project.tmpl* to point to the installation location. If the files are extensible, set ConfigName to the name of your set of files instead, and make sure ConfigRootDir is set to the directory that is used for the *imboot* configuration root on your machine.

Parameter Settings and Feature Symbols

Parameter settings and feature symbols go in *Imake.tmpl* or *Project.tmpl*, depending on whether they are general-purpose or project-specific values. Choose default values that reflect the likely choice on the widest variety of machines, and use the vendor files to override the defaults as necessary.

To create a new parameter, define a default value using a *cpp* macro, then set a *make* variable to the value of the macro:

```
#ifndef LexCmd
#define LexCmd lex
#endif
#ifndef LexLib
#define LexLib -ll
#endif

   LEX = LexCmd
LEXLIB = LexLib
```

Feature symbols are similar except that there's no corresponding *make* variable:

```
#ifndef HasPutenv
#define HasPutenv NO
#endif
```

In either case, you can override the macro value if necessary in the site or vendor file:

```
#ifndef LexCmd
#define LexCmd flex /* use GNU flex instead */
#endif
#ifndef LexLib
#define LexLib -lfl /* use GNU flex library instead */
#endif

#ifndef HasPutenv
#define HasPutenv YES
#endif
```

Rule Syntax

This section briefly discusses rule syntax and the various parts of a rule. For more information, see Chapter 12.

Rules are defined as *cpp* macros. General-purpose rules go in *Imake.rules*. Project-specific rules go in *Project.tmpl*. Following is a simple example that illustrates some basic rule-writing principles.

```
1: /*
2:  * BuildProgram() builds the program "prog" from the
3:  * given object files and libraries.  It may be
```

```
 4:  * invoked multiple times in the same Imakefile to
 5:  * build several different programs.
 6:  *
 7:  * Arguments:
 8:  * prog program name
 9:  * objs object files from which program is built
10:  * libs libraries needed to link program
11:  *
12:  * Targets produced:
13:  * prog build this program
14:  * all      build prog (and any others in Imakefile)
15:  * clean    remove program (and others in Imakefile)
16:  */
17:
18: #ifndef BuildProgram
19: #define BuildProgram(prog,objs,libs)                   @@\
20: all:: prog                                             @@\
21: prog: objs                                             @@\
22:     $(CC) -o prog objs $(LDOPTS) libs $(LDLIBS)        @@\
23: StuffToClean(prog)
24: #endif /* BuildProgram */
```

Lines   Meaning

1–16   Comment describing the purpose of the rule. Especially helpful to those unfamiliar with rule syntax.

19–23   Rule definition. All lines of the definition but the last are terminated by a special sequence @@\ signifying that the rule definition continues onto the next line.

19   The rule begins with a #define directive specifying the rule name and parameter list. There should be no spaces from the beginning of the rule name to the end of the parameter list. Separate multiple parameters by commas.

20–23   The body of the rule. This determines what the rule expands to. Parameter values passed to a rule when it's invoked are substituted into the body of the rule as it's expanded, and apply to that invocation only.

21–22   Main target entry built by rule (the entry named after the program).

- Line 21 specifies that prog depends on its object files. The target name is followed by a single colon. To allow a target name to be associated with multiple entries in a *Makefile*, use a double colon instead. (all, clean, and install targets are likely candidates for double colons.)

- Line 22 specifies the command used to perform the final link step.

    Command lines must be indented by a tab, not spaces.

CC, LDOPTS, and LDLIBS are configuration parameters—*make* variables defined elsewhere in the configuration files. The values of these variables apply to all invocations of the rule.

18, 24 #ifndef and #endif directives to protect the definition given on lines 19–23 so the definition can be overridden by one occurring earlier in configuration file processing.

- All rule definitions should be surrounded by #ifndef and #endif.

- The #ifndef and #endif lines are not part of the macro definition and do not end with the @@\ sequence.

- The #endif is followed by a comment repeating the name of the rule. This is not required, but makes it easier to find the end of a complex rule.

20   This line generates an all target entry.

- all is dependent on prog, so *make all* builds the program.

- The all target entry precedes the prog entry so all (not prog) becomes the default target when BuildProgram() is the first rule invoked in the *Imakefile*.

- A double colon is used so multiple entries may be associated with the all target. For instance, if you invoke BuildProgram() several times in the *Imakefile*, each invocation generates an all entry.

23   Rule definitions can invoke other rules, which are expanded in turn to generate additional target entries. In this case, StuffToClean() generates a clean target entry to remove the final executable.

If you want to use shell programming constructs in a rule there are additional considerations. Here's a simple rule that removes *.o* files from directories named by the dirs parameter:

```
 1: /*
 2:  * Remove object files from the named directories
 3:  */
 4:
 5: #ifndef CleanObjects
 6: #define CleanObjects(dirs)                              @@\
 7: cleanobjs::                                             @@\
 8:     for i in dirs ;                          \          @@\
 9:     do                                       \          @@\
10:         echo "removing object files in $$i..." ;  \    @@\
11:         (cd $$i; $(RM) *.o) ;                \          @@\
12:     done
13: #endif /* CleanObjects */
```

The rule illustrates the following conventions to be aware of:

- Refer to shell variables using two $-signs (e.g., $$i on lines 10, 11).

- Multiple-command constructs require special care:

  — Multiple commands in a command sequence should be separated by semi-colons as necessary to keep the shell from running them together.

  — Command sequences that continue over several lines should be joined by backslashes placed after all but the last line. The backslashes go after the commands on the line but before the @@\ marker.

  — The cd and $(RM) commands on line 11 are enclosed within (and) to force them to execute in a subshell. This isolates the effect of the cd so the current directory is restored after the subshell terminates.

G

Basics of make and cpp

This appendix is a brief introduction to some basic concepts of *make* and *cpp* that will help you understand *imake*. Since *imake* produces Makefiles, you need to understand a little about *make*. *imake* uses *cpp* to do most of its work, so you should also understand something about *cpp*.

For more information on either program, see the references suggested in Appendix I, *Other Sources of Information*.

Basics of make

make operates by reading a file named *Makefile* that functions as a kind of script specifying how to build targets you're interested in, such as programs or libraries. The *Makefile* contains entries that provide specifics for target building. The form of an entry is:

```
target: dependencies
    commands
```

target names the thing you want to build. *dependencies* lists the things that *target* depends on. For example, if the object file *src.o* is built from the source file *src.c*, *src.o* depends on *src.c*. *make* uses dependencies to determine whether it needs to do anything. If a target is newer than all its dependencies (as determined from the last modified time of each), the target is assumed to be up to date. If the target is older than any of its dependencies (or if the target doesn't exist), it needs to be rebuilt. When *make* determines that a target is out of date, it executes the *commands* part of the entry to bring the target up to date. *commands* may contain more than one line; each line must be indented with a tab (not spaces).

For example, if a program *prog* is built from source files *a.c* and *b.c*, the target entry might look like this:

```
prog: a.o b.o
    cc -o prog a.o b.o
```

This specifies that *prog* is the target, that the object files *a.o* and *b.o* are the dependencies, and that to build the program we run the C compiler to link it from the object files.

There are some dependencies here we haven't specified: *a.o* and *b.o* are built from *a.c* and *b.c* and therefore depend on them. We don't need to list those dependencies explicitly because *make* has built-in knowledge about the relationship between *.c* files and *.o* files, and how to compile the former to produce the latter.

If you write a lot of program-building entries in a *Makefile*, you'll have many instances of the C compiler's name. To substitute another C compiler like *gcc*, you have to edit each instance. *make* allows you to use variables to alleviate this difficulty. So, you could use the variable CC, and assign it a value like this:

```
CC = cc
```

Then you refer to it either as $(CC) or ${CC}. The two forms are equivalent, although this handbook always uses the first form. A revised *Makefile* using the variable looks like this:

```
CC = cc
prog: a.o b.o
    $(CC) -o prog a.o b.o
```

To change the C compiler, you just change the value assigned to CC.

Note that what I'm calling *make* variables are sometimes referred to in other *make* documentation as *make* macros. *cpp* has macros, too; to avoid confusion, in this handbook the word "macro" always means a *cpp* macro, not a *make* macro.

It's not an error to refer to a variable that hasn't been assigned a value. Undefined variables implicitly have an empty value.

When you invoke *make*, you can specify particular targets you want built. If you don't name any, *make* builds the first target listed in the *Makefile*.

In addition to target names, you can specify options on the command line. One that's especially useful is *−n*, which tells *make* to show you the commands it would execute to bring the targets named on the command line up to date, without actually executing those commands.

make is picky about where you put tabs and spaces. Do not indent command lines in a target entry with spaces (use tabs). Do not indent variable assignments with tabs (use spaces).

Comments may be placed in a *Makefile*; they begin with a # character and continue until the end of the line:

```
# This is a comment
```

Basics of cpp

The C preprocessor *cpp* performs several operations on its input that are important for *imake*'s purposes, such as macro definition, file inclusion, and conditional testing. All of these operations are triggered by lines beginning with # followed by a keyword. These are called preprocessing directives.

Macro Definition

cpp allows a macro to be defined and given a value such that further instances of the macro name in the input are replaced by the macro value in the output. For example, given the following definition:

```
#define BinDir /usr/local/bin
```

then the input:

```
BinDir/program
```

is transformed to this in the output:

```
/usr/local/bin/program
```

Macros may be defined in terms of other macros:

```
#define YES 1
#define OUI YES
```

Given these definitions, the value of OUI is 1.

Macros may be defined with parameters. When the macro is invoked later, the arguments in the invocation are substituted for the parameters in the definition. Thus the following input:

```
#define Append(a,b) cat a >> b
Append(current,archive)
```

produces this output:

```
cat current >> archive
```

Macros may be defined with the empty value:

```
#define EmptyMacro
```

This is useful in conjunction with conditional tests for which you only need to know whether or not a symbol is defined.

Long macro definitions may be spread across lines by using backslashes to indicate continuation:

```
#define LongMacro This\
is\
a\
long\
value
```

There is no backslash on the last line. The backslashes and the newlines following them are deleted when the definition is processed. For the preceding example, the value of LongMacro is Thisisalongvalue.

Although you can split a macro definition across lines, you cannot split a macro invocation. The following invocations are unlikely to produce a useful result, if indeed your *cpp* doesn't simply consider them illegal:

```
Long\
Macro

Append(current,\
archive)
```

Macros may be undefined:

```
#undef MacroName
```

Macros may be defined or undefined from the *cpp* command line with the *−D* and *−U* options. The following command defines DEBUG, defines TMPDIR to have a value of "/usr/tmp", and makes sure unix is undefined (some *cpp*s predefine it by default):

```
% cpp -DDEBUG '-DTMPDIR="/usr/tmp"' -Uunix
```

File Inclusion

When *cpp* encounters a directive that takes either of the following forms, it inserts the contents of `filename` into the input stream:

```
#include <filename>
#include "filename"
```

If `filename` is surrounded by angle brackets (< and >), *cpp* looks for the file in the include-file directories named on the *cpp* command line using *−I* arguments (and in a list of standard directories). For instance, if *cpp* is invoked like this:

```
% cpp -I/usr/include -I/var/include
```

it will look first in */usr/include*, then in */var/include*, and then in the standard directories.

If `filename` is surrounded by double quotes rather than angle brackets, *cpp* looks in the current directory first before searching the other directories.

A directive of the form:

```
#include MacroName
```

inserts the file named by `MacroName` if its value is of the form `<filename>` or `"filename"`.

Conditional Testing

cpp allows a primitive form of flow control using conditional constructs:

```
1)  #if condition        2)  #ifdef symbol        3)  #ifndef symbol
        stuff                    stuff                    stuff
    #endif                   #endif                   #endif
```

In the first form, when `condition` is true (non-zero), `stuff` is processed (and ignored otherwise). In the second form, `stuff` is processed if `symbol` has previously been defined in a #define statement. The third form is like the second, but `stuff` is processed if `symbol` is not defined.

Conditionals may have an #else clause:

```
#if condition
    stuff
#else
    other-stuff
#endif
```

If `condition` is true, `stuff` is processed, otherwise `other-stuff` is processed.

The following two constructs are equivalent:

```
#ifdef symbol
#if defined(symbol)
```

So are these:

```
#ifndef symbol
#if !defined(symbol)
```

Comments

Comments may be written by surrounding them with /* and */:

```
/* this is a comment */
```

A comment doesn't have to begin and end on the same line:

```
/*
 * this is a 3-line comment
 */
```

H

A Little History

imake is often thought to have been developed for the X Window System. It's true that the two have been closely associated through all releases of X11, but that's not how *imake* came into being.

Todd Brunhoff wrote *imake* at the Tektronix Research Labs in about 1982–1984 while developing operating systems for a research platform called Magnolia. This was a 68010-based, dual-processor computer with 40MB disk, 2MB memory, a 19-inch black-and-white display, and a proprietary window system. *imake* was first used to help port Berkeley UNIX to this machine. Writing correct Makefiles by hand was difficult and time-consuming, but it was relatively simple to generate them using *imake*.

Later, during development of X11R1 at MIT, Brunhoff rewrote *imake* to support multiple platforms (the design it retains today), and engineered the first X11 configuration files. The rewrite was intended to allow R1 to be configured more easily, but acceptance of *imake* was far from automatic: "Most everyone was incredulous about the usefulness of this cryptic software beast, and getting everyone to buy into it was very difficult," says Brunhoff.

Nevertheless, *imake* proved its worth. X11R1 became the first publicly available project configured with it, and later releases continued to use *imake*. Jim Fulton wrote *xmkmf* and maintained the configuration files from X11R2 through X11R4. Other X Consortium staff took over from Fulton as Keepers of the Files after X11R4, and retain the major oversight for them today.

When asked to comment on the preceding account, Fulton said, "I'd almost be tempted to mention that Brunhoff and Fulton now disclaim all knowledge of *imake* and stare blankly when asked about it."

Joining in this sentiment, Brunhoff added, "Fulton and Brunhoff have suffered terribly from their intimate association with *imake* and are known to display various nervous tics when the subject is broached. They now can only find employment with regional traveling carnivals, but do maintain their email addresses."

I

Other Sources of Information

The references listed below serve as useful sources of information for *imake*, *make*, *cpp*, and the X11 configuration files. Sources noted below as being "available on the archive site" can be accessed with a Web browser; use the following URL to get to an index page:

```
http://www.primate.wisc.edu/software/imake-stuff
```

Alternatively, connect via anonymous FTP to *ftp.primate.wisc.edu* and look in the */software/imake-stuff* directory.

Books and Papers

- *Managing Projects with make* (2nd edition), Andrew Oram and Steve Talbott. O'Reilly & Associates, Inc., 1991. The standard reference for *make*.

- *The C Programming Language* (2nd edition), Brian W. Kernighan and Dennis M. Ritchie. Prentice Hall, 1988. The standard reference for the C language. Includes information on *cpp*.

- *Configuration Management in the X Window System*, Jim Fulton. A general description of *imake* as used for X11. This paper is included in the X11R5 distribution in *mit/doc/config/usenixws/paper.ms*. It's also available on the archive site.

- *Using Imake to Configure the X Window System*, Paul DuBois. The main body of this paper has been superseded (by this handbook), but the appendix contains a catalog of rules provided by the X11 configuration files. Much of the information remains current even though the paper was written for X11R4. Available on the archive site.

- *Using imake with Motif,* Paul DuBois. This paper discusses some of the issues involved in using *imake* to configure the Motif 2.0 distibution and other Motif-based projects. Available on the archive site.

- *Minotaur Passage,* Paul DuBois. This passage is taken from the first edition of *Software Portability with imake.* It describes a particularly intricate intertwining of the information in the generic and project-specific sections of the X11R5 configuration files. (This intertwining has since been unravelled beginning with the X11R6 files.) Available on the archive site.

The *imake* Mailing List

imake-talk is a mailing list for discussing software configuration with *imake.* As such, the list is intended for questions about how *imake* works, how configuration files work, special problems that come up when configuring software on particular platforms, etc.

To subscribe to *imake-talk,* send the following in the body (not the subject line) of an email message to *imake-talk-request@primate.wisc.edu:*

```
subscribe imake-talk
```

Other Online Information Sources

The *SunOS to HP-UX 9.05 Porting Guide* contains some information about using *imake* on HP-UX systems (see Chapter 3 and Appendix A of the *Guide*). The *Guide* is available at:

```
http://www.interworks.org/Tech/sun_hpux_port
```

J

Using imake with OpenWindows

Sun supplies versions of *imake*, *xmkmf*, and the *imake* configuration files on its systems that have been modified from standard X11 versions. Presumably the aim of these modifications is to make *imake* easier to use under Solaris and Open-Windows, but the modified tools have been the cause of some difficulty over the years. This appendix describes how to overcome these difficulties. Its aims are twofold:

- To make it easier to use Sun's *imake/xmkmf* setup with the configuration files that Sun supplies.

- To make it easier to use Sun's *imake/xmkmf* setup with other configuration files, such as the standard X11 files.

Version Numbers

Table J–1 shows some of the (for our purposes) more important versions of Solaris, SunOS, and OpenWindows, and how they correspond. At OpenWindows 2.0, *imake* support is X11R4-based. Beginning with OpenWindows 3.3, *imake* support is X11R5-based (with some R6 modifications), with the exception that *xmkmf* is based on the OW 2.0 version of *xmkmf*. Beginning with OpenWindows 3.4, Motif header files and libraries are included for Common Desktop Environment (CDE) support.

Table J–1: Relationship Between Solaris, SunOS, and OpenWindows Version Numbers

Solaris	SunOS	OpenWindows	Comment
1.0	4.1.1B	2.0	*imake* tools are X11R4-based
1.1	4.1.3	3.0	
2.0	5.0	3.0.1	SunOS becomes SVR4-based
2.2	5.2	3.2	Last version with X11R4-based *imake* tools
2.3	5.3	3.3	*imake* tools become X11R5-based (+X11R6 mods)
2.4	5.4	3.4	Motif header files and libraries now included
2.5	5.5	3.5	Current version

Sun's *imake* tools are installed under */usr/openwin*, so I'll refer to them in terms of the OpenWindows version in which they first appeared. For example, "OW 2.0 *imake*" means the *imake* included with OpenWindows versions 2.0 through 3.2, whereas "OW 3.3 *imake*" means the *imake* included with OpenWindows versions 3.3 and up. If you don't know what version of OpenWindows you have, run *uname −r* to find out your SunOS version number, then use the table to determine the corresponding OpenWindows version.

Assumptions

In this appendix, I make the following assumptions about directory and file locations:

- The OPENWINHOME environment variable has a value of */usr/openwin*. (If the value is different on your system, substitute that value whenever you see */usr/openwin* below.)

- *imake* and *xmkmf* are located in */usr/openwin/bin* (and also in */usr/openwin/bin/xview*, which is a symlink to */usr/openwin/bin*). I assume that your search path is set up so that you get the OpenWindows versions of *imake* or *xmkmf*, not versions installed somewhere else such as */usr/bin/X11* or */usr/X11R6.1/bin*.

- The configuration files are located in */usr/openwin/lib/config*.

Problems

Briefly, you can expect severe problems if you have the OW 2.0 tools (i.e., Open-Windows earlier than 3.3):

- Use of the environment variable OPENWINHOME by *imake* may cause configuration files not to be found.

- *xmkmf* passes incorrect arguments to *imake*.

- The configuration files don't know where any of the OpenWindows stuff is.

- The OW 2.0 tools don't handle XCOMM or NullParameter.

Sun straightened out most of these problems in later releases. Therefore, you can expect fewer difficulties if you have the OW 3.3 tools (i.e., OpenWindows 3.3 or later), which behave much more reasonably. The main problems are these:

- *xmkmf* (still) passes incorrect arguments to *imake* (although in a different way).

- The wrong *install* command can be selected.

- The configuration files don't know how to find any CDE stuff.

There are other miscellaneous issues as well, such as that no version of OW *xmkmf* knows about the *−a* option that X11 *xmkmf* understands from R5 on.

The causes of these problems and how to deal with them are described in the sections following. Some of the solutions involve replacing Sun's tools. For instance, each Sun version of *xmkmf* has one or more problems, although the particular problems are different for each version. For purposes of illustration, I show what the problems are and how to edit *xmkmf* to fix them. But I recommend instead that you just grab an already-modified version that fixes the problems and also adds *−a* option support. See the section "Obtaining Replacement Tools" for instructions on how to get these alternate versions.

I advise you to make a backup copy of any file you modify or program you replace, in case you make a mistake or want to undo your actions. That also allows you to *diff* the original file with your modified copy later to see what you did.

Fixing OpenWindows 2.0 imake Support

This section describes what you need to do to make the OW 2.0 tools usable.

Problem: Use of the environment variable OPENWINHOME by OW 2.0 *imake* may cause configuration files not to be found.

Description: Standard X11 *imake* looks for *−Ipathname* in its argument list to find out the pathname of the directory in which the configuration files are located. OpenWindows *imake* is nonstandard because it also uses OPENWINHOME to locate configuration files. The 2.0 and 3.3 versions of OW *imake* differ somewhat, though.

OW 3.3 *imake* looks in the *lib/config* directory under OPENWINHOME if that environment variable is set and no *–I* argument is given. OPENWINHOME typically has a
value of */usr/openwin,* so the effect is that *imake* defaults to looking in
/usr/openwin/lib/config for configuration files when no *–I* argument is given. This
makes it easier to invoke *imake* if you're using Sun's configuration files. Since you
can override the use of OPENWINHOME by specifying *–I* on the command line to
specify any set of configuration files you want, OW 3.3 *imake* presents no special
problems.

However, OW 2.0 *imake* is less cooperative. It insists on looking under OPENWIN-
HOME if that variable is set. It does this even if you specify an *–I* argument on the
command line. This slavish dependence on OPENWINHOME makes *–I* useless for
indicating where the configuration files are. If you only want to use the Open-
Windows configuration files, that may not be a problem. But if you want to use
any other files, you can't easily do so. Any *imake* that makes this difficult must be
considered broken.

If you don't know which version of *imake* you have, make sure OPENWINHOME is
set, then run the following command:

```
% imake -v -s/dev/null -T/dev/null -f/dev/null -I/abc
```

This command tells *imake* to display the *cpp* command it uses to generate Makefiles. (You can safely run this *imake* command anywhere, because the */dev/null*
arguments keep it from actually creating any files.) If you see only *–I/abc* in the
cpp command, you're okay. If you see *–I/usr/openwin/lib/config* preceding *–I/abc*,
your *imake* is broken.

There are two workarounds for a broken *imake*, although both are problematic:

• If you unset OPENWINHOME, *imake* uses command-line *–I* arguments in the normal way. This is a poor solution because it breaks any other programs that
  assume OPENWINHOME has the correct value. One of these is the OW 2.0
  xmkmf, so this is a serious problem.

• If you set the environment variable IMAKEINCLUDE to an *–I* argument that
  specifies where to look for configuration files, IMAKEINCLUDE takes precedence even over OPENWINHOME. This is a poor solution if you routinely use different sets of configuration files because you have to change the value every
  time you want to specify a different set.

A better solution to the problem is to leave OPENWINHOME set but replace Sun's
imake with the one from X11R6.1. However, note that replacing OW 2.0 *imake* is
not sufficient; you also need to fix *xmkmf* and the configuration files, as described
below.

Problem: *xmkmf* passes incorrect arguments to *imake*.

Description: OW 2.0 *xmkmf* determines which arguments to pass to *imake* in a section that looks like this:

```
if   [ -n "$topdir" ]; then
    args="-I$topdir/config -DTOPDIR=$topdir -DCURDIR=$curdir"
elif [ -n "$OPENWINHOME" ]; then
    args="-DUseInstalled "$OPENWINHOME/lib/config
else
    args="-DUseInstalled "/usr/lib/X11/config
fi
```

The first case handles using configuration files located within the X11 source tree, and does not concern us here. The second and third cases determine whether to use installed OpenWindows or X11 configuration files. If OPENWINHOME is set, *xmkmf* tells *imake* to use the OpenWindows files. Otherwise *xmkmf* specifies the standard X11 files in */usr/lib/X11/config*. *−DUseInstalled* is passed in both cases to indicate use of installed configuration files. (This is important so that a subsequent *make Makefile* command continues to use the same installed files as those that were used to build the *Makefile* in the first place.)

The error in the *xmkmf* fragment just shown is that neither of the last two cases specifies *−I* before the configuration directory pathname. This causes *imake* not to interpret them as locations in which to look for configuration files. To fix this, add −I before the pathnames:

```
if   [ -n "$topdir" ]; then
    args="-I$topdir/config -DTOPDIR=$topdir -DCURDIR=$curdir"
elif [ -n "$OPENWINHOME" ]; then
    args="-DUseInstalled "-I$OPENWINHOME/lib/config
else
    args="-DUseInstalled "-I/usr/lib/X11/config
fi
```

Problem: The OW 2.0 configuration files don't know where any of the Open-Windows stuff is.

Description: OW 2.0 OpenWindows configuration files are essentially identical to the corresponding X11R4 files. In fact, they are so close that the parameters indicating where to find things like X11 header files and libraries have the same values as in the X11R4 files. That's a problem, because OpenWindows locates those files under the */usr/openwin* hierarchy. Consequently, any *Makefile* built using the OW 2.0 configuration files won't be able to find anything having to do with Open-Windows, and therefore probably won't build applications successfully.

To fix this problem, add the following lines to *site.def* to tell the configuration files about the */usr/openwin* hierarchy:

```
#ifndef OpenWinHome
#define OpenWinHome /usr/openwin
#endif

OPENWINHOME = OpenWinHome

#ifndef BinDir
#define BinDir $(OPENWINHOME)/bin
#endif

#ifndef LibDir
#define LibDir $(OPENWINHOME)/lib
#endif

#ifndef IncRoot
#define IncRoot $(OPENWINHOME)/include
#endif

#ifndef StandardIncludes
#define StandardIncludes -I$(INCROOT)
#endif

#ifndef ExtraLoadFlags
#define ExtraLoadFlags -L$(OPENWINHOME)/lib
#endif
```

The OW 3.3 configuration files don't have this problem (as long as OPENWINHOME is set correctly in your environment), because *site.def* contains the following line:

```
#define ProjectRoot $(OPENWINHOME)
```

This line equates `ProjectRoot` to the value of OPENWINHOME. Location parameters for OpenWindows-related stuff are anchored to `ProjectRoot`, so they get the correct values.

The next two problems are not Sun-specific; they occur with any X11R4-based configuration files if you're building Makefiles from Imakefiles that were written assuming the use of configuration files based on R5 or later. Since OW 2.0 *imake* tools are R4-based, they're subject to these two problems.

Problem: XCOMM is not handled correctly by the OW 2.0 *imake* tools.

Description: As of X11R5, XCOMM is used for writing comments that should appear in a *Makefile*. For example:

```
XCOMM this is a comment
```

When the above line is written in an *Imakefile*, XCOMM is supposed to be translated to #, resulting in a line in the *Makefile* that looks like this:

```
# this is a comment
```

However, the OW 2.0 *imake* tools are X11R4-based and don't know about XCOMM, resulting in literal instances of XCOMM in your Makefiles.

The best way to address the problem is to replace *imake* with the current version from X11R6.1. R6.1 *imake* handles XCOMM internally. Another strategy that often works (and may be easier) is to add the following lines to the top of *Imake.tmpl*:

```
#ifndef XCOMM
#define XCOMM #
#endif
```

There is a widely-circulated patch to *xmkmf* that adds -DXCOMM=/**/# to the arguments passed to *imake*. That's only half a solution: it causes XCOMM to be processed when you run *xmkmf*, but not if you run *make Makefile* later.

Problem: NullParameter is not handled correctly by the OW 2.0 *imake* tools.

Description: NullParameter originally appeared in X11R5, defined as the empty token. It's used in rule invocations to indicate explicitly that an argument is empty. However, the OW 2.0 *imake* tools are X11R4-based and don't know about Null-Parameter, resulting in literal instances of NullParameter in your Makefiles. To fix the problem, add the following line to your *Imake.rules* file:

```
#define NullParameter
```

Fixing OpenWindows 3.3 imake Support

The OW 3.3 tools are pretty usable as supplied by Sun. This section describes some things you can do to make them more usable.

Problem: *xmkmf* passes incorrect arguments to *imake*.

Description: OW 3.3 *xmkmf* determines which arguments to pass to *imake* in a section that looks like this:

```
if   [ -n "$topdir" ]; then
    args="-I$topdir/config -DTOPDIR=$topdir -DCURDIR=$curdir"
elif [ -n "$OPENWINHOME" ]; then
    args=" "-I$OPENWINHOME/lib/config
else
    args=" "-I/usr/lib/X11/config
fi
```

The first case handles using configuration files located within the X11 source tree, and does not concern us here. The second and third cases determine whether to use installed OpenWindows or X11 configuration files. If OPENWINHOME is set, *xmkmf* tells *imake* to use the OpenWindows files. Otherwise *xmkmf* specifies the standard X11 files in */usr/lib/X11/config*. There are no missing −*I*'s in the second and third cases (as there are with the OW 2.0 *xmkmf*), but notice that -DUse-Installed has been deleted. My guess is that Sun intends this not to matter for the OpenWindows case, because Sun defines UseInstalled in *site.def* to force it on. However, the definition is incorrect; see discussion below. At any rate, it's important not to delete -DUseInstalled for the X11 case because the X11 files expect it to be passed on the command line. If *xmkmf* doesn't specify that argument, any subsequent *make Makefile* command won't find the installed X11 files. To fix the problem, change the fragment just shown to restore the -DUse-Installed arguments:

```
if  [ -n "$topdir" ]; then
    args="-I$topdir/config -DTOPDIR=$topdir -DCURDIR=$curdir"
elif [ -n "$OPENWINHOME" ]; then
    args="-DUseInstalled "-I$OPENWINHOME/lib/config
else
    args="-DUseInstalled "-I/usr/lib/X11/config
fi
```

In addition to modifying OW 3.3 *xmkmf*, you should fix OW 3.3 *site.def*, which defines UseInstalled incorrectly. The relevant line looks like this:

```
#define UseInstalled YES
```

There are two problems here:

- The definition is misleading. As written, the definition seems to imply that if you changed the value to NO, it would make a difference. But it wouldn't: the configuration files never test the value of UseInstalled, they only test whether or not it's defined. UseInstalled should not be defined as YES or NO; it should simply be defined as nothing or left undefined.

- Defining UseInstalled unconditionally (as is done above) may result in "macro redefinition" errors if *imake* happens to be invoked with *–DUseInstalled* on the command line (as it will be if you run *make Makefile* later).

You could get around these problems by rewriting the definition as follows:

```
#ifndef UseInstalled
#define UseInstalled
#endif
```

But you're better off to remove the definition from *site.def* entirely. If you've made the change to *xmkmf* shown above, *xmkmf* defines UseInstalled for you anyway.

Problem: InstallCmd in the OW 3.3 configuration files may select the wrong *install* command.

Description: The value of of InstallCmd is simply install. Depending on how your search path is set up, you may get either the System V-based */usr/sbin/install* or the BSD-based */usr/ucb/install*. The install rules in the configuration files expect a BSD version, so change the value of InstallCmd in *sun.cf* to explictly select the proper one as follows:

```
#define InstallCmd /usr/ucb/install
```

Problem: The OW 3.3 configuration files don't know how to find any CDE stuff.

Description: Those systems on which Sun ships CDE Motif include Motif libraries and header files, but the configuration files do not include any CDE support. If you wish to develop applications under CDE Motif, you must modify your Open-Windows configuration files. For a set of patches to the files that make the appropriate changes, see the section "Obtaining Replacement Tools."

Miscellaneous Issues

This section describes what to do about various other issues that don't fall into the categories already discussed.

Problem: *xmkmf* (all OW versions) doesn't understand the −*a* option.

Description: Beginning with X11R5, standard X11 *xmkmf* takes a −*a* argument that tells it to run the following commands after generating the *Makefile*:

```
make Makefiles
make includes
make depend
```

Sun's *xmkmf* was initially based on X11R4 *xmkmf*, and subsequent versions have never been updated to provide this functionality. See "Obtaining Replacement Tools" to obtain a version that understands −*a*.

Problem: The OW 3.3 configuration files don't support *gcc*.

Description: Sun stopped including a C compiler with their systems as of SunOS 5.x. It's possible to get *gcc* for free, but the configuration files shipped with OW 3.3 aren't set up to use it very well. See the section "Obtaining Replacement Tools" for some notes on changes you can make to your configuration files to add *gcc* support.

Obtaining Replacement Tools

Replacement or auxiliary tools that make it easier to use *imake* under Open-Windows are available at either of these locations:

```
http://www.primate.wisc.edu/software/imake-stuff
ftp://ftp.primate.wisc.edu/software/imake-stuff
```

The tools are provided in the form of a *tar* file that has been *gzip*'ed (*openwin-support.tar.gz*) or *compress*'ed (*openwin-support.tar.Z*). Transfer the one you want and run *gunzip* (or *uncompress*) to recover *openwin-support.tar*. Then extract the files:

```
% tar xf openwin-support.tar
```

The *tar* command unpacks the distribution into a directory *openwin-support* that contains the following:

- A version of *xmkmf* that doesn't have the problems of the OW 2.0 and 3.3 *xmkmf*, and that understands the *−a* option.

- Binaries of the X11R6.1 versions of *imake* and *makedepend* for BSD-based SunOS 4.x and System V-based SunOS 5.x.

- Configuration file modifications. These include an addendum for OW 2.0 *site.def* to let the 2.0 configuration files know about the OpenWindows hierarchy, a set of patches for the OW 3.3 configuration files to add CDE support, and notes on using the OW 3.3 configuration files with *gcc*.

- Installation instructions.

Acknowledgments

The following people provided assistance in determining how various versions of OpenWindows behave or supplied examples of what they did to make *imake* work under OpenWindows: Jayachander Balakrishna, Philip Brown, John Evans, Bob Friesenhahn, Charlie Havener, James McIninch, Howard Moftich, Monty Solomon, Adam Stein, and Larry Virden.

The table of system version numbers was derived from a more extensive table in Casper Dik's Solaris FAQ, which is available in plain text or HTML forms at:

```
ftp://ftp.fwi.uva.nl/pub/solaris/solaris2.faq
http://www.fwi.uva.nl/pub/solaris/solaris2.html
```

Index

About the Author

Paul DuBois is a programmer at the Wisconsin Regional Primate Research Center at the University of Wisconsin-Madison. He leads a quiet life with few interests outside of family, church, and programming.

Colophon

Our look is the result of reader comments, our own experimentation, and feedback from distribution channels. Distinctive covers complement our distinctive approach to technical topics, breathing personality and life into potentially dry subjects. UNIX and its attendant programs can be unruly beasts. Nutshell Handbooks help you tame them.

The animal featured on the cover of *Software Portability with imake* is the boa constrictor, a snake of a Boidae family. Boa constrictors are typically gray or silver with a series of brown or deep red saddles along their backs. They are found in the warmest parts of America, from Mexico to Argentina, and can reach lengths of up to 18 feet. Their young are born live, an average brood consisting of 30 to 50 one-foot snakes. The Boids, which include boas, anacondas, and pythons, are the giants of the snake world.

Boas feed on birds, reptiles, and mammals. A constrictor will seize prey with its mouth, swiftly coil around it, and tighten the grip so that the victim cannot expand its chest to breathe. Contrary to popular rumor or belief, boa constrictors pose little threat to humans. When a boa perceives danger, it will usually flee or threaten by hissing with a sound that can be heard over 100 feet away.

Edie Freedman designed the cover of this book, using a 19th-century engraving from the Dover Pictorial Archive. The cover layout was produced with Quark XPress 3.3 using the ITC Garamond font.

The inside layout was designed by Edie Freedman and Nancy Priest and implemented in gtroff by Lenny Muellner. The text and heading fonts are ITC Garamond Light and Garamond Book. The illustrations that appear in the book were created in Macromedia Freehand 5.0 by Chris Reilley.

More Titles from O'Reilly

UNIX Tools

Programming with GNU Software

By Mike Loukides & Andy Oram
1st Edition December 1996
260 pages, ISBN 1-56592-112-7

This book and CD combination is a complete package for programmers who are new to UNIX or who would like to make better use of the system. The tools come from Cygnus Support, Inc., and Cyclic Software, companies that provide support for free software. Contents include GNU Emacs, *gcc*, C and C++ libraries, *gdb*, RCS, and *make*. The book provides an introduction to all these tools for a C programmer.

Applying RCS and SCCS

By Don Bolinger & Tan Bronson
1st Edition September 1995
528 pages, ISBN 1-56592-117-8

Applying RCS and SCCS is a thorough introduction to these two systems, viewed as tools for project management. This book takes the reader from basic source control of a single file, through working with multiple releases of a software project, to coordinating multiple developers. It also presents TCCS, a representative "front-end" that addresses problems RCS and SCCS can't handle alone, such as managing groups of files, developing for multiple platforms, and linking public and private development areas.

lex & yacc , 2nd edition

By John Levine, Tony Mason & Doug Brown
2nd Edition October 1992
366 pages, ISBN 1-56592-000-7

This book shows programmers how to use two UNIX utilities, lex and yacc, in program development. The second edition contains completely revised tutorial sections for novice users and reference sections for advanced users. This edition is twice the size of the first, has an expanded index, and covers Bison and Flex.

Managing Projects with make

By Andrew Oram & Steve Talbott
2nd Edition October 1991
152 pages, ISBN 0-937175-90-0

make is one of UNIX's greatest contributions to software development, and this book is the clearest description of *make* ever written. It describes all the basic features of *make* and provides guidelines on meeting the needs of large, modern projects. Also contains a description of free products that contain major enhancements to *make*.

Porting UNIX Software

By Greg Lehey
1st Edition November 1995
538 pages, ISBN 1-56592-126-7

This book deals with the whole life cycle of porting, from setting up a source tree on your system to correcting platform differences and even testing the executable after it's built. It exhaustively discusses the differences between versions of UNIX and the areas where porters tend to have problems.

Exploring Expect

By Don Libes
1st Edition December 1994
602 pages, ISBN 1-56592-090-2

Written by the author of Expect, this is the first book to explain how this part of the UNIX toolbox can be used to automate Telnet, FTP, passwd, rlogin, and hundreds of other interactive applications. Based on Tcl (Tool Command Language), Expect lets you automate interactive applications that have previously been extremely difficult to handle with any scripting language.

UNIX Tools

Writing GNU Emacs Extensions

By Bob Glickstein
1st Edition April 1997
236 pages, ISBN 1-56592-261-1

This book introduces Emacs Lisp and tells you how to make the editor do whatever you want, whether it's altering the way text scrolls or inventing a whole new "major mode." Topics progress from simple to complex, from lists, symbols, and keyboard commands to syntax tables, macro templates, and error recovery.

UNIX Power Tools, 2nd Edition

By Jerry Peek, Tim O'Reilly & Mike Loukides
2nd Edition August 1997
1120 pages, Includes CD-ROM
ISBN 1-56592-260-3

Loaded with even more practical advice about almost every aspect of UNIX, this new second edition of *UNIX Power Tools* addresses the technology that UNIX users face today. You'll find increased coverage of POSIX utilities, including GNU versions, greater *bash* and *tcsh* shell coverage, more emphasis on Perl, and a CD-ROM that contains the best freeware available.

Tcl/Tk Tools

By Mark Harrison
1st Edition September 1997
678 pages, Includes CD-ROM
ISBN 1-56592-218-2

One of the greatest strengths of Tcl/Tk is the range of extensions written for it. This book clearly documents the most popular and robust extensions—by the people who created them—and contains information on configuration, debugging, and other important tasks. The CD-ROM includes Tcl/Tk, the extensions, and other tools documented in the text both in source form and as binaries for Solaris and Linux.

UNIX Basics

sed & awk, 2nd Edition

By Dale Dougherty & Arnold Robbins
2nd Edition March 1997
432 pages, ISBN 1-56592-225-5

sed & awk describes two text manipulation programs that are mainstays of the UNIX programmer's toolbox. This new edition covers the *sed* and *awk* programs as they are now mandated by the POSIX standard and includes discussion of the GNU versions of these programs.

SCO UNIX in a Nutshell

By Ellie Cutler & the staff of O'Reilly & Associates
1st Edition February 1994
590 pages, ISBN 1-56592-037-6

The desktop reference to SCO UNIX and Open Desktop®, this version of *UNIX in a Nutshell* shows you what's under the hood of your SCO system. It isn't a scaled-down quick reference of common commands, but a complete reference containing all user, programming, administration, and networking commands.

What You Need to Know: When You Can't Find Your UNIX System Administrator

By Linda Mui
1st Edition April 1995
156 pages, ISBN 1-56592-104-6

This book is written for UNIX users, who are often cast adrift in a confusing environment. It provides the background and practical solutions you need to solve problems you're likely to encounter—problems with logging in, printing, sharing files, running programs, managing space resources, etc. It also describes the kind of info to gather when you're asking for a diagnosis from a busy sys admin. And, it gives you a list of site-specific information that you should know, as well as a place to write it down.

O'REILLY™

TO ORDER: **800-998-9938** • *order@oreilly.com* • *http://www.oreilly.com/*

OUR PRODUCTS ARE AVAILABLE AT A BOOKSTORE OR SOFTWARE STORE NEAR YOU.

FOR INFORMATION: **800-998-9938** • **707-829-0515** • *info@oreilly.com*

UNIX Basics

Learning the UNIX Operating System, 4th Edition

By Jerry Peek, Grace Todino & John Strang
4th Edition December 1997
106 pages, ISBN 1-56592-390-1

If you are new to UNIX, this concise introduction will tell you just what you need to get started and no more. The new fourth edition covers the Linux operating system and is an ideal primer for someone just starting with UNIX or Linux, as well as for Mac and PC users who encounter a UNIX system on the Internet. This classic book, still the most effective introduction to UNIX in print, now includes a quick-reference card.

Learning GNU Emacs, 2nd Edition

By Debra Cameron, Bill Rosenblatt &
Eric Raymond
2nd Edition September 1996
560 pages, ISBN 1-56592-152-6

Learning GNU Emacs is an introduction to Version 19.30 of the GNU Emacs editor, one of the most widely used and powerful editors available under UNIX. It provides a solid introduction to basic editing, a look at several important "editing modes" (special Emacs features for editing specific types of documents, including email, Usenet News, and the World Wide Web), and a brief introduction to customization and Emacs LISP programming. The book is aimed at new Emacs users, whether or not they are programmers. Includes quick-reference card.

Learning the bash Shell, 2nd Edition

By Cameron Newham & Bill Rosenblatt
2nd Edition January 1998
336 pages, ISBN 1-56592-347-2

This second edition covers all of the features of bash Version 2.0, while still applying to bash Version 1.x. It includes one-dimensional arrays, parameter expansion, more pattern-matching operations, new commands, security improvements, additions to ReadLine, improved configuration and installation, and an additional programming aid, the bash shell debugger.

Learning the Korn Shell

By Bill Rosenblatt
1st Edition June 1993
360 pages, ISBN 1-56592-054-6

This Nutshell Handbook is a thorough introduction to the Korn shell, both as a user interface and as a programming language. The Korn shell is a program that interprets UNIX commands. It has many features that aren't found in other shells, including command history. This book provides a clear and concise explanation of the Korn shell's features. It explains ksh string operations, co-processes, signals and signal handling, and command-line interpretation. The book also includes real-life programming examples and a Korn shell debugger called kshdb, the only known implementation of a shell debugger anywhere.

Using csh and tcsh

By Paul DuBois
1st Edition August 1995
242 pages, ISBN 1-56592-132-1

Using csh and tcsh describes from the beginning how to use these shells interactively to get your work done faster with less typing. You'll learn how to make your prompt tell you where you are (no more pwd); use what you've typed before (history); type long command lines with few keystrokes (command and filename completion); remind yourself of filenames when in the middle of typing a command; and edit a botched command without retyping it.

Learning the vi Editor, 5th Edition

By Linda Lamb
5th Edition October 1990
192 pages, ISBN 0-937175-67-6

This book is a complete guide to text editing with vi, the editor available on nearly every UNIX system. Early chapters cover the basics; later chapters explain more advanced editing tools, such as ex commands and global search and replacement.

O'REILLY™

TO ORDER: **800-998-9938** • **order@oreilly.com** • **http://www.oreilly.com/**

OUR PRODUCTS ARE AVAILABLE AT A BOOKSTORE OR SOFTWARE STORE NEAR YOU.

FOR INFORMATION: **800-998-9938** • **707-829-0515** • **info@oreilly.com**

UNIX Basics

UNIX in a Nutshell: System V Edition

By Daniel Gilly &
the staff of O'Reilly & Associates
2nd Edition June 1992
444 pages, ISBN 1-56592-001-5

You may have seen UNIX quick-reference guides, but you've never seen anything like *UNIX in a Nutshell*. Not a scaled-down quick reference of common commands, *UNIX in a Nutshell* is a complete reference containing all commands and options, along with generous descriptions and examples that put the commands in context. For all but the thorniest UNIX problems, this one reference should be all the documentation you need. Covers System V, Releases 3 and 4, and Solaris 2.0.

Volume 3M: X Window System User's Guide, Motif Edition

By Valerie Quercia & Tim O'Reilly
2nd Edition January 1993
956 pages, ISBN 1-56592-015-5

The *X Window System User's Guide, Motif Edition* orients the new user to window system concepts and provides detailed tutorials for many client programs, including the *xterm* terminal emulator and the *twm, uwm,* and *mwm* window managers. Later chapters explain how to customize the X environment. Revised for Motif 1.2 and X11 Release 5.

UNIX in a Nutshell, Deluxe Edition

By Daniel Gilly, et al.
1st Edition August 1998 (est.)
444 pages (est.), Includes CD-ROM & book
ISBN 1-56592-406-1

This deluxe package includes the bestseller, *UNIX in a Nutshell, System V Edition,* plus a powerhouse of online UNIX books from O'Reilly, including *UNIX in a Nutshell, System V Edition*; the complete text of *UNIX Power Tools, 2nd Edition*; *Learning the UNIX Operating System, 4th Edition*; *Learning the vi Editor, 5th Edition*; *sed & awk, 2nd Edition*; *Learning the Korn Shell,* as well as *UNIX in a Nutshell.*

How to stay in touch with O'Reilly

1. Visit Our Award-Winning Web Site

http://www.oreilly.com/

★ "Top 100 Sites on the Web" —*PC Magazine*
★ "Top 5% Web sites" —*Point Communications*
★ "3-Star site" —*The McKinley Group*

Our web site contains a library of comprehensiveproduct information (including book excerpts and tables of contents), downloadable software, background articles, interviews with technology leaders, links to relevant sites, book cover art, and more. File us in your Bookmarks or Hotlist!

2. Join Our Email Mailing Lists

New Product Releases

To receive automatic email with brief descriptions of all new O'Reilly products as they are released, send email to:
listproc@online.oreilly.com
Put the following information in the first line of your message (*not* in the Subject field):
subscribe oreilly-news

O'Reilly Events

If you'd also like us to send information about trade show events, special promotions, and other O'Reilly events, send email to:
listproc@online.oreilly.com
Put the following information in the first line of your message (*not* in the Subject field):
subscribe oreilly-events

3. Get Examples from Our Books via FTP

There are two ways to access an archive of example files from our books:

Regular FTP

• ftp to:
  ftp.oreilly.com
  (login: anonymous
  password: your email address)
• Point your web browser to:
  ftp://ftp.oreilly.com/

FTPMAIL

• Send an email message to:
  ftpmail@online.oreilly.com
  (Write "help" in the message body)

4. Contact Us via Email

order@oreilly.com
  To place a book or software order online. Good for North American and international customers.

subscriptions@oreilly.com
  To place an order for any of our newsletters or periodicals.

books@oreilly.com
  General questions about any of our books.

software@oreilly.com
  For general questions and product information about our software. Check out O'Reilly Software Online at **http://software.oreilly.com/** for software and technical support information. Registered O'Reilly software users send your questions to: **website-support@oreilly.com**

cs@oreilly.com
  For answers to problems regarding your order or our products.

booktech@oreilly.com
  For book content technical questions or corrections.

proposals@oreilly.com
  To submit new book or software proposals to our editors and product managers.

international@oreilly.com
  For information about our international distributors or translation queries. For a list of our distributors outside of North America check out:
  http://www.oreilly.com/www/order/country.html

O'Reilly & Associates, Inc.
101 Morris Street, Sebastopol, CA 95472 USA
TEL   707-829-0515 or 800-998-9938
          (6am to 5pm PST)
FAX   707-829-0104

International Distributors

UK, EUROPE, MIDDLE EAST AND NORTHERN AFRICA (EXCEPT FRANCE, GERMANY, SWITZERLAND, & AUSTRIA)

INQUIRIES

International Thomson Publishing Europe
Berkshire House
168-173 High Holborn
London WC1V 7AA
United Kingdom
Telephone: 44-171-497-1422
Fax: 44-171-497-1426
Email: itpint@itps.co.uk

ORDERS

International Thomson Publishing Services, Ltd.
Cheriton House, North Way
Andover, Hampshire SP10 5BE
United Kingdom
Telephone: 44-264-342-832 (UK)
Telephone: 44-264-342-806 (outside UK)
Fax: 44-264-364418 (UK)
Fax: 44-264-342761 (outside UK)
UK & Eire orders: itpuk@itps.co.uk
International orders: itpint@itps.co.uk

FRANCE

Editions Eyrolles
61 bd Saint-Germain
75240 Paris Cedex 05
France
Fax: 33-01-44-41-11-44

FRENCH LANGUAGE BOOKS

All countries except Canada
Telephone: 33-01-44-41-46-16
Email: geodif@eyrolles.com
English language books
Telephone: 33-01-44-41-11-87
Email: distribution@eyrolles.com

GERMANY, SWITZERLAND, AND AUSTRIA

INQUIRIES

O'Reilly Verlag
Balthasarstr. 81
D-50670 Köln
Germany
Telephone: 49-221-97-31-60-0
Fax: 49-221-97-31-60-8
Email: anfragen@oreilly.de

ORDERS

International Thomson Publishing
Königswinterer Straße 418
53227 Bonn, Germany
Telephone: 49-228-97024 0
Fax: 49-228-441342
Email: order@oreilly.de

JAPAN

O'Reilly Japan, Inc.
Kiyoshige Building 2F
12-Banchi, Sanei-cho
Shinjuku-ku
Tokyo 160-0008 Japan
Telephone: 81-3-3356-5227
Fax: 81-3-3356-5261
Email: kenji@oreilly.com

INDIA

Computer Bookshop (India) PVT. Ltd.
190 Dr. D.N. Road, Fort
Bombay 400 001 India
Telephone: 91-22-207-0989
Fax: 91-22-262-3551
Email: cbsbom@giasbm01.vsnl.net.in

HONG KONG

City Discount Subscription Service Ltd.
Unit D, 3rd Floor, Yan's Tower
27 Wong Chuk Hang Road
Aberdeen, Hong Kong
Telephone: 852-2580-3539
Fax: 852-2580-6463
Email: citydis@ppn.com.hk

KOREA

Hanbit Media, Inc.
Sonyoung Bldg. 202
Yeksam-dong 736-36
Kangnam-ku
Seoul, Korea
Telephone: 822-554-9610
Fax: 822-556-0363
Email: hant93@chollian.dacom.co.kr

SINGAPORE, MALAYSIA, AND THAILAND

Addison Wesley Longman Singapore PTE Ltd.
25 First Lok Yang Road
Singapore 629734
Telephone: 65-268-2666
Fax: 65-268-7023
Email: daniel@longman.com.sg

PHILIPPINES

Mutual Books, Inc.
429-D Shaw Boulevard
Mandaluyong City, Metro
Manila, Philippines
Telephone: 632-725-7538
Fax: 632-721-3056
Email: mbikikog@mnl.sequel.net

CHINA

Ron's DataCom Co., Ltd.
79 Dongwu Avenue
Dongxihu District
Wuhan 430040
China
Telephone: 86-27-83892568
Fax: 86-27-83222108
Email: hongfeng@public.wh.hb.cn

ALL OTHER ASIAN COUNTRIES

O'Reilly & Associates, Inc.
101 Morris Street
Sebastopol, CA 95472 USA
Telephone: 707-829-0515
Fax: 707-829-0104
Email: order@oreilly.com

AUSTRALIA

WoodsLane Pty. Ltd.
7/5 Vuko Place, Warriewood NSW 2102
P.O. Box 935
Mona Vale NSW 2103
Australia
Telephone: 61-2-9970-5111
Fax: 61-2-9970-5002
Email: info@woodslane.com.au

NEW ZEALAND

Woodslane New Zealand Ltd.
21 Cooks Street (P.O. Box 575)
Waganui, New Zealand
Telephone: 64-6-347-6543
Fax: 64-6-345-4840
Email: info@woodslane.com.au

THE AMERICAS

McGraw-Hill Interamericana Editores, S.A. de C.V.
Cedro No. 512
Col. Atlampa 06450
Mexico, D.F.
Telephone: 52-5-541-3155
Fax: 52-5-541-4913
Email: mcgraw-hill@infosel.net.mx

SOUTH AFRICA

International Thomson Publishing South Africa
Building 18, Constantia Park
138 Sixteenth Road
P.O. Box 2459
Halfway House, 1685 South Africa
Telephone: 27-11-805-4819
Fax: 27-11-805-3648

O'REILLY™

TO ORDER: **800-998-9938** • **order@oreilly.com** • **http://www.oreilly.com/**

OUR PRODUCTS ARE AVAILABLE AT A BOOKSTORE OR SOFTWARE STORE NEAR YOU.

FOR INFORMATION: **800-998-9938** • **707-829-0515** • **info@oreilly.com**